A DOCUMENTARY HISTORY OF THE ITALIAN AMERICANS

A DOCUMENTARY HISTORY OF THE ITALIAN AMERICANS

EDITED BY WAYNE MOQUIN
WITH CHARLES VAN DOREN

Consulting Editor: Francis A. J. Ianni

PRAEGER PUBLISHERS
New York · Washington

Published in the United States of America in 1974
by Praeger Publishers, Inc.
111 Fourth Avenue, New York, N.Y. 10003, U.S.A.

© 1974 by Praeger Publishers, Inc.

COPYRIGHT NOTICES AND PERMISSIONS

The copyright notices and permissions are listed below and on page v, which constitutes an extension of this copyright page.

The editors wish to express their gratitude for permission to reprint material from the following sources:

Library of Congress Cataloging in Publication Data
Moquin, Wayne, comp.
  A documentary history of the Italian Americans.

  Bibliography: p. 433.
  1. Italians in the United States—History—Addresses, essays, lectures.
I. Van Doren, Charles Lincoln, 1926–   joint comp. II. Title.
E184.18M66   917.3'06'51   72-91348
ISBN 0 275 19720 4

Printed in the United States of America

CONTENTS

Introduction   xi
PART ONE: THE ITALIAN AMERICAN PRESENCE IN THE NEW
   WORLD, 1492–1850   1
Columbus Discovers the New World   3
John Cabot and the Discovery of North America   7
The Voyages of Amerigo Vespucci   10
Verrazzano's Description of New York Harbor   17
Enrico di Tonti in the Mississippi Valley   19
Eusebio Kino's Exploration of California   23
Filippo Mazzei and American Independence   26
Italian Opera in America   *Lorenzo Da Ponte*   31
Indian Agent at Fort Snelling   *Lawrence Taliaferro*   34

PART TWO: IMMIGRATION AND THE PATTERNS OF
   SETTLEMENT, 1850–1929   37
Italian Life in New York   39
Chicago's Italian Colony   *Alessandro Mastro-Valerio*   45
Italian Immigrants in Boston   49
Immigrants in Cities   55
Italian Immigration into the South   59
Italians of California   64
The Farm Colony at Vineland, New Jersey   67
The Effect of Emigration upon Italy   *Antonio Mangano*   73
A Farm Colony in North Carolina   *Felice Ferrero*   81
Piedmontese on the Mississippi   85
Italian Progress in the United States   *Alberto Pecorini*   89

PART THREE: MAKING A LIVING, 1890–1930   97
Enslavement of Italian Immigrants   99
The Padrone System: A Federal View   105
Vines and Wines of California   Andrea Sbarboro   111
Forced Labor in West Virginia   Gino C. Speranza   117
Italian Competition for Black Labor in the South   122
The Italian Working Women of New York   Adriana Spadoni   126
Tontitown, Arkansas: The Work of Pietro Bandini   131
Americanization Through Affluence   136
The Track Gangs   140
  1. The "Wop" in the Track Gang   Dominic Ciolli   141
  2. When the Boss Went Too Far   Cesidio Simboli   146
The Differences Between Americans and Italians   Stefano Miele   150
Amadeo P. Giannini and the Bank of America   153
Amedeo Obici, America's "Peanut King"   Dominick Lamonica   158

PART FOUR: THE QUASI-PUBLIC UTILITY: ORGANIZED CRIME AND
  THE ITALIAN AMERICAN, 1890–1973   163
The New Orleans Mafia   Henry Cabot Lodge   167
Report of the White Hand Society   171
Black Hand, Mafia, and Camorra   174
How the United States Fosters the Black Hand   Frank M. White   179
Imported Crime   Arthur Train   184
Last Statement in Court   Bartolomeo Vanzetti   189
An Unfair Press   194
Al Capone: Public Benefactor   197
  1. Public Service Is My Motto   Al Capone   198
  2. Alcohol and Al Capone   Frederick Lewis Allen   200
The Castellamarese War of 1930–31   205
Crime as an American Way of Life   Daniel Bell   219
The Structure of Organized Crime   229
How We Italians Discovered America and Kept It Clean and
  Pure While Giving It Lots of Singers, Judges, and Other
  Swell People   Nicholas Pileggi   235
The Mafia Craze   Vincent Teresa   243

PART FIVE: THE CONTROVERSY OVER ITALIAN IMMIGRATION:
  VIOLENCE AND POLEMIC, 1890–1924   253
The New Orleans Lynching, March 14, 1891   255
"What Shall We Do with the 'Dago'?"   259
Italians Can Be Americanized   Joseph A. Senner   264
Italian Feeling on American Lynching   Augusto Pierantoni   268
How It Feels to Be a Problem   Gino Speranza   271
The Flower of Her Peasantry   John Foster Carr   278
The Non-Americanization of Immigrants   Luigi Carnovale   283
Immigration and Labor   Constantine Panunzio   287
Italophobia   291

PART SIX: EMERGENCE OF THE ITALIAN AMERICAN 295
Little Italy, 1888 299
Italians Should Be Republicans 304
Italian Children in the Primary Grades Jane Addams 306
Feast Days in Little Italy Jacob Riis 313
The Italian Theater of New York Hutchins Hapgood 317
Italian Associations of New York Antonio Mangano 321
A Survey of Boston's Italians Robert A. Woods 326
The Sons of Italy 329
American Priests for Italian Missions 331
The Foreign Language Press 335
The American Mission of Frances Xavier Cabrini 338
A Sicilian Colony in Manhattan Gaspare Cusumano 343
Americanization and Reaction Alfonso A. Costa 346
Michelangelo in Newark 350
Americanization in Chicago 355
My Neighborhood Edward Corsi 358
The Speech of Little Italy Anthony M. Turano 362
The Odyssey of a Wop John Fante 366
Mayor La Guardia of New York 372
Italian Culture for the Second Generation Mario Petruzzelli 376
No. 38 Becomes a Citizen Max Ascoli 379
Little Italy on June 10, 1940 385
Pride in American Citizenship Attilio Piccirilli 389
Italian Americans, Fascism, and the War
Constantine M. Panunzio 392
Loyalty of Italian Americans Vito Marcantonio 399
Italian Americans Vote Republican Vincent Tortora 401
The Process of Americanization Laura Fermi 405
Italian Americans of Boston's North End
Norman Thomas di Giovanni 410
Little Italy Seventy-five Years Later Pietro Di Donato 414
Italo-American Teen-Age Culture Francis A. J. Ianni 419
Italian American Sports Heroes Maurice R. Marchello 425
Italian Americans Today Richard Gambino 428
Bibliography 433
Fiction Readings 435
Index 437

Sections of illustrations follow pages 116 and 228.

INTRODUCTION

The selections in the first chapter of this book testify to the longstanding involvement of Italians with the United States. Immigration statistics kept since 1820 (though not always accurately) reveal that Italy, by sending more than 5,199,000 persons to America, is the second largest contributor of foreign-born U.S. citizens outside the Western Hemisphere. (Germany is first.) But in contrast to the Germans, English, Irish, Scots, and Scandinavians, some of whom began arriving in appreciable numbers in the seventeenth century and who continued coming until after World War I, the great bulk of Italian immigration was concentrated in the period between 1875 and 1925. In other words, the Italians were a major part of the "new immigration," as it came to be called, that coincided with the rapid industrtialization of the United States following the Civil War.

Despite the size of the Italian American population, there has been strikingly little historical and sociological research on this group until recently. This has been largely because of the lateness of the immigration. Every immigrant group has had to establish itself more or less securely before reflecting on and reconstructing its own history. The most basic task in any such reconstruction is the collecting and studying of the sources—the newspapers, magazines, letters, parish and organizational papers, and other documents—that came out of the life of the particular ethnic group. This work of collecting, evaluating, cataloguing, and translating is best done by those who belong to the community in question—in this case the Italian Americans.

To date the job has only been begun. The Immigration Archives of the University of Minnesota under the directorship of Professor Rudolph Vecoli; the Center for Migration Studies, on Staten Island, under Silvano M. Tomasi; and the Istituto di Studi Americani, at the University of Florence, Italy, directed by Professor Pietro Russo, are among the leading agencies collecting the masses of source material that tell the stories of America's many Italian communities. These efforts at source research are fundamental for the study of Italian American history, for they are the key to revealing the life of Italian American communities from within.

The present condition of Italian American research being what it is, this volume can only be regarded as a preliminary attempt to document the diversity of Italian American life (and not always from within). No ethnic group in the United States is an undifferentiated entity. Each, particularly one so large as the Italian Americans, manifests all the diversity of the society in which it lives. There are Italian American paupers, laborers, white-collar workers, and millionaires; bankers, industrialists, and stock brokers; garage-owners, grocers, bakers, miners, and truck-drivers; actors, athletes, professors, clergy, lawyers, and physicians; farmers, factory workers, criminals, politicians, policemen, and judges. For the millions of unheralded Italian Americans, there are dozens whose names are frequently before the public, from Nick Buoniconti of the Miami Dolphins to Judge John Sirica of the Federal District Court in Washington, D.C. To explore Italian American society in depth is beyond the scope of this volume. We have had to be satisfied with merely indicating the diversity of the general experience of Italian American communities.

Needless to say, we could not have compiled this book unaided. We are grateful to the libraries of the University of Minnesota and the University of Illinois for the generous use of their facilities. Professor Pietro Russo was kind enough to consult with us in Florence, Italy, and to offer useful material and suggestions. And a special word of appreciation must go to our consulting editor, Professor Francis A. J. Ianni of Teachers College, Columbia University, for his advice on topics and sources, as well as for reading and commenting on the selections. The editorial matter and the points of view expressed therein are, naturally, our own responsibility.

Chicago
December 1973

Part One

THE ITALIAN AMERICAN PRESENCE IN THE NEW WORLD, 1492–1850

Because Italians were numerically so conspicuous in the "new immigration" after 1880, it is sometimes forgotten that Italian American history is as old as American history itself. No ethnic group, save the American Indian, has played a longer or more constant role in the history of the Western Hemisphere. Italians were discoverers, explorers, colonists, and frontiersmen. Today, they are citizens in every part of the United States.

The names of Columbus, Vespucci, Verrazzano, and Caboto are well-known. Less familiar are the many Italians who were present in the Spanish, French, Dutch, and English colonies that are today parts of the United States. Fray Marcos de Niza, who explored New Mexico in 1538 searching for the seven cities of Cíbola, was a native of Savoy. The Jesuit missionary Eusebio Kino, born in Segno, Italy, worked among the Indians in Sonora and Arizona in the late seventeenth century. By 1610, there were Italian colonists in Jamestown, Virginia. In 1657, a group of Waldenses from Piedmont, fleeing religious persecution, settled in New Amsterdam. During the same decade, Italian Catholics arrived in Maryland. Of the Italians who served France in America, none is better known than Enrico di Tonti, the associate of La Salle in exploration of the Mississippi Valley. Shortly after the founding of New Orleans in 1718, an Italian colony developed there.

In the decades after the War of Independence, Italians were

attracted to nearly all parts of the United States. Many of them —tradesmen, artists, artisans, musicians, teachers—settled along the more populous East Coast. But the lower Mississippi Valley became home for many others. The first Roman Catholic bishop of St. Louis was Giuseppe Rosati, a native of Sora, near Naples. By 1850, there were Italians from Maine to California, in all settled areas, and at several frontier outposts.

The total number of Italians in America from 1600 to 1850 was not very large, thousands in a population that grew from five million in 1800 to twenty-three million by 1850. The names of most of them have disappeared from history except as they are preserved in local newspapers, church registries, court houses, and cemeteries. Others earned a measure of fame and deserve more attention than they usually receive in our history books: Filippo Mazzei, the physician-horticulturalist and friend of Thomas Jefferson; Francesco Vigo, aide-de-camp of George Rogers Clark during the American Revolution; Count Paolo Andreani, who explored the Upper Midwest in 1791; Lorenzo Da Ponte, promoter of Italian language and opera in New York; Adelina Patti, the opera singer; Francesco Scala, director of the U.S. Marine band; the artists Giuseppe Cerachi, Michel Felice Corné, Constantino Brumidi; and Giacomo Beltrami, who explored the sources of the Mississippi River in 1823. The selections in this chapter pinpoint a few of these early Italian Americans and their activities.

COLUMBUS DISCOVERS THE NEW WORLD

[Disagreements persist over the ancestry of Christopher Columbus, but it is undisputed that he was born in Genoa, Italy, about 1451. Seagoing became his career early in life, and by 1474, he was planning a westward voyage across the Atlantic. Under the sponsorship of Ferdinand and Isabella, monarchs of the newly united Spain, his expedition of three ships left Palos, Spain, on August 3, 1492, stopped at the Canary Islands, and after ten weeks sighted land. San Salvador in the Bahamas was the first landfall. Over the next dozen years, Columbus made three more voyages, each time enlarging his area of exploration and finally touching the mainland of Central America on his last trip in 1502–4. The selection reprinted here is from a letter Columbus wrote on March 14, 1493, to Lord Rafael Sanchez, treasurer of Aragon, telling what he had found on the first voyage. By this date, Columbus was back in the Iberian Peninsula where he was received with great honors by the King of Portugal and by the monarchs of Spain.]

Knowing that it will afford you pleasure to learn that I have brought my undertaking to a successful termination, I have decided upon writing you this letter to acquaint you with all the events which have occurred in my voyage, and the discoveries which have resulted from it. Thirty-three days after my departure from [Gomera] I reached the Indian Sea, where I discovered many islands, thickly peopled, of which I took possession without resistance in the name of our most illustrious monarch, by public proclamation and with unfurled banners. To the first of these islands, which is called by the Indians Guanahani, I gave the name of the blessed Savior (San

From R. H. Major, ed., *Select Letters of Christopher Columbus* (London, 1847), pp. 1–17.

Salvador), relying upon whose protection I had reached this as well as the other islands; to each of these I also gave a name, ordering that one should be called Santa Maria de la Conception, another Fernandina, the third Isabella, the fourth Juana [Cuba], and so with all the rest. . . .

As soon as we arrived at that, which as I have said was named Juana, I proceeded along its coast a short distance westward and found it to be so large and apparently without termination that I could not suppose it to be an island, but the continental province of Cathay. Seeing, however, no towns or populous places on the sea-coast, but only a few detached houses and cottages, with whose inhabitants I was unable to communicate because they fled as soon as they saw us, I went further on, thinking that in my progress I should certainly find some city or village.

At length, after proceeding a great way and finding that nothing new presented itself and that the line of coast was leading us north-ward (which I wished to avoid because it was winter, and it was my intention to move southward, and because, moreover, the winds were contrary), I resolved not to attempt any further progress but rather to turn back and retrace my course to a certain bay that I had observed, and from which I afterward dispatched two of our men to ascertain whether there were a king or any cities in that province. These men reconnoitered the country for three days and found a most numerous population and great numbers of houses, though small and built without any regard to order; with which information they returned to us. In the meantime I had learned from some Indians whom I had seized that that country was certainly an island, and therefore I sailed toward the east, coasting to the distance of 322 miles, which brought us to the extremity of it; from this point I saw lying eastward another island, 54 miles distant from Juana, to which I gave the name of Española [Hispaniola]. I went thither and steered my course eastward as I had done at Juana, even to the distance of 564 miles along the north coast. . . .

In that island also, which I have before said we named Española, there are mountains of very great size and beauty, vast plains, groves, and very fruitful fields, admirably adapted for tillage, pasture, and habitation. The convenience and excellence of the harbors in this island and the abundance of the rivers, so in-dispensable to the health of man, surpass anything that would be believed by one who had not seen it. The trees, herbage, and fruits of Española are very different from those of Juana, and, moreover, it abounds in various kinds of spices, gold, and other metals. . . .

But the extent of Española is greater than all Spain from Catalonia to Fontarabia, which is easily proved, because one of its four sides which I myself coasted in a direct line, from west to east, measures 540 miles. This island is to be regarded with special interest and not to be slighted; for although as I have said I took possession of all these islands in the name of our invincible King, and the government of them is unreservedly committed to His Said Majesty, yet there was one large town in Española of which especially I took possession, situated in a remarkably favorable spot and in every way convenient for the purposes of gain and commerce. To this town I gave the name of Navidad del Señor, and ordered a fortress to be built there, which must by this time be completed, in which I left as many men as I thought necessary, with all sorts of arms and enough provisions for more than a year. I also left them one caravel and skillful workmen, both in shipbuilding and other arts, and engaged the favor and friendship of the king of the island in their behalf, to a degree that would not be believed, for these people are so amiable and friendly that even the king took a pride in calling me his brother. But supposing their feelings should become changed and they should wish to injure those who have remained in the fortress, they could not do so, for they have no arms, they go naked, and are moreover too cowardly; so that those who hold the said fortress can easily keep the whole island in check, without any pressing danger to themselves, provided they do not transgress the directions and regulations which I have given them. . . .

Finally, to compress into few words the entire summary of my voyage and speedy return and of the advantages derivable therefrom, I promise, that with a little assistance afforded me by our most invincible sovereigns, I will procure them as much gold as they need, as great a quantity of spices, of cotton, and of mastic (which is only found in Chios), and as many men for the service of the navy as Their Majesties may require. I promise also rhubarb and other sorts of drugs, which I am persuaded the men whom I have left in the aforesaid fortress have found already and will continue to find; for I myself have tarried nowhere longer than I was compelled to do by the winds, except in the city of Navidad, while I provided for the building of the fortress and took the necessary precautions for the perfect security of the men I left there.

Although all I have related may appear to be wonderful and unheard of, yet the results of my voyage would have been more astonishing if I had had at my disposal such ships as I required. But these great and marvelous results are not to be attributed to any merit of mine but to the holy Christian faith and to the piety and religion of our sovereigns; for that which the unaided intellect of man could not compass, the Spirit of God has granted to human exertions, for God is wont to hear the prayers of His servants who love His precepts even to the performance of apparent impossibilities. Thus it has happened to me in the present instance, who have accomplished a task to which the powers of mortal men had never hitherto attained; for if there have been those who have anywhere written or spoken of these islands, they have done so with doubts and conjectures, and no one has ever asserted that he has seen them, on which account their writings have been looked upon as little else than fables.

Therefore, let the King and Queen, our Princes, and their most happy kingdoms, and all the other provinces of Christendom render thanks to our Lord and Savior Jesus Christ, who has granted us so great a victory and such prosperity. Let processions be made and sacred feasts be held and the temples be adorned with festive boughs. Let Christ rejoice on earth, as He rejoices in heaven in the prospect of the salvation of the souls of so many nations hitherto lost. Let us also rejoice, as well on account of the exaltation of our faith as on account of the increase of our temporal prosperity, of which not only Spain but all Christendom will be partakers.

JOHN CABOT AND
THE DISCOVERY OF
NORTH AMERICA

[John Cabot, or
Giovanni Caboto, was born, like Columbus, in Genoa, about 1450,
but is considered a Venetian, having become a citizen of that
republic by 1476. He worked out of Venice on Mediterranean
trading ships. The exact year of his arrival in England is not known,
but he was certainly there by 1495, hoping to find support in this
northern maritime nation for an expedition across the Atlantic. On
March 5, 1496, Henry VII granted letters patent to Cabot and his
sons for such a voyage. He left Bristol in the ship *Matthew* on May 2,
1497, following a course nearly along the fifty-first parallel of
latitude. On June 24, land was sighted, but whether at Belle Isle,
Newfoundland, or Labrador we do not know. Cabot then returned
to England and prepared for a new expedition consisting of five
ships. After departing from Bristol in May, 1498, one of the ships
soon returned. The other four, one of which carried Cabot, were
never heard from again. Cabot's explorations have been much less
heralded than those of Columbus, probably because his work did
not immediately lead to an expansion of trade or empire by Britain.
The letter reprinted here was written by Raimondo di Soncino,
minister to England from Milan, to the Duke of Milan on December
18, 1497.]

Perhaps even in the press of so much business Your Excellency
will not be sorry to learn that His Majesty has gained part of Asia
without a stroke of the sword. In this kingdom is a low-class
Venetian called Master Zoanne Caboto, a man of considerable
ability, most skilful in navigation, who saw that the Most Serene

From A. W. Lawrence and Jean Young, eds., *Narratives of the Discovery of America*
(New York, 1931), pp. 272–76.

Kings, first the Portuguese and then the Spanish, had occupied unknown islands, and thought to make a similar acquisition for His Majesty. And having obtained the royal grants which gave him the profitable control of the lands found by him, the right of possession being reserved to the Crown, he committed himself to Fortune and departed in a little ship from the port of Bristol, in the western part of this kingdom, with eighteen persons. Passing Ireland, which lies more to the west, and then rising towards the north, he began to navigate to the oriental countries. Leaving the north on his right for some days, and wandering considerably, he came at last to *terra firma*, where he planted the royal banner, took possession for this sovereign, collected certain tokens and returned.

The said Master Zoanne, as he is a foreigner and poor, would not be believed if his partners, who are nearly all Englishmen and from Bristol, did not testify to the truth of what he tells. This Master Zoanne has the representation of the world on a map, and also on a solid globe, which he has made, and he shows by them where he arrived, and going towards the Orient he has passed much of the Tanais country. And they say that the land is fertile and temperate, and think that brazil wood and silks grow there, and they declare that the sea there is full of fish that can be taken not only with nets but with fishing-baskets, a stone being placed in the basket to sink it in the water, and this I have heard Master Zoanne tell. And the said Englishmen, his partners, say that they can bring so many fish that this kingdom will have no more business with Iceland, with which country it has a very great trade in the fish called stock-fish.

But Master Zoanne has his thoughts directed to a greater undertaking, for he thinks of going from the place which he has occupied farther along the coast towards the Orient until he is opposite an island he calls Cipango, situate in the equinoctial region, where he believes all the spices of the world grow, and there are also gems. And he says that he was once at Mecca, where from remote countries spices are carried by caravans, and that those carrying them, being asked where those spices grew, said they did not know, but that other caravans came to their homes with this merchandise from remote countries, and these too say that they receive them from other remote countries. And he argues that if the oriental people tell those of the south that these things are from places remote from them, and thus from hand to hand, it follows (assuming the rotundity of the earth) that the last fetch them from the north, towards the west. And he tells this in a way that makes me believe it, since to do so costs me no more than it does. And what is a greater thing, His Majesty here, who is wise and not prodigal, also places confidence in what he says, and since his return has provided well for him, as this Master Zoanne tells me. And in the spring, it is said, His Majesty will arm some ships and will give them all the criminals so that he may go to that country and plant a colony.

In this way he hopes to make London a greater place for spices than Alexandria. And the principals in the business are citizens of Bristol, great mariners, who, now that they know where to go, say that the voyage will not take more than fifteen days, nor do they ever have storms after leaving Ireland. I have also talked with a Burgundian, a companion of Master Zoanne, who affirms the same and who is willing to go, since the Admiral (as Master Zoanne is already styled) has given him an island, and he has given another to some barber of his, a Genoese from Castiglione, and they both consider themselves Counts while my Lord the Admiral thinks himself no less than a Prince. I believe too that some poor Italian friars will go on the voyage, all of whom have the promise of being bishops. And I, having become a friend of the Admiral's, if I wished to go, could have an archbishopric, but it has occurred to me that the benefices Your Excellency has reserved for me would be a surer thing, and I beg that if any become vacant during my absence you will give me possession of them, taking care that they are not usurped in the meantime by others, whose presence enables them to be more urgent in their claims than I, who am reduced in this country to eat ten or twelve courses at every meal and stay three hours at table each time, twice a day, for the love of Your Excellency. To whom I humbly commend myself.

THE VOYAGES OF AMERIGO VESPUCCI

[The man after whom the Americas were named was born in Florence in 1454. After 1491, he lived in Seville, Spain, working as an agent for the Medici bankers. Whether Vespucci made two or four voyages to the New World is uncertain since there are two contradictory sources of information, both from his own hand. The one excerpted here, a letter of September 4, 1504, to Pier Soderini at Florence, describes four voyages. Other letters cite only two, and that number seems to be accepted currently. If so, Vespucci sailed to America from May, 1499 to June, 1500 under the auspices of Spain, and from May, 1501 to July, 1502 for Portugal. In both cases, he sailed along the Caribbean and Atlantic coasts of South America, discovering the bay of Rio de Janeiro and reaching the Rio de la Plata. This selection describes a possible earlier voyage in 1497–98 to the Gulf of Mexico and the southeast coast of what is now the United States.]

Your Magnificence shall know that the motive of my coming into this realm of Spain was to traffic in merchandise: and that I pursued this intent about four years: during which I saw and knew the inconstant shiftings of Fortune: and how she kept changing those frail and transitory benefits: and how at one time she holds man on the summit of the wheel, and at another time drives him back from her, and despoils him of what may be called his borrowed riches: so that, knowing the continuous toil which man undergoes to win them, submitting himself to so many anxieties and risks, I resolved to abandon trade, and to fix my aim upon something more praiseworthy and stable: whence it was that I made preparation

for going to see part of the world and its wonders: and herefor
the time and place presented themselves most opportunely to me:
which was that the King Don Ferrando of Castile being about to
despatch four ships to discover new lands towards the west, I
was chosen by his Highness to go in that fleet to aid in making
discovery: and we set out from the port of Cadiz on the 10 day of
May 1497, and took our route through the great gulph of the
Ocean-sea: in which voyage we were eighteen months (*engaged*):
and discovered much continental land and innumerable islands,
and great part of them inhabited: whereas there is no mention
made by the ancient writers of them: I believe, because they
had no knowledge thereof: . . . and so we sailed on till at the end
of 37 days we reached a land which we deemed to be a continent:
which is distant westwardly from the isles of Canary about a
thousand leagues beyond the inhabited region within the torrid
zone: for we found the North Pole at an elevation of 16 degrees
above its horizon, and (*it was*) westward, according to the shewing
of our instruments, 75 degrees from the isles of Canary: whereat
we anchored with our ships a league and a half from land: and
we put out our boats freighted with men and arms: we made
towards the land, and before we reached it, had sight of a great
number of people who were going along the shore: by which we were
much rejoiced: and we observed that they were a naked race: they
shewed themselves to stand in fear of us: I believe (*it was*) because
they saw us clothed and of other appearance (*than their own*): they
all withdrew to a hill, and for whatsoever signals we made to them
of peace and of friendliness, they would not come to parley with us:
so that, as the night was now coming on, and as the ships were
anchored in a dangerous place, being on a rough and shelterless
coast, we decided to remove from there the next day, and to go in
search of some harbor or bay, where we might place our ships in
safety: and we sailed with the maestrale wind, thus running
along the coast with the land ever in sight, continually in our
course observing people along the shore: till after having navigated
for two days, we found a place sufficiently secure for the ships, and
anchored half a league from land, on which we saw a very great
number of people: and this same day we put to land with the
boats, and sprang on shore full 40 men in good trim: and still
the land's people appeared shy of converse with us, and we were
unable to encourage them so much as to make them come to speak
with us: and this day we laboured so greatly in giving them of
our wares, such as rattles and mirrors, beads, *spalline*, and other
trifles, that some of them took confidence and came to discourse
with us: and after having made good friends with them, the night
coming on, we took our leave of them and returned to the ships:
and the next day when the dawn appeared we saw that there were
infinite numbers of people upon the beach, and they had their women
and children with them: we went ashore, and found that they were

all laden with their worldly goods which are suchlike as, in its (*proper*) place, shall be related: and before we reached the land, many of them jumped into the sea and came swimming to receive us at a bowshot's length (*from the shore*), for they are very great swimmers, with as much confidence as if they had for a long time been acquainted with us: and we were pleased with this their confidence. For so much as we learned of their manner of life and customs, it was that they go entirely naked, as well the men as the women. . . . They are of medium stature, very well proportioned: their flesh is of a colour that verges into red like a lion's mane: and I believe that if they went clothed, they would be as white as we: they have not any hair upon the body, except the hair of the head which is long and black, and especially in the women, whom it renders handsome: in aspect they are not very good-looking, because they have broad faces, so that they would seem Tartar-like: they let no hair grow on their eyebrows, nor on their eyelids, nor elsewhere, except the hair of the head: for they hold hairiness to be a filthy thing: they are very lightfooted in walking and in running, as well the men as the women: so that a woman recks nothing of running a league or two, as many times we saw them do: and herein they have a very great advantage over us Christians: they swim (*with an expertness*) beyond all belief, and the women better than the men: for we have many times found and seen them swimming two leagues out at sea without anything to rest upon. Their arms are bows and arrows very well made, save that (*the arrows*) are not (*tipped*) with iron nor any other kind of hard metal: and instead of iron they put animals' or fishes' teeth, or a spike of tough wood, with the point hardened by fire: they are sure marksmen, for they hit whatever they aim at: and in some places the women use these bows: they have other weapons, such as fireharded spears, and also clubs with knobs, beautifully carved. Warfare is used amongst them, which they carry on against people not of their own language, very cruelly, without granting life to any one, except (*to reserve him*) for greater suffering. When they go to war, they take their women with them, not that these may fight, but because they carry behind them their worldly goods, for a woman carries on her back for thirty or forty leagues a load which no man could bear: as we have many times seen them do. They are not accustomed to have any Captain, nor do they go in any ordered array, for every one is lord of himself: and the cause of their wars is not for lust of dominion, nor of extending their frontiers, nor for inordinate covetousness, but for some ancient enmity which in by-gone times arose amongst them: and when asked why they made war, they knew not any other reason to give than that they did so to avenge the death of their ancestors, or of their parents: these people have neither King, nor Lord, nor do they yield obedience to any one, for they live in their own liberty: and how they be stirred up to go to war is (*this*) that when the enemies have slain or captured any of them, his oldest kinsman rises up and goes about the highways haranguing them to go with him and avenge the death of such his kinsman: and so are they stirred up by fellow-feeling: they have no judicial system, nor do they punish the ill-doer: nor does the father, nor the mother chastise the children: and marvellously (*seldom*) or never did we see any dispute among them: in their conversation they appear simple, and they are very cunning and acute in that which concerns them: they speak little and in a low tone: they use the same articulations as we, since they form their utterances either with the palate, or with the teeth, or on the lips: except that they give different names to things. Many are the varieties of tongues: for in every 100 leagues we found a change of language, so that they are not understandable each to the other. . . . In fine, they live and are contented with that which nature gives them. The wealth that we enjoy in this our Europe and elsewhere, such as gold, jewels, pearls, and other riches, they hold as nothing: and although they have them in their own lands, they do not labour to obtain them, nor do they value them. They are liberal in giving, for it is rarely they deny you anything: and on the other hand, liberal in asking, when they shew themselves your friends. . . . At this beginning, we saw nothing in the land of much profit, except some show of gold: I believe the cause of it was that we did not know the language: but in so far as concerns the situation and condition of the land, it could not be better: we decided to leave that place, and to go further on, continuously coasting the shore: upon which we made frequent descents, and held converse with a great number of people. . . . This land is very populous, and full of inhabitants, and of numberless rivers (*and*) animals: few (*of which*) resemble ours, excepting lions, panthers, stags, pigs, goats, and deer: and even these have some dissimilarities of form: they have no horses nor mules, nor, saving your reverence, asses nor dogs, nor any kind of sheep or oxen: but so numerous are the other animals which they have, and all are savage, and of none do they make use for their service, that they could not be counted. What shall we say of others (*such as*) birds? which are so numerous, and of so many kinds, and of such various-coloured plumages, that it is a marvel to behold them. The soil is very pleasant and fruitful, full of immense woods and forests: and it is always green, for the foliage never drops off. The fruits are so many that they are numberless and entirely different from ours. This land is within the torrid zone, close to or just under the parallel described by the Tropic of Cancer: where the pole of the horizon has an elevation of 23 degrees, at the extremity of the second climate. Many tribes came to see us, and wondered at our faces and our whiteness: and they asked us whence we came: and we gave them to understand that we had come from heaven, and that we were going to see the world, and they believed it. In this land we placed baptismal fonts, and an infinite (*number of*) people were baptised, and they called us in their language Carabi, which means men of great wisdom. We took our departure from that port: and the province is called Lariab: and we navigated along the coast, always in sight of land, until we had run 870 leagues of it, still going in the direction of the maestrale (*north-west*) making in our course many halts, and holding intercourse with many peoples: and in several places we obtained gold by barter but not much in quantity, for we had done enough in discovering the land and learning that they had gold. We had now been thirteen months on the voyage: and the vessels and the tackling were already much damaged, and the men worn out by fatigue: we decided by general council to haul our ships on land and examine them for the purpose of stanching leaks, as they made much water, and of caulking and tarring them afresh, and (*then*) returning towards Spain: and when we came to this determination, we were close to a harbour the best in the world: into which we entered with our vessels: where we found an immense number of people: who received us with much friendliness: and on the shore we made a bastion with our boats and with barrels and casks, and our artillery which commanded every point: and our ships having been unloaded and lightened, we drew them upon land, and repaired them in everything that was needful: and the land's people gave us very great assistance. Continually furnished us with their victuals: so that in this port we tasted little of our own, which suited our game well: for the stock of provisions which we had for our return-passage was little and of sorry kind: where (*i.e., there*) we remained 37 days: and went many times to their villages? where they paid us the greatest honour: and (*now*) desiring to depart upon our voyage, they made complaint to us how at certain times of the year there came from over the sea to this their land, a race of people very cruel, and enemies of theirs: and (*who*) by means of treachery or of violence slew many of them, and ate them: and some they made captives, and carried them away to their houses, or country: and how they could scarcely contrive to defend themselves from them, making signs to us that (*those*) were an island-people and lived out in the sea about a hundred leagues away: and so piteously did they tell us this that we believed them: and we promised to avenge them of so much wrong: and they remained overjoyed herewith: and many of them offered to come along with us, but we did not wish to take them for many reasons, save that we took seven of them, on condition that they should come (*i.e., return home*) afterwards in (*their own*) canoes because we did not desire to be obliged to take them back to their country. They were contented: and so we departed from those people, leaving them very friendly towards us: and having repaired our ships, and sailing for seven days out to sea between north-east and east: and at the end of the seven days we came upon the islands, which were many, some (*of them*) inhabited, and others deserted: and we anchored at one of them: where we saw a numerous people who called it Iti: and having manned our boats with strong crews, and (*taken ammunition for*) three cannon-shots in each, we made for land: where we found (*assembled*) about 400 men, and many women, and all naked like the former (*peoples*). They were of good bodily presence, and seemed right warlike men: for they were armed with their weapons, which are bows, arrows, and lances: and most of them had square wooden targets: and bore them in such wise that they did not impede the drawing of the bow: and when we had come with our boats to about a bowshot of the land, they all sprang into the water to shoot their arrows at us and to prevent us from leaping upon shore: and they all had their bodies painted of various colours, and (*were*) plumed with feathers: and the interpreters who were with us told us that when (*those*) displayed themselves so painted and plumed, it was to betoken that they wanted to fight: and so much did they persist in preventing us from landing, that we were compelled to play with our artillery: and when they heard the explosion, and saw one of them fall dead, they all drew back to the land: wherefore, forming our council, we resolved that 42 of our men should spring on shore, and, if they waited for us, fight them: thus having leaped to land with our weapons, they advanced towards us, and we fought for about an hour, for we had but little advantage of them, except that our arbalasters and gunners killed some of them, and they wounded certain of our men: and this was because they did not stand to receive us within reach of lance-thrust or sword-blow: and so much vigour did we put forth at last, that we came to sword-play, and when they tasted our weapons, they betook themselves to flight through the mountains and the forests, and left us conquerors of the field with many of them dead and a good number wounded: and for that day we took no other pains to pursue them, because we were very weary, and we returned to our ships, with so much gladness on the part of the seven men who had come with us that they could not contain themselves (*for joy*): and when the next day arrived, we beheld coming across the land a great number of people, with signals of battle, continually sounding horns, and various other instruments which they use in their wars: and all (*of them*) painted and feathered, so that it was a very strange sight to behold them: wherefore all the ships held council, and it was resolved that since this people desired hostility with us, we should proceed to encounter them and try by every means to make them friends: in case they would not have our friendship, that we should treat them as foes, and so many of them as we might be able to capture should all be our slaves: and having armed ourselves as best we could, we advanced towards the shore, and they sought not to hinder us from landing, I believe from fear of the cannons: and we jumped on land, 57 men in four squadrons, each one (*consisting of*) a captain and his company:

and we came to blows with them: and after a long battle (*in which*) many of them (*were*) slain, we put them to flight, and pursued them to a village, having made about 250 of them captives, and we burnt the village, and returned to our ships with victory and 250 prisoners, leaving many of them dead and wounded, and of ours there were no more than one killed, and 22 wounded, who all escaped (*i.e., recovered*), God be thanked. We arranged our departure, and seven men, of whom five were wounded, took an island-canoe, and with seven prisoners that we gave them, four women and three men, returned to their (*own*) country full of gladness, wondering at our strength: and we thereon made sail for Spain with 222 captive slaves: and reached the port of Calis (*Cadiz*) on the 15th day of October, 1498, where we were well received and sold our slaves. Such is what befell me, most noteworthy, in this my first voyage.

VERRAZZANO'S DESCRIPTION OF NEW YORK HARBOR

[Born near Greve in Tuscany in 1485, Giovanni da Verrazzano moved to Dieppe, France, about 1506 to pursue what became a successful maritime career. He made several voyages to the Middle East, and in 1508 sailed to Newfoundland. Obtaining support from the French king, François I, Verrazzano left for the New World aboard *La Dauphine* in January 1524, ostensibly to search for a water passage to the Orient. Sighting land at Cape Fear, North Carolina, he sailed first south, then, to avoid contacting any Spaniards who might be in the vicinity, turned north. On April 17, *La Dauphine* entered New York harbor. Verrazzano's account of his discovery, including his encounter with Wampanoag Indians, follows. He later continued his voyage, going up along the coast of Maine, before returning to France on July 8, 1524. Verrazzano made at least two more voyages across the Atlantic, but he did not return from the last. Wading ashore on the island of Guadeloupe in 1528, he was killed by a number of Carib Indians.]

At the end of a hundred leagues we found a very agreeable situation located within two small prominent hills, in the midst of which flowed to the sea a very great river, which was deep within the mouth; and from the sea to the hills of that [place] with the rising of the tides, which we found eight feet, any laden ship might have passed. On account of being anchored off the coast in good shelter, we did not wish to adventure in without knowledge of the entrances. We were with the small boat, entering the said river to the land,

From *Fifteenth Annual Report* of the American Scenic and Historic Preservation Society (Albany, N.Y.), 1910.

which we found much populated. The people, almost like the others [which they had seen further south], clothed with the feathers of birds of various colors, came toward us joyfully, uttering very great exclamations of admiration, showing us where we could land with the boat more safely. We entered said river, within the land, about half a league, where we saw it made a very beautiful lake with a circuit of about three leagues; through which they [the Indians] went, going from one and another part to the number of XXX [30] of their little barges, with innumerable people, who passed from one shore and the other in order to see us. In an instant, as is wont to happen in navigation, a gale of unfavorable wind blowing in from the sea, we were forced to return to the ship, leaving the said land with much regret because of its commodiousness and beauty, thinking it was not without some properties of value, all of its hills showing indications of minerals.

The anchor raised, sailing toward the east, as thus the land turned, having traveled LXXX [80] leagues always in sight of it, we discovered an island triangular in form, distant ten leagues from the continent, in size like the island of Rhodes, full of hills, covered with trees, much populated [judging] by the continuous fires along all the surrounding shore which we saw they made. We baptized it in the name of your most illustrious mother. . . .

ENRICO DI TONTI IN THE MISSISSIPPI VALLEY

[Tonti, son of a
Neapolitan banker-in-exile, was probably born in Gaeta in 1674.
From age 18, his whole life was a career of military service for
France. He enlisted for duty in the New World under La Salle in
1678; after 1680, he lived in the Mississippi Valley and Tonti can
be credited as the founder of Illinois. In 1682, he and La Salle
descended the Mississippi River to the Gulf of Mexico. Having
returned north, he oversaw the building of Fort St. Louis at
present day Starved Rock in 1682–83. After La Salle's death, Tonti
remained in the Illinois country until 1700, when he went south to
a newly formed colony in Louisiana. He died there, only four years
later, on September 6, 1704. The following selection is taken from
Tonti's *Memoir on La Salle's Discoveries 1678–1690* written in 1693.
It covers events from 1678 through the descent of the Mississippi
in 1682.]

After having been eight years in the French service, by land and
by sea, and having had a hand shot off in Sicily by a grenade,
I resolved to return to France to solicit employment. At that time
the late M. Cavelier de La Salle came to court, a man of great
intelligence and merit, who sought to obtain leave from the court
to explore the Gulf of Mexico by traversing the countries of North
America. Having obtained of the King the permission he desired
through the favor of the late M. Colbert and M. de Seignelai, the
late Monseigneur the Prince of Conti, who was acquainted with him
and who honored me with his favor, sent me to ask him to be

From Louis Phelps Kellogg, ed., *Early Narratives of the Northwest 1634–1699* (New York,
1917), pp. 283–322.

allowed to accompany him in his long journeys, to which he very willingly assented.

We sailed from Rochelle on the 14th of July, 1678, and arrived at Quebec on the 15th of September following. We recruited there for some days, and after having taken leave of M. the Count de Frontenac, governor general of the country, ascended the St. Lawrence as far as Fort Frontenac, 120 leagues from Quebec, on the banks of the Lake of Frontenac, which is about 300 leagues around, and after staying there four days, we embarked in a boat of forty tons to cross this lake, and on Christmas day we found ourselves opposite a village called Tsonnontouan, to which M. de La Salle sent some canoes to procure Indian corn for our subsistence. From thence we sailed towards Niagara, intending to look for a suitable place above the Falls where a boat might be built. The winds were so contrary that we could not approach it nearer than nine leagues, which determined us to go by land. We found there some cabins of the Iroquois, who received us well. We slept there, and the next day we went three leagues further up to look for a good place to build a boat. There we encamped.

The boat in which we came was lost on the coast through the obstinacy of the pilot, whom M. de La Salle had ordered to bring it ashore. The crew and the things in it were saved. M. de La Salle determined to return to Fort Frontenac over the ice, and I remained in command at Niagara with a Recollect Father [Louis Hennepin] and thirty men. The bark was completed in the spring. M. de La Salle joined us with two other Recollect Fathers and several men, to aid in bringing this bark up, on account of the rapids, which I was not able to ascend on account of the weakness of my crew. He directed me to wait for him at the extremity of Lake Erie, at a place called Detroit, 120 leagues from Niagara, to join there some Frenchmen whom he had sent off the last autumn. I went in advance in a bark canoe, and when we were near Detroit the ship came up. We got into it, and continued our voyage as far as Missilimakinak, where we arrived at the end of August, having crossed two lakes larger than that of Frontenac.

We remained there some days to rest ourselves, and as M. de La Salle intended to go to the Illinois, he sent me to the Sault Sainte-Marie, where Lake Superior discharges itself into Lake Huron, to look for some of his men who had deserted, and himself set sail on the Lake of the Islinois. Having arrived at Poutouatamis, an Islinois village, the calumet was sung, a ceremony of theirs during which large presents are given and received, and in which a post is placed in the midst of the assembly, where those who wish to make known their great deeds in war, striking the post, declaim on the deeds they have done. This ceremony regularly takes place in the presence of those with whom they wish to make alliance, and the calumet is among the savages the symbol of peace. M. de La Salle sent his ship back to Niagara to fetch the things he wanted, and, embarking in a canoe, continued his voyage to the Miamis River. There he commenced building a house.

In the meantime I came up with the deserters, and kept on my way to within thirty leagues of the Miamis River, where I was obliged to leave my men, in order to hunt, our provisions failing us. I then went on to join M. de La Salle. When I arrived he told me he wished that all the men had come with me in order to proceed to the Islinois. I retraced my way to find them. But the wind increasing, we were forced to land, and the violence of the waves was such that our canoe was upset. We were, however, saved, but everything that was in the canoe was lost, and for want of provisions we lived for three days on acorns. I sent word of what had happened to M. de La Salle. He directed me to join him. I went in my little canoe. As soon as I arrived we ascended twenty-five leagues, as far as the portage, where the men whom I had left behind joined us. We made the portage, which is about two leagues in length, and came to the source of the Islinois River. We embarked there and descended the river for 100 leagues. When we arrived at the village of the savages, they were absent hunting and as we had no provisions we opened some caches of Indian corn.

During this journey some of our Frenchmen, fatigued, determined to leave us, but that night was so cold that their plan was broken up. We continued our route, in order to join the savages, and found them thirty leagues below the village. When they saw us they thought we were Iroquois, and therefore put themselves on the defensive and made their women run into the woods; but when they recognized us, the women with their children were called back and the calumet was danced to M. de La Salle and me, in order to mark their desire to live in peace with us. We gave them some merchandise for the corn which we had taken in their village.

This was on the 3d of January, 1679. It was necessary to fortify ourselves for the winter. Applying ourselves to it, we made a fort which was called Crèvecœur. Part of our people deserted and they even put poison into our kettle. M. de La Salle was poisoned, but he was saved by some antidote a friend had given to him in France. The desertion of these men gave us less annoyance than the effect which it had on the minds of the savages, for the enemies of M. de La Salle had spread a report among the Islinois that we were friends of the Iroquois, who are their greatest enemies. . . . We reached Missilimakinak about Corpus Christi in 1680 [1681]. M. de La Salle arrived some time afterwards, on his way to seek us at the Illinois, with M. de La Forest. He was very glad to see us again, and notwithstanding all reverses, we made new preparations to continue the exploration which he had undertaken. I therefore embarked with him for Fort Frontenac, to bring things that we should need for the expedition. Father Zénoble accompanied us thither. When we came to Lake Frontenac, M. de La Salle went forward, and I waited for his boat at the village of Teyagon. When it arrived there I embarked for the Islinois. When we came to the Miamis River I assembled some Frenchmen and savages for the exploration, and M. de La Salle joined us in December.

We went in canoes to the River Chicaou, where there is a portage which joins that of the Islinois. The rivers being frozen we made sledges and dragged our baggage to a point thirty leagues below the village of Islinois, and there, finding the navigation open, we arrived at the end of January at the River Mississipy [Feb. 6, 1682]. We proceeded on our course, and . . . arrived at the sea on the 7th of April [1682].

M. de La Salle sent canoes to inspect the channels. Some went to the channel on the right hand, some to the left, and M. de La Salle chose that in the centre. In the evening each made his report, that is to say, that the channels were very fine, wide, and deep. We encamped on the right bank, erected the arms of the King, and returned several times to inspect the channels. The same report was made.

This river is 800 leagues long, without rapids, to wit, 400 from the country of the Sioux, and 400 from the mouth of the Islinois River to the sea. The banks are almost uninhabitable, on account of the spring floods. The woods are chiefly poplar, the country one of canes and briars and of trees torn up by the roots; but a league or two from the river, is the most beautiful country in the world, prairies, open woods of mulberry trees, vines, and fruits that we are not acquainted with. The savages gather the Indian corn twice in the year. In the lower course of the river, the part which might be settled, is where the river makes a course north and south, for there, in many places, every now and then it has bluffs on the right and left.

The river is only navigable for ships as far as the village of Nadesche, for above that place the river winds too much; but this would not prevent one's setting out from the country above with pirogues and flatboats, to proceed from the Ouabache to the sea. There are but few beavers, but to make amends, there is a large number of buffaloes or bears, large wolves, stags, *sibolas* [buffalo], hinds, and roe deer in abundance; and some lead mines, with less than one-third refuse. As these savages are stationary, and have some habits of subordination, they might be obliged to make silk in order to procure necessaries for themselves, if the eggs of silkworms were brought to them from France, for the forests are full of mulberry trees. This would be a valuable trade.

EUSEBIO KINO'S EXPLORATION OF CALIFORNIA

[Eusebio Francisco Kino was born in Segno, Italy, in 1645 and entered the Jesuit order at the age of 20. He came to Mexico to work as a missionary among the Indians in 1681, first in Lower California, and then among the Pimo Indians in Primeria Alta (now southern Arizona and northern Sonora). Based at Mission Dolores from 1687 until his death in 1711, Kino explored and charted much of the Southwest. His most significant work in cartography was the preparation of maps between 1698 and 1701 proving that California was not an island, as had been believed. Apart from his explorations, he was able to found about twenty missions, of which the best known is San Xavier del Bac near Tucson, Arizona. Following Kino's pioneering efforts, other Italian Jesuits came to the Southwest, among them Juan Mario de Salvatierra, Francesco Saveria Saetta, Francesco M. Piccolo, and Jesus Lombardi, who was killed in the 1680 Indian revolt at Santa Fe. The selection below contains Kino's assertions about California in a short chapter entitled "Cogent Reasons and Clear Arguments Which Establish the Certainty of the Land Passage to California."]

In case there should be some incredulous persons or someone ignorant of it, the continuity of these lands with California would be rendered certain and proved by the seven following convincing reasons or arguments:

1st. Because thus I saw it on October 9, 1698, from the neighboring high mountain of Santa Clara. And again in March of the past

Herbert E. Bolton, ed., *Kino's Historical Memoir of Primeria Alta* (Cleveland, 1919), Vol. I, Chapter 8.

year, 1701, we saw this connection and passage by land to California, in the company of Father Rector Juan María de Salvatierra, for his Reverence came with ten soldiers and other persons to see this demonstrated, since some had contradicted us.

2d. Because in four other journeys inland which I have made, travelling fifty leagues to the northwest of the said hill of Santa Clara, which is near to and to the eastward of the arm and head of the Sea of California, and afterwards in going ten leagues more to the westward, along the Rio Grande, to where it unites with the Colorado River, and from this confluence forty leagues more to the southwest, along the same Colorado River to its mouth, no Sea of California has been found or seen, for it does not rise higher than barely to the latitude of thirty-two degrees. Hence it is plainly to be inferred that Drake, besides many other modern cosmographers, in their various printed maps, with notable discredit to cosmography, deceive themselves as well as others, by extending this sea, or arm, or strait of the Sea of California from thirty-two to forty-six degrees, making it thereby an island, and the largest in the world, whereas it is not an island but a peninsula.

3d. Because in this journey inland when I was saying mass on March 11 at the above-mentioned mouth of the Colorado River, in company with Father Rector Manuel Gonzales, the sun rose above more than thirty leagues of sea, at the head of this Californian arm or gulf. At the same time, from the same estuary we saw to the westward thirty leagues more of continuous land, as many more to the south and southwest, and many more to the north, northwest, and northeast. Therefore, this sea does not extend to the north.

4th. Because the natives nearest to that estuary, Quiquimas as well as Cutganes and Coanopas, both this time and on other occasions, gave us various blue shells which are found only on the opposite coast and on the other, or South Sea, where the ship from China comes. And they gave us this time some little pots which shortly before they had brought from that opposite coast, travelling ten leagues from the west by continuous land.

5th. Because these natives and others who came to see us from far to the southwest gave us various reports of the fathers of our Company, telling us that they wore our costumes and vestments, and that they lived down there to the souhward with the other Spaniards at Loreto Concho, where the Guimies and Edues, or Laimones Indians obtained their food, and where Father Rector Juan María de Salvatierra and others were. And I having purposely asked them if those Guimies and Edues Indians down there planted maize, and what foods they lived on, they answered us that they did not plant maize nor beans, etc., but that their food was game, the deer, the hare, the mountain goat, the *pitajaya*, the *tuna*, the *mescal*, and other wild fruits, and that the Indians to the westward had blue shells, all being things and reports which it was plain to me were true, since I was there and lived with those Indians seventeen years ago.

6th. Because now in this journey inland and on other occasions I have found various things—little trees, fruit, incense, etc.—all species which are peculiar to California alone, and samples of which I bring, to celebrate with the incense, by the favor of heaven, this Easter and Holy Week, and to place five good grains of incense in the Paschal candle. Moreover, near this estuary we already have found some words of the Guimia language which I learned there, while missionary and rector of that mission of California, although unworthy, in the two trienniums of Fathers Provincial Bernardo Pardo and Luys del Canto, from the year 1681 to that of 1685.

7th. Because the ancient maps with good reason showed California as a peninsula and not as an island, as well as some modern ones, among them the universal map of my Father master of mathematics in the University of Ingolstadt, which is in my possession. He dedicated it to our Father San Ygnacio and to San Francisco Xavier, with this inscription: *de Universo Terrarum Orbe Opime Meritis* [To the well deserving of the whole world].

And if some hostile and obstinate persons should maintain that some Quiquima Indians say that farther west the sea still extends to the northwest, these Quiquimas speak of the other sea, on the opposite coast, and not of this our Sea of California, of which, as some call it Red Sea, we may say, because we have found this passage, *Aparuit terra arida, et in Mari Rubro via sine inpedimento* [Dry land appeared and in the Red Sea a way without hindrance], as says the Church on August 8, on the day of the saints who have the Gospel: *Euntes in mundum universum. Predicate Evangelium omni creaturæ* [Go ye into all the world and preach the Gospel unto every creature].

FILIPPO MAZZEI AND AMERICAN INDEPENDENCE

[Mazzei, a native of Tuscany, was a physician, horticulturalist, and political philosopher. Brought to Virginia in 1773 along with a group of Italian farm workers, he was supposed to spend his time on agricultural experiments to improve the productivity of the colony. But he soon became involved in the political agitation against England, and from 1774 to 1781 he devoted most of his time to helping the movement for independence. In 1779, Governor Patrick Henry of Virginia commissioned Mazzei to return to Tuscany to ask for a loan and supplies to aid in the war against England. The mission was not successful, although Mazzei remained in Italy four years, but he did publicize the American cause. During his stay in Florence, he conferred frequently with the Grand Duke, Leopold, and wrote him a series of letters urging aid for the Americans. The following letter, of August 26, 1782, was writen at a time when the success of the Revolution was fairly well assured. Mazzei returned to Virginia in 1783 and remained for nearly two years. Although a citizen of Virginia, he was unable to gain political prominence there after the war. He therefore sailed again for Europe in 1785, never to see the United States again.]

Your Royal Highness' most humble servant, Filippo Mazzei, realizing that the hour of his departure is approaching, has deemed it his duty humbly to submit this last memorandum, before presenting himself personally before Your Royal Highness, to receive the honor of your commands.

In his last memorandum he mentioned that the cabinet of the

From *William and Mary College Quarterly Historical Magazine*, October, 1942, pp. 369–74.

King of England had agreed to recognize the independence of America without any reservations in the event that General Carleton were not successful in persuading Americans to make some face-saving concessions. In the postscript he mentioned the upheaval which occurred in the ministry, adding that if this produced any change in their resolution with regard to America, he would take the liberty to inform Your Royal Highness of it. He also stated that no more than fifteen and perhaps only eight days would elapse before he could produce unequivocal proofs in support of his statements. A protracted period of indisposition did not permit him to do so within the time indicated, and he, therefore, asks permission to do so now, in order that from his letters Your Royal Highness may, at any future time, see how events have borne out all he has written. The extraordinary power of your memory will enable you to recall what he has had the honor of communicating to you orally.

On the tenth of last month General Conway and the Duke of Richmond in their desire to show Parliament that Mr. Fox and other colleagues had had no just reasons for absenting themselves from the ministry, not only gave ample proof that the resolution had been adopted by the council, but also indicated that there was no intention to modify this or any other measure that had already been agreed upon. Furthermore, they added that if any changes were made, they too would resign. But the most positive proof that could be presented is the statement made in Parliament by Count Shelburne, since he is the present Prime Minister, and the open enemy of the absolute independence of Americans. He declared that, although he personally still thought that as soon as the absolute independence of America was recognized, the splendor of England's glory would forever become obscured, he had nevertheless yielded to the majority in the council.

In order to understand the opinion of the English nation on this subject, it is sufficient to know that all those ministers (both those who resigned and those who remained in office) who maintained, as they still do, that it is necessary to recognize the absolute independence of America, enjoy the esteem and trust of the nation, while Lord Shelburne has lost all his popularity. On the other hand, according to persons who should be better informed or more truthful, His Majesty in the conversations he has had with this minister, is said to have assured Shelburne that he would support him only so long as he continued to be with the King's party against the absolute independence of America. But these conversations are pure fabrications which are devoid of truth and common sense. Although the King's party has done everything possible to conceal the true motives that led to the appointment of Lord Shelburne as Prime Minister, a circumstance that resulted in a split in the new ministry, it is known that the appointment was made in an effort to stop the execution of a plan which tended to diminish the influence of the Crown. The writer has positive information on this point, and submits as proof the fact that Lord Shelburne's last speech was no less equivocal than the responsories of oracles. Those who resigned from the Ministry accused him of inconsistency and duplicity. Mr. Fox in particular, while praising the sentiments of some of his friends who remained in office, condemned their lack of foresight and predicted that they would in time become wise and follow his example.

It is not certain whether the royal court will win its point. Judging by appearances, the chances are that it will win, since there is no longer any talk of changing the present Parliament, the majority of whose members favors the former ministry.

As for the independence of America, there is now no reason why the English should give another humiliating proof of their weakness by recognizing America before agreeing on a general peace. From General Carleton's dispatches Englishmen have seen that this would not help them to obtain a truce from America.

The ill-considered statements that England will never, at any cost, recognize America's independence, come from persons whose minds are distorted by passion, or who suffer from political short-sightedness, for it is quite clear that such a step, however hard it may be, is inevitable.

The writer begs Your Royal Highness to permit him to speak frankly of the situation in America in consideration of the fact that up to now all his predictions have been borne out, even though in his conversations and letters he may have merely suggested to Your Royal Highness the probability and not the certainty of these events. He is induced to do this solely through his desire to feel that he has done all he could decently do to persuade Your Royal Highness to look with less indifference upon those means which may tend to preserve the good will of the *only* country whose friendship may be of great benefit to the commerce and *all* the industries of your States. Despite the war, the power of America increases by great strides, and the writer has recently received authentic proofs of this fact from Virginia, Philadelphia, and from Mr. Adams, the Minister to Holland.

For still some time to come any major European sea power, that is willing uselessly to sacrifice more than it can ever gain, can harm Americans along their seaboard, but a combination of all Europe can no longer take from them their independence.

It must not be presumed that the belligerent powers of Europe will make peace only on the condition that England and America end their disputes, for England would immediately offer America treaties of alliance and commerce which will in no way tend to limit the independence of Americans.

But even if such a peace should be concluded, and England should refuse to deal with America as an independent power, Americans would immediately stop all foreign trade for which they have no absolute need. Their frigates and privateers would do much harm to the English for whom commerce is a vital need. Since England has no privateers, she would be obliged to bear the expenses of a naval warfare to give what can at best be imperfect protection to its own commerce.

America produces everything. By merely shifting the workers who are now engaged in the production of the immense quantities of raw materials that are shipped abroad, she can easily manufacture any article. If it is true that Americans prefer agricultural pursuits to any other, it must be remembered that that is due to force of habit and to the fact that they look upon farming as a more pleasant occupation. Furthermore, there are large tracts of excellent land which are very profitable. This project has been under consideration for some time. The writer was told that he was the first to propose it. The fact is that the writer made the proposal as soon as he received from Dr. Franklin the reply mentioned in his first memorandum. In that reply Dr. Franklin stated that at that time Congress had not even thought of entering into trade relations with European powers. The writer's proposal was submitted to Congress by Mr. Jefferson, whom I have repeatedly mentioned; Dr. Franklin expressed himself as holding the same opinion as the writer. The suggestion would have been adopted the following year had France not hastened to accept the proposals received from Americans. France accepted only because she heard that England herself, following the total defeat of General Burgoyne because of his having ventured too far inland, was about to propose conditions of settlement. This situation invariably arises whenever the enemy commits such errors.

A few months ago the improved morale of the English occasioned by the change in the ministry proved nothing but a pure and fleeting delusion. The result of the battle of April 12, merely caused a respite from the evils; it was not a favorable turn in the tide of events. Serious consideration is being given in England to the means of avoiding total disaster, and of retrieving as much as possible their lost trade with America. It is not true that they are deceiving themselves in believing that they can obtain from America any concession which would infringe upon her rank as a sovereign nation. They are fully convinced of this fact, despite their efforts to lead various courts into believing the contrary. Their object is to discourage these courts from acquiring for their respective states the commerce with America without which English industries can never again flourish as in the past. All Englishmen agree on this point.

Besides, they deceive themselves in thinking that they can retrieve a considerable part of America's trade; the wounds inflicted are too deep and too recent. If ever private persons in America should, by force of habit, permit themselves to resume trade relations, their legislative bodies would enact laws to stop them.

The means to carry this out are not wanting. Before the writer's departure from Virginia, this state was considering the advisability of placing high tariffs on English manufactures that might be imported after the restoration of peace. It was proposed to use the revenue to indemnify persons who suffered losses by a method of warfare unworthy of civilized nations. It is very probable that the other states will follow the example of Virginia, as they have done in other matters.

England cannot long delay to give up her ill-founded claims on America. It is certain that Americans will be tacitly or openly grateful to those who have aided them, or at least shown a disposition to do so. They will make a clear distinction between friendly people and those who have shown themselves opposed or indifferent to them.

In this last memorandum, the writer has deemed it his duty to call Your Royal Highness' attention to the matters herein recited in order that Your Royal Highness may in your wisdom be better able to judge whether it is more expedient to you to profess a complete indifference toward the friendship of the American states in general and of Virginia in particular, or to give evidence of your appreciation of it. Your Royal Highness could do so in various ways, without at all compromising yourself.

If the affectionate veneration in which the writer has always held your person and his great desire to merit your benevolence, as well as the means he has used to deserve it, are deemed worthy of a gracious reward, he begs that it be in the form of an audience, longer than usual, before his departure, for which purpose he will present himself at the public audience. Meanwhile, with the greatest deference and with profound veneration, he has the honor to remain Your Royal Highness' most humble servant, etc.

ITALIAN OPERA IN AMERICA

Lorenzo Da Ponte

[Having gained a great reputation as librettist for Mozart, Da Ponte came to the United States in 1805 and was considered one of the most cosmopolitan residents of New York City for the next three decades. A native of Venice, he had been a clergyman, but involvement in scandal forced him to flee to Austria in 1779. His collaborations with Mozart in the 1780's produced such masterpieces as *The Marriage of Figaro, Don Giovanni,* and *Cosí Fan Tutte.* In America he tried his hand at making a living in several ways, but was most successful when promoting the Italian language and culture. He taught Italian privately for several years, and in 1825 was appointed the first professor of Italian at Columbia College. He also undertook to run a bookstore selling works of Italian literature. In 1825, he began importing Italian opera companies as described in the selection below. By 1833, he had raised enough money for an opera house, but this enterprise was unsuccessful. Da Ponte died at the age of 89, in 1838.]

Though, to my joy, I could see the interest in Italian letters increasing daily both in New York and other cities of the Union, I still thought there was another way of making them both more widely spread and more highly esteemed; but, to tell the truth, I did not dare to hope for such a thing. What, therefore, was my delight, when a number of persons assured me that the famous Garzia, with his incomparable daughter and several other Italian singers, was coming from London to America, and in fact to New York, to

From Arthur Livingston, ed., *Memoirs of Lorenzo Da Ponte* (Philadelphia, 1929), Part 5.

establish the Italian opera there—the *desideratum* of my greatest zeal?

He came, in truth, and the effect was prodigious. Unimaginable the enthusiasm in the cultivated portions of the public aroused by our music when executed by singers of most perfect taste and highest merit. The *Barbiere di Siviglia* of the universally admired and praised Rossini, was the opera fortunate enough to plant the first root of the great tree of Italian music in New York [Nov. 29, 1825, premiere].

A short time before our singers were to arrive, a young American, a youth of much talent, and a great lover of the noble art of music, was talking of it with friends of his one day in my presence, and as it were *ex cathedra*. Finding his notions erroneous, I remarked in jest:

"Silence, King Solomon! You know nothing of music yet!"

That excellent young man felt a flash of anger, but I begged him to be calm and promised soon to convince him. Sometime later Garzia arrived. The "Barber of Seville" of the Rossini mentioned was announced for the opening night. I took him to the fifth performance, with others of my pupils, and that admirable music caught them up, along with the rest of the audience, into a sort of ecstatic spell. Having observed from their perfect silence, the expressions on their faces and in their eyes, and their constant clapping of hands, the marvelous effect that music had had on them, I approached my sceptic, when the performance was over, and asked him what he thought of it: "Mr. Da Ponte," he said generously, "you are right. I confess with real pleasure that I did not know an iota about music." Not far different the impressions of the first performance on all those who did not have their ears lined with that sheepskin of which drums are made, or some particular interest in speaking ill of it—(a newspaper critic of the dishonest tribe honored Italian music with the name of "monstrous")—whether to give the palm to the music of other countries, or to praise to the stars the clucking of some amorous hen. But despite such prattling, the delight in our music in New York was so constant, that few were the evenings when the theatre was not filled with a large and select audience; and that happened, when it happened, I believe, through lack of poise in the Spanish conductor.

How great an interest I took in the continuance and success of such an enterprise is too easy to imagine to require words of mine. I clearly foresaw the many enormous advantages our literature would derive from it and how it would tend to propagate our language through the attractiveness of the Italian Opera which, in the eyes of every cultivated nation of the world, is the noblest and most pleasurable of all the many spectacles the human intelligence ever invented, and to the perfecting of which the noblest arts have vied with one another in contributing.

But however beautiful, however esteemed, the operas set to

music by Rossini might be, it seemed to me that to give fewer performances of them and alternate them with those of other composers would be a most profitable thing, both for the reputation of the excellent Rossini and for the treasury of the producers. A good fowl is certainly an appetizing dish; but it was served often enough by the Marchioness of Montferrat at the dinners which she gave the King of France, to prompt that Majesty to inquire whether hens were all one could find in that country. I mentioned the point to Garzia; he liked it; and at my suggesting to him my *Don Giovanni* set to music by the immortal Mozart, he uttered another cry of joy and said nothing but this:

"If we have enough actors to give *Don Giovanni*, let us give it soon. It's the best opera in the world!"

I was as happy as could be at such an answer, both because I hoped for an excellent success, and from a keen desire, natural enough in me, to see some drama of mine presented on the stage in America. But looking over the field, we discovered that the company lacked a singer capable of playing the part of Don Ottavio. I undertook to find him myself, and I did find him; and then when the manager of the Opera refused to incur additional expense, between me, my pupils and my friends, we provided the money to pay him; and *Don Giovanni* appeared on the stage [May 23, 1826, premiere].

I was not disappointed in my hopes. Everything pleased, everything was admired and praised—words, music, actors, performance; and the beautiful, brilliant and amiable daughter was as distinguished, and shone as brilliantly, in the part of Zerlinetta as her father seemed incomparable in the part of Don Giovanni. Varying, in truth, were opinions in the audience as to the transcendent merit of those two rare portents in the realm of harmony. Some preferred Rossini, some the German, nor could I say with assurance which had the more partisans, *Il Barbiere di Siviglia* or *Don Giovanni*. It should be observed, however, that Mozart, either because he is no more or because he was not an Italian, not only has no enemies, but is exalted to the heights for his supreme merit by impartial judges and connoisseurs; whereas Rossini has a very goodly party of enemies, some because they are envious of his renown, others through malice inborn and an accursed instinct to criticize and to depreciate anything remarkable that Italy produces.

INDIAN AGENT
AT FORT SNELLING
Lawrence Taliaferro

[The Taliaferros of
Virginia were an established family by the time Lawrence was born
in 1794. Four brothers, John, Francis, James, and Lawrence, had
emigrated to Virginia from Genoa, Italy, in 1637. After serving in the
War of 1812, the Lawrence described in this selection pursued a
military career in Chicago; Chillicothe, Ohio; and Green Bay, Wisconsin. Appointed Indian agent by President Monroe in 1819, he was
responsible for overseeing the Sioux and Chippewa tribes from present day Minneapolis. Taliaferro was very successful in dealing with
the Indians, and they regarded him as a trusted friend. His enemies
in the West, those who sought to take advantage of the tribes—the
traders and Astor's American Fur Company—failed to dislodge him
from his post. He remained in Minnesota until 1839, when he moved
to Bedford, Pennsylvania. Except for a period of military service,
1857–63, he lived in retirement. The account below is taken from
Taliaferro's autobiography of 1864, written in the third person.]

Lieut. Taliaferro was noted for his proficiency in military tactics in
the battalion and evolutions of the line, and so reported on the
confidential inspection reports by Inspector General Wood, in July,
1818, when he left his post on a four months sick leave for the
Bedford Springs, in Pennsylvania. On his recovery, he passed on to
Washington city, where he paid his respects to the President, his
patron friend and connection. Here the President was pleased to
say: "He wished Lieut. Taliaferro to resign his position in the army;
he had heard a good report of him; he was above his rank; promo-

tion was too slow; that he wanted his services in a responsible civil capacity, where he would have more command of his time; go home to your mother, and remain until you hear from me." He was gratefully and politely thanked. On the 27th of March, following, the Secretary of War, John C. Calhoun, forwarded to his address at Fredericksburg the appointment of Agent of Indian Affairs at St. Peter's near the Falls of St. Anthony. The office was duly accepted, and he, after filing his bonds, left to join the expedition under Colonel Leavenworth, already ordered with his regiment, the Fifth Infantry, to lake post at the junction of the St. Peter and Mississippi. The Agent, however, repaired to St. Louis, and reported to Governor William Clark, Superintendent of Indian Affairs, and late companion of Lewis to the Columbia River. From St. Louis he keel-boated with the Winnebago Agent, N. Boilvin, as far as Prairie du Chien. Here falling in with a government boat, proceeded on this slow mode of conveyance, in company with an escort of Indians, headed by Tah-ma-ha—or, The Pike—sometimes called the "Burn," a one-eyed Indian, a great friend of the Americans in the war of 1812, who described many interesting scenes on the Mississippi, and on board the American gun boats. He possessed both cunning and much intelligence. His remarks upon the conduct of the Indians, and British traders who instigated them to acts of hostility against the United States, which confirmed the truth of much that had been previously stated in the public prints.

It may be remarked in this connection, that the new agent was not only apparently well received by the agents and traders, and citizens of Prairie du Chien, but rather obsequiously so by the former—in fact these felt their guilt being in the main yet British subjects. Among these was Joseph Rolette, agent of the American Fur Company, who seemed most desirous of feeling the pulse of the agent by many proffered acts of kindness and civilities, all of which was understood and properly appreciated.

The agent proceeded onward to his post—visiting the villages of Wabasha, Red Wing, at the head of Lake Pepin and Petite Corbeau or Little Crow, addressing the chiefs of each town as to the nature of his appointment and the reasons why the President had sent troops to erect a fort at St. Peters, and location of an agent to conduct the affairs of the Dakota nation, in connection with the chiefs of the "Seven fires;" that apparently their new father might seem to them young, but that he had an old soldier's head, and an honest heart, determined to cause the Indian trade to be well conducted for their benefit on principles of equal justice to all. . . .

The Indian country was more or less agitated east of the Mississippi, but west all was tranquil. In the midst of many perplexities, single-handed and alone, the Agent was consoled by many testimonials of well done, good and faithful servant. He was secure in the confidence of all honest men. Jackson was at the head of the government and the agent had been one of his old soldiers. His

Eagle eye saw all things, small, and great. His written message to the Little Crow, chief second of all the Sioux, showed he perfectly understood Indian wants and Indian character. "My Son, I have received your talk at the hands of your agent, Mr. Taliaferro. When he speaks, open your ears and listen, for you hear my words. You say truly 'we have both been warriors.' The war club is again buried deep in the ground. I am again your friend and the friend of your Nation —let us smoke the same pipe and eat out of the same dish. War is hurtful to any Nation. Keep the 'Seven fires' of your Nation in peace and good order, and I will try and do the same with the twenty-seven fires of my Nation. Make your wants known to your faithful agent and you will hear from your true friend speedily."

Doctor John Gale, of the army, writing from Council Bluffs, on the Missouri, says: "The whole army on this frontier unite in the belief that the government has for once an honest, efficient agent for Indian affairs. You know, my dear fellow, that I am too proud to flatter any man—yet it is refreshing to see the Indian department rapidly brought out of chaos and made a highly respectable branch of the government. You need not be surprised ere long to see ex-Ministers, ex-Governors, ex-Judges and Members of Congress, seeking for admission into it. I tell you, my old messmate and friend, you are a most fortunate civil appointment for the government, though I was one among many that regretted the resignation of one whose turn of mind seemed so well adapted to the army. Colonel Kearney and other officers now enroute for your Post, can give you an account of Indian affairs in this quarter—much *gas* but nothing real as to results."

Previous to 1835 the agent importuned the President to assign a sub-agent for the Chippewas of the Upper Mississippi and its tributaries, urging as a reason the remoteness of the Sault Ste Marie and the difficulties of the route. After some time a Mr. George Peterson, a Chippewa half-blood and brother-in-law of Henry R. Schoolcraft and agent for the Chippewas, was appointed and unfortunately located at Lapointe, Lake Superior. He proved of unsteady habits, consequently his people had no respect for him. After him a Mr. Symon or Simon, a discharged soldier, secured the situation and he, like his predecessor, drank more whiskey than the Indians. Maj. Dallam was offered the appointment, but after an investigation of the general condition of the Indians and the character of their traders, declined to serve. Finally Miles Vineyard, of Illinois, accepted and entered on his duties. Notwithstanding these efforts to be relieved from the visits of these people they still kept up (at all risks) their habits of seeing their friend the agent and the Military Post at Fort Snelling.

Part Two

IMMIGRATION AND THE PATTERNS OF SETTLEMENT, 1850–1929

Between 1820 and 1929 more than 4,600,000 Italians emigrated to the United States. This is a migration second only to the large German migration of the same period. The great majority of the Italian immigrants did not arrive until after 1880, however, hence their inclusion in the statistics of the "new immigration" from eastern and southern Europe. The immigration records kept by the Federal Government as of 1820 are not strictly accurate, especially for the early years, but they serve as an excellent guide to the relative number of arrivals from the many European nations. Only once before 1854 did more than 1,000 Italians arrive in any one year—in 1833, after the 1831–32 revolutions in France which spilled over into the Italian states. Not until 1870 were there more than 2,000 arrivals in any one year. Through the mid-1880's most of the newcomers were from the cities of northern Italy, but gradually, due to the breakdown of the land tenure system, overpopulation, and the failure of the government to meet pressing economic difficulties, the source of immigration shifted to the Mezzogiorno, the provinces of southern Italy. By 1900, for the first time, more than 100,000 Italians came to American shores in one year. For fifteen years that number was consistently exceeded, with 285,731 entering in the peak year 1907, and 283,738 in 1914. During and after World War I, immigration dropped markedly. Only in 1921, in a rush to get in under the wire as Congress prepared to halt or severely restrict the flow of immigrants, were there again more than 200,000 newcomers from Italy. In 1924 the Reed-Johnson Immigration Act was passed and signed by President Coolidge curtailing the century-old pattern of relatively free admission to the United States.

More than eighty per cent of the Italians who came to the United States after the Civil War settled in the northeast quarter of the country—from New York to Minnesota and north of the Mason-Dixon line—largely in the cities. "Little Italies" mushroomed in all major cities, with New York City becoming the first choice for Italian immigrants. By 1920, there were more than half a million in New York State, while Pennsylvania had 220,000, New Jersey, 157,000, and Massachusetts 117,000. It was another decade before Illinois exceeded the 100,000 mark. West of the Mississippi, Louisiana and California claimed more Italians than other states.

While such figures indicate that Italians became mostly urban dwellers, every state had its contingent of Italian immigrants. They worked on the iron range of Minnesota, in the coal mines of West Virginia and Kentucky, in the gold mines of California, and in the silver mines of Nevada. Italian immigrants took to the land as farmers in every state; and there were rural communities in Alabama, Arkansas, California, Colorado, Connecticut, Delaware, Louisiana, Maryland, Mississippi, Missouri, New Jersey, New York, North Carolina, Rhode Island, Tennessee, Utah, Texas, Virginia, Wisconsin, and Wyoming. The most famous of their farm communities were Vineland, New Jersey; Tontitown, Arkansas; and the Italian-Swiss Colony in northern California.

The selections in this chapter concern the general characteristics of the Italian immigration: its causes, the effects on Italy, and life in some of the immigrant communities.

ITALIAN LIFE IN
NEW YORK

[There had been a
colony of Italians living in New York City all during the 19th
century. For most of the century it was a small colony of Northern
Italians, numbering only a few hundred as late as 1850; but by
1881, there were more than 20,000 Italians in Manhattan, and the
"Little Italy" around Mulberry Street had become the prototype of
similar colonies in other parts of the city. In the 1870's, the tide
of immigration began to swell, and the new arrivals came predominantly from southern Italy. The selection below describes the
Italians of Manhattan in the early years of the "new immigration."]

The fact that Italian immigration is constantly on the increase in
New York makes it expedient to consider both the condition
and status of these future citizens of the republic. The higher walks
of American life, in art, science, commerce, literature, and society,
have, as is well known, long included many talented and charming
Italians; but an article under the above title must necessarily
deal with the subject in its lower and more recent aspect. During
the year 1879 seven thousand two hundred Italian immigrants were
landed at this port, one-third of which number remained in the city,
and there are now over twenty thousand Italians scattered among
the population of New York. The more recently arrived herd
together in colonies, such as those in Baxter and Mott streets,
in Eleventh Street, in Yorkville, and in Hoboken. Many of the most
important industries of the city are in the hands of Italians as
employers and employed, such as the manufacture of macaroni, of
objects of art, confectionery, artificial flowers; and Italian workmen
may be found everywhere mingled with those of other nationalities.

From *Harper's Magazine*, April, 1881.

It is no uncommon thing to see at noon some swarthy Italian, engaged on a building in process of erection, resting and dining from his tin kettle, while his brown-skinned wife sits by his side, brave in her gold earrings and beads, with a red flower in her hair, all of which at home were kept for feast days. But here in America increased wages make every day a feast day in the matter of food and raiment; and why, indeed, should not the architectural principle of beauty supplementing necessity be applied even to the daily round of hod-carrying? Teresa from the Ligurian mountains is certainly a more picturesque object than Bridget from Cork, and quite as worthy of incorporation in our new civilization. She is a better wife and mother, and under equal circumstances far outstrips the latter in that improvement of her condition evoked by the activity of the New World. Her children attend the public schools, and develop very early an amount of energy and initiative which, added to the quick intuition of Italian blood, makes them valuable factors in the population. That the Italians are an idle and thriftless people is a superstition which time will remove from the American mind. A little kindly guidance and teaching can mould them into almost any form. But capital is the first necessity of the individual. Is it to be wondered at, therefore, that the poor untried souls that wander from their village or mountain homes, with no advice but that of the parish priest, no knowledge of the country to which they are going but the vague though dazzling remembrance that somebody's uncle or brother once went to Buenos Ayres and returned with a fortune, no pecuniary resource but that which results from the sale of their little farms or the wife's heritage of gold beads, and no intellectual capital but the primitive methods of farming handed down by their ancestors, should drift into listless and hopeless poverty? Their emigration is frequently in the hands of shrewd compatriots, who manage to land them on our shores in a robbed and plundered condition.

On the other hand, the thrifty *bourgeois* who brings with him the knowledge of a trade, and some little capital to aid him in getting a footing, very soon begins to prosper, and lay by money with which to return and dazzle the eyes of his poorer neighbors, demoralizing his native town by filling its inhabitants with yearnings toward the El Dorado of "Nuova York." Such a man, confectioner, hairdresser, or grocer, purchases a villa, sets up his carriage, and to all appearance purposes spending his life in elegant leisure; but the greed of money-getting which he has brought back from the New World surges restlessly within him, and he breaks up his establishment, and returns to New York to live behind his shop in some damp, unwholesome den, that he may add a few more dollars to his store, and too often his avarice is rewarded by the contraction of a disease which presently gives his hard-earned American dollars into the hands of his relatives in Italy. There is an element of chance in the success of Italians which makes emigration with them a matter of more risk than with other nationalities of more prudence and foresight. The idyllic life of an Italian hill-side or of a dreaming medieval town is but poor preparation for the hand-to-hand struggle for bread of an overcrowded city. Hence the papers of the peninsula teem with protests and warnings from the pens of intelligent Italians in America against the thoughtless abandonment of home and country on the uncertain prospect of success across the ocean.

The fruit trade is in the hands of Italians in all its branches, from the Broadway shop with its inclined plane of glowing color, to the stand at a street corner. Among the last the well-to-do fruit-merchant has a substantial wooden booth, which he locks up in dull times, removing his stock. In winter he also roasts chest-nuts and pea-nuts, and in summer dispenses slices of water-melon and *aqua cedrata* to the *gamins* of the New York thoroughfares, just as he once did to the small lazzaroni of Naples or the fisherboys of Venice. With the poorer members of the guild the little table which holds the stock in trade is the family hearth-stone, about which the children play all day, the women gossip over their lace pillows, and the men lounge in the lazy, happy ways of the peninsula. At night the flaring lamps make the dusky faces and the masses of fruit glow in a way that adds much to the picturesqueness of our streets. These fruit-merchants are from all parts of Italy, and always converse cheerfully with any one who can speak their language, with the exception of an occasional sulky youth who declines to tell where he came from, thereby inviting the suspicion that he has fled to escape the conscription. That they suffer much during our long cold winters is not to be doubted, but the patience of their characters and the deprivations to which they have always been accustomed make them philosophic and stolid. As soon as they begin to prosper, the fatalism of poverty gives place to the elastic independence of success, and their faces soon lose their characteristic mournfulness. I have seen young Italian peasants walking about the city, evidently just landed, and clad in their Sunday best—Giovanni in his broad hat, dark blue jacket, and leggings, and Lisa with her massive braids and gay shawl, open-eyed and wide-mouthed in the face of the wonderful civilization they are to belong to in the future. The elevated railroad especially seems to offer them much food for speculation—a kind of type of the headlong recklessness of Nuova York, so unlike the sleepy old ways of the market-town which has hitherto bounded their vision.

There are two Italian newspapers in New York—*L'Eco d'Italia* and *Il Republicano*. There are also three societies for mutual assistance—the "Fratellanza Italiana," the "Ticinese," and the "Bersaglieri." When a member of the Fratellanza dies, his wife receives a hundred dollars; when a wife dies, the husband receives fifty dollars; and a physician is provided for sick members of the society. It gives a ball every winter and a picnic in summer, which are made the occasion of patriotic demonstrations that serve to keep alive the love of Italy in the hearts of her expatriated children. Many of the heroes of '48 are to be found leading quiet, humble lives in New York. Many a one who was with Garibaldi and the Thousand in Sicily, or entered freed Venice with Victor Emanuel, now earns bread for wife and child in modest by-ways of life here in the great city. Now and then one of the king's soldiers, after serving all through the wars, drops down in his shop or work-room, and is buried by his former comrades, awaiting their turn to rejoin King Galantuomo.

There is something pathetically noble in this quiet heroism of work-day life after the glory and action of the past. I met the other day in a flower factory, stamping patterns for artificial flowers, an old Carbonaro who had left his country twenty-two years before —one of the old conspirators against the Austrians who followed in the footsteps of Silvio Pellico and the Ruffinis. He was gray-haired and gray-bearded, but his eyes flashed with the fire of youth when we talked of Italy, and grew humid and bright when he told me of his constant longing for his country, and his feeling that he should never see it again. It was a suggestive picture, this fine old Italian head, framed by the scarlet and yellow of the flowers about him, while the sunlight and the brilliant American air streamed over it from the open window, and two young Italians, dark-eyed and stalwart, paused in their work and came near to listen. It was the Italy of Europe twenty years back brought face to face with the Italy of America to-day. In another room, pretty, low-browed Italian girls were at work making leaves—girls from Genoa, Pavia, and other cities of the north, who replied shyly when addressed in their native tongue. Italians are especially fitted for this department of industry; indeed, their quick instinct for beauty shows itself in every form of delicate handiwork.

In the second generation many Italians easily pass for Americans, and prefer to do so, since a most unjust and unwarranted prejudice against Italians exists in many quarters, and interfere with their success in their trades and callings. It is much to be regretted that the sins of a few turbulent and quarrelsome Neapolitans and Calabrians should be visited upon the heads of their quiet, gentle, and hardworking compatriots. All Italians are proud and high-spirited, but yield easily to kindness, and are only defiant and revengeful when ill-treated. . . .

I fail to find that Italians here retain their national habits of enjoyment or their love of feast-day finery. True, I have seen *contadine* in gold beads and ear-rings sitting on their door-steps on Sunday afternoons, and I have watched a large family making merry over a handful of boiled corn, just as they did at home, and I have seen the Genoese matrons dress one another's hair of a Sunday morning in the old fashion. But the indifferentism and stolidity of the country react upon them. There seems to be little of the open-air cooking, the polenta and fish stalls, the soup and macaroni

booths, that breed conviviality in the Italian streets. They apparently
eat in their own homes, after the New World fashion.

Undoubtedly much of the recklessness with which Italians are
charged in New York is the result of the sudden removal of
religious influences from their lives. At home there is a church
always open and at hand, and the bells constantly remind them
of the near resting-place for soul and body. When their homes are
noisy and uncomfortable, they can find peace and quiet in the cool
dark churches; and when they are on the verge of quarrel or
crime, and the hand involuntarily seeks the knife, the twilight
angelus or the evening bell for the dead softens the angry heart and
silences the quick tongue. Here the only escape from the crowded
rooms is in the equally crowded yard, or the door-step, or the
rum-shop. The only entirely Italian Catholic church in New York,
I believe, is that of San Antonio di Padova, in Sullivan Street,
attended by a superior class of Italians, all apparently prosperous
and at peace with their surroundings.

In the days of political persecution and struggle in Italy, America
was the republican ideal and Utopia toward which the longing eyes
of all agitators and revolutionists turned. When self-banished or
exiled by government, they were apt to seek their fortunes in
America, often concealing their identity and possible rank, and
taking their places among the workers of the republic. Among
these was Garibaldi, who passed some time here in the suburbs of
New York, earning his living like many another honest toiler,
and awaiting the right moment to strike the death-blow at tyranny.
To study the Italian character in its finer *nuances*, the analyst should
not limit his investigations to the broad generalizations of the
Italian quarters, but should prosecute his researches in out-of-the-
way down-town thoroughfares, where isolated shops with Italian
names over their doors stimulate curiosity. In these dingy places,
among dusty crimping-pins, pomatum-pots, and ghastly heads of
human hair, half-worn clothing, the refuse of pawnbrokers' shops,
you may meet characters that would not have been unworthy the
attention of Balzac, and would eagerly have been numbered by
Champfleury among his "Excentriques." I have one in my mind
whose short round person, tall dilapidated hat, profuse jewelry,
red face, keen gray eyes, and ready tongue fully qualify him for
the title of the Figaro of Canal Street.

Another interesting class of Italians is found in the people
attached to the opera—the chorus-singers and ballet-dancers,
engaged also for spectacular dramas. It is in a measure a migratory
population, crossing the ocean in the season, and recrossing when
the demand for its labor ceases. Many chorus-singers who remain
in New York follow different trades out of the opera season, and
sing sometimes in the theatres when incidental music is required.
By singers New York is regarded chiefly as a market in which they
can dispose of their talents to greater pecuniary advantage than in

Europe, and they endure the peculiar contingencies of American life simply in order to lay by capital with which to enjoy life in Italy. A season in America is always looked forward to as the means of accumulating a fortune, and not for any artistic value. I have heard of more than one Italian who, after a successful engagement in New York, has invited sundry compatriots to a supper at Moretti's, and announced his intention of shaking the dust of America from his shoes for evermore, being satisfied to retire on his gains, or to sing only for love of art and the applause of artists in the dingy opera-houses of Italy. The climate of America with its sudden changes kills the Italian bodies, and the moral atmosphere chills their souls—notably among artists. The "Caffè Moretti" has for years been the *foyer* of operatic artists, and no review of Italian life in New York would be complete without a mention of it. For many years they have dined, and supped, and drank their native wines in this dingy, smoke-blackened place, forgetting for the nonce that they were in America, and, coming away, have left their portraits behind them, large and small, fresh and new, or old and smoke dried, hanging side by side on the wall to cheer the hearts of the brother artists who should follow after them to the New World, and find a moment's respite from home-sickness over Signor Moretti's Lachryma Christi and macaroni cooked in the good Milanese fashion. In view of the general assimilation of Italians with their American surroundings, it is surprising and delightful to find a place that retains so picturesque and Italian a flavor.

Since the abolishment of the *padrone* system one sees few child-musicians, and the wandering minstrels are chiefly half-grown boys and young men, who pass their summers playing on steamboats and at watering-places. It is gratifying to feel that one of the disgraces of modern and enlightened Italy has been wiped from the national record by the strong hand of governmental authority.

CHICAGO'S ITALIAN COLONY

Alessandro Mastro-Valerio

[As in New York,
northern Italians founded the Italian settlement in Chicago and
dominated it until the 1880's, when large numbers of southern
Italians began to arrive. Already a thriving industrial city, Chicago
offered jobs in railroads, meat packing plants, farm implement
companies, and many other rapidly expanding industries. It also
offered the immigrants dismal poverty conditions in Near West-
side tenements. In 1850, there were only 100 Italians in Chicago, but
forty-five years later, there were many thousands. By then, most
of the city's Italians lived very near what is today the downtown
business districts and many resided in the neighborhood of Jane
Addams's Hull House on Halsted Street. This selection was written
by Alessandro Mastro-Valerio in 1895, three years after he founded
an unsuccessful agricultural colony at Daphne, Alabama. In 1898,
he founded and became editor of *La Tribuna Italia Transatlantica*
in Chicago.]

The Italians of Chicago number 25,000, mostly belonging to the
peasant class. Those who have grown with the town are in
prosperous circumstances; and, with few exceptions, they came from
the north of Italy, and particularly from the Riviera. They do not,
for the most part, form an intelligent class. They are neither
entrepreneurs nor producers. They have not been identified with
the wonderful, intelligent progress of the city; but they have grown
rich with it from the increase in value of real estate, or from
their business of selling fruit. The children are no better than their
parents. A case was discovered recently of a young Italian worth

From *Hull House Maps and Papers* (New York, 1895), pp. 131–39.

$100,000 who was contented to be simply a policeman. Behind bar-
room counters, there are young Italians who are worth even more
money. Some of the present generation deserve praise because they
have entered the liberal professions or legitimate manufacturing
enterprises. The Italian colony consists of professional men,—news-
paper-men, bankers, publicans, employment agents, lawyers, interpreters, midwives, musicians, artisans, laborers, sweaters' victims,
grocers, bakers, butchers, barbers, merchants, etc., all of which are
necessary one to another and cannot bear separation without dis-
organization. It is a town within a town, a stream, a rivulet in the
sea, of such intense force of cohesion that it cannot be broken, as
the mighty ocean cannot break the Gulf Stream.

The immigrant Italians are lodged by Italian innkeepers, and
fed by Italian *restaurateurs*. Italian publicans quench their thirst.
Italian employment agents or "bosses" find them work, and group
them and take them to the country, where, in the majority of
cases, they board them, and act as interpreters between the contractor and them. Italian agents or bankers send their money to
their families in Italy, and sell them tickets for the latter when
they come to join them in America. Italian doctors are called in
case of sickness, and Italian druggists furnish the curative drugs,
which must bear Italian names in order to be trusted. Italians
manufacture macaroni as nearly as possible like that of Italy; and
Italian grocers furnish cheese, oil, olives, bologna, bread, and many
other Italian delicacies or necessaries. Their priests must be
Italians; also their lawyers and their undertakers. These streams
and rivulets run into the midst of the *mare magnum* of Chicago,
about South Clark Street, and Third, Fourth, Pacific, and Sherman
Avenues, and Dearborn Street between Harrison and the Twelfth
Street viaduct; about Illinois, Michigan, Indiana, and La Salle
Streets, where the Italian Church of the Assumption is located;
about West Indiana, Ohio, Huron, Sangamon, and North Halsted
Streets, and Milwaukee and Austin Avenues; about South Halsted,
Ewing, Forquer, DeKoven, and Twelfth Streets and the river.
Smaller streams run in other directions. Each is well marked, and
bears, more or less, a reputation of its own.

The charge of filthiness, so often made against Italians of this
class, is to be attributed partly to their special condition of life
in the crowded tenement houses of our American towns, which
are the reverse of hygienic in their construction, both in regard to
the material used, which is poor and easily impregnable, and as
to the disposition of space, which does not conduce to healthful
living. The accusers ought to consider that those Italian immigrants
come from the open country, or from villages where the houses
are built of stonemasonry less easily heated and cooled, and having
wide corridors differently disposed with doors and windows, which
give room for plenty of light and air. The promiscuity of sex and
of strange people force sighs from the hearts of Italian women,

mothers of girls, on first setting foot into the "infernal bolges" of South Clark Street and Fourth Avenue. *"Madonna mia, qui debbo vivere?"* I have heard sigh an Italian woman on one of these occasions, looking at her girls, while her heart was full of dismay. It is the custom of my part of Italy to whitewash the houses with lime in September, and before Easter, or in May, at the time of moving. It is also the custom that, on the Saturday before Easter, the priest goes in *pompa magna* to bless the houses of the district assigned to him, one by one. For such an occasion the houses of even the poorest people are made clean from roof to cellar in honor of the sanctity of the visitor who comes to bless the buildings, the persons, and the animals in the stable, in the name of God; therefore he is received with marked and religious reverence. Presents of eggs and money are made to him; the eggs are taken care of by the priest's servant maid, who attends in her picturesque peasant's costume, and puts them in a straw basket. A boy responds to the Latin prayers, and puts the money into a silver bucket containing the blessed water and the sprinkler. When a boy, I often attended to act in this capacity, and I remember with pleasure the neat appearance of the poorest houses. When I found myself in an American tenement house, inhabited by Italians, at the sight of the filth that appeared before me I could not help thinking with a sense of *ripianto amarissimo* of the houses of the same people as I have seen them on those good Saturdays. Most certainly the same conditions would not exist among these people on a farm in the country.

The greed of gain which has developed among the Italians causes most of the women to employ all their spare time in sewing clothing, in order to add their little share to the earnings of the husband and sons. This is a serious detriment to them, and is one cause of their filthy homes, which they have no time to care for. By reason of the same greed, boys and girls are sent to sell newspapers in the streets, and sometimes to beg. The skilled Italian in Chicago gets as much money as the American skilled laborer. The unskilled Italian laborer gets from $1.00 to $1.75 a day. As I have stated before, they economize in every way they can; but when the occasion arises which pleases them, they spend their money like water. They are hard workers, and not inclined to be vicious. Their women are notably virtuous.

L'Italia, the leading Italian newspaper of Chicago, inaugurated with its first number a veritable crusade against the two offences of ragpicking and sending boys and girls in the streets, and was instrumental in holding a mass-meeting for compulsory education in Chicago, which was part of a movement in the course of which the principle of compulsory education was adopted by the Board of Education, led by the late Charles Kominsky. The mass-meeting ended in the appointment of a committee of prominent Italians to call upon Mayor Cregier and upon the council, requesting the interference of the police in the ragpicking of the Italians. Briefly speaking, an ordinance was passed and enforced; but the ragpickers formed a sort of political association, and let the party in power understand that they were voters who would vote against that party at the next election if the interference of the police in their occupation was not stopped. Immediately the police, by secret orders, let the ragpickers alone. No lobbyists at Washington could have worked the scheme more effectually. This will answer the question whether Italians have Americanized themselves, and to what extent.

ITALIAN IMMIGRANTS IN BOSTON

[In the 1890's, the Italians replaced the Irish as Boston's unwanted ethnic invasion. In addition to providing a sizeable labor force in the factories and fields of Massachusetts, they became prime targets of the American nativist sentiment that was focused in Boston. By 1900, three years after the following article was written, there were 13,738 Italians in Boston. The selection was written by Frederick O. Bushee of South End House, a Boston settlement house established to aid immigrants.]

Throughout the entire city of Boston one can hardly find a more interesting or picturesque spot than the old North End. It is interesting from an historical standpoint, while the strange and heterogeneous character of its inhabitants makes up its picturesqueness.

North Street, formerly known as Ann, Fifth, and Ship Streets, was among the first to be settled in Boston and was one of the few important streets in the town. It was on North Square that the old North Church was located in which the Mathers (Increase, Cotton, and Samuel) successively ministered; and at the foot of North Square there still stands an old-fashioned wooden structure which was for thirty years the home of Paul Revere. Instead, however, of the sturdy patriots of English descent who once resided here, immigrants from Italy throng the streets. . . .

As North Street was one of the oldest streets in Boston, it did not long remain a fashionable one. It lost its American features as

From *Arena*, April, 1897.

soon as immigration commenced in the first half of this century. The Irish and Italians have successively held this region on the east, while the Jews have occupied a large portion of the district immediately west of the dividing line of Hanover Street. Portuguese, Russians, Swedes, and a few representatives of other nationalities are also found in the neighborhood.

The North End has seemed to be the natural rendezvous for every new accession of immigrants until they earn their promotion to some more fashionable part of the city or are crowded out by the persistent pressure of newcomers. For many years after their famine the Irish held undisputed sway of the region; and they seemed to be especially opposed to the advent of foreigners into their territory. Their contest with the Italians was sharp, but they were finally obliged to yield, as the Americans had done before them; and now, with the exception of a few who have taken refuge in houses of their own, they have been driven to the outskirts or have taken up their abode in other parts of the city. Of all the nationalities in this part of the city the Italians are much the most numerous, and are becoming relatively more and more so. The most prosperous are purchasing houses in the neighborhood, and others of them are permeating the territory of the Jews so rapidly that the Italians will soon become possessors of the entire district if their numbers continue to increase.

At present they number about eighteen thousand, although the residence of many is so transient that it is difficult to count them accurately. The single men move from city to city with little inconvenience, and they visit their own country frequently. The last six years have witnessed a growth by immigration in the Italian population which is certainly remarkable, and which would seem to many alarming, for in 1890 they numbered less than five thousand. Comparatively few of the Italians are old residents. None are recorded as living in Boston before the census of 1855, and their growth was very gradual until 1880, when they numbered one thousand two hundred and seventy-seven. From that time until the present their numbers have doubled every five years, with the exception of the last five years, when they nearly quadrupled their numbers. In 1880 they formed one per cent of the foreign population in Boston. In 1890 they had grown to three per cent. And at the present time they form approximately eleven per cent of the foreign born. Such a movement in immigration as this has not been witnessed in Boston since the Irish famine of 1846, when nearly fifty thousand Irish settled in Boston in a single decade. The Italians and the Slavonic races now, however, form the bulk of that immigration which is on the increase in our Eastern cities.

If the North End is more picturesque than formerly, it has become so at a sacrifice to its industry. Groups of idlers may always be seen on pleasant days about North Square, the centre of Italian activity. The men are of an olive complexion, short of stature, with prominent cheek-bones and round heads. They uniformly wear low felt hats and ill-fitting clothes, and not infrequently adorn themselves with earrings. The women, with their gayly-colored headdress and huge ear-drops, are even more noticeable than the men, and, when walking through the streets with large baskets or bundles on their heads, they remind us strongly of the European peasantry.

There are three general types represented among the Italians. The Genoese, or northern type, number six or seven thousand. They have a slight mixture of Teutonic blood, and most nearly resemble our own type. The southern Italians, represented principally by the Neapolitans and Calabrians, make up nearly one-half of the colony. The Sicilians, a darker-complexioned type, number about three thousand, but are not confined so closely to this section of the city. . . .

Life on North Street begins very early in the day. Four or five o'clock in the morning is the time for rising. Some are apparently in the same situation as the youth of an inert disposition who got up early in the morning that he might have more time to loaf; but many have work, especially in the summer, and all would work if they could.

In Italy breakfast consists chiefly of milk, bread, and coffee. In this country some sort of meat is added to the list unless poverty prevents. Cereals also are eaten. Beef is much too dear in Italy to be common, and is not most frequently used here. Pork or chicken better suits one accustomed to a vegetable diet. After a light breakfast those who have employment are off to their work. Even then this section is not at all deserted; it is less populous, that is all. Those who are not fortunate enough to have employment are soon loitering about the streets or gathered into the various saloons for a social time. The four or five saloons in the vicinity, with such names as Scipione, Petruccio, Generio, etc., over the doors, are a real product of the colony. It is not until we come to the very outskirts of the district that the familiar names of Sullivan, O'Brien, and Keefe again appear.

In Italy a man can buy a large glass of wine for a cent, and then order an indefinite amount of water, and sit in the saloon for the rest of the day. Here he pays five cents for a glass of beer, is not expected to order more than one glass of water, and is not really welcome for more than two or three hours, unless he continues to patronize the bar. This custom is not so convenient for the loafers, but it means that the saloon-keeper, like the laborer, is on a higher scale of profit than when at home. The saloons in this neighborhood differ from most saloons in that gaming rather than drinking is the chief attraction. Some of the idlers are interested in pool, but most of them gather around the card tables. They play for the drinks. It is only courteous to the proprietor that they should do so. Sometimes five or ten cents is staked, but this is not usually done except in lotteries. During the summer months the saloons do not fill up until evening, but in winter they are frequented throughout the day, not entirely on account of the cold, but because of the enforced idleness during that part of the year.

Apparently the only amusement for those who remain outside the salon is eating. Aside from fruit in summer, crabs, razor-fish, and boiled sweet corn are sold; and in winter, hot baked potatoes. Razor-fish and crabs are eaten from the shell, apparently with great relish. The crab-man sells a large basketful each day, and takes in about one dollar and fifty cents, at the rate of three crabs for five cents. Women go into the sweet-corn business. Mrs. Costa has been endeavoring to support herself and five small children by selling boiled sweet corn at the rate of two ears for one cent. It is needless to say that Mrs. Costa was "at home" to charity visitors even before the season closed. Pears and bananas may often be bought toward evening at the rate of two dozen for five cents. This cheap food supply is a great convenience to some, and often furnishes all the meal that is eaten, for the Italian goes without his dinner if he has no money; he does not beg.

The dinner of the ordinary Italian is made up largely of macaroni, French or Italian bread, and usually some meat and potato. That form of flour preparation known as spaghetti is most frequently used. This is boiled whole and served as a first course. The Italian experiences no difficulty whatever in eating this slippery food, for he merely sucks it into his mouth from his fork in a very unconventional if not elegant manner. The better class of Italians drink wine at their meals, preferably of their own manufacture. Sometimes it is purchased from a neighboring saloon, but they consider this a very inferior quality compared with that made in their own country. Fruit or a few dried olives, which very much resemble a small prune, are sometimes eaten for dessert. Supper does not differ very much from dinner for the workmen. Some kind of vegetable food constitutes their principal diet.

In the Italian colony the afternoon is spent much like the forenoon. The women, who have been indoors at their work, are now sitting on the doorsteps gossiping with a neighbor; but they do not go far from home nor make themselves conspicuous. The man here is lord of the household, and wife and daughter are guarded with a jealousy which insures a greater domestic virtue among the women than is always exhibited by the men.

The baker's cart makes its daily rounds to-day, and, in addition to his regular stock, the baker has brought a barrel of Italian bread, stale but still good, which he offers for fifty cents, barrel and all. But he is unable to sell it. The Italian makes no uncertain provision for the future. He buys only when he has to, and then as cheaply as possible. Occasionally a Jew wanders over from the village across the way with an armful of clothing to sell. Although he offers a coat for forty cents, and a waistcoat for fifteen cents, he fares no better than the baker, and goes away disgusted because the "Dago" wants to buy his clothing for nothing. But this is the accusation which, though in a less degree, the Jew makes against the world in general, so we must make some allowance.

A little after six o'clock the men begin to return from their work, and the village soon assumes its normal size. In the evening the saloons again furnish entertainment for the majority; but their accommodations are limited, and overflow meetings are held in the public eating-houses or in private rooms. The more retired the spot, the more excessive becomes the gambling and the more frequently do quarrels occur, though the drinking may be less.

The one Italian theatre, consisting of a marionette show, is the only regular place of amusement, and this is too dull to be popular, even for an Italian who has little else to do. We enter the dance halls expecting to find Italians there; but these are principally Irish affairs. Few Italians are present, for by common consent the two races associate as little as possible. "Only the decent ones are allowed," according to the dancers. "If any Italians come in who do not behave, we just fire 'em out." The Italians frequently have dances of their own on festive occasions, which are more elaborate affairs. But they are not always harmonious, and readily give occasions for quarrels on account of some jealousy or fancied slight.

By nine o'clock most of the women have disappeared from the streets, and all the girls are within doors, for the street-walkers are not of the Italian race. If the morrow is a working day, the men retire from the street by ten o'clock, and only the saloons and dance halls remain active. At eleven o'clock the saloons are closed. The dance halls keep open until midnight.

Although a majority disappear early from the streets, the district does not become quiet until long after; and the noise commences again so early in the morning that there are but few hours of rest. It is not the usual din of a city which reaches one's ears, but rather the peculiar hum of voices and stir of living beings. There is a certain unsettled state, a feeling of restlessness which haunts us continually. Men without homes, and whole families, trying to adapt themselves to their strange surroundings cause the unrest. . . .

The Italians show a considerable tendency toward isolation, chiefly on account of their language, and this tendency increases an already difficult problem. Not till the second generation do they become really Americanized, but then they are quite transformed through their new environment. The schools, the street life, and especially the use of the English language bring them into closer touch with American life. Their dread of appearing strange before their playmates stimulates them to imitate American ways, and soon their home becomes the single link which binds them to Italy. Even their euphonious names become distasteful to them, and a Marondotti wishes he were a Smith or a Brown. The home life is but little changed in the new surroundings, for it seldom comes in contact with outside influences. Its influence is always Italian. Macaroni continues to be the Italian's food unto the second and third generations.

To sum up, we have in the Italians a large colony of immigrants held together by a combination of clannishness and ignorance, the latter of which separates them also from within on account of differences in dialects and habits; a people who are physically strong but intellectually untrained; perhaps no worse morally than ourselves, yet who offend and shock us because their vices are of a different nature from our own.

The Italians are not the most desirable nor are they the worst immigrants with which we have to deal. They represent, perhaps, an average of the difficulties which confront us in the problem of the assimilation of races.

It is only by a careful study of the people themselves and an observation of their actual life amongst us that we shall be enabled to judge of them correctly and estimate their contributions to American life.

IMMIGRANTS
IN CITIES

[Italian immigrants, like the general American population, settled in the cities where jobs were more plentiful. More than eighty per cent of the Italians who immigrated after 1880 settled in urban areas and, today, they are still as concentrated in the cities. Because urban America since the Civil War has been largely a matter of unplanned sprawl with services that lagged far behind population demands, a great deal of inner city congestion and overcrowding resulted. In 1905, G. E. Di Palma Castiglione discussed the problems resulting from such urban concentrations of people.]

The concentration of the Italians in the large cities is as detrimental to themselves as it is to the United States. The peasant who establishes himself in a large American city cannot be anything but a laborer; all of his technical qualities are lost both to himself and to the country which harbors him. The Italian peasant, who has had centuries of experience in tilling the land, who understands all kinds of cultivation, who is not only expert in viniculture, but also in the culture of all the vegetables and fruits of his new country, is giving but the minimum part of his productive habits, i.e., his physical force.

The evils of concentration do not consist only in this dispersion of energy, or rather this mistaken employment of forces; they are not only economic evils, but they extend also to the moral and political fields. In fact, the Italian immigrant as a laborer, alter-

From "Italian Immigration into the United States 1901-4," in: *American Journal of Sociology*, September, 1905.

nating only between stone-breaking and ditching, remains an alien to the country. The immigrant, to whatever nationality he may belong, does not feel himself a part of the collectivity as long as no ties, first economic, then moral, are formed to attach him to the new soil. The laborer cannot form these ties while he remains a machine, pure and simple, furnishing only brute force, and no special interest can be felt in the work he accomplishes. Thus the Italian immigrant, thrust into the large cities, surrounded and out-classed by those who do not understand him and whom he does not understand, shuts himself in with his fellow-countrymen and re-mains indifferent to all that happens outside of the quarters in-habitated by them. Although renouncing the idea of repatriation, because he knows the economic conditions in his own country for-bid, and becoming an American citizen, he remains always a stranger to the new country.

The crowding into the large American cities brings other harmful effects. The cost of living in the northern states, and especially in the large centers, is very high, while the wages, on account of the greater competition, are relatively low. This lack of equilibrium imposes upon the Italian large material sacrifices which deplete him physically and lower him socially. The high rents force him to live in the worst quarters and in restricted space. In the Italian quarters of New York and Philadelphia can be seen the alleged lodging-houses, with seven or eight or even ten persons occupying one bedroom. Families of seven or more members crowd into houses containing only two rooms, one of which is the kitchen. This mode of existence, apart from the fact that it is fruitful in the de-velopment and extension of infectious diseases, renders the people vile in their personal habits, and, as has been alluded to before, makes them appear repulsive to the Americans. If these material condi-tions influence the Italians to feel no sincere or profound attach-ment to the adopted country, on the other hand they influence the native American to disdain the newcomers, thus causing a reciprocal psychologic state of mind which is a powerful obstacle in the way of assimilation.

But the influence of this agglomeration of the Italians goes still farther, for, besides the evils already spoken of, it furnishes an effective stimulus for the development and deepening of moral corruption. Among Italian immigrants, as among all others, there are certain elements which belong to no class, having lived the life of all, with no trade or capacity for honest work of any kind. Such people have no moral curb or scruple, and prey upon the others. They find in the swarming Italian quarters of the large American cities fruitful fields in which to exercise their baneful powers for the despoliation of their countrymen, who, ignorant and ingenuous, become their ready victims. In the guise of agents, solicitors, or journalists, they extort money. As founders of gambling dens and houses of ill-fame, they organize schemes of blackmail and other crimes. It is among these people that the ward politicians find their agents. The existence of people like these depends upon the crowded conditions referred to. The number of such individuals is not large, but they are indefatigable propagators of corruption among the immigrants.

Thus are conditions formed which, while placing obstacles in the way of reciprocal advantage, ruin the Italian immigrant morally, materially, and physically.

It is not the large number of Italian immigrants which constitutes a peril for the United States. The immigrants are young, honest, strong, and overflowing with energy; they possess potentially all the factors to represent an increase of development of the American people. The real danger is their concentration in the large cities, their defective distribution in the territory of the republic, which renders impossible their proper utilization, and forms an ever-increasing plethora of labor in the more populous states, while at other points there is a large and unsatisfied need of laboring-men.

The problem is not, as some are inclined to think, to find means for limiting or stopping the immigratory current, but to avoid the evils of concentration, and to find a way effectually to distribute the mass of immigration.

What causes provoke the concentration of Italians in the large cities? Why is it that these peasants prefer to live in crowded centers, rather than to scatter over the country, where they would be able to continue the art of agriculture and find the most appropriate outlet for their energies? Looking for the causes of this phenomenon will aid powerfully to solve the problem, and a brief survey of present and former conditions reveals the two principal causes: (a) the poverty of the Italian immigrants; (b) their previous mode of existence.

As has been demonstrated, the average amount of capital of the newcomer is a sum which, at the most, enables him to live without work ten or twelve days. If work be not found in that limited period, he must turn for help to his countrymen or to public charity. He has no time—aside from all other difficulties encountered, such as ignorance of the language, difference in all the conditions of life, etc., etc.—to study the advantage or disadvantage of points in the United States where he might be able to develop his activities. Even if he knew before landing that the South or West was adapted to his needs, his lack of funds would prevent his using that knowledge. Furthermore, the same lack of money forbids him to choose work in the fields, for, although better paid, it depends upon circumstances, which he has neither time nor money to command, and the fact that the land can be bought at a low price must be neglected, while he is glad to secure any kind of work which will provide for his present needs.

In addition to the economic causes, there is another, far more complex, because derived from habits of life which have obtained for centuries. The population of southern Italy is composed in great part of peasant farm laborers massed in large boroughs, which might be called cities, not for the perfection and complexity of their municipal and social life, but for their number of inhabitants. In order to live in these crowded haunts and mix with their fellows, the peasants walk morning and night several miles to and from the fields. They leave their homes long before dawn and return after sunset. This custom arose in feudal days, when the organization for public safety was deficient, and existed in those communities until the foundation of Italian unity, thus forming tendencies and psychological conditions in the peasant peculiar to him.

A study of the character of the southern Italians shows that they cannot live isolated; the conditions indicated above have formed in them the necessity of living in homogeneous groups, to reunite with their own kind. At the same time, they have acquired great diffidence toward the outside world of all who do not belong to the nucleus in which they were born and bred. Such tendencies, however, with the conditions which created them, are slowly passing away, but are yet strong enough to influence the deliberations of the individual, and especially in his choice of a mode of life.

This fear of isolation and this distrust of strangers become stronger and deeper in a new, strange country, and the peasant, although provided with money enough to buy and stock a small farm, finds in his own social needs a powerful obstacle to the realization of such a plan; but, joined with a sufficient number of his own countrymen in similar financial conditions, he does not hesitate to choose the farm.

These, then, are the principal reasons which account for the agglomeration of Italians in large cities. Suppressing them, the resulting evil will necessarily cease to exist.

The means best adapted to solving this problem would appear to be the formation of colonizing societies which should propose to found agricultural colonies composed of Italian peasants. It is well known that the greater part of the good arable land, once the property of the government, has been pre-empted, and has become the property of railroad companies and private individuals; but we are still far from the time in which all the good land will be under cultivation. Large areas await the hard and continued work of the laborer to be productive. As stated above, most of these lands belong to private corporations or individuals, and these should, in their own interests, favor the colonizing idea and aid in realizing it.

ITALIAN IMMIGRATION INTO THE SOUTH

[Before the
Civil War, the overwhelming majority of immigrants of all nationalities settled north of the Mason-Dixon line, the slave labor system
being a deterrent to southern settlement. After 1865, however, the
southern states made organized attempts to encourage immigration
to help the region recover from the devastation of war. The success
of the South's immigrant bureaus was never overwhelming, but, after
1880, many Italians ventured there mainly from Naples to New
Orleans. In Arkansas and Louisiana, they comprised the largest
foreign-born group. They founded farm colonies in a number of
states, and some native southerners looked upon Italians as a
possible replacement for black labor. Prior to Tontitown, the most
ambitious Italian settlement was at Sunnyside, also in Arkansas, but
that colony finally failed. The following selection assesses the South's
need for Italian immigration.]

The South needs white labor, but does the South want the immigrant? This is a question which is agitating business men throughout the Southern States. The negro population has proved unequal
to the task of furnishing an increasing supply of efficient labor, and
the negro must be supplemented—perhaps to some extent supplanted—by the white man. But is the immigrant of today the kind
of white man whom the South stands ready to welcome? . . .

The South should most carefully consider this problem of immigration. From no other source can the Southern States obtain
their labor which they need; and yet, with the negro already on

From "Italian Immigration into the South," by Emily Fogg Meade, in: *South Atlantic
Quarterly*, July, 1905.

the land, to bring in the Italian and the Slav may greatly add to social and economic difficulties, now almost insurmountable. . . .

To the ordinary American the Italian is a dirty, undersized individual, who engages in degrading labor shunned by Americans, and who is often a member of the Mafia, and as such likely at any moment to draw a knife and stab you in the back. The newspapers are to blame for this impression. They are quick to publish sensational tales of disorder, strikes and murders, but overlook the significant facts that show progress among these newcomers. Only recently have articles been written showing an appreciation of this frugal, moral and industrious people.

Hitherto, in America, the Italian immigrant has settled in the city, and here he has not had a fair chance to show what good was in him. Essentially a country dweller, life in New York and Chicago too often worked upon him for evil. Several reasons may be advanced in explanation of this tendency to settle in the city. While nearly all the Southern Italians come from rural districts, they do not live on isolated farms, but are crowded together in closely-built villages, going to work every day on their little farms in the surrounding country. They are a gregarious people, and this characteristic, added to their ignorance of English, causes them on landing in the United States to seek their own people. They know nothing of our farms, and their long years of painful effort, when the taxes were so heavy that after paying them they had scarcely anything left, make them think farming is unprofitable. They wish to find remunerative labor, but as they are unskilled workmen, they are obliged to go to work on the railroad, on construction of large buildings, about mines, as street sweepers, and in factories. Because of this tendency Americans have failed to recognize that these apparently unskilled laborers are really skillful farmers of the kind needed in many parts of the country. This may be shown by the success of Italians who have been settled in Southern New Jersey for the past thirty-five years, long enough for a second generation to grow up.

There are two types of settlements in Southern New Jersey, Vineland and its vicinity, founded by Signor Secchi di Casale, to which the Italians came under leadership; and Hammonton, which is of special interest because of its natural, unorganized development. In both cases the Italians have become successful farmers and good citizens.

For many years the pine barrens of New Jersey were considered worthless. Within the last twenty-five years, however, there has been a growing appreciation of the real value of the sandy soil, which requires a fertilizer, moisture, and above all, thorough cultivation. When properly treated, it produces excellent crops of fruits and vegetables, sweet potatoes being a specialty. This land could not compete with the productive West in growing heavy crops, but the healthful climate attracted New Yorkers and New Englanders who disliked long, cold winters, or who had contracted lung or throat diseases. Land was cheap, but it was hard work to clear it, for it had to be grubbed out. Besides the pine growth, it was covered with scrub oaks and a thick undergrowth. There were also swamps to drain. A cheap labor force was required, and it was here that the first Italians who came to Hammonton became of value. When many acres of land were planted in berries, pickers were needed. Italians who are used to gathering olives are admirable berry-pickers. Accordingly it became customary to bring Italian families from Philadelphia for the berry season.

A few Italians came to Hammonton before 1865, but it was not until after the war when the demand for fresh fruit and vegetables arose, that the possibilities of New Jersey soil became apparent, and a direct immigration began. Among the first to come had been a Charles Campanella from a small town in north eastern Sicily, near Messina: Mr. Campanella first brought over his brother, and, as the two prospered, they were followed by relatives and friends, until now more than half the inhabitants of that town are in the United States, and other Italians from the rural disricts about Naples have been the forerunners of many others from their native towns. Some of the pickers also have been pleased with the country life and the opportunity to buy cheap land and have settled here. The main object of the Italian is always to make a home. If he comes without his family, he finds work at the neighboring brick yard, on the railroad or on a farm, and saves until he has enough to buy land. When he has his family with him, they may live in one room in the house of another Italian, until they save enough for a home. If the land is wild land, the Italian takes his leisure time to clear it. When the land is finally placed under cultivation, he asks one of the building and loan associations for a loan, which is usually enough to build a house. He gradually pays off the debt, and often buys new land in this way. Italians have bought out many of the old settlers since 1880. The sons of the farmers went west or to the cities, and the older generations having retired or died, the farms were sold to the newcomers.

On the small farms the work is frequently done by the women and children, while the father continues his work at the brick yard or at the factories, or on the railroad. In most cases the Italian farmer, in addition to managing his own place, plows and clears land for American farmers, and works at odd jobs during the winter to increase the family income. Frequently the whole family goes as berry pickers to the better strawberry region further south, as well as for later crops in Hammonton. Cranberry picking is considered so remunerative that well-to-do Italians leave their farms to earn $75 for a good season.

The average holding of Italians is 14.6 acres. The principal selling crop is berries with sometimes sweet and white potatoes, tomatoes, peaches, and pears. Grapes are extensively grown for their own use,

but the sour wine made from them is occasionally sold in Philadelphia. The Italian works the New Jersey soil with great success.
His careful hoeing and fertilizing, his continuous patient work, his
family labor, and his few wants, make it possible for him to derive
a comfortable living where an American would starve. . . .

Many parts of the South are still covered with pine forests,
similar to those in New Jersey. Before settlements are made, the
roots and underbrush must be grubbed, and the swamps drained.
The climate of the South is less rigorous than that of New Jersey,
and is better suited to immigrants from Southern Europe. The
products are much the same. The negroes of the South have paid
little attention to home gardens, and in many parts of the South
localities are entirely without the fruit and vegetables that might
be so easily grown. Whenever Italian farmers have settled, their
gardens are always models. They have introduced some of their own
vegetables to Americans, and they adopt American plants, for
instance, asparagus, celery and rhubarb. Several thousand Italian
farmers are already located in the South. In Louisiana they are
used in the sugar cane region with success. . . . There are strawberry growers in Independence, La., farmers about Greenville, Miss.,
truck farmers near Memphis, and many Texan cities, and vine
growers about Mobile. . . .

Many small settlements at the North, and notably one at Alexandria, Virginia, have been the result of railroad work. The Italian
laborers have been sent to these regions, and they have remained
to make a home after the railroad work was done. A colony at
Bryan, Texas, now numbering over 500, was founded in this way.
The Italians were working on a branch of the Houston and Texas
railroad. They were given inducements to buy land on the Brazos
River, and have since sent for their relatives. At Rosetta, Pa., the
workers in the quarries, have small farms. Even in the coal regions,
Italian miners are redeeming some waste land of the railroad.

These facts suggest that the most successful placing of Italian
families in the South will result from the combination of small
farms, and opportunities to work on railroads or in factories. The
mills in need of men spinners, can offer the inducements of small
farms. Railroads that are making extensions and wish to build up
a population along their lines can promise cheap land which can
be developed while the railroad work is carried on, and offer a
permanent home for the future. Whenever a few Italians are successfully located, they always act as advertisers to the people at
home.

Some system must be devised to arrange for the advancing of
money in such a way that it will not seem too heavy a lien on
the immigrant's future. Large manufacturers and planters can
afford to make the payments; the railroads should be induced to
do something, but that will not solve the difficulty. Building
and loan associations are sadly lacking south of the Mason and

Dixon line. Some similar organization on a large scale could be utilized. Immigrants are coming in increasing numbers this spring. The sale of return tickets has already been very large and the steamship companies are beginning to feel that their accommodations will be inadequate. It is important that the South should share in the distribution of these willing workers.

ITALIANS OF CALIFORNIA

[West of the Mississippi, California proved the strongest magnet for Italian immigrants. The colonies that emerged there, both in San Francisco and in rural areas between 1850 and 1900, consisted primarily of northern Italians—many of them from wine growing regions of Italy. The Gold Rush first drew them to the West Coast: in the decade 1850–60, the Italian population increased tenfold (from 228 to 2800). It grew steadily every decade thereafter until by 1900, there were at least 30,000 Italians in the state. Perhaps there may even have been as many as the 60,000 cited in the following article by Marius J. Spinello, instructor in Italian language at the University of California.]

California has nearly sixty thousand Italian citizens and I am in a position to assert and maintain that the economic conditions of the Italian population in this state are incomparably better than those of the Italians in the east. The greater prosperity the Italian enjoys in California is not accidental; it is the result of causes which any organization for the development of the state ought to divulge, through the Italian papers in the east, if we think that the Italians are as good citizens as any that come to our shores. Moreover, by investigating, discovering, and making those reasons known, we would not only proclaim to the world in a most convincing manner the possibilities of the state, but we would also at the same time do justice to a much abused, misrepresented and undervalued portion of our population.

From *Sunset*, January, 1905.

San Francisco has many a brilliant and highly respected professional man of Italian birth or parentage. The beautiful orchards, vineyards and gardens planted by Italians on the shifting sand dunes of San Francisco, of San Mateo, in Santa Clara valley, around Stockton, Napa, Fresno, Tulare, Los Angeles, and on the slopes of the Sierras, tell us what the sturdy sons of the noble nation to which the world is indebted for all that makes life worth living, can do wherever their lot is cast, and especially under the mild and benignant sky of California. Everywhere, we are told, the most well-kept vineyards, most luxuriant and profitable orchards belong to Italians. The Swiss-Italian colony of Asti is another eloquent proof of what we may expect from the Italians in the land where they can have free and fair play by the side of other settlers.

The taxes collected from the Italians of California represent over $12,000,000 worth of property, real and personal. The American reference agencies have registered over eight hundred Italian business houses with a credit varying from $500 to $500,000. These facts are indisputable and show us how materially prosperous our Italian population is in California. In view of their number, the aggregate capital owned and managed by them is equally as considerable as that in the hands of the representatives of any other nationality on Californian soil. This enormous accumulation of capital is primarily due to the uncommon energy, sobriety and faithfulness which characterize the Italians, despite their decadent writers; but, when we compare their achievements here with their achievements in the east, the rapidity of their success must be recognized as due also to the youth, and to the inexhaustible wealth of this state.

The eastern Italian comes from the same country and stock from which the California Italian comes, but though very successful, he has not been able to accomplish so much in so short a time. Why? Because, in the east, he found the country thickly populated and had to begin his climbing at the lowest step of the ladder, while the people who had come before him, were well-nigh the top. In California, on the other hand, he came as early as the rest of the early settlers and started alongside of them. Here, he met with no race prejudice. The virgin soil was as responsive to his toiling as it was to the labors of others. And today he finds himself on equal footing with all the other inhabitants of California. He figures as a most successful wine grower, as a prosperous farmer, as a shrewd and far-seeing business man, as a weighty capitalist, as a distinguished and well-beloved professional man, and a most public-spirited citizen. He is appreciated and respected by his fellow citizens as much as any other honest, law-abiding, industrious and intelligent Californian.

The residents of this state who have noticed, as I have, the excellent qualities of the Italian immigrants will, I am sure, welcome among us as many of them as are willing to come. Our boundless rich fields are waiting for the hands of those who, even in New England, are looked upon as the most skilful and painstaking cultivators in the country. Around New Haven, Connecticut, my former home, the Italian farms are places of great attraction. The Americans flock to see them as they would to see and admire beautiful historical monuments. Our state, with its miles and miles of unsettled territory, needs settlers to develop its unspeakable resources, to bring out its hidden treasures; and the healthy Italian race, which is three or four times as prolific as the New England Yankee, ought to be encouraged to come here.

The California Promotion Committee ought to enter upon a plan of propaganda whereby the numerous Italian colonies in the east may learn just what California has in store for all those of their members who are willing to exchange the barrenness of city life for the peace and comfort of easily acquired homes in the land of gold and sunshine. Pamphlets ought to be printed in Italian, setting forth the advantages and the rewards which California holds out to the dutiful, sober, and willing immigrant. Courses of lectures should be held in the largest Italian colonies, where hundreds of hands are looking for honest employment. The diplomatic representatives of the Italian government ought to be interested in the movement, because they could, better than any one else, direct the steps of their compatriots.

THE FARM COLONY
AT VINELAND,
NEW JERSEY

[Of the more
than sixty Italian agricultural communities in the United States,
Vineland is probably the best known and one of the most successful.
This article, describing the settlement, was written by Kellogg
Durand on the thirtieth anniversary of its founding.]

The two races amongst whom . . . colonization experiments have
recently been made, are those giving us their greatest numbers—the
Jews and the Italians. Nearly one hundred and fifty thousand Jews
were admitted to the United States last year, and, approximately
three hundred thousand Italians. If these two races could be attracted to the soil, to the cultivation of our vast farming lands, the
importance of the movement would be beyond estimate.

I have had occasion to visit the oldest and most notable experiments in Jewish and Italian colonization, those in southern New
Jersey, and this article . . . is based on the results of my personal
observations among the colonists of these two peoples. The Jew is
temperamentally, characteristically, physically, traditionally, and
historically different from the Italian. It could not be otherwise,
therefore, than that their colonization efforts should be along different though parallel lines, and that their work should of necessity be
viewed from different standpoints. Geographically these experiments
in South Jersey are near together, but in no other respect. In this
article I shall discuss the Italian colonies. . . .

The story of the first Italian land colony in southern New Jersey

From "Immigrants on the Land: Italian Colonies," in: *The Chautauquan*, March, 1908.

is soon told. It was founded by an Italian political refugee to this country, Signor Secchi de Casale. This man had established the first Italian newspaper in New York, called *L'Eco d'Italia*, through which he had endeavored to keep alive the flame of Italian patriotism among the Italians who were then in the United States. He was a disciple of Mazzini and a companion of Garibaldi and other Italian patriots who were instrumental in the union of Italy and with whom he had fought for her independence.

In the year 1849, after the unsuccessful attempt to form a Roman republic, he and several of his companions in the Cause migrated to New York. De Casale lived with Garibaldi in the village of Stapleton, Staten Island, in a house still standing. As the Italians in this country increased, de Casale found his interest in the welfare of his immigrant countrymen growing and their need was at that time so apparent to him that he felt called upon to suggest some legitimate and wise channel for the expression of their energies and for the development of their abilities.

As a reward for his services to the Italians in America, King Victor Emanuel later knighted de Casale.

While his efforts were constant in many directions, the most important accomplishment of his life was the establishment of an agricultural colony near Vineland, New Jersey.

Mr. Charles Landis, the founder of the city of Vineland, coöperated with Chevalier de Casale in his colonization scheme. The first group of peasants brought here in a body were sent to the colony in 1878, although a few years previous to this time certain individual Italians had exploited the work of berry picking in the vicinity, notably at Hammonton. From these beginnings grew the somewhat extended Italian colonization that we find today.

On the whole, the district of South Jersey is drear and unlovely; it is flat and hill-less, covered with scrub oak, stunted pine, and in many places consists chiefly of large swamps. For years it lay in its primal state because few American farmers had the energy to apply themselves to its improvement and reclamation. Certain towns on the railway there were, small and not very prosperous, and with these as a basis, the work of the immigrant colonists has gone on. The surface soil for the most part is light and sandy, often white like the sand of sea-beaches, but there is a sub-soil which is fairly rich, and on the whole it has been proved adaptable for certain crops. Grapes, sweet potatoes, beans, and tomatoes all grow admirably throughout this belt, and peaches and other fruits have been satisfactorily grown in certain sections.

Italian peasants born and accustomed to intensely hard work took hold of the great task of reclaiming the difficult lands that surrounded their settlements, and by dint of patience and great labor they have learned what crops can be depended upon. With the berries, the beans, and the sweet potatoes, and later the grapes, for a beginning, the early colonists developed farms of remarkable prosperity. American settlers who had once occupied farms in the neighborhood grew discouraged and many of them left, allured by the call of the town, or the more fertile fields of the middle west. These deserted plantations were quickly occupied by the olive-skinned newcomers, and today the farms once occupied by Americans are worked side by side with the farms of the brothers of the Italian pioneers who themselves cleared away the virgin tangles and made the sandy, barren dunes fertile.

Since the first settlers took up their living these Italian colonists have slowly increased until today they number some thousands. Not a large population, perhaps when compared to our aggregate Italian population, but these colonies are only experiments, samples as it were, and in many other sections are similar experiments. Taken together the results are important. For convenience we are noting the story of South Jersey, but there are other colonies in California, in Louisiana, in Connecticut, in Massachusetts, Rhode Island, Pennsylvania, New York, in Tennessee, and Texas. These have each sprung up independently, without special attention but the readiness shown by the colonists to adapt themselves to the soil is clear indication of what may be expected when the government undertakes in a systematic way the work of settling the Italians on the soil throughout the country in such places as their labor is most needed.

No people coming to America can live as economically as do the Italians. Their standard of living is by no means in conformity with that general condition of comfort that is called the "American standard of living." Ultimately, however, the Italians desire things which are foreign to them at home and gradually they raise their own standards. But at the outset the rigid economy they practice is a help.

The Italians start in life absolutely independent. Families come down from the cities, Philadelphia and New York, as berry pickers. They acquire a little money and a small, crude shack in which they live until they have paid off all indebtedness and get a little ahead, when they begin to build their own homes. The Jews, on the other hand, invariably start with a burden of debt to carry for their land and for their homes, and the cost of living to the Jew is always greater than to the Italian. He must have his wine at Passover and he must support his Talmud-Torah and his lodge, and oftentimes he is sending money home to Russia to bring over the remainder of his family, and it is a number of years before he finds himself on a clear footing. The Italian, in the meantime, free of debt, forging ahead by small steps, succeeds in acquiring his house and land free from all debt.

The Italian, more than any other alien, comes to America with the idea of saving a sum of money sufficient to enable him to return to his native land for the remainder of his life. But the immigrants who have been a few years in this country acquire certain habits and customs which they are unable to take back with them to Italy, and rather than repudiate these, they prefer to bring their families to America. Each year more and more Italian families are thus brought to America by Italian immigrants who have established themselves in this country and who, contrary to their early expectations, have renounced their early ambition of returning to Italy, and are now only desirous of making a permanent home in this country. This is a phenomenon, however, which is only acquired unconsciously with their Americanization.

The comparative agricultural conditions in America and in Italy are tremendously in favor of America. At home the Italian peasant has lived for many generations in towns which are in many cases the outgrowths of burgs and feudal castles under whose protection they were originally built. The peasants go out in the early morning to the farms and gardens, the fields and vineyards, which sometimes are distant several miles, and return at evening. This regime carries with it certain discomforts and physical disadvantages resulting from lack of proper and comfortable houses, from excessive toil, and such heavy taxation as leaves a residue of profit so small that the comforts and many of the necessities of life, are impossible. This toilsome regime has been the direct cause of the low standard of living which the Italians bring with them, but which in this country enables the Italian to more readily adjust himself to a difficult and stubborn environment and to reclaim land which ordinary American farmers have despaired of. Italian peasants who come to New York are, for the most part, entirely ignorant of the agricultural possibilities of this country. To them America is New York, but when offered a safe conduct to the soil in the agricultural districts, the Italian finds the advantages of American country life far in excess of any dreams he may have cherished. The comforts and independence afforded the American farmer, even the Americanized immigrant farmer, appeal to him, and he willingly undertakes the most difficult and disagreeable of work for a period of years in order that he may win the position of an American citizen. This ideal which is so easily placed before him is stimulating to good citizenship, to industrious labor, and to rapid, though not too rapid Americanization.

One of the great difficulties in the establishment of agricultural colonies in any section of the country is in the matter of securing a ready market for the crops. The South Jersey colonists do not have this difficulty to contend with. The grape juice companies in and near Vineland use not only all the grapes which all of the colonists in that section can produce, but many more.

The most profitable crop of all, however, is probably that of sweet potatoes. The Vineland brand of sweet potatoes brings from twenty-five cents to one dollar more in the market than any other brand. Some of the Italian farmers make as much as eight hundred dollars a season, from six acres of sweet potatoes. The Allivine Company, also near Vineland, has an enormous cannery. This cannery offers an adequate market for all the sweet potatoes, lima beans, and tomatoes that the colonists can raise. The canning of sweet potatoes is carried on on an enormous scale. Every inducement is made to encourage the colonists (Jewish and Italian alike) to raise more of these products each year, and yet the demand is entirely out of proportion to the supply. This cannery employs two hundred hands and runs three months in the year, from the middle of August to the middle of November. Its output is sometimes as high as thirty thousand cans of tomatoes a day. The machinery is most perfect and tomatoes are canned at the rate of forty-two cans a minute.

The labor employed is mostly Italian, men and women. Rough work of the cannery is generally undertaken by Italians. The skinning of tomatoes, for example, which is unskilled labor and fairly remunerative, will not be touched by Jewish girls—it hurts their hands; and while the work really is perfectly clean, it looks nasty; it also hurts their hands, owing to the fact that the tomatoes are acid and the water out of which they have to be taken is hot. The Italian women are paid at the rate of three cents a bucket for skinning these tomatoes and the average woman makes anywhere from seventy-five cents to two dollars a day. Occasionally an expert worker will make three dollars a day. Here as in many other cases the Italians come bringing their entire families and it is common to see a man and woman and several children at work filling buckets with the skinned tomatoes. The company pays farmers eight dollars a ton for the tomatoes which they bring in. To stimulate tomato raising the Allivine Company furnish the local farmers with manure and fertilizer at low rates, sometimes cost price, exacting in return promises from the farmers that they will put in so many acres of tomatoes for the following season. It is rare, however, to find a farmer who abides by his promise and puts in as many crops of tomatoes as the company prescribed. They utilize their fertilizers for other crops. Sometimes they take a chance on another crop being more successful, as, for example, sweet potatoes. One year several farmers made a good deal of money from their sweet potato crops, so the next year instead of putting in a reasonable number of sweet potatoes and a reasonable number of tomatoes and other crops, they, so to speak, put all of their eggs in one basket by devoting themselves very largely to sweet potatoes. If they do this for several years successively, there is danger of a sweet potato "slump," in which case they will lose heavily.

The canning of sweet potatoes is an industry which the Allivine Company has been developing extensively, and they are restricted in the matter of more extensive development only through the lack of supply of sweet potatoes. In the west and middle west where sweet potatoes are not grown, there is a tremendous demand for canned sweet potatoes. For the so-called "prime sweets," that is to say, the first size, largest sweet potatoes, the farmers receive five dollars a barrel. They have had heretofore no market for their small potatoes but now the Allivine Company pays seventy-five cents a barrel for them.

Although the Allivine Farm is closer to Jewish colonies than to the Italian it is a boon to both peoples. It is sufficiently near to the Italians to offer a ready market for their produce and at the same time to give employment to pickers in season, and indoor work during the canning of the crops. The Allivine Farm, which is run in conjunction with the cannery and vice versa, not only serves as a model for the foreign farmers of the region but gives employment to a large number, who are frequently glad of such an opportunity for apprenticeship. . . .

THE EFFECT OF EMIGRATION UPON ITALY

Antonio Mangano

[In 1907, Antonio Mangano, a Protestant clergyman and a native of Calabria, returned to Italy to study the profound effects emigration was having on the country. His findings were published in a series of five articles following his return to the United States in 1908. This selection is from an article on the emigration of the Italian labor force.]

A labor movement of such huge proportions as that in progress to-day in the southern provinces of Italy cannot fail to be fraught with good and evil results to the whole country and its inhabitants. The first and most natural effect, however, has been an increase in wages for the agricultural laborers in sections where the supply of workers is low because of the large numbers who have emigrated. Twenty or more years ago, when these provinces contained the tens of thousands of toilers who are now using their strength for the industrial prosperity of other countries, it was the *contadino's* part to beg the landowner for a day's work, and to accept without a murmur two *carini* or sixteen cents a day, and all manner of haughtiness and arrogance with it. Over-population and a high birth rate rendered the supply of labor greater than the demand and the more favored class took advantage of this. But when it was known that great railways were to be built across the American continent, that our cities were in need of laborers, and that they would receive from five to seven, and even ten times as much for their toil as at home, the most adventurous crossed the ocean, and soon the

From *Charities*, April 4, 1908.

money they sent back proved their success. Then the spirits of men began to rise; the little stream became a mighty river.

The landowners at first paid little heed to this steady outflow of men. There were still plenty whom necessity made willing to till their fields from dawn till dark at the old wage. But when, in 1905, the Abruzzi and Molise lost in round numbers 50,000 men and 10,000 women; the Campagna 65,000 men and 19,000 women; the Basilicata 17,000 men and 1,600 women; Calabria 56,000 men and 8,000 women; and Sicily 81,000 men and 25,000 women, the tables turned, competition shifted from the employee to the employer, and the land-owners were compelled to offer two or three francs a day in order to secure men to raise the most necessary crops. Twenty years ago, from sixteen to twenty-five cents a day was the usual wage of a peasant. To-day, as a direct result of emigration, wages have increased fifty per cent, and in some localities men cannot be hired for less than three times the amount they formerly received. In this way peasants who have never left their homes are benefited by the emigration of others. And even at this increased wage, the land-holders are lamenting the fact that many of their fields lie unworked because of the lack of hands to cultivate the soil and tend the vineyards, and they are begging the government to pass laws restricting peasant emigration.

Emigration and its results is a live topic of conversation among all classes of society in Italy. I have witnessed many a hot discussion in the town secretary's office when I was gleaning statistics. Several men always followed the stranger into the office and stood by, interested listeners until appealed to for their opinions. I was surprised to discover how well posted nine out of every ten are, with definite, well thought-out convictions, favorable or unfavorable to the movement according to their social position. A southern landlord in the province of Molise told me, with bristling mustache and school as soon as they could decipher the letters from America and keen flashing eyes, that every year he is finding it more difficult to secure laborers to raise his wheat, and he is compelled to pay such as are available three times as much as he ever did before.

"Why, my dear sir," said he, "we have simply come to the utmost limit in these parts. We cannot go on in this way any longer. The government must help us, and that very soon. We poor landholders are at the mercy of the few able-bodied men who remain. But (with a deprecatory shrug) we cannot expect anything from the government at Rome. They do not think of us; they are engrossed too much in the interests of northern Italy."

I turned to Pietro, a brawny workman, who stood listening and smiling to himself, with his hands in his pockets.

"Well, and what do you think of this emigration to America?" I asked.

He straightened involuntarily, the hands came out of his pockets to assist his rapid gesticulatory Italian.

"Ah! Signor, emigration is one great blessing to our country. What would all of these people do here, except to live more wretchedly, if that were possible, while the *latifondisti* (landowners) are fattening upon their life-blood! The fact is, if it hadn't been for emigration, we must have ended by eating one another up. Once there was no money in this town. Now we all have a little and we poor *contadini* don't have to go to the *padrone* and beg a loan and pay him fifty per cent on it. No! No! No one can doubt that emigration is a great blessing!"

These answers are from opposite points of view, but each voiced the feeling of his class I found upon making similar inquiry in all the forty or fifty towns I visited. Once I did find an affable *civile* who looked at the subject apart from his own personal interests. The usual discussion was waxing hot, when he ended it by this impartial remark: "Emigration is indeed a blessing for the one who emigrates, for he can earn more money and his family can live more comfortably. But for the country, it is an evil, for we are fast losing our working population."

The belated introduction of machinery in farm work is directly due to emigration. Progressive landowners who study the situation are beginning to realize that to work their soil with profit, or even at all, the machines must take the place of departed laborers, and so throughout the province of Molise and elsewhere are found here and there modern reapers, thrashers, ploughs and cultivators, objects of wonder to the entire country-side. This use of modern implements is still too new to see any great changes in agriculture, and their cost makes such tools too expensive for the small landowner or peasant proprietor. . . .

Another point of interest to me was to discover what change, if any, had been made in the life and manners of the returned emigrant; how he is regarded by those who knew him before and after, so to speak. The consensus of opinion seemed to be that the returned emigrant dresses and carries himself much better than formerly, that he is intellectually awakened, has more cleanly habits, more life and spirit, and that he will not, as a rule, be willing to put his neck under the yoke again and be content with his former life. His visit to his native land is of short duration, usually during the dull winter season, and he returns to America in the spring though there are those who remain two or three years.

Only last month I was talking with a well known Italian banker and commission merchant of Naples, who was in New York on a brief business trip. He told me that the hundreds of thousands of Italian laborers who left our shores last November during the financial panic and consequent industrial depression, are causing the Italian government grave concern. Thousands are congregated at Naples, rapidly depleting the food-supply, hardly adequate for the inhabitants because of abandoned, untilled fields, and absolutely refusing to comply with the government's request that they return to their own little hill-towns. Instead, these returned emigrants are demanding that the government furnish them work on public improvements,—quite American this sounds,—for the winter months. It is probable that nearly all of these will return to America, as the steamship companies report exceedingly large steerage lists booked for April and May sailings from Genoa and Naples to New York.

I believe one of the most wholesome effects of emigration is this "more life and spirit" just mentioned, for here are the hopeful beginnings of a proper appreciation of the dignity and worth of a man and his work. The *contadini's* contact with democratic, individualistic America with its opportunities for every industrious man, no matter how lowly his birth, to become a successful, respected citizen, is creating self-respect and ambition. A spirit of hope and independence is stirring these down-trodden masses, who have been considered no better than pack-animals for centuries, and they are awakening at last to their right and the possibility of progress. That which socialism has not been able to do in any sane way, emigration is doing in a most natural manner. There are some phases of this transition which are quite amusing, and to which it is most difficult for those who once lorded it over these poor people to accommodate themselves.

In the little town of Pulsano on the beautiful, spacious Gulf of Taranto, I roused the genial communal secretary from his midday nap. He good-naturedly showed me the registers and spoke at length of the numbers who had emigrated and of those who had returned. "Do you observe any change in the returned emigrant?" I asked. His answer was both laughable and pathetic. He nearly wept as he told me of the utter lack of respect shown by returned emigrants towards their former superiors. Said he: "I have always been good to these people and helped them, even when they were going away. Then they were very humble and always came into my office with great fear, hat in hand, hardly daring to lift their eyes from the floor. When they return, they come in here and look on me as no better than themselves. They do not even take off their hats. I can hardly endure it. Respect is due, if not to myself, at least to my official position. But in America they lose all respectfulness."

I sympathized heartily with him. It is a pity that life in America should cause the Italian to lose any of his charming native politeness, but the returned emigrant does not distinguish between servile, unmanly obsequiousness and common courtesy. Just because the *civile* and upper classes have always treated him with contempt, he considers it a mark of his equality to fail in respect to them when he returns. It is a characteristic of half knowledge, and of contact with a people who recognize no strict class distinctions, by whom all who work hard and earn an honest livelihood are held in high esteem, and only the indolent and dishonest are despised. . . .

Possibly more important than any of the effects so far mentioned, is the impulse which emigration has given to popular education. Italy has many large universities. Those of Bologna and Naples have been famous seats of learning for centuries. The University of Naples has over four thousand students enrolled; Bologna and Turin number thousands more, and the various other institutions of learning are taxed to their utmost capacity. But while this is true, I visited towns where from seventy-five per cent to ninety per cent of the population can neither read nor write. Education was not furnished for all until recently; it was the privilege of the more fortunate classes who could afford to pay for it. Thirty years ago in my own native town of nearly fifteen thousand inhabitants, there were but six of us, all boys of different families, who had a private teacher, the only children in that entire town who were receiving any schooling. There is a national law which makes at least a primary education compulsory, but since educational matters are left entirely in the hands of the communes, and these being always short of funds are obliged to keep down expenses, school appropriations suffer because of a lack of appreciation of the value of education.

Here again emigration is accomplishing what laws could not. When the first emigrants came here from Italy, it was necessary to depend upon the *padrone* or some town official to read and answer the letters from America. This had a two-fold disadvantage. In the first place, such services would always have to be well paid for in fruit, eggs, cheese or money; but, what was more difficult to endure, family secrets became common property of the town. If the head of the family sent home five hundred francs, the whole town knew of it in a few hours, and the women discussed that and the other contents of the letter as they gathered at the common *fountain* to fill their water jars or at the public *fontanile* to wash their clothes. Manifestly, the best way to avoid this was to have some one in the family learn to read and write. Thus, not because education was really desired, but because it supplied a need, thousands of children were given a primary education, but they left school as soon as they could decipher the letters from America and write a reply.

At the present time, however, the Italian in America sees the value of fuller instruction. He sees the advantage that the man who can read and write and figure has over the illiterate. One is the boss, the other digs in the ditch. The Irish overseer works apparently only with pencil and paper, while the Italian swings a pick or breaks his back toiling with a short shovel under the hot sun, or in the rain; and so, as he works, he resolves, as every good father should, that he will make it possible for his children to have an education and take a higher position in the world than he can. So, if his children are in Italy, he sends back word that they all be sent to school. Consequently the schools in the southern provinces are crowded to overflowing. I visited several of them. What a contrast with our magnificently built and equipped public schools! The wretched rooms; rough, crude old benches; no heat in cold weather; no means of ventilation; children dirty and unkempt; and odors so strong I hardly dared take a long breath until out again in the open air! And yet, as I talked with the teachers, I was impressed with the keen enthusiasm with which they do their work under such unfavorable conditions, and the heroic sacrifice many of them are making for the sake of the children entrusted to them.

One of the most important and far-reaching results of emigration is the change in ownership of landed property. Twenty years ago there were very few *contadini* who owned a foot of land. All the soil belonged to the great land barons who left the management of their estates to agents and passed their days in idleness and pleasure in the capitals of Europe. Naturally the one ideal which the landless *contadino* cherished was that some day he might become the owner of a few acres and a little *torre* or hut in which he and his family could dwell, free from harassing rents. But in those days, for a peasant to scrape enough together to purchase even an eighty dollar hut and a strip of land, was absolutely out of the question. Finally the way opened. The great America needed these sturdy sons of toil. From the Calabrian and Sicilian mountains they went by thousands. They had had good training in simple living and hard work. They could live in shanties, eat dry bread and macaroni, do satisfactory work, and at the same time put by the greater part of their earnings. They had learned long ago how to save every *centesimo*. Soon money began to pour into Italy and the post office banks were full of the emigrants' savings. Naturally the first thought was to possess the coveted hut and piece of land, and it is noteworthy that in sections where the peasant has never been a landowner before, the greatest efforts are put forth in order to join the ranks of the property holders. . . .

Were these the only results of emigration, it is evident that Italy could well afford to help on the throng that is annually crossing the ocean. But this is only half the picture. Certain evil results are everywhere apparent, and cause grave concern to the government, to patriotic statesmen and to all who love that fair land. The southern provinces, particularly the Basilicata, Abruzzi, Calabria, Sicily, and more recently Bari, are rapidly losing their working population, that which produces feed for the nation, and for export trade. And, as a consequence, whole sections are fast becoming depopulated, towns are abandoned and landholders are everywhere saying that they cannot find anyone to cultivate the soil,—"*Ci manca la mano d'opera*,"—"We lack the working hand,"—is the universal cry. "The young men have all gone to America." As one man put it, "We are rearing good strong men to spend their strength for America." I passed through town after town where I scarcely saw an able-bodied man. Only the old men, women and children are left. . . .

And what becomes of the women and children left in Italy without their natural protectors? Italian girls and women, even of the peasant class, have always been carefully guarded. The knife of father, brother or husband is ready to avenge any insult to their honor. But while these are far across the sea, the direst things often happen. The prefect of Cosenza, Calabria, told me that he considered this one of the most serious phases of the emigration problem in the south. Said he: "Years ago we had family order here. Children were brought up to obey their parents. To-day, we are confronted with prostitution among a class of women who formerly in spite of their poverty were respectable. Then, too, infanticide is rapidly making itself felt, an evil entirely unknown here a few years ago."

The number of illegitimate children is steadily increasing. When it is remembered that even in 1901 the percentage of families without a head, due either to death or emigration, was for the kingdom, 9.10; for the province of Basilicata, 22.7; and for Calabria, 29.1; and that it is the strongest, sturdiest men of from twenty-one to fifty years who emigrate, it is evident that there is serious danger of race degeneration in the near future.

These conditions are bad enough in themselves, but the evil does not stop with them. Children brought into the world under such circumstances are not only deprived of the strict control and discipline of a father, but they have no proper chance for moral development, and grow up without any restraint. This will not be conducive to good manhood or good citizenship, to say the least.

Another menace is the spread of disease, especially tuberculosis, among the southern provinces. Contracted by emigrants who live in crowded, unhealthy tenement houses in America, or work in our subways or in factories, it is carried back to Italy where it was almost unknown a few years ago, but where it is now growing rapidly. The Italians have not yet learned how to cope with it successfully. . . .

It stands to reason that when towns have been steadily diminishing for twenty years, anywhere from ten to fifty per cent or even more, as Amalfi, from 10,000 to 3,000, many emigrants cannot be returning to live. When once an immigrant brings his family across the ocean, or marries here and children come to bless him, he is by that very fact anchored here, for his children's sake if for no other reason. I know a prosperous laboring man in Brooklyn with a wife and eight children. The wife said to me not long ago: "Mike and I would like to return to our own town. We have there a little house of two rooms and a nice piece of ground which bears figs, olives and grapes. We two could live very comfortably and enjoy the sunshine and the open air. Here I am shut up in this house from one week's end to the other. The most I can do is to go across the street on Sunday to see my neighbors. But how can we go back to Italy with our children? We cannot support them there, and what would they do? Here they can get an education and become something. *Al paesello nostro, non c'è nulla.* In our little town there is nothing, so we must remain here for their sakes."

There might be a possibility for the single man's return, but he is usually quite young, and his free life amid the glitter and glamour of our cities unfits him for the dull, simple routine of his mountain home. Among these there is an increase of the drink habit and this with other vices learned here, is carried back when they return for a visit. Their example is demoralizing, for they scorn work while their money lasts and spend their time in the wine-shops, drinking and gambling.

The young Italian of more strength of character does not find it possible to remain in Italy either. In Rome I met a patriotic young fellow who had been in the United States and had learned to read and write English at a night school. Hundreds of bright young Italians are doing the same thing, and others are learning trades in our industrial night schools. He had returned to serve for three years in the Italian army. He told me that in America he was earning two dollars a day as a blacksmith. "Italy no good," said he, "I stay in America. America good country for the workman."

This is the growing conviction of most of those who come from the rural sections and, for this reason, there is no certainty that the money which has been sent back is destined to remain in Italy. In fact, there is recent evidence to the contrary. Just before I left Rome, I was talking with an official high in government circles, who is in a position to know the facts. He told me gravely that even now money is being withdrawn and returned again to America. "Only last month," said he, "I received a communication from one of our consuls in the western part of the United States where the Italian population is not large either, warning me of this. He reported that in the past year he has recalled from various postal banks in the south, sums totaling 2,000,000 *lire* ($400,000) for Italians in his district."

This, together with the fact that the number of emigrant women and children is increasing, and that Italians are acquiring property and becoming successful in business in our cities, means that the Italians are in America to stay. Italy has lost them; she is in danger also of losing the money she hoped would recompense her, and she is beginning to feel that she must do something to induce her children to return, or, at least, to retain those who remain.

A FARM COLONY
IN NORTH CAROLINA

Felice Ferrero

[Since the individual immigrant rarely had sufficient funds to buy land on his own, frequent attempts were made to establish farm colonies and thus reduce the population congestion in the cities. One such experiment, launched around the turn of the century, was the colony at St. Helena, near Wilmington, North Carolina. This account of St. Helena is from an article by journalist Felice Ferrero, a native of Florence, who traveled extensively in the United States.]

The suggestion that the immigrant buy a farm or take up a claim is empty. He has no money to buy or to travel; he does not trust the land seller, and he does not want to go and live a lonely life among strangers who do not understand him. A few of the most adventurous immigrants will buy in later years and work their own land; but their number is so small that it can hardly have any value as a factor in a "back to the country" movement. . . .

The real problem is, therefore, to find a way of inducing immigrants, no matter how low their resources may be, to move on to the country as soon as they land. Perhaps not many people have so far given serious effort to reach its solution; but at least one attempt has been made, and since it is both successful and in process of extension, it is worthy of notice and of imitation. The desire of a wealthy North Carolinian to foster the interests and the development of his state, furthered by his innate philanthropic tendencies, was the prime motive of the enterprise. Incidentally it appeared that the attempt might resolve itself at the same time into

From "A New St. Helena," in: *Survey*, November 6, 1909.

a good business venture, and a help in settling this embarrassing question of city congestion. Greater all-round satisfaction could hardly be demanded.

The present situation in North Carolina, a situation representative of all southern states without mineral resources, may be thus briefly described—immense tracts of excellent soil and no hands to work it. Upon these fertile lands grow vast forests of pine and cedars; water stagnates in impassable swamps; mosquitoes and malaria prosper —wild, desolate solitudes through which the train speeds for miles on a single track road without sight of a house. The land is good, but who could venture into such a wilderness without money and the collaboration of railroads and agents to dispose of the products that sufficient means might with time bring forth from the ground?

Hugh MacRae, the southern gentleman referred to, has organized a company to colonize such a region. Since no farmers could be obtained in the vicinity to brave the task of overcoming its primeval conditions, he resorted to foreign help. He chose it of one kind, to avoid conflicts of nationality, and made his first trial with Italian peasants, whose persistence, thrift, and willingness he already knew. To allure this foreign help so far from any of its centers of gravitation—North Carolina is a state where Italians are practically unknown—two inducements were held out that would appeal to any human being, the prospect of living among fellow country-men and the promise of good gains. So rose the colony of St. Helena in the swamps north of Wilmington, N. C., not far from the Atlantic coast. St. Helena is a composite name adopted by the colonists themselves, Helena for the popular queen of Italy, sanctified to satisfy a desire latent in those simple peasant souls to keep good with the royalty of heaven also. Chosen to be the godmother of a new village, the holy Helena must feel herself in duty bound to stand sponsor for it, even though it be merely an earthly coincidence that selected her rather than some one other of her twenty-five thousand companions in beatitude.

Into St. Helena only Italian farmers are admitted, and only northern Italians. In fact, those there present, about 300 in number, are all from the same Venetian provinces. This insures to them the society of fellowmen of the same dialect, the same habits, the same tastes, the same methods of work, and guarantees to them that which is so necessary to pioneers struggling against the wilderness—the support of one's kind. . . .

The company's contract with the immigrants was made so that to each immigrant it sells a small farm of ten, fifteen, twenty acres, according to the size of his family and his working capacity. The unit size is ten acres. The price for the farm is thirty dollars an acre. While this sum may at first glance seem high for land "as is," utterly unimproved, the fertility of the region and its mild climate, which knows no frost and makes possible the raising of crops throughout the winter, justifies the price; indeed, results show that such an amount is actually very low. The company builds for the immigrant—and at his expense—a small, but well-constructed bungalow of three rooms, costing $250. It gives him also the implements and animals needed for a successful start. For all this the company requests no payment in advance. If an immigrant begins with ten acres, his debt will be about $600, aside from the money that he may have borrowed for his voyage.

Supplied with a house and the requisite tools, the peasant finds himself face to face with his ten-acre swamp, heavily wooded. Long, weary toil must yet be his before he can get crops from his land. While in high rubber boots he fells his trees and stumps his fields, he must also eat. The company has provided for this as well. All the wood he cuts it buys, at the rate of ninety cents a cord, which gives a revenue of a dollar to a dollar and a half per day to every laborer. When he has cleared and sowed his land, he may cut wood in the nearby forests and thus keep up his supply until it is time for him to reap his first crop. Steady hard work and sometimes also disease await the pioneer during the first year; but in all contingencies the company stands by him. If he is stricken by the insidious fever of the marshes, the company will take care of him; if he cannot stand the climate, or if he grows discouraged, it will provide him with means to go back to his home, freeing him from all responsibilities imposed upon him by the compact.

If he can withstand the dangers and the strain of the first year, however, recompense follows promptly. His land gives him four crops of vegetables annually. An expert agriculturist, whom the company keeps on the spot, helps him choose the right thing for the right time, and to get as much from the land as it will possibly yield; the cultivation is highly intensive and strictly scientific. Then the produce is carried to New York by fast trains, in refrigerating cars, and marketed by the expert agents of the company. Thus, the expert cultivating insures the maximum yield, and the expert selling, the maximum returns for the crop. Of these returns the company generally keeps one-half, and the other half goes to the farmer. Some farmers have been able to pay off most of their debt and to accumulate a little pile besides, and the life of the colony barely counts four years. What more attractive inducement could be held out to a foreign peasant, whose life has been a miserable *via crucis* through debts and want, than the prospect of becoming within five or six years the independent proprietor of a farm, able to give him an annual income of $1,500 or more?

When the farmer has paid off his debt his farm is his own, in his own right. He has been able to acquire it without investing a penny. Hold out the vision of such a future to the great mass of peasants who pass through Ellis Island every month, and see how many of them, ready to seize fortune by the hair, will eagerly turn their backs upon the city!

St. Helena is now a neat little village of 300 inhabitants. It has a station on the Atlantic Coast Line, where the express trains, with direct Pullman service to and from New York, stop regularly. It has a little church, plain but good-looking, dedicated to St. Joseph. Its curé, Rev. Donati, a Tuscan who has recently come to the colony, is as yet a sort of itinerant pastor, serving as in the primitive church. He has no house, sleeps with some friendly family, takes his meals with his parishioners in turn. They gladly invite him to their simple table—a table where what seems luxury has taken the place of the scarcity they knew across the sea. There is always meat on the table since wild rabbits are plentiful in the woods and poultry on the farms. There will be wine also as soon as the newly planted vines, the long lines of which border the different fields, begin to bear; the vines are looked after with as much care as the children,—or more,—says one of the colonists. . . .

There are instances in St. Helena of how active and business-like and how much-respected, the roughest and apparently poorest immigrant material may become, if the proper chance be given. A needier and more unattractive looking crowd than the St. Helena colonists on their arrival, could hardly be pictured; yet this crowd has rapidly gained general consideration, and even high esteem, among the population of the surrounding country and in the city of Wilmington. The colonists had to go to Burgaw, three miles away, for provisions. This they found very inconvenient and promptly devised a remedy. They organized themselves into a co-operative society—each contributed a small share—and started a small general store. Note, this general store does not belong to any private individual; it is run for the benefit of the community, by a small committee of trustees chosen among the colonists. It is now so well regarded in the business world of Wilmington, that any order from it to a wholesale firm is honored at once without guarantee. Its bills have always been paid upon presentation, and its credit is as excellent as its reputation for good management. To the colonists the store sells the goods at just enough above wholesale prices to pay the expenses of operation.

There was talk in St. Helena recently of organizing a similar co-operative enterprise for the purchase of agricultural machinery, farm animals, and other stock requiring a comparatively large outlay of capital. This system of co-operative association for agricultural enterprises was brought by the colonists directly from Italy where it is widely practiced, but in Italy the initiative in such organizations is generally taken by some well-meaning and philanthropic person of higher standing—perhaps the village doctor, or the parson, or a benevolently inclined proprietor—who also looks after the business management. The fact that the practice has been so readily and successfully applied in St. Helena by the peasants themselves, shows that in these humble personalities there are sometimes qualities of observation and executive capabilities that await only opportunity for effective expression.

PIEDMONTESE ON THE MISSISSIPPI

[At the same time that German and Scandinavian immigrants were pouring into the Great Lakes region to seek farmland, a group of northern Italians living at Galena, Illinois, moved northward and founded the settlement of Genoa, Wisconsin. These Piedmontese cleared land that had been considered unfit for farming and turned it, beginning in 1863, into a prosperous agricultural colony. Alexander E. Cance, a member of the U.S. Immigration Commission, wrote the following report on the Genoa community.]

Southward from St. Paul, the Mississippi winds its way between banks that frequently rise abruptly, almost perpendicularly, from the water's edge to a height of several hundred feet. The traveler over the Burlington Railroad, which closely hugs the east brink of the river, has noticed numerous coves or pockets, a few acres in extent, marking the place where some small tributary creek has cut its way down through the rocky barrier to reach the level of the great river. Through these narrow defiles or coulées, the woodsmen and farmers living back on the uplands were accustomed to bring their produce to the river for barter or shipment. In time, little villages grew up in these narrow openings, huddled, disorderly hamlets, poorly laid out, depending for their existence on the traffic between the back country farmers and the rivermen. One of these hamlets is Genoa. About 200 persons live in the village, 1,000 in the township; 207 families, of whom forty-four are of Italian descent. . . .

The first arrivals came immediately from Galena, Ill., whither,

From *Survey*, September 2, 1911.

fifty years ago, they had somehow come together from various parts of the globe—one from South America, another from the California mines, a third from a picturesque career in Africa. Genoa was selected for settlement because one of their number, who had gone on an exploring trip up the river, brought back news that he had found the duplicate of his Piedmont home. They chose the site because it looked like Switzerland, and renamed it Genoa. The colony grew slowly; there was no colonization and no considerable influx of immigrants at any one time. The settlers are all from Piedmont or Lombardy, Italy, and practically all the foreign-born arrived before 1890. . . .

Dairying is perhaps the most important present industry. The impetus came with the introduction of the creamery between 1885 and 1890. The dairy region of Vernon county is practically included in the tract of rough, hilly territory, some twelve miles wide, lying along the river and including Genoa township. This section is well adapted to grass, despite the insufficient supply of running water, and some cattle have been raised since the inception of the settlement. But dairying did not enter largely into the pioneer farming system; it was confined chiefly to the few pounds of butter which the farmer's wife had difficulty in exchanging for groceries at the village store. Cows were seldom milked in winter either by Italians or Americans, and in summer butter was frequently a drug on the market at eight to ten cents a pound.

The dairy industry was developed in the Italian settlement exactly as it developed elsewhere in Wisconsin. The creamery made the Wisconsin farmer a dairyman after the opening of the Minnesota wheat lands and the ravages of the chinch bug had wrought havoc with his wheat growing. The central feature is a farmer's co-operative creamery, really a joint stock company in which the patrons, Italian, German, and American dairymen, are shareholders. The cream is separated from the milk by hand or power separators before it leaves the farm; a cream collector hauls it to the creamery, where a hired butter-maker determines by test and weight the amount of butter-fat in each farmer's cream, and churns it. Cream is paid for on a butter-fat basis, the patron receiving his check every two weeks. The butter is sold by the co-operative company, and any surplus is returned as dividends to the stockholders in proportion to the shares held. Last year the dividends were 11 per cent on the par value of the outstanding stock. Since the patrons hold shares roughly corresponding to the quantity of cream delivered, the division of surplus is fairly equable.

The Italians have been fairly successful dairymen and stock raisers. Their dairy herds range from three to sixteen milk cows and about the same number of young cattle. In addition to an average of 200 pounds of butter made and consumed yearly at home, the income from dairy cows runs from fifty to nearly five hundred dollars for each farm. Not a large average, surely, for there are no pure bred or high grade herds, but comparing well with the income of other patrons in the vicinity. While the principles of breeding are not well understood, the Italian farmer takes great pride in his herd. . . .

It is a significant fact that these Italians are buying and operating modern farm implements of the most approved models with as great efficiency as their neighbors, the Scandinavians and Germans. Two and three-horse plows, drills, corn cultivators, and disc harrows are employed; mowing machines, hay tedders, and horse forks are used in haying; every farmer has a self-binder, and no field is so steep or uneven that the grain must be cut or bound by hand. The ordinary outlay for farm machinery on a 120-acre farm is between four and five hundred dollars. Hay loaders and gang plows cannot be operated successfully on the hillsides, and manure spreaders have not yet been introduced.

The farmsteads of the Piedmontese in Wisconsin present a better appearance and represent a larger outlay of capital than those of any group of Italians known to the writer. The houses, even on the small farms, are neat, well-constructed, and comfortable. On the larger farms, many of them are of brick or of stone, some of them erected years ago. Most of them are surrounded with well-cared-for lawns, ornamented with shrubbery and native trees. The big basement barns, the granaries, the tobacco sheds, the corn cribs, the tool sheds, and the milk houses on the greater number of farms give a picture of thrift and prosperity that one seldom associates with an Italian farmstead. The Italian has made sure, if slow, progress. The log granary or the hog house, he tells you, was his dwelling house for twenty years. He built his new barn out of stone which he and his son quarried, and every timber and rafter he hewed out of trees that grew in his wood lot; it was put up the year following a very profitable tobacco crop, and paid for as soon as the cupola was in place. Not one of the forty farmers brought any large amount of material wealth with him to the community. Every one endured many discomforts and inconveniences in order to become independent. And with the majority economic independence is a religion. An Italian rarely goes into debt for anything less than an economic necessity. For example, one rarely finds a top buggy or a bicycle that is not fully paid for. The American frequently contracts debt for luxuries, very often for comforts; the Italian, as a rule, never. . . .

This Wisconsin settlement is one of the very few Italian communities where the Italian and the Italian-American are not regarded nor spoken of as Italians, but as fellow citizens. Most of them speak fluent English, the young people all do, and converse intelligently, frankly, and without suspicion, on agriculture, politics, or topics of current interest. They attend strictly to their farming, and display more intelligence and real knowledge of diversified agriculture than any group of Italians investigated. They remind one of the German and German-Swiss farmers who have proved so successful both as farmers and as citizens. They have confidence in themselves, and the community feels that they can and do take their places and assume the responsibilities of citizenship shoulder to shoulder with the non-Italians in the neighborhood.

It may be that the environing conditions—natural and social— have molded this community differently from others where the opportunity for race isolation was afforded and conformity to the traditional type of agriculture was the line of least resistance. At any rate, Genoa exemplifies the adaptability of the North Italian, and illustrates his capacity for diversified agriculture and for American rural life as it has developed in our mid-western states. The community has not yet begun to live abundantly, or to enjoy fully its evident prosperity. On the other hand, who shall say that the great rank and file of American farmers has advanced farther or more rapidly in rural wealth, welfare, or well-rounded citizenship than this small group of Italian fellow citizens?

ITALIAN PROGRESS IN THE UNITED STATES

Alberto Pecorini

[By 1910, so many Italian immigrants had come to America that they had established a sizeable and permanent place for themselves. The first generation, born in Italy, were in some measure becoming "Americanized." They were making economic progress and achieving social stability. In the article from which this selection comes, journalist Alberto Pecorini noted the changes that had taken place in the Italian immigration since the 1880's.]

On the whole, . . . the Italian outlook in the United States is encouraging. First of all, Italian immigration is improving. The day of the organ-grinder, once the only representative of his race, has passed forever, and that of the ignorant peasant is rapidly passing. Illiteracy is diminishing, and with it the evils of which it has been the principal cause. The Italians who have come to New York in recent years—and, as has been noted, conditions among the Italians here are approximately those in other American cities—have not all been mere manual laborers, but in a large measure representatives of the different trades. There are today in the city fifteen thousand Italian tailors, many of them employed in the best establishments of Fifth Avenue and Broadway, earning from $40 to $100 per week. Almost one half of the barbers in New York are Italians, and satisfaction with cleanliness and skill is general. There are thousands of printers, mechanics, bricklayers, electricians and carpenters at work here, and their employers will testify that they are among the most sober, honest and industrious of workmen.

From "The Italians in the United States," in: *Forum*, January, 1911.

The rising movement among the Italians has been noticed especially in trade and industry. The retail fruit business is to a large extent, and the artificial flower industry almost entirely, in their hands. Italian hotels and restaurants are popular with Americans, and the Italian 50-cent *table d'hôte* is conceded to be the best to be had for that amount. Italians are prominent in the contracting business, although contractors generally can not be considered the most desirable class of Italians, many of them being utterly uneducated and taking advantage of the ignorance of the laborers of their race. Italian importers and merchants are no longer small storekeepers, importing a few barrels of wine or boxes of macaroni from their native villages, to be distributed among purchasers from the same villages; they are members of well-organized and powerful firms, with offices on Broadway and elsewhere side by side with those of important American merchants and importers. Four-fifths of all the trade between Italy and the United States, which amounts to $100,000,000 per year, passes through New York, and the greater part of it is controlled by Italians, from the importation of raw silk to that of lemons, olive oil and macaroni.

The number of Italian bankers doing a legitimate business among their countrymen in New York, especially since the enactment of the law compelling them to give a bond to the state, is increasing every day. There are at present more than a hundred of these bankers in New York; and, while most of their business is that of steamship agents and notaries public, there are several important financial institutions among them. One of these, founded in 1865, occupies fine quarters in Wall Street. The number of the bankers of the old irresponsible type is rapidly decreasing, partly on account of the decrease of ignorance among the Italian masses, but more particularly because of the establishment here of the Italian Savings Bank and of an agency of the Bank of Naples. On the first of the year the Savings Bank held total deposits of $2,395,750.71, divided among 11,170 depositors. The agency of the Bank of Naples, which was established by the Italian Government to facilitate the transfer of money from Italian immigrants here to their families at home, under normal conditions sends to Italy $5,000,000 annually —and about $2,000,000 is sent each year through the Post Office. Italian business men have in the banking field, as their particular financial organ, the Savoy Trust Company, founded five years ago as the Italian-American Trust Company. This institution has a capital of $500,000; and, although during the panic of 1907 its deposits dwindled to an insignificant amount, it weathered the storm, and is prospering today in its handsome offices on Broadway, with deposits of $2,000,000. An institution that is inspiring and directing Italian trade in New York is the Italian Chamber of Commerce, which, in existence for many years, has recently been reorganized and is now controlled by younger and more capable men.

Italian professional men are involved in the general uplift. The lawyers of today, although many of them are bad enough, are a great improvement upon their fellows of only ten years ago. Formerly, when actions were brought for damages in case of accident, the lawyer who appeared for the complainant was in the pay of the individual or corporation responsible for the casualty; he would accept ridiculously small compensation on behalf of his client, and then divide that with the unfortunate laborer who had been injured, or with his family in the event of his death. This practice, once the rule, still exists as an exception. There are almost 400 Italian physicians in New York, and by far the majority of them are respectable and able men. Competition among them has been somewhat severe in the past, and it is yet to some extent. However the Italian Medical Association of New York was recently formed, with headquarters in the Metropolitan Building, and at its first annual banquet, held at the Hotel Astor, the Italian doctors demonstrated that vast possibilities exist among them for serious, organized effort for the good of the Italian masses.

The professional men suggest the artists. There are, of course, the Italian operatic "stars," who are attracted by the high prices offered by the American impresarios, but who do not come to stay. Those artists who remain are the musicians, the teachers of music and the decorators. The musicians have already made their presence felt, having practically abolished the monopoly held for years by German bands and orchestras; the decorators are already asserting themselves as against artists of other nationalities, and their work may be seen in the handsomest theatres, and the finest hotels. And among the artists, may I be pardoned if I mention the cooks? They claim that theirs comes first among the *beaux arts*, and a great many of us agree with them. Well, Italian cooks are already employed in large numbers in the most fashionable restaurants and hotels, and the day is not far off when they will destroy the monopoly of the French *chefs des cuisines* as they ended that of the German musicians.

That the Italian Government has done a great deal for the Italian immigrants in America cannot be denied. The Society for Italian Immigrants, which protects ignorant arrivals from thieves and swindlers and gives them food and shelter for 50 cents a day until they may find work, is largely subsidized by the Italian Government, as is the Home for Italian Immigrants, established by the St. Raphael Society under the presidency of Archbishop Farley. The Italian Government also maintains an Italian labor bureau in New York for the distribution of immigration, and an Italian inspectorate of immigration informs the Government at Rome of the conditions of labor in this country. The Italian Government further has subscribed $60,000 toward the fund for the erection of an Italian hospital in New York.

The Roman Catholic Church is, of course, the most important religious agency among the Italians in America. There are about fifty Italian churches of this denomination and more than eighty priests in New York. Various Protestant denominations have also established churches and missions throughout the Italian quarters, twenty of which are now in operation. Grace Episcopal Church, the Methodist Episcopal Church of Jefferson Park, and the Presbyterian Church in University Place, have been particularly successful in social work among the Italians. Settlement work exclusively among Italians, both in Manhattan and Brooklyn, has had a far-reaching influence, the Richmond Hill House in the former borough being a centre of activity.

The most important educational centre for Italians in New York at present is the great English and trade school, recently established by the Children's Aid Society in the two large buildings formerly used by the Five Points House of Industry, in Worth Street. Here nearly 500 Italians of both sexes may be found every evening. There are classes in English, stenography, typewriting, sewing, cooking, sign painting and printing, as well as a gymnasium, club rooms, a library and a large auditorium. The Young Men's Christian Association has also done a great deal in the way of evening classes for Italians, half the membership of the Bowery branch, for instance, being of that race. The Italians are further receiving efficient help from the Board of Education in the matter of evening schools and lectures in Italian, and it is a cause for regret that these schools and lectures are not patronized as are those in the Jewish quarters. For the last eight years there has been an Italian member of the Board of Education.

It is to be regretted that the Italian press, by reason of a mistaken idea of patriotism, is not serving as an interpreter of American life and ideals to its constituency. Nevertheless the Italian press has followed the general movement forward, though it has not led it. There are six Italian daily newspapers in New York with a circulation varying from 10,000 to 30,000 copies per day. About half of these newspapers have a larger circulation out of than in the city, and all have special agents hunting for subscribers in the smaller towns, the mining districts and the labor camps. The first Italian newspapers consisted merely of translations from American journals, and even now the Italian press has no local news service of its own, while almost every daily imposes upon itself a great sacrifice for its cable service from Italy. While a great part of the advertising of the Italian newspapers comes from steamship companies, professional men, importers and merchants, there is still too large a proportion from fake doctors, real estate swindlers, and alleged brokers who sell to the immigrant the stock of companies that do not exist. However, there are two Italian dailies that enjoy the distinction of having refused money offered for political support at the last municipal election, and of having helped the Fusion cause without recompense—a startling reform in Italian journalism. It is to be hoped that in the future the Italian press may not con-

fine its benevolent activities to the providing of the city with monuments to Italian worthies, but that it will attempt to instruct the
Italian masses with regard to their duties in their new environment.

That Italians today are coming to America in families in much
larger numbers than ever before is a most encouraging sign. Accustomed and attached to family life, the Italian is lost without it.
The proportion of Italian women coming to the country is much
greater than it was, and Italian life in American cities is little by
little losing the appearance of impermanence it presented when a
smaller number of families, each with a large number of men
boarders, was the rule. Another encouraging feature of the situation
is that Italian books are coming into the United States in much
larger quantities than in the past, one dealer in Broadway having
imported as many as a million volumes last year, three-fourths of
which were fairy tales and popular novels, the literary pabulum of
artisan families in Italy. The Italian uplift in New York may
further be said to have found expression in the formation of an
up-to-date men's club, with a handsome house near Fifth Avenue.
The Italian Club has more than 350 members, with an initiation fee
of $100, and it boasts of having sold $600 worth of champagne to its
members last New Year's Eve—thus measuring a long step forward
in the arts of civilization. . . .

The small percentage of Italians engaged in agriculture in this
country have developed in three distinct fields—truck farming, extensive agriculture, and fruit raising. During the last ten years a
considerable number of farms, abandoned by Americans who have
gone west or entered business in the cities, have been occupied by
Italians in Western New York and the New England States. Truck
farming has been carried on to a greater extent, however, in New
Jersey, Pennsylvania and the Carolinas. In Ohio there are Italian
truck farmers in the vicinity of Cincinnati and Cleveland, and fruits
are raised by Italians in large quantities near the former city. The
vicinity of Chicago, in Illinois, has also a large number of Italian
farmers, many of whom make sausages after the Italian fashion,
which, being sold in the east, seriously menace the trade in the imported Italian kind. Recently the Long Island railroad has established an experimental agricultural station, where Italians have been
successfully raising vegetables. Long Island, like New Jersey, Western New York and the lower part of the Connecticut Valley, will in
the next few years see an even greater number of Italian farmers
raising vegetables on land neglected or abandoned by native Americans.

The second field in which the Italian has been tried out as an
agricultural laborer in the United States is in what I have termed
extensive agriculture. Italians are not numerous in the wheat and
corn fields of the Dakotas and Kansas, but they have gone in considerable numbers to the cotton, sugar cane, and tobacco fields of
the south and south-west. Of the 30,000 Italians in Louisiana,

about one-half are working on sugar and cotton plantations. Reports from the famous farm colony of Sunny Side, in Arkansas, founded by the late Austin Corbin, in which many Italians are employed, show that in spite of adverse conditions they are much more than holding their own in competition with the negro. Very few Italians have penetrated into Alabama, although they are raising vegetables and tobacco in two agricultural colonies in that state. Texas, on the contrary, is a wide open and inviting field for the Italian, and already 15,000 of them are engaged in agriculture there.

It is, however, in fruit culture that the Italian agriculturist has been the most successful in the New World. Almost every Italian owning a farm raises fruit to some extent, but the great fruit-bearing country for them is California, in which state are 60,000 Italians, of whom fully one-half are engaged in agriculture. Vines of all kinds have been imported from the most celebrated wine-producing districts of Europe, and for the last few years the American tourist has been drinking London claret produced by the Italian in California.

As to the future of the Italian engaged in agriculture, the country need have no misgivings; for he loves the soil and his most ardent desire is to own his little piece of land as soon as possible. The need of the urban Italian is a civic need. There are only a little more than 15,000 voters among the half million Italians in New York, approximately 3 per cent, while the proportion among other foreign nationalities varies from 15 per cent to 25 per cent. The naturalized Italians are mostly of the class of laborers, small storekeepers and petty contractors. The better elements have not as yet identified themselves with the community in which they live, in which their children were born, in which they own millions of dollars' worth of real estate, and pay millions annually in taxes. There is not an Italian holding an important municipal office. These conditions are abnormal, unhealthful, and they may become disastrous; they must be changed. Desirable Italian residents must become American citizens, and must take away the direction of their politics and the protection of their interests from the dealers in votes. Thus far relations between the Italian voter and the political parties have existed only at election time, and the better class of Italians have lost confidence in them.

To get votes is political propaganda; to make citizens an educational process. Citizens are needed far more than voters. To organize all educational agencies at present working among the Italians, and make them transform this inert, dead mass into a living progressive force, is an immediate necessity. A million unassimilated Italians in New York, with three millions in the United States, only a few years hence, will not tend to lessen the burden of government in the city or the nation. The problem of making a citizen of the Italian is not an insoluble one. It is only a question of going to work with a sincere desire to help, not to exploit; recognizing the bad side of Italian-American life, but giving full credit for the good. The Italian is certainly capable of contributing his full quota to the best life of the Republic, and it should be the task of earnest Americans to bring that consummation about. Only thus may what seems now a peril be made a blessing.

Part Three

MAKING A LIVING, 1890–1930

Italians, like immigrants from all nations, came to the United States to make money. The economy of Italy faltered badly between 1870 and 1900, particularly in the Mezzogiorno: overpopulation inflated the labor supply; the breakdown of the land tenure system combined with archaic farming practices and exhausted soil to impoverish agriculture; wages were low; and the poor were overtaxed. At first, Italians sought jobs in neighboring European countries—France and Germany—and southern Italians even went to the northern Italian cities for employment. Many thousands went to Argentina and Brazil, but by the end of the nineteenth century the tide had shifted in favor of the United States, where industrialization was rapidly expanding the economy, and wages were offered that were unthinkable in Italy.

For large numbers of Italians the goal of emigration was to make enough money to be able to return home, live comfortably, and perhaps buy land or a small business. Some worked in America during times of prosperity, then returned home with their savings during slack seasons. There developed a sizeable two-way traffic across the Atlantic as these "birds of passage" wended their way back and forth. A permanent return to Italy "some day" may have been in the minds of most of the immigrants, but as the years passed, the "birds of passage" became fewer in number. The great majority stayed in the United States permanently, and many who tried to adjust themselves to their native land could not: they had become too Americanized, and they returned here.

Most of those who did find jobs in the United States, whether they ever returned to Italy or not, did manage, even on meagre earnings (from an American point of view), to send back money to support families or to bring wives and children over. These remittances proved a financial boon to Italy, so much so that the Italian government encouraged emigration. By 1914, nearly three-quarters of a billion dollars had been sent to Italy from her immigrants in this country.

When the immigrants from the Mezzogiorno arrived, they found themselves at the bottom of the economic ladder, a position the Irish had occupied for most of the later nineteenth century, in the cities of the eastern seaboard. The Italians became a major part of the foundation on which America's industrial might was built. They worked in the mines, the steel plants, the packing houses, the textile plants, the fields, and on the railroads—everywhere that common laborers were needed. In an era of powerless unions, low pay, and ruthless industrialists, the Italians endured the worst of working and living conditions that America had to offer. In addition, they were often victimized by their own *padroni*, or bosses, many of whom were not above taking advantage of fellow countrymen for the sake of financial gain. When used as strikebreakers, the Italians were abused by other workers for undermining the unions. When they joined in a strike, they were vilified by society as anarchists, radicals, and criminals determined to destroy America. All this of course they shared with other members of the "new immigration"— Poles, Greeks, Slavs, Czechs, Jews, etc.—but the Italian share was larger because there were more of them.

Although most of the Italian immigrants in America made their way as common laborers, some were engaged in other pursuits— as shopkeepers, restaurant owners, wholesalers, tailors, barbers, newspaper publishers, and farmers. Many engaged in truck farming, reclaiming what had been considered worthless land and, like the Japanese in California, turning it into highly productive acreage. And some few immigrants were very successful financially—Amadeo P. Giannini, founder of the Bank of America, and Andrea Sbarbaro, founder of the Italian Swiss Colony, to name only two.

ENSLAVEMENT OF ITALIAN IMMIGRANTS

[Most of the Italians who came to the United States in the last quarter of the nineteenth century were males under 45 years of age, most of whom became common laborers in mines, factories, fields, and on the railroads. The *padroni* were the agents for their employment; the intermediaries who obtained the jobs, took men to where they worked, relayed to them their wages, and saw to housing and food. The drawbacks and evils of the padrone system were examined in an article by a fellow Italian.]

Tradition, more than wealth, divides the Italian immigrants into laborers and contractors, and subjugates the laborers to the contractors. In the course of time some accidental changes may occur in the personnel of the two classes. The laborious and thrifty peasant of South Italy may become a shopkeeper and importer, and his son may graduate as a lawyer or a physician; the political exile from Romagna or Tuscany may become a saloon-keeper and a contractor; and teachers and members of other professions may turn street-sweepers or common laborers. Yet the initial differences in most cases become hereditary, and ultimately grow into social institutions.

The territorial divisions of Italy are reproduced by the distribution of the Italian immigrants through the States. The tailor from Naples and Palermo, the weaver from Lombardy, the hat-maker from Piedmont, all follow the tracks of those who have preceded them. When a workman earns enough to support a family and feels sure of steady employment, he generally buys a house on monthly payments and settles permanently in this country. But the common laborer—the house-painter, the stone-cutter, the job-printer—wanders from one State to another, contriving to live the whole year round on the small savings of a few working months. He has, therefore, little inducement to remain. The wages of the unskilled laborer are entirely arbitrary, the people from Southern Italy receiving as a rule lower wages than their Northern colleagues, even when working side by side with them.

The industry of the Italian laborer and the benefits to this country which accrue from his work cannot be disputed. He tills the soil, builds railroads, bores mountains, drains swamps, opens here and there to the industry of American workmen new fields which would not perhaps be opened but for his cheap labor. It is a mistake to believe that he causes the lowering of wages; this is due to the increase of the capitalists controlling great interests. It is equally unjust to speak of him as a pauper laborer. He becomes a pauper on landing because he receives no help, no guarantee of life and independence, and he necessarily falls a victim to the Italian contractor and the contractor's American partner or employer. There are people who would like to keep him out of this country; it would be more reasonable to keep out the contractor.

The Italian laborer does more than his share of work and receives less than his share of earnings; for as a matter of fact, the laws enacted with regard to this matter oppress the laborer and assist rather than hamper the contractor. Even supposing that the contractor does not succeed in importing contract labor, he finds in the market a large number of men entirely at his mercy, with not even the weak support of a promise to defend themselves against his greed. The few dollars which the immigrant possesses on landing are skilfully taken out of his pocket by the hotel-keeper before the hotel-keeper gives him a chance to work. When he is reduced to absolute indigence, the lowest kind of work imaginable is offered him and he has to accept it. He walks through Mulberry Street and sees a crowd around a bar in a basement. He enters the basement and finds a man employing men for a company. He adds his name to the list without knowing anything about the work he will be called upon to do, or about the place where he is to be transported, or about the terms of his engagement. Perhaps, however, he passes a banker's establishment and stops to read on a paper displayed at the window a demand for two hundred laborers, supplemented with the significant assurance that the place of work is not far distant. He enters, enlists, takes his chances, and falls in the snare set for him.

I once witnessed the departure of a party of laborers and I shall never forget the sight. In foul Mulberry Street a half-dozen carts were being loaded with bundles of the poorest clothes and rags. One man after another brought his things; women and children lounged about, and the men gathered together in small groups, chattering about the work, their hopes, and their fears. For these men *fear*. They have heard of the deceit practised upon those who have preceded them and of their sufferings. Each man carried a tin box containing stale bread and pieces of loathsome cheese and sausage, his provision for the journey. Some had invested whatever money they had in buying more of such food, because, as they told me, everything was so much dearer at the contractor's store. The sausage, for instance, which, rotten as it was, cost them four cents a pound in New York was sold for twenty cents a pound at the place of their work. Presently our conversation was interrupted by the appearance of the contractor; the groups dissolved, the men took leave of their wives and friends, kissed once more their children, and made a rush for the carts. Then the train started for the railroad station, where the laborers were to be taken to their unknown destination. Of course, this destination and the wages and the nature of the work have been agreed upon in some informal way. But the contract is a sham. I do not believe there is a single instance in which a contract was honestly fulfilled by the contractor. When we think of law-breakers we instinctively refer to the lowest classes. But the contractors are systematic law-breakers. As a rule, the laborer is faithful to the letter of his engagement, even when he feels wronged or deceived.

The contractor is sure to depart from the terms of the contract either as to wages, or hours of labor, or the very nature of the work. Contractors have been known to promise employment, to pocket their fees, and then to lead the men to lonely places and abandon them. Some employment agencies agree with the employers that the men shall be dismissed under pretext after a fortnight or two of work, in order that the agents may receive new fees from fresh recruits. As a rule, however, the men obtain more work than they want or can stand. The contractor, who has acted thus far as an employment agent, now assumes his real functions. Him alone the employer (a railroad or some other company) recognizes, and all wages are paid to him. He curtails these for his own benefit, first by ten or twenty per cent or more, and he retains another portion to reimburse himself for the money he has spent for railway fares and other items. Wages are generally paid at the end of the second fortnight; the first fortnight they remain unpaid till the end of the work, in guarantee of the fulfillment of the contract by the laborer. Meanwhile the men have to live, and to obtain food they increase their debt with the contractor, who keeps a "pluck-me store," where the laborers are bound to purchase all their provisions, inclusive of the straw on which they sleep. The prices charged are from twenty-five to one hundred per cent and upward above the cost of the goods to the seller, and the quality is as bad as the price is high. At sunset the work ceases and the men retire to a shanty, very much like the steerage of a third-class emigrant ship, the men being packed together in unclean and narrow berths. The shanty is no shelter from wind or rain. Only recently the shanty where the Chicago National Gas-Pipe Company huddled its Italian workmen, near Logansport, Ind., was blown down by a wind-storm and several men were killed. Neither the number nor the names of the dead were known, as Italian laborers are designated only by figures.

The brutality of the contractors toward their subjects baffles description. The contractor is a strongly-built, powerful man; he has acquired the habit of command, is well armed, protected by the authorities, supported by such of his employees as he chooses to favor, and, sad to say, by the people, who are hostile to the laborers. He often keeps guards armed with Winchester rifles to prevent his men from running away. His power has the essential characteristics of a government. He fines his men and beats and punishes them for any attempted resistance to his self-constituted authority. On Sunday he may either force them to attend church service or keep them at work. I have been told of contractors who taxed their men to make birthday presents to their wives. A feudal lord would not have expected more from his vassals.

There are numerous cases where the contractor objects to paying wages. One day last July, as I was walking in King's Bridge, near New York City, I met two laborers loitering in the rear of their shanty. They were evidently afraid to talk, and it was with much difficulty that I learned from them that they were the only members of a gang of about two hundred who had dared to strike work, because their contractor had employed them for three months without paying them. I made my way to the shanty and entered into conversation with a woman who was engaged in cooking. She told me, with tears, that she had saved a little money and had invested it in feeding the men. "Now, if the contractor will not pay us," she said, "I shall be ruined." I denounced the outrage in the Italian press of New York, but ineffectually. A few days later some Italians who worked in a locality near Deal Lake, New Jersey, failing to receive their wages, captured the contractor and shut him up in the shanty, where he remained a prisoner until the county sheriff came with a *posse* to his rescue. I could mention a half-dozen more such cases, all recent. The latest came to my knowledge in Cleveland, Ohio. A contractor had run away with the money, and neither the press nor an attorney employed by the men succeeded in compelling the company which employed him to pay the workmen. Old laborers have the same tale to tell. Nearly all have the same experience. Every one will grant that robbing a poor man of his well-earned wages is a shameful crime; yet in no instance, to my knowledge, has a contractor been made to suffer for his fraud. He generally disappears for a few days and starts again in another place. In this way many, no doubt, have been enriched.

But this is not the worst form of outrage of which contractors are guilty. There have been cases where Italian laborers have suffered actual slavery, and in trying to escape have been fired upon by the guards and murdered, as happened not long ago in the Adirondacks. A similar case was told to me by one of the victims. He said:

> We started from New York on November 3, 1891, under the guidance of two bosses. We had been told we should go to Connecticut to work on a railroad and earn one dollar and seventy-five cents per day. We were taken, instead to South Carolina, first to a place called Lambs(?) and then after a month or so to the "Tom Tom" sulphate mines. The railroad fare was eight dollars and eighty-five cents; this sum, as well as the price of our tools, nearly three dollars, we owed the bosses. We were received by an armed guard, which kept constant watch over us, accompanying us every morning from the barracks to the mines and at night again from the work to our shanty. . . . Part of our pay went toward the extinction of our debt; the rest was spent for as much food as we could get at the "pluck-me" store. We got only so much as would keep us from starvation. Things cost us more than twice or three times their regular price. Our daily fare was coffee and bread for breakfast, rice with lard or soup at dinner-time, and cheese or sausage for supper. Yet we were not able to pay off our debt; so after a while we were given only bread, and with this only to sustain us we had to go through our daily work. By and by we became exhausted, and some of us got sick. Then we decided to try, at the risk of our lives, to escape. Some of us ran away, eluding the guards. After a run of an hour I was exhausted and decided to stay for the night in the woods. We were, however, soon surprised by the appearance of the bosses and two guards. They thrust guns in our faces and ordered us to return to work or they would shoot us down. We answered that we would rather die than resume our former life in the mine. The bosses then sent for two black policemen, who insisted that we should follow them. We went before a judge, who was sitting in a barroom. The judge asked if there was any written contract, and when he heard that there wasn't, said he would let us go free. But the bosses, the policemen, and the judge then held a short consultation, and the result was that the bosses paid some money (I believe it was forty-five dollars), the policemen put the manacles on our wrists, and we were marched off. At last, on April 1, we were all dismissed on account of the hot weather. My comrades took the train for New York. I had only one dollar, and with this, not knowing either the country or the language, I had to walk to New York. After forty-two days I arrived in the city utterly exhausted. . . .

At best, the workman, after years of hard labor, saves just enough money to purchase his return ticket, or possibly a hundred dollars more to pay off the debts contracted in his absence by his family, or to buy up the small farm which was foreclosed by the government because he failed to pay the land tax. The boss or contractor, the hotel-keeper, the salon-keeper, and the banker accumulate fortunes and buy villas or palaces in their native towns, whither they eventually return after the time has passed when their sentence to punishment is no longer valid, covered with all the honor and glory accruing from the possession of wealth.

THE PADRONE SYSTEM:
A FEDERAL VIEW

[If the *padroni* were looked upon by American authorities as an evil, they were, for thousands of Italian workers, a necessary evil. Predatory as some of the *padroni* were, they, nevertheless, were instrumental in bringing many immigrants to America, arranging for jobs, sending remittances back to Italy, and generally helping the newcomers to adjust to America. Both the Italian and American governments, viewing the padrone system as exploiting the immigrants, wanted to do away with it. The history and operation of the system was the subject of an industrial commission report in 1901.]

In the period of industrial recovery following the Civil War, there was a pressing demand for labor. Special legislation was even invoked to aid in supplying this demand. Thus the act of 1864, for the encouragement of immigration, gave manufacturers and contractors the right to import foreign laborers under contract. Speculation in cheap labor ensued; agents were sent to foreign countries in search for workmen. The unenlightened peasants of Italy were the easiest victims of this speculation. Their coming, in fact, was not of their own accord, as was the case with the people of northern Europe, but they came usually under contract.

This difference between the Italian immigrant and the northern people, and the reason for their having been so easily exploited, is brought out by their illiteracy and ignorance of the English language.

From *Reports of the Industrial Commission on Immigration and Education*, Vol. 15. Washington, 1901, pp. 430–36.

The great bulk of Italian immigration has come from southern Italy, the provinces, Abruzzi, Avellino, Basilicata, Sicily, Calabria, and Naples. Almost the whole number from these provinces are of the peasant class, accustomed to hard work and meager fare. Their illiteracy is very high. In 1899 the illiteracy for all races of immigrants was 22.9 percent, while for the immigrants from southern Italy it was 57.3 percent, and for northern Italy the illiteracy was only 11.4 percent, showing clearly the contrast between this ignorant peasant class of unskilled laborers and the skilled workmen from the manufacturing centers of northern Italy. In 1900 the percentage of illiteracy for these immigrants was 54.5 in contrast to 24.2 for all races and 11.8 for the northern Italians.

This illiteracy is brought out by the investigation of the United States Department of Labor of the Italians in Chicago (*Ninth Special Report*, p. 383). Out of 4,553 persons ten years of age and over, 2,752, or 60.44 percent, were found to be illiterates. Among 2,812 males, 51.96 percent were illiterate; and of 1,741 females, 1,291 or 74.15 percent, were illiterate. As to the literacy itself of the 39.56 percent who were literate, only 18.21 percent could read and write English and Italian, while 54.80 percent could read and write Italian only. More than this, the literate males who could read and write Italian only were 60.55 percent of the literates, which shows how very unfavorably the Italians are situated when they enter industrial activities under American conditions.

The same investigation showed that of the number of persons of foreign birth and ten years of age and over, 58.62 percent were able to speak English and 47.38 percent were not able to speak English. . . .

Some form of contract was then necessary to induce these people to leave their country, for by temperament they were not the self-reliant people of the north who came of their own volition. The dread of change, the fear of coming to a strange and unknown land had to be counteracted by material inducements. It was thus that they came, not in search of work but under contract for several years, and thus were assured in advance of permanent work at what seemed to them high wages.

At this earliest stage in the Italian immigration the padrone was the agent of the contractor or manufacturer. Laborers were demanded, and he acted simply as the agent in supplying specific demands. The manufacturer or contractor was of another nationality, but in looking for cheap labor he had recourse to an Italian already in this country. This Italian, undertaking to supply the number of laborers called for, went or sent to Italy for the number, who entered upon a contract binding themselves to service for from one to three years, and in rare instances even for seven years. At the same time he furnished transportation and took care of them upon landing here until they were sent to the work for which they were contracted. It was thus that the padrone was merely a middleman, the man who stood between the contractor and the men. He was looked upon by the men as their representatives, not as their employer, and upon him they depended.

Under this early system there were numerous ways in which the padrone could make money. In the first place, he had a commission from the men as well as from the contractor for furnishing the men, and commission on their passage. Upon getting them here he had a profit from boarding them until they went to work. This was deducted from their prospective earnings. After that the padrone usually furnished food and shelter for them while at work. This privilege was usually given free by the contractor who furnished shelter and for which the padrone charged rent. Then there was also the commission from sending money back to Italy; and finally the commission on the return passage after the contract had been completed.

But the padrone par excellence was not an agent and did not act for the contractor. He acted primarily upon his own initiative and for himself. Instead of waiting for a call for men, he would upon his own responsibility engage Italians to come, and contract for their labor for a certain number of years. After having brought them here he would farm them out to anyone who wanted them. He boarded them, received their wages, and paid them what he saw fit. Sometimes a laborer would receive $40 a year and as often only $40 for two years. Under this system the padrone occasionally would buy outright a minor from his or her parents.

Men, women, and children were thus brought into the country, the boys to become bootblacks, newsboys, or strolling musicians. In this stage the padrone system most closely resembled the system as it existed in Italy, which meant in general the employment of children, or minors, in the "roving professions," such as strolling musicians, performers on the harp or hand organ, and street acrobats. These persons were under the direction of a master or padrone more or less inhuman, to whom belonged all the earnings of these persons.

This system flourished most widely during the decade 1870–1880, and under its influence Italian immigration was stimulated to such an extent that the flow soon equaled the demand. The sphere of the padrone then changed. His work of inducing immigration was no longer necessary; immigrants came without having previously made contracts, and governmental action was aimed at preventing the importation of contract labor. Under these two influences—the great increase in immigration and governmental opposition—the character of the padrone has changed.

As a result of this demand for laborers and the activities of the padroni the Italian immigrants have been largely males, and until recent years have not come by families, as have the other nationalities, notably the German and Scandinavian people. . . .

Under these changed conditions it is probable that the padrone has very little to do with bringing Italians into the country, since it is no longer necessary to have a contract to bring them in, and because it is even unsafe according to federal statutes. The padrone is now nothing more than an employment agent, and exists only because of the immigrants and their illiteracy and ignorance of American institutions. He procures his subjects at the port, upon their landing, by promising them steady work at high wages. If the immigrant does not get under the control of the padrone by this means, the immigrant need only go to the colony of his race in any of the large cities, where he will readily be picked up by one of the padroni and promised employment.

By this means the newcomers are attached to the padrone, who is able to fulfill his promises, because he "stands in" with the contractors, he knows officials and bosses of the railroads, and he is thus in a way to furnish employment for his fellow countrymen who cannot speak English and have no other way of finding employment. It may then be said that the padrone system no longer exists, and that the successor to the padrone is an employment agency, which collects the labor only after it has already arrived in this country, and makes its profit through commissions and keeping boarders.

As Dr. Egisto Rossi, of the Italian Immigration Bureau, has summed up the situation, "The padrone system, or bossism, can be defined as the forced tribute which the newly arrived pays to those who are already acquainted with the ways and language of the country."

Though the character of the padrone is now that of an employment agent, it is undoubtedly true that no Italian has an employment agency license. But it is also true that in nine years there has never been a prosecution of an Italian for carrying on an employment agency without a license. His mode of operation is to go to the regular licensed agencies or to the contractors and furnish the men desired. The padrone also has no office of his own.

But the padrone does not employ the men alone and upon his own responsibility. He works together with the Italian banker, who is a somewhat more responsible party than the padrone; at least the men have more faith in him, because it is through him that they send money back to Italy, and with whom they keep their small savings. It is through the banker that the call is made for the number of men who are wanted, and it is in his office where the arrangements with the men are made. He may advance the money for transportation, and even the commission if the men do not have the money. The padrone takes charge of the men in the capacity of a boss, takes them to the place of work, runs the boardinghouse or shanty store at the place of work, and acts as interpreter for the contractor.

The padroni may be divided into several classes. The first class is the small boss who furnishes many odd jobs for individuals. The next class is the boss who regularly supplies contractors and others with laborers in large numbers. This is the largest class and really stands for the padrone as he at present exists. Finally, there are bosses who at the same time are independent contractors. But this is the exception, for the padrone, it may be said, is never a foreman and just as rarely an independent contractor. His work is to act as an interpreter for the foreman and run the boarding-house or shanty store.

For furnishing employment he receives a commission from the laborer. This commission depends upon the (1) length of the period of employment; (2) the wages to be received; and (3) whether they board themselves. If they board themselves, the commission is higher and varies from $1 to $10 a head. For a job of five or six months the commission may even rise to $10. In some cases the wages are paid to the padrone, but this is only when the contractor is dishonest and receives a share from the padrone. But if the contractor is honest, he knows that the people are generally cheated, and so he pays the men direct, deducting, however, the board and other charges as shown by the padrone.

Under this system the padrone is in combination with the Italian banker, who furnishes the money to pay for transportation, for the erection of shanties when they are not provided by the contractor, and to buy provisions. All this money is then deducted from the earnings of the men. The profits derived from the venture are finally shared by the padrone with the banker, who, however, finds his chief source of gain in holding the savings of the laborers, sending their money to Italy, and changing the money from American to Italian, in which process great shrinkage usually takes place.

The padrone has a further hold upon these people as a result of irregular employment. During the winter there is almost no employment at all. This means that during the greater part of five months these people are without work. When work is plentiful, the laborer who boards with his boss is said to be fortunate if he can save more than one-half of his earnings. Some of these earnings are sent to Italy or frequently squandered, so that the laborer often finds himself in winter without resources of his own. In such cases he finds it convenient to go [to] the boarding-house of the boss or banker, where he remains until spring, when it is understood that he shall enter the employ of the boss. . . .

Occasionally, Italians are employed through padroni in the endeavor to break a strike. For example, in the lockout in 1892–93 of the granite cutters, Mr. Duncan testified before the Commission that Italians were employed to take the places of the union men. But he said that they were inefficient and had to drift out of the work because of the minimum wage rate established by the union and the desire of the employer to have only the most profitable men. The general secretary-treasurer of the Granite Cutters' National Union describes a padrone system in New York City which was prepared to supply men to employers in the granite-cutting trade. The union has an eight-hour day with $4 in New York. The padrone gathers the Italians, who comply with the state law by declaring their intentions for citizenship.

These men pay the padrone $12 commission, $6 remaining on deposit as a guaranty that at the end of the week the man supplied with work shall return $6 to the padrone; if not, his employment ceases. These $6 per man per week are paid by the padrone to the contractor, who has thus employed men at $3 under a $4 law in New York, which provides that mechanics employed in the state upon municipal, county, or state work shall be paid the prevailing rate of wages and work the prevailing hours. This is one of the very rare instances where skilled labor is furnished in New York by the padrone system, and it cannot be taken as representative of the system.

The Italian immigrant, however, does not always limit himself to becoming a common laborer on railroad work and other excavations, but often becomes an artisan. Insofar as he becomes an artisan he comes in conflict with American workmen, but the conflict is less sharp than formerly, because the American unions are organizing Italian labor. The Italians themselves are coming to understand the importance of organized labor. This is noticeable especially among the Italian hod carriers, masons, and stonecutters; and where this feeling and sense of organization has developed there is no opportunity for the padrone system.

VINES AND WINES OF CALIFORNIA

Andrea Sbarboro

[Born at Acero, near Genoa, Sbarboro came to the United States with his parents as a child. By 1875, he had worked his way up from a grocery store clerk to a successful banker in San Francisco. In 1881, he talked some of his fellow immigrants into forming a community to establish vineyards at Asti. After several years of near failure, by 1890, the Italian Swiss Colony, with Pietro Rossi as chief winemaker, became an enormous success. Within ten years, the company had its own national marketing system and began winning international fame for the quality of its wines. In 1900, Sbarboro authored the following article on the importance of the winemaking industry for California.]

Among the many economic resources of California, none is more valuable, and none holds greater promise for the material development of the State, than the culture of the grape and its preparation in various forms for the use of consumers. Viticulture in other parts of our country is seemingly little more than an avocation, a matter of side interest among agriculturists; but here in the Golden State it is an established and extended industry, and destined to grow to vast proportions not far in the future. The wine industry alone already gives employment to over ten thousand people.

The origin of the industry in California is of especial interest, being due to the pioneers of the Church, who laid here the religious foundations. The first missionaries, who had been accus-

From *Overland Monthly*, January, 1900.

tomed in their native country to the use of wine, both at the mass
and on the table, when they arrived here to civilize the Indians
found an abundance of everything with which to satisfy their
appetites, with the exception of that which they most desired
—wine. However, being scientific men, they readily ascertained that
the soil and climate of California were very similar to those of
Spain and Italy, and they soon discovered that the grape-vine could
grow here as well as in those countries of the Old World. Their
opinion was fortified by the fact that wild grapes grew profusely
on nearly all the hillsides of California. They were not long in
writing to their brethren who were preparing to leave the old
country for California to bring with them cuttings from grapevines. The Missionaries set these out in different parts of the State
and to their satisfaction found that grapes grew as luxuriantly here
as they did in their native land, and made as good wine. The first
varieties of grapes were called the "Mission," as they were brought
here by the Missionaries.

The oldest vineyard was planted in Sonoma County, although
there recently died a single vine at Santa Barbara which was
supposed to be over one hundred years old and produced over
one ton of grapes.

The setting out of new vineyards which was pushed to an
extreme for a decade or two, has been discontinued until recently,
for the reason that the grape industry had been brought down
so low by unreasonable competition that in some cases it did not
pay the farmer to gather his grapes. But within the past two
years the price of grapes has advanced to such a figure that this
season new vineyards are being set out in some parts of the State,
especially in the northern part of Sonoma County, where, by-the-
bye, that dreadful insect, phylloxera, has never appeared. This pest
has done a great deal of damage in some parts of the State, notably
in Napa County, which was once the banner grape-producing county
of the State, but now produces not one quarter of its former crop.
However, many vineyards are now being set out with resistant
vines, which are not affected by the phylloxera, and as the demand
for wines is rapidly increasing, both for home consumption and
the supplying of the European market, and in our new possessions
of Cuba, Porto Rico, and the Philippines, where there are a large
number of wine-drinking people, it is expected that hereafter the
grape industry will increase from year to year and eventually
become the principal industry of California. . . .

The largest vineyard in the State was set out by the late Leland
Stanford at Vina, Tehama County; in the Sacramento Valley. It
was the desire of this great man to make wine on a large scale,
and thus to show the people of the world what California could
produce; but, while he understood financiering and the building of
railroads, he did not understand the viticultural industry, and the

result was, unfortunately for this State, that he selected a place where only the poorest kind of wine-grapes could be produced. He set out a vineyard of about four thousand acres on a flat land subject to irrigation; but while the crop of grapes produced was large, the quality of the wine was such that it was only fit for distilling into brandy, which is now made on a large scale and is of a very superior quality.

The revenue derived from this immense tract of land has been turned over by that noble lady, Mrs. Stanford, as part of the endowment of the Leland Stanford Junior University, at Palo Alto.

The next largest vineyard in the State is that owned by the Italian-Swiss Agricultural Colony, at Asti, in upper Sonoma County. This vineyard is now composed of nearly two thousand acres and was selected by persons who had made a life study and had large experience in the production of wine in Italy. It is composed of rolling hills, and while the Stanford vineyard produces as much as ten tons of grapes to the acre, the Asti vineyard produces only an average of two tons to the acre. But the hills having a sunny exposure and the soil being volcanic, it produces the very finest quality of dry wines, and it was principally due to these wines that California was enabled to compete favorably with the wine-producing countries of Europe at the exhibitions of Bordeaux, in France, and Genoa and Turin, in Italy, where California wines were awarded gold medals and highest praise.

For many years the Mission was the only grape raised in California, and it produced a heavy wine with such an alcoholic strength that it found little favor with the general public; but in the early sixties the Legislature of California, appreciating the viticultural importance of a State which could produce good wine, made a liberal appropriation, and sent Colonel A. Haraszthy to Europe for the purpose of bringing here a large variety of grape-cuttings from the best wine-producing districts of Europe. These in time were set out in different parts of the State, and were found to give satisfactory results. . . .

The viticultural industry of California must eventually become the greatest industry of the State, as important as it is in France, which industry was the principal means by which the enormous war debt imposed by Bismarck in 1870 was paid. California has a territory larger than the kingdom of Italy, where with a population of thirty-two million inhabitants there is produced annually about one billion gallons of wine. Grapes can be successfully grown in every county of this State; the northern part produces in perfection the dry wines of Bordeaux, in France, and of Florence, in Piemonte, Italy,—such as Cabernet, Burgundy, Sauternes, Riesling, Barbera, Chianti, Baralo, etc., while in the southern part of the State, the sweet wines of Spain, Portugal, and Sicily, such as Sherry, Port, Muscatel, Madeira, and Marsala, come to such perfection that when properly made and adequately aged and placed side by side with the wines from the mother country, they cannot be distinguished from them. It follows that we can produce in this State just as much wine as is now grown in Italy,—that is to say, one billion gallons per annum,—representing a value of three hundred million dollars. Instead of that, we are now producing barely thirty million gallons per annum, representing about nine million dollars. . . .

While California is the only State in the Union where fine wines can be grown and in unlimited quantities, still our grape-growers for several years past have not been adequately remunerated for their labor. The principal reason for this has been that many people have gone into the wine-making business without any knowledge of the science of wine-making. The result has been that in past years a large quantity of poor wine has been thrown on the market at ruinous prices. With the low prices for wine naturally followed the low prices for grapes. Add to this the competition of trade, and the final result has been very unsatisfactory, both to the grape-grower and to the wine-maker. This condition of affairs, however, is rapidly changing. Like all other affairs of life, it is coming to the test of the survival of the fittest. Those people who have ventured to go into wine-making without the proper knowledge, have gone or are rapidly going to the wall. This enables the truly scientific wine-maker to produce a finer quality of wine and obtain a fair remuneration for his labor and capital invested, and furthermore, by the production of fine wines, the consumption is materially increased.

This year, thanks to the liberal offer made by Mr. Henry J. Crocker to pay fourteen dollars a ton for the dry-wine grapes of the State, and the short crop produced, the price of grapes has been held at such a figure as to pay liberally the grape-grower, and at the same time to keep out of the market the incompetent wine-maker. The result is that the vintage of 1899 will be one of the best the State has ever produced. In fact, notwithstanding the war which is made by some people against the development of industries by combinations on a large scale, I believe that if the grape-growers and the good wine-makers, together with the legitimate wine-dealers of this State, would unite their forces and form a combination, the three branches of the industry—that is to say, the grape-growers, wine-makers, and wine-dealers—would be materially benefited, while consumers of wine could be supplied with a better article without enhancement in price, and the sale both in the United States and in foreign lands would be very considerably increased.

I am a firm believer in co-operation in whatever branches of industry,—in finance, as well as in agriculture and manufactures. The time has passed when the people of the country sympathized with the poor stage-driver because he lost his occupation on account of the building of the railroad. For one person thrown out of employment, one hundred now find remunerative positions in other branches of industry.

Especially in this new country, where so many million acres of land have never been touched by the plow, I do believe that the joining of forces for the development of new industries would be beneficial to humanity.

A splendid illustration of the effect of co-operation is given by the organization of the Italian-Swiss Agricultural Colony. It was formed on the plan of the building and loan associations which have procured homes for millions of people in the United States and have taught the lesson of thrift and economy to wage-earners.

In 1881, the promoters of the colony, most of them practical viticulturists from Italy, seeing the brilliant future of the viticultural industry of California, formed a co-operative association, issuing two thousand shares of stock. Each share paid into the common fund one dollar a month, making a total of two thousand dollars per month. As soon as ten thousand dollars had been accumulated in the treasury, a committee was appointed to go over the State and select a tract of land suitable for growing the best varieties of grapes. The committee, after having examined over forty tracts of land which had been offered, selected a tract of fifteen hundred acres which had been formerly used as a sheep-ranch in the beautiful Russian River Valley, near Cloverdale. They immediately set to work to dig up the trees by the root, plow the land, and set out grapevines, which they carefully selected from the best varieties from different parts of Europe.

The result has been that in less than twenty years the colonists have changed the sheep-ranch into a beautiful vineyard of two thousand acres, erected one of the largest wineries in the State, built a settlement for one hundred families, erected a schoolhouse where many children, most of them born on the premises, already attend, have a railroad station, post-office, and telephone, and have laid the foundation for a new city. Their business has increased to such an extent that they have already set out a vineyard for the production of sweet-wine grapes, built a winery and created a settlement for Madera, in the county of that name, and have also recently purchased a new winery at Fulton, Sonoma County.

The results show the effect of co-operation. The members of the colony paid into the treasury of the corporation one hundred and sixty thousand dollars. The property which is now owned by the colonists is worth nearly two million dollars. It pays a reasonable rate of interest annually to its members and continues to add lands and improvements to its holdings from year to year for the benefit of all of its members. Had it not been for the principle of co-operation,—or trusts, if you please,—the tract of land at Asti would probably still be used for a sheep-pasture, and employment would not have been supplied to the thousands of people who are now earning a good living through the enterprise of this colony. Thousands of similar enterprises could be successfully inaugurated in California.

Because Italians were numerically so conspicuous in the "new immigration" after 1880, it is sometimes forgotten that Italian American history is as old as American history itself. Christopher Columbus, born in Genoa, Italy, about 1451, planted the Spanish flag in the New World in 1492. Since that day, Italians and Italian Americans have been helping to shape the history of the Western Hemisphere.

The continents of the New World were named in honor of Amerigo Vespucci, a Florentine by birth, who made several important voyages to the new lands discovered by Columbus.

Based at Mission Dolores from 1687 until his death in 1711, Father Eusebio Francisco Kino explored and charted much of the Southwest. His most significant work in cartography was the preparation of maps proving that California was not an island, as had been believed. Apart from his explorations, he was able to found about twenty missions, of which the best known is San Xavier del Bac near Tucson, Arizona.

Like other immigrants entering the United States toward the end of the nineteenth century and in the early years of the twentieth century, many Italians sailed into New York harbor on crowded ships.

Once the immigrants had landed at Ellis Island, they were given a series of tests and examinations, including a literacy test. The immigrant had to be able to read twenty words in any language or he would be sent back.

New York Public Library Picture Collection

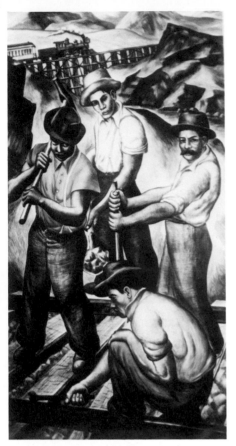

In the period after 1890, the Italians, along with other "new immigrants," provided a substantial part of the labor force for the canals and rail lines then under construction. It was a temporary way to make a living, but life on the "track gangs" was neither pleasant nor easy. Often the immigrants were as much victims as beneficiaries of the opportunities available to them in the "land of opportunity."

After two naturalized Italian immigrants, Nicola Sacco and Bartolomeo Vanzetti, were arrested for the 1920 murder of the paymaster and a guard at a shoe factory in South Braintree, Massachusetts, extreme xenophobia, antiradicalism, and anti-Communism became widespread among Americans. The evidence convicting Sacco and Vanzetti was circumstantial, but such was the hostility of the court and the public that a guilty verdict was inevitable. In 1927, after six years of appeals that failed, they were finally executed.

Little Italy in Manhattan in New York City, like other Italian communities in major cities, could be the scene of gala festivals. More often, however, it was filled with the daily problems of poverty that afflicted immigrant ghettos everywhere.

After serving five terms as mayor of Cleveland, Ohio, Anthony J. Celebrezze was appointed Secretary of Health, Education, and Welfare by President John F. Kennedy.

John A. Volpe, pictured here with President Lyndon B. Johnson, has had a long and distinguished career in public service. After three terms as Governor of Massachusetts, he became Secretary of Transportation and, recently, went to Rome as the American Ambassador to Italy.

Wide World Photos

John Orlando Pastore, a popular senator from Rhode Island, is pictured here delivering a fiery speech to the Democratic National Convention at Atlantic City, New Jersey, in 1964.

Enrico Caruso, perhaps the best known of many Italian opera stars, is shown here performing in Verdi's *La forza del destino* in 1918.

FORCED LABOR IN WEST VIRGINIA

Gino C. Speranza

[American-born Gino Speranza, as an officer of the Society for the Protection of Italian Immigrants, investigated the working conditions in several labor camps in the West Virginia counties of Kanawha, Raleigh, Clay, and Wirt. The publicity resulting from the publication of some of his findings in journal and newspaper articles helped to ameliorate the worst of the conditions described. The society itself sent agents into the camps to establish schools for the immigrants and to hear grievances.]

It is a far cry from Harmon's Camp in the lonely mountains of Raleigh County, West Virginia, to New York City, yet it speaks well for the unceasing vigilance of our militant philanthropy that a cry from that camp in the wilderness was heard and heeded. The adventures of the twenty-three Italian laborers who were sent to Raleigh County from New York reads like a page from the history of the Middle Ages, except that the splendid animal courage of those days is replaced here by the all-absorbing sordid interest of money-making.

In the early part of March, 1903, twenty-three Italians were shipped (I use the word advisedly) from New York by one of those numberless "bankers" who infest the Italian colony, to Beckley, West Virginia, to work on a railroad in process of building in the Piney Creek District. They were told, as is often done and as must be done to induce men to go to that region, that Beckley was a few hours from New York and the approximate

From *Outlook*, June 13, 1903.

cost of transportation would be eighty cents. When they arrived at Beckley, after a journey of nearly two days, hungry, bewildered, and conscious already that they had been betrayed, they were driven to Harmon's Camp, some four miles from town. Those who have not been to the West Virginian labor camps can hardly understand how lonely and isolated some of them are. Even though geographically near each other, they are completely shut in by high mountains, and the surrounding country is practically un-inhabited. Conscious of having been sold by the agents in New York, the lonesomeness of the camp naturally increased the apprehension of the laborers. But they started in on the work of drilling and grading, even though the work was not as it had been represented. Perhaps they worked because the presence of some armed guards and the sight of the contractor with a revolver ostentatiously stuck in his breast pocket was not reassuring. More-over, to make matters worse, though they were at liberty to "buy anywhere," they had to buy from the camp commissary, no matter how extortionate the prices were, as the nearest store was miles away. The day came when such conditions grew unbearable and the men left; they were not paid, but it seemed better to lose money than to remain. The contractor, however, having advanced transportation, was not going to stand a loss if he could help it. It is true that the Governor of West Virginia, stirred by constant complaints of abuse, had urged the use of legal process in such cases rather than a recourse to force. However hampered legally the contractor might be, the storekeeper had a ready remedy under the "Boarding-House Law" of West Virginia, which gives the right of arrest for non-payment of board. It did not matter that it applied with doubtful propriety to shanty board in a camp, once an accom-modating squire could be found to grant a warrant. And so the twenty-three "insurgents" were arrested and locked over night in the Grand Jury room at the County Court-House at Beckley, on the charge of non-payment of board. The next morning enters the contractor; he is a private citizen, he is not an officer, he is not even a party of record to the proceedings. What right has he in that Grand Jury room used as a jail? And when the prisoners, in the actual custody of the law, refuse to go back to his camp, he and his henchman, in that room set apart for what has been called "the bulwark of Anglo-Saxon liberty," proceed to bind six of the prisoners with ropes. I cite from the sworn statement of one of the men: "He had tied my wrists and had thrown the rope around my neck, when I shouted to the storekeeper, who was present and spoke Italian, 'Not this, not this! It is Holy Week and I know Christ's hands were tied, but there was no rope around his neck.'" Thereupon the contractor, convinced that the binding of the arms was sufficient, bunched together six of the bound men and marched them out into the public street. There, before "the whole town," not excluding certain sworn officers of the law, seeing that the prisoners still refused to march back to camp, the contractor hitched the rope by which they were tied to a mule, urging it on. The squire who had issued the warrant of arrest fortunately appeared then and cut the men free. Praise be to him for this act! But why did he urge these men to go back, as he did, with that brute of a contractor, and why did he, instead of trying the prisoners then and there according to law, go back to camp with them and help to induce them to "work out" their "board" and transportation? Why did he not take action against the contractor caught *in flagrante?* Why was there no entry made in his official docket of the disposition of this case till months after? Why did not the Prosecuting Officer at Beckley, who knew of this barbarity, take any action until two months after the event, when a society six hundred miles away submitted to him evidence which he could have gathered fifty yards from his office; and even then why did he merely promise to submit "this small matter" to the next Grand Jury?

Of the twenty-two of the men who worked out their "debts," one escaped and cannot be traced; eleven walked practically all the way from Charleston, West Virginia, to Washington, District of Columbia; two I found in a Washington hospital; the others had money enough to return to New York.

I have given this case at length, not because it is an example of exceptional cruelty and lawlessness, but because it is an uncommonly well substantiated and corroborated case of the system of intimidation in force in some labor camps of West Virginia, ranging from the silent intimidation of armed guards to an active terrorism of blows and abuse, of which the general public knows nothing.

It was in the latter part of April, 1903, that I was sent by the Society for the Protection of Italian Immigrants of New York to investigate a large number of complaints of alleged maltreatment suffered by Italians in certain counties of West Virginia. That State is developing her splendid resources of coal and lumber, and this necessitates the building of railroads for the transportation of such products. The demand for labor is tremendous and the supply totally inadequate. If it is true that too many immigrants come to our shores, it hardly holds good for West Virginia. There capital is in danger of becoming paralyzed from lack of the labor supply. To supply the feverish demand, laborers of all conditions and classes have been literally dumped into that State by the brokers in human flesh in the cities—not only men unfit for the hard work required, but a lawless and criminal element as well. The problem for the contractor does not end with the getting of the men to West Virginia; an even harder task is to keep them there, for the isolation of the camps, the absence of human intercourse, and the hardships of life create a feeling of discontent among the laborers almost from the first day. It is not strange, under these circumstances, therefore, that contractors should resort to methods both to get and to keep laborers which are in defiance of law and repugnant to the moral sense. The temptation to illegitimate practices is further strengthened by the method employed of advancing transportation for the men. Thus, two hundred laborers at $10 each means an investment of $2,000; if the men become dissatisfied and leave, it means a clear loss to the contractor. Yet, however strong the temptation, it cannot justify acts of restraint which in practice amount to white slavery. The use of armed guards around the camps is notorious. Worse yet, the evidence seems to show that the men are charged for the expense of such unlawful surveillance.

Cases of brutality are frequent and inexcusable. One may find some palliation for the unlawful restraint exercised over men who wish to escape before they have "worked out" their transportation. But what can be said in extenuation of such acts of brutality as those of men felled with blows from iron bars or gun butts, or marched at the point of rifles and cursed and beaten if unable to keep up with the pace of the mounted overseers? I have before me the sworn declaration of one Girardi—a bright young Piedmontese, who had been employed by Boxley & Co. near Kayford. He was ordered to lift a heavy stone, and asked a negro co-laborer to help him. His was not, evidently, a permissible request, as his foreman, on hearing it, called him a vile name and thrust a revolver in his face. Thereupon Girardi lifted the stone, at the cost of a very bad rupture. That man to this day has had no redress.

"Tired of abuse," reads the sworn statement of another laborer, "we decided to escape from the camp; we had proceeded but a short distance when we were overtaken by several men armed with rifles and revolvers, who drove us back. One of the pursuing band took from me an iron rod which I held over my shoulder, over which I had slung my valise, and with it repeatedly struck several of my companions." Another, a splendid type of hardy Calabrian, described under oath the following picture: "My attention was drawn to the other side of the creek, where an Italian was shouting for help—appealing to us as fellow-countrymen to aid him. He had been felled by a blow of a heavy stick dealt him by one of the guards. Cervi, my friend, and I tried to cross over to help him, but were prevented by our boss, who drove us back at the point of a pistol; all I dared do was to shout to him not to resist or he would be killed, and to go back; the man who had struck him lifted him bodily by his coat and pushed him on, striking him every time he stumbled or fell from exhaustion." . . .

It is a reasonable presumption that contractors do not engage men with the express purpose of maltreating them, for it is a plain business principle that dissatisfied men make poor workers. I believe, therefore, that, with some few exceptions, these abuses are to a great extent due to that lack of mutual confidence and more especially of mutual understanding which is the basis of much of the unrest and spirit of reprisal in the labor situation. This lack of mutual understanding is especially evident in the relations between American employers and Italian laborers. It is not merely ignorance of the language, it is rather a lack of clear-sightedness and perception as regards what counts with these foreign laborers. Employers of Italian labor too often forget that their employees are proverbially sensitive, but are also susceptible to kind treatment. Courtesy and kindness will hold these men even in distant and isolated camps much better than curses and forcible threats. As a purely business proposition, the employment of a capable and honest interpreter or confidential secretary who knows both Italian and American ways, to whom laborers could go, would be a better and cheaper investment for contractors than the maintenance of armed guards or brutal foremen. As it is, not only in West Virginia but wherever Italian labor is employed the Italian is at the mercy of the middleman, without any right of appeal. Whether it be the fraud of his own countryman, the banker-agent who sells his labor under false pretenses, or the extortion of his countryman, the camp storekeeper to whom the contractor lets the commissary privileges, whether it be the "rake-off" of the foreman or the peculations of the paymaster, whether it be the brutality of the boss or the unlawful order of the gang-foreman—no matter what the injustice may be, the laborer has no opportunity to appeal to his employer, either because the employer recognizes the decision of his middleman as final or because he will not "bother with details." While this system, popularly called the "padrone system," is tolerated by contractors, abuses will continue. Much, however, can be done to lessen its evils by institutions like the Society for the Protection of Italian Immigrants, a society administered by Americans, which aims to destroy the padrone system by competing with padrones, using legitimate methods in supplying laborers and safeguarding their rights.

The responsibility, in the last instance, however, rests on the employers. Their duty to the men should not cease with the payment of agreed wages; without a careful, businesslike, and humane supervision, workmen are very likely to be abused by the middlemen. Especially is this true of the foreign workman, whose helplessness in the face of unlawful and brutal treatment such as that in West Virginia would almost justify an extra-judicial reprisal. Certainly it is of vital importance that these numberless foreign laborers who come to us should learn, as a first step towards assimilation, that Americanism means honesty, regard for law, fair play, and plain dealing.

ITALIAN COMPETITION FOR BLACK LABOR IN THE SOUTH

[The efforts of Southern states to attract large numbers of immigrants after 1865 were never very successful, but of those who did come to the region, Italians were the most numerous. White native Southerners hoped that the Italians would replace the blacks in the cotton fields. This hope was not to be realized, however, for the Italians wanted to own their own land; they were not willing to be tenant farmers for other whites on a permanent basis. The initial success of the Italians in the South led Alfred Stone, a wealthy Delta cotton planter, to write the following article expressing his sanguine expectations for the Italian farmers.]

In respect of its influence upon trade balances, and as a factor in our general commercial supremacy, cotton is probably the most valuable American agricultural commodity. The association of the negro with the production of this crop is so fixed in the public mind that it is as a cotton grower that his economic importance in this country is chiefly measured. Not unnaturally this association has resulted in fixing in the public mind the idea of the absolute dependence of the Southern crop upon negro labor. This idea has been fostered to an unwholesome extent in both sections of the country, and its constant emphasis is largely responsible for the ignoring of a movement destined to threaten the conceded supremacy of the negro in his oldest American field. This movement is the immigration of foreign whites to the Southern States, and to my mind it possesses more significance for the

From "The Italian Cotton Growers: The Negroes' Problem," in: *South Atlantic Quarterly*, January, 1905.

negro's future than any other economic factor that touches his life today.

There is no other section of equal area in the United States in which the negro has enjoyed so nearly an absolute monopoly of the field of manual labor as in the riparian lands of the Mississippi river and its tributaries in the States of Mississippi, Louisiana, and Arkansas. In the various counties and parishes of this large section the proportion of negroes to whites runs from three or four to one to more than fifteen to one. Every consideration of climate, soil, and economic condition tended to render absolute the hold of the negro agriculturist; yet right here the white man, in the person of the Italian immigrant, has proved his ability to more than meet the negro upon his most favored ground. The experiment with Italians in this section is not a large one, but the number of these people engaged in cotton growing is constantly increasing. Indeed, the matter has long since passed the experimental stage. Measured by whatever standard may be applied the Italian has demonstrated his superiority over the negro as an agriculturist. I am not now discussing the merits of the two as tenants, or weighing their respective advantages from the planter's point of view. I have reference merely to the ability of the Italian to produce more cotton on a given acreage than the negro, and to gather a greater percentage of it without outside assistance.

The cause of this superiority is not far to seek. Given equal soil and equal climatic conditions for growing cotton, and the odds are with the man who cultivates his crop best and most carefully. The Italian works more constantly than the negro, and, after one or two years' experience, cultivates more intelligently. In comparing the two it is scarcely necessary to go beyond the appearance of their respective premises and fields to gain an insight into the difference between them. The general condition of the plantation premises occupied by negroes, under whatever system of cultivation, has been an eyesore in the cotton States for more than a generation. The spectacle of broken-down fences, patchwork outhouses, half-cultivated fields, and garden spots rank with weeds, is too familiar to the traveler through the Southern States to need description here. The destructive propensity of the negro constitutes today a serious problem on many a well ordered plantation. On the property in which the writer is interested the effort to maintain the premises of the negro tenants in keeping with the general appearance of the plantation seems yearly to become a more hopeless undertaking. It seems difficult to escape the conclusion that back of all this lie the characteristics that apparently have always been a curse to the race—whether in Africa, the Southern States, or the West Indies—shiftlessness and improvidence.

On the other hand, the appearance of the Italian cotton grower's immediate surroundings, working on the same tenant system as the negro, is alone sufficient to tell the story of the difference between the ultimate end and purpose of the labor of the two. The contrast is not alone in the things that appeal to the eye; it is much more emphasized in the respective uses made of the same material and opportunities. From the garden spot which the negro allows to grow up in weeds, the Italian will supply his family from early spring until late fall, and also market enough largely to carry him through the winter. I have seen the ceilings of their houses literally covered with strings of dried butter beans, pepper, okra, and other garden products, while the walls would be hung with corn, sun-cured in the roasting ear stage. In the rear of a well-kept house would be erected a wood shed, and in it could be seen enough fire wood, sawed and ready for use, to run the family through the winter months. These people did not wait till half-frozen feet compelled attention to the question of fuel, and then tear down the fence to supply their wants. Nor would they be found drifting about near the close of each season, in an aimless effort to satisfy an unreasoned desire to "move,"—to make the next crop somewhere else.

It is always difficult to get a negro to plant and properly culti-vate the outer edges of his field—the extreme ends of his rows, his ditch banks, etc. The Italian is so jealous of the use of every foot for which he pays rent that he will cultivate with a hoe places too small to be worked with a plough, and derive a revenue from spots to which a negro would not give a moment's thought. I have seen them cultivate right down to the water's edge the banks of bayous that had never before been touched by the plough. I have seen them walk through their fields and search out every skipped place in every row and carefully put in seed, to secure a perfect stand. I have seen them make more cotton per acre than the negro on the adjoining cut, gather it from two to four weeks earlier, and then put in the extra time earning money by picking in the negro's field.

It is not within the scope of this article to discuss the use of his opportunities by the Italian, as contrasted with the negro's neglect of his. But the frugality and thrift of the former offer a contrast to the latter's careless, spendthrift ways no less striking than that between the methods of cultivation of the two. Given a soil as fertile as the alluvial land to which I have referred, and people who apply the methods of the Italian to its cultivation will soon own the fields they till. And this is what they are doing —buying land and paying for it. Handicapped as they are at first, by ignorance of the language and ignorance of the cultivation of the plant they raise, still they are becoming property owners, tax-payers, and citizens. . . .

I have referred here to a small portion of the cotton belt, one with which I am personally familiar. But the entire South is turn-ing its attention to white immigration. It is being encouraged through the organized efforts of business associations and transportation companies, while there are well defined movements in some States toward the creation of State immigration bureaus. The climate is here, and the soil—and the need for labor; it is a mere question of time before the story of the immigration to the West will be repeated in the South.

What is the significance of all this to the negro? To my mind here at last the white man has become the negro's problem. His problem, because the wisest leaders among his own people agree with his most sensible white advisers upon two points vital to his future in this country; that the home of the mass of the race must remain in the Southern States, and that its destiny must be worked out upon the soil. The field of the negro's activities thus becomes doubly circumscribed, and any invasion of that field by the white man must present for him a serious aspect. I would not be understood as attempting to set up a "scarehead" here. There is no danger of an inrush of foreigners buying up all the land in the South, and leaving none for the negro. Not at all. But with every encroachment by the white man upon the negro's ancient field, there follows a corresponding diminution of the latter's opportunities in that field. If the negro this year produces sixty-five per cent of our cotton, and twenty years hence is producing but forty-five per cent, then certainly the two decades would mark for him a distinct loss of ground.

How rapid this movement may become it is of course impossible to forecast. It may be many years before the negro, as a race, will be in any wise visibly affected by it. But henceforth it can no more be ignored than can the progress of any other economic struggle between the black race and the Caucasian. The man who argues that the negro agriculturist today fills a place that cannot be wrested from him by the white man—that because he is today essential to the production of the country's greatest crop, he is therefore essential for all time—displays as little wisdom as does he who contends that the negro will some day altogether cease to be a factor of economic value in American industrial life.

THE ITALIAN WORKING WOMEN OF NEW YORK

Adriana Spadoni

[The single greatest hindrance to the success of organized labor during the era of mass immigration was the oversupply of workers. For employers, it was a buyer's market. If a strike was called, strikebreakers were brought in with police protection, and the strikers lost their jobs. For the millions of immigrants in poverty, the benefits of unionization were far less evident than the simple economics of "No work, no eat." The unionization of Italian women had a further difficulty: the men behind the women wanted to keep the money coming in at all costs. For the male-dominated society of Italian immigrants, this issue proved an almost insurmountable obstacle to the labor movement, as is explained in the following selection.]

The southern Italian immigrant has long been an economic problem. But the southern Italian woman did not attract attention until five or six years ago, when, like a snag, she began to protrude from the troubled waters of labor organizations. Even then the possible dangers from the Italian working woman did not loom large or near. She belonged to the most despised race among the immigrants, the one with perhaps the lowest economic standards. And all the time she was creeping farther and farther into the labor fields.

In November, 1909, she came suddenly to the surface. The biggest and possibly the most important strike in the history of women's labor was called—the strike of the shirt-waist makers. It involved thousands of women and girls. It lasted three months and proved that women had come into the labor world to stay

From *Colliers*, March 23, 1912.

and were able to fight their battles. Thousands of women—American, Irish, Jewish—suffered and starved for their union ideals. Only the Italian girls refused to go out. Not only that, but by hundreds they slipped quietly into the vacant places and labor unions stood helpless.

The supply was unlimited. In Manhattan alone there are approximately 60,000 Italian women of working age. Practically the entire number are southern Italians. No one knew anything about the Italian working woman, what her ideals were, to what stimuli she would react. The abstract ideas of unionism, community spirit, welfare of the whole—ideas that would have supported a body of Jewish girls through months of suffering—were presented to her. The Italian girl looked out of her big brown eyes and continued to fill the places of the striking waist makers. Nothing stopped her. From her silent persistence, abstract arguments bounced back like harmless rubber balls. She appeared gentle, malleable. In reality she was like rock. Those at the head of the movement for better conditions saw all their efforts about to be nullified by this brown, ignorant, silent woman who would not listen, and when she did could not or would not understand.

Something had to be done and done quickly. The Women's Trade Union League heard of Arturo Caroti and asked him to help. Signor Caroti is a writer, a lecturer, and a Socialist. At the time he was manager of a cooperative store of the Silk Weavers' Union in Hoboken, New Jersey. He gave up his management and allied himself with the Women's Trade Union League in Manhattan.

"There is only thing we can do now in the emergency," he explained. "We must *buy* them off."

That was the key to the problem.

To the average American, living in a city that has a large Italian population of this class, the Italian is either an object of sentimental pity or one of prejudice. He is supposed to be either a poverty-stricken victim of European conditions, a creature of violent temper, but hidden artistic possibilities, or a plotting Camorrist. No attention is paid to the almost racial difference beween the north and the south. In reality, the southern Italian immigrant, as he invests New York, Chicago, Pittsburgh, the mills of the South and the mines of the North, is driven by one single idea—money.

He is the Jew of the West without Hebrew ideals and community spirit. The southern Italian lives, dreams, and thinks of money. He is in America for the purpose of making it, and for that alone. The "frightful European conditions" he left behind are the conditions to which he hopes to return. To be the "galantuomo" of his native village is his ideal. At present he digs ditches on a Western railroad and lives on $4.85 a month, or pushes a huckster's cart on Mulberry Street; but some day he will loll before the tavern door and expatiate on the glories of America to admiring friends. In the meantime he herds his family of nine into three rooms and takes boarders.

He works early and late and starves—but he saves money. He is often looked upon as a pauper by outsiders, when in reality he has a bank account of four figures. He has no respect for the law which forces him to send his children to school, but he has a tremendous respect for the law that compels a child to support its parents. Everybody belonging to him must work. He is like a starving man let loose among unlimited food supplies. He not only gathers and carries away a load too great for his own strength, but forces those who belong to him to do the same. And his women belong to him as much as his feather bed and the copper saucepans he brought with him from the home land. As a thinking, human being, acting independently, the southern Italian immigrant woman does not exist. She obeys absolutely the will of her nearest male relative and he is driven by the concrete vision of a dollar. No increase in wages in future years, no improved conditions in his own work, much less the indirect benefits of improved conditions in other lines, weighs for a second against the actual daily wage he can obtain at the moment.

These were conditions that Caroti had to face alone in 1909. So, knowing the people, he said: "Buy them off now. After we will think." A fund was raised, and Caroti began buying Italian women and girls to stay away from the striking shops. The few men concerned in the strike, mostly pressers, were handled in the same way; five dollars a week if married, three and a half if single. The plan was effective and worked well in cases where the girls were not making much more than that at their tables. But the supply of "scabs" did not seem to decrease. As fast as one woman was prevailed upon to keep away, another was ready to take her place. Those who had been bought off passed along the good news, and others, grateful for the blessings of this wonderful country, joined the strike breakers. In the crisis, no matter how unskilled, they were sure of getting work and of holding it long enough to be bought off.

With such a drain upon it the fund began to give out. Then the male relatives of the "scabs" descended upon the Women's Trade Union League's headquarters and demanded the wages of their women. Angry fathers and brothers threatened Signor Caroti, demanding that he make payment or meet the consequences. On the walls of the Women's Trade Union League's headquarters there is still a chalked warning: "Pay, Caroti, or you die"—exactly the kind of thing that makes scareheads in the press. But Arturo Caroti is not an American journalist and he knew his people. As he says: "Afraid? I know them. When they came to my office I pointed to the wall: 'Look what some fool writes.' Bah!" Like a child threatening the passer-by with his toy pistol, the grumbling relatives went home. Later, after working hours, when the women were in, Signor Caroti visited the homes and "talked and talked and talked." . . . .

As Signor Caroti estimates it, of the 60,000 Italian women in New York above working age, fully 30,000 are actually employed outside their homes in such work. Of these fully 50 per cent are married. Of the other 30,000 another 15,000 work in their homes as much of the year as they can get work. Like a relief brigade, they can be called on—60,000 women skilled in the work required, with the lowest possible economic standards of living—absolutely at the command of their men, who are incapable of grasping an abstract idea, and will fight blindly till they drop for their new right— which is the right to hold fast to the concrete dollar before them. When this was made clear once for all, organized women's labor saw that something must be done, and done quickly. Some wall must be built to stem the next flood. With complete trust in Signor Caroti they put the matter into his hands. In December, 1910, he began his long and difficult task of organizing the Italian working girls. His plan and method are best explained in his own words:

"The history of labor unionism in Italy shows that it was a growth outward from purely social groups. It was an evolution. First men came together for mutual pleasure and recreation. In time their common interests bound them. Slowly the trade union grew. Among the women it will have to be the same. The spirit of cooperation will have to grow from a basis which the girls understand. That is; the social. When they get used to the idea of organization in this way—the reason does not matter—we will have gone a long step. To get them to stand together for any purpose of their own, independent of the influence of their masters, is something. They will absorb the spirit. In time—the union ideals."

For this purpose the Italian Women's Mutual Benefit Society was evolved, and a fund was raised to supply Signor Caroti with an assistant. To build the society on a practical basis and give it a concrete value in the eyes of its members, it was put in the form of a kind of lodge, furnishing free doctors in case of illness. The dues were fixed as ten cents a month to throw the matter beyond the pale of charity and at the same time not cause high dues to be an excuse for not joining. In time sick benefits will be added, and the whole worked slowly into a strong mutual benefit scheme.

In this way, by the indirect methods of monthly parties, the work proceeded. Under the sugar-coated pills of music, recitations, and dancing, with never a word "union" mentioned, the Italian girl began to swallow and slowly assimilate the spirit of cooperative action.

It was in December, 1910, that Signor Caroti began this work, chipping single-handed the mountain of conservatism. What has been accomplished? Viewed in actual numbers by those who have no idea of the difficulties to be overcome, very little. But to those who understand the conditions that the Women's Trade Union League and Signor Caroti had to face, a miracle. Now, barely fourteen months after the first step was taken, the Mutual Benefit Society numbers two hundred regular members, and this year another club, for factory girls only, was organized, and in the three weeks of its life has grown to forty-five members. Under the direction of Mrs. Weyl and Miss Miller of Greenwich House, this club, by means of the long year of preparatory work, is now ready for more than music and dancing and recitations, with carefully concealed principles wrapped in Socialist poetry. It meets once a week for regular lectures on hygiene, working conditions, economics. There is no hiding the real motive, the intention to improve and bring the Italian working woman up to the standard of economic consciousness of other nations.

It is being done; slowly but surely the wedge has entered. A year ago the girls looked suspiciously at efforts to induce them to come to the Mutual Benefit meetings. At one of the early meetings I overheard two girls talking. Their faces were sharp with mistrust.

"What's it for? Why did they wish us to have a good time?"

"Oh, come on, join; it can't hurt you. It's only ten cents, and if you get sick you'll get a doctor and medicine, and afterward they're going to give us clothes and get us jobs and get us more money."

"Sure I'll join."

Now only a little over a year later, in the opinion of Signor Caroti, there is a group of Italian girls in this same district that was to be reached then only by promises of personal gain, who to-day, if occasion demanded, could organize and control the Little Italy of Mott and Sullivan and Thompson Streets.

What effect will it have on the economic conditions of New York when employers can no longer rely on an unlimited supply of skillful workers ever waiting to take the empty places? When he can no longer hang out a sign and in a single hour have a steady procession from the tenements of the various Italian districts to carry back into their dark, unventilated homes the clothes, the feathers, the flowers, the food, the unbelievable things he gives to be done to save himself rent, and because he knows he *can get them done* by women who will continue to work when he has cut the prices below the scorn of a Jew? When he knows that every steamer brings more, who, when they have been here only a few days, will underbid those who have been here a few months, until his schedule of wages are a farce—or a tragedy, according to the point of view?

TONTITOWN, ARKANSAS: THE WORK OF PIETRO BANDINI

[Under the sponsorship of Austin Corbin, president of the Long Island Railroad, an Italian agricultural colony was started in 1895, at Sunnyside, Arkansas. For a number of reasons, including Corbin's death, the enterprise failed. In the wake of this failure, a young immigrant priest, Pietro Bandini, went to Arkansas to help his fellow Italians out of their predicament. In 1898, on credit, they purchased 900 acres in northwest Arkansas and established a farming community named after Enrico di Tonti. Tontitown remains today a striking agricultural success, with canning factories and marketing faculties nearby. Its early history is recounted in the following article.]

In the midst of a crowd of noisy, eager peasant immigrants that were disgorged upon the Battery Pier from an Italian steamer some twenty-one years ago, walked a man in the garb of a priest. His face was very thoughtful and earnest as he watched the bewilderment of these newcomers at their journey's end. Now and then he addressed one of them with a low-spoken Italian phrase, or quieted the wails of some frightened, straying child. He stood on the pier until the last fantastically clad stranger with the last bit of preposterous luggage had vanished into the mystery of streets that stretched away from the other side of Battery Park, and then he too turned and left the water-front. The priest was Father Bandini, and he had come to America on a mission—to investigate and to better the conditions of his countrymen who drift untutored to these shores.

From "A Safe Way to Get on the Soil," by Anita Moore, in: *World's Work*, June, 1912.

What Father Bandini found out is a familiar tale to us now—the helplessness of the alien in the hands of glib porters and hotel-keepers, the loss of his small store of savings to the pretended friend who offers to find him a job in return for a competence, the inevitable drifting toward slum-life, and the daily round of hard street-labor to ward off starvation—all this is a scandal too old to bear repeating. Father Bandini went to work at once to find a remedy. The fact that seemed to him important was that the large majority of his countrymen had come from small farms at home. For that reason the priest felt that the only hope for them was to get them on the land and let them earn their bread in their accustomed way. The big obstacle that confronted this theory, however, was the social, pleasure-loving nature of the Italians which would make the isolated life of the ordinary American farmer intolerable to them.

Father Bandini's solution was to put a whole colony of these Italians on the land in one place, thus restoring the community life and the hopefulness of their former homes. The success of his experiment puts before social workers a new solution of the whole immigration problem. It also offers "a way out" to the man of small means who wants to get back to the land—be he Italian, or German, or just plain American. Here are the facts of this interesting experiment:

Father Bandini, once having decided on a plan of colonization, plunged immediately into a study of government bulletins about climatic and agricultural conditions in various parts of the United States and at last decided upon the region of the Ozark Mountains in Arkansas, where the 1,500 foot elevation insures a healthful climate and where the seasons are long and open. The land had no very encouraging crop-record, but a test of the soil gave promise of fair productivity under the proper cultural conditions.

To this country in March, 1898, Father Bandini came with a band of twenty-six hardy and all but penniless families. They picked out a tract of 300 acres in Washington County, within six miles of the St. Louis and San Francisco Railroad, and they purchased the land at $15 an acre. The scheme was not coöperative. The land was divided into lots varying in size from 5 to 20 acres, and each man paid what he could for his share—$10, $15, $25—and gave his note and a mortgage on the land for the balance, Father Bandini personally endorsing each note. They called their settlement Tonti-town in honor of an early Italian immigrant, Enrico Tonti, who had served as Lieutenant to La Salle and had established a small military post near the Arkansas River. . . .

The colony is now fourteen years old. It numbers 700 inhabitants, and owns 4,760 acres of good productive land, all clear of encumbrance, the value of which has increased from the original $15 paid for it to $50, $100, and even $150 an acre. In the village there are a modern hotel, three stores, a post-office, a land office, or town hall, and a school—St. Mary's Academy—which contains five large, well-equipped class rooms, several living rooms for the three Sisters of Mercy and the two young women teachers, and a gymnasium. Here 130 children are enrolled.

The good priest who caused all this prosperity has kept constantly before his people the secret of their success. "One of the great dangers which threaten the farmers in America," he says to them "is that they may become land poor. Forty acres is all that one man can profitably till. With twenty acres he can support a large family in comfort and save a little money. With forty acres he can become a man of means if he is industrious."

The Tontitown colonists follow this teaching. They build up their land by rotation of crops and fertilization. With the long open seasons they grow two or three crops of the same vegetables in the same season. Thus, for instance, they plant early spring onions for the market between rows of young peach trees or grapevines. After the onions have been harvested for the market, string beans are planted on the same ground. When the string beans have been marketed, the same ground is planted with some nitrogen producing crop—such as cow peas. The cow peas are used as fodder for the cattle, thus providing a fertilizer directly and indirectly— the productivity of the soil is increased, yet it has yielded three crops and nourished an orchard or vineyard.

The first year that the young apple orchards produced a full crop, fruit in the Ozark mountain region was most abundant. Commission men bought apples in the orchards from the native farmers at 60 cents a barrel—20 cents a bushel. The Tontitown people bought and installed two fairly large fruit evaporators and established canneries and cider and vinegar factories. They fancy-packed their choicest apples and sold them at good prices. The seconds they canned or evaporated; the culls and parings they used for cider, then ran the pulp through the presses again with water and made vinegar; and at last the pulp was put back on the land for fertilizer. In all they received at the rate of $6 a barrel for their fruit as against the 60 cents received by the American farmers.

They ship their choice peaches, and the seconds are canned or evaporated. Every farmer has a vineyard of from four to eight acres which yields him returns from $500 to $600 per acre. The grapes are made into wine. One man alone makes 1,500 gallons of wine every season. The Tontitown wine is a fine domestic vintage that finds a ready market at $1 a gallon.

By his energy and initiative Father Bandini has promoted the establishing of other industries besides agriculture. Tontitown now possesses brickyards and limekilns. Three creameries profitably handle the milk; one of these creameries is devoted to butter making and the other two to cheese manufacturing. There are also a broom factory, a brickyard, a blacksmith shop, and a cobbler's shop.

The best proof of the triumph of Father Bandini's theory, however, lies probably not so much in a record of material achievement as in evidence of the satisfaction of the inhabitants. One formal statement of this satisfaction, because of its quaint phraseology, is too good to omit:

> I, the undersigned, a resident of Tontitown from its very beginning, about fourteen (14) years ago, was not formerly a farmer, neither am I an expert farmer at present; yet I am glad to state that I am very well satisfied and pleased of my position and pleased with the crops I get from my farm, on which I raised almost everything I tried to.
>
> Last year we had an exceptional dry season for a few months; had not a drop of rain for four months; yet from my little vineyard of 70 vines I got 6,200 pounds of first class grapes.
>
> On a surface of three-fourth of an acre I had a ton and a half of hay, 12 bushels of beans.
>
> On another acre I raised sweet potatoes, on an average of 488 bushels an acre, extremely large; 40 bushels of Irish potatoes; 500 pounds of beans and half a ton of hay.
>
> In consequence of the drought, as said above, the crop of strawberries and oats was light, but corn we had in abundance.
>
> (Signed) ADRIANO MORSANI.
> Tontitown, Ark., February 8, 1912.

Perhaps the greatest asset of the community is in the development of its children. They are healthy physically, morally, and intellectually. Of the children of the original families who first settled in Tontitown, nine girls—now grown to young women—are established as school teachers, holding University, State, or second grade certificates. Three sisters, who lost their father during the first year of the colony, have just built and furnished a little cottage for their mother, besides which they have finished paying for the farm which their father had bought before his death. Two of the first boys—now quite grown up—purchased eighty acres of land in 1910 and that spring planted twenty acres in strawberries. From the berries in the spring of 1911 and their fall crops of potatoes, hay, and corn they realized enough to pay for their farm.

The best part of the story of Tontitown is that it is only an introduction to a great extension of the colonization plan. In 1911, Faher Bandini went back to Italy and there he told his story to all who would listen. He enlisted the sympathies of the Pope, the Prime Minister, and the Queen Mother, and of several societies and organizations, all of which are pledged to do what they can to direct the flux of emigration away from the old channels and into the safe and pleasant outlet of our Western country. As an evidence of their earnestness a new little colony has already sprung up in Arkansas which the good priest is now fostering with the same devotion that he lavished on Tontitown.

That is what Father Bandini has done for his countrymen. What he has done to help solve some of the most momentous problems that confront us can be stated almost as definitely.

He has again illustrated the value of intensive cultivation of the soil. His success also suggests that farm colonies may be the simplest means by which the poor man can get on the land, and that colonization on a large scale may yet empty the city slums by putting the agricultural immigrant at once in touch with the opportunity to practice the only kind of productive industry for which he is fitted.

AMERICANIZATION THROUGH AFFLUENCE

[For the immigrant, the chief pathway to assimilation has been economic security: sufficient affluence to enter the middle class. Coming from the more affluent region of Italy, the northern Italians, who flocked to California, had an advantage over their fellow countrymen from the Mezzogiorno. The northerners were frequently artisans, tradesmen, knowledgeable farmers, or professional men. The California Italians spoken of in this selection were just such northerners, several of whom became enormously successful and prosperous in their American callings.]

The first thing that the Italian immigrant does after arrival is to go to work. He may have a good education in the home country—although the chances are against this—but no matter what his attainments or education, the immigrant does not hesitate at what is offered. It may be the most menial service, but not a moment is lost. Having satisfied his ambition to work, the next ambition is to save money. Some of the immigrants have borrowed the funds with which to come, and these debts are scrupulously paid. The next ambition, usually, is to send money to Italy to bring out sweetheart or wife that the new home may be founded. The next ambition is to go into business or to own some land. Always the Italian is saving and planning to get ahead in the world. Ten years usually suffice to remove him from the necessity of working for others, but he works just as hard or harder for himself. Always he has money for use in an emergency.

From "Old Wine in New Bottles," by Winfield Scott, in: *Sunset*, May, 1913.

This saving habit of the north Italian was emphasized in striking fashion shortly after the San Francisco fire of 1906. The Italian quarter which then, as now, contained about 35,000 people, was swept out of existence. When rehabilitation started, the Italians were first to build. The "Latin Quarter" of San Francisco was rebuilt long before many American landowners thought of removing the ruins from their property. The money came in part from the Italian banking institutions, and in part from the actual cash savings carried by the Italians themselves and not deposited in any bank. There is food for thought in the fact that only the Chinese were prepared to build as quickly as the Italians. The Chinese district would have been set in order quite as fast as the Latin quarter, had there not been some delays as to where the Chinese would locate. It is not forgotten, even now, that when reconstruction began, the Italians were ready with the money.

After the founding of the immigrant's home comes the family and the education of the children. Here is where the Italian is a "stickler." His children must have better advantages than he has had. At the school, his children meet the children of all nations. Here is started the transformation of the Italian into an American. The children inevitably neglect the use of Italian as their knowledge of English develops. Quite frequently the first generation intermarries with some other nationality. Even if the first generation marries with Italian blood, the second generation speaks English habitually, and is as apt to marry with some other nationality as with Italian. The Italian is so no longer. He has become Americanized. . . .

After the immigrant learns something of the language and the customs of the adopted country, he branches out into business. There is no line of commercial endeavor in which the Italians are not to be found. Four of the banks of San Francisco are controlled by them, the Italian American Bank, the Bank of Italy, the Fugazi Bank, and the Columbus Loan and Savings Society.

Nor do these banks embrace all of the financial responsibility or activities of the Italian people. The Italian mercantile houses are depositors in all of the commercial banks of San Francisco. The people use the savings banks operated by people of all nations. It is noteworthy to say in this connection, however, that five of the most successful building and loan societies ever organized in California were managed by an Italian, Andrea Sbarboro. They built 25,000 homes and paid out over $6,000,000 and were conducted on the best plane. Their successful manager was rewarded by a decoration from the King of Italy, in recognition of his services to the Italian people.

As might be expected, the Italians naturally enter the fruit and wine business. Wherever they go they plant a tree or a vine. Even on Telegraph Hill in San Francisco, where an American would never think of planting anything, the Italians have their family vegetable gardens with the steep slope terraced off. To make something grow appears to be almost a passion with them. They have control of the fruit and vegetable business of San Francisco and most of California. They are fruit packers of the highest order. The gardening business belongs to them, and what an Italian can make grow, starting with a stretch of bare sand or waste land, is amazing. The California Fruit Canners' Association was grouped around the establishment of an Italian, Fontana. In the vineyard business the Italian-Swiss Colony, founded by Andrea Sbarboro, and the Italian Vineyard Company of southern California, started by an Italian, are monumentally large enterprises. Neither are they confined by any limits. Chocolate manufacture has been carried on successfully in California since 1852 by an Italian concern. In macaroni manufacture they have but one competitor anywhere in California. The marble business belongs to them. They are manufacturers and traders in almost every conceivable line. They are artisans, blacksmiths, carpenters, machinists and so on. In merchandising they have held their own. Their chamber of commerce is organized to aid business relations between California and the mother country. They are the leaders of the fishing industry. Wherever they go, whatever they do, they utilize to the ultimate the resources of the industry in which they engage. If they are ranchers, they farm every foot of ground. If gardeners, they know more about water and fertilizers than any of their neighbors. Among themselves and with their neighbors they are not inclined to litigation. Indeed, no less litigious class of people are to be found in California.

Many Italian names are on the list of men who are artists. In politics they have produced A. Caminetti, former congressman, and the son of a miner. In law their most shining example, perhaps, is Justice F. M. Angellotti, of the State Supreme Court and the son of a fishmonger. In medicine no men stand higher than Di Vecchi and Sartori, both educated Italians of the best class.

Instancing the rise of Italians to positions of wealth and prominence, many exemplars might be given. There is Andrea Sbarboro, president of the Italian American Bank, an organizer of the California Promotion Board and for ten years president of the chamber of commerce of San Francisco, who started his career as a boy peddling toys on a New York ferry-boat. F. Daneri, one of the leading merchants of his time, was self-made. Schiappa-Pietra, who accumulated a fortune of over $2,000,000 in Ventura county land, started as a ranch hand. Secundo Guasti, the president of the Italian Vineyard Company, started as a cellerman. He lives in a $150,000 replica of a famous Italian palace. His company owns several thousand acres of vineyard. The father of Dr. Giannini, one of the leading Italians of San Francisco, was a vegetable gardener. L. Scatena, president of the Bank of Italy, was a vegetable man. M. J. Fontana, whose great cannery on North Beach formed the nucleus of the California Fruit Canners' Association, began in California as a bootblack. There is a romance in the lives of these men and in the lives of hundreds of others. All that they have asked is a man's chance in a man's country. All that they have wanted at first was an opportunity to work. The rest has been achieved by their own efforts.

THE TRACK GANGS

[In the middle decades of the nineteenth century, the Irish provided a substantial part of the labor force to build the canals and rail lines. After 1890, the Italians, along with other "new immigrants," took their place. The railroads needed the workers and sought them out by the thousands. As a result, small colonies of Italians were soon found in many cities and towns of the Midwest and Far West. Life on the "track gang" was neither pleasant nor easy, as the following selections testify. It was a temporary way to make a living, but in the process, the immigrants were often as much victims as they were laborers.]

From: 1. *Immigrants in America Review*, July, 1916.
2. *World Outlook*, October, 1917.

1. THE "WOP" IN THE TRACK GANG

Dominic Ciolli

I am a medical student in one of our Eastern universities, Italian born, who arrived in this country with my parents when hardly more than an infant. My father underwent the usual struggle of the immigrant, and by dint of perseverance and hard work has been able to make a living for himself and family, and now even possesses property as well. However, like thousands of other college students, it has been necessary for me to assist myself by working during the summer vacations. Through the aid of friends, railroad employees, I was able to obtain a position with one of the great trunk lines. I was to work as a track laborer, but because I possessed more than the average education of a track employee I was to be allowed privileges more characteristic of a track foreman as regarded habitation and food.

I was granted a position early in June. My home was a considerable distance from the gang to which I had been assigned, and the seven-hour journey required to arrive at my destination brought me in the Indiana town at 4 A.M. From thence I tramped out to a large string of dilapidated box cars, the home of the track gang, arriving here at 5 o'clock. The men had left for work some time before, so I spent the time inspecting the surroundings. There were nine cars, six for the half hundred men, one for the hand cars, one for the tools, and the last for the padrone and the timekeeper. I was to be allowed to live with them. Ours was the only car possessing windows. On both sides of the cars, on the ground, were rusty, perforated tin boxes, propped up by stones. These were stoves. Heaps of rubbish covered the ground, and the general appearance of the immediate surroundings, combined with the undefinable

stench, gave me an idea of the interior of these commodious dwell-
ings.

When the men returned, about four that evening, I inquired
why they had left so early that morning, and was informed by the
boss that there was no use beginning work after five. "If we let
them go to work at seven, they will become lazy, and will not do
enough work. Then the men higher up will discharge me." So he
played the tyrant, and his tyranny was condoned and valued by his
superiors. He had been twenty-six years in the service, longer than
the majority of foremen, and he was proud of his reputation.

Immediately after their return, the men began to gather wood
from surrounding places. They cooked their meals in blackened
kettles, devouring more soot than food. By half past seven, the men
had retired, for they had to rise at three next morning, in order to
boil their coffee for breakfast and prepare their bread and water
lunches, for it must be remembered they worked some distance
from the cars. I could not help reflecting, in view of what I had
observed, upon the hardships that the men were plainly undergoing.

But that was only the beginning. I was going to see another phase
of railroad life the following day. Though the men had arisen at
three, I remained in bed until four—the laborer that cooked the
foreman's breakfast, preparing mine as well. I looked out of the
door and saw men scurrying here and there, rushing for water,
washing, dressing, eating. Many of them were already awaiting the
call of the padrone. They reminded of a band of gypsies, lank, lean
and tired-looking. Instead of the sturdy men who came to this
country to better themselves, there were to be found the gaunt,
pale, emaciated remains of a former healthy manhood. The reason
was to be presented that day.

Sharply at five o'clock, the boss leaped from his car and began
swearing and cursing at the men. The poor laborers trembled and
hurried. In a moment five hand cars were on the rails. After riding
six miles, we arrived at our destination, and amidst cursing and
swearing the men took the cars off the track and began to tear
up the old rails. In a few seconds, the sweat was rolling in streams.
The rails were heavy and the men worked with might and main
throughout the forenoon. There was no let up—no mercy. From
shortly after five to twelve, almost seven hours, the men labored
without rest. "The beasts," said the padrone, "must not be given
a rest. Otherwise they will step over me." As those men silently
appealed to him for mercy, I was filled with pity, and often during
the day I was tempted to beg the padrone to let them rest, but
how could I approach a raging maniac? He was the type railroads
wanted. He had obtained more work from his men than many another foreman, and a slave-driver is a success on the railroad.

And after seven hours of the hardest labor, how did they replenish their spent energies? The younger men had sausages and bread, the older men satisfying themselves with bread alone. Yet with coffee in the morning and bread at noon, these men worked for ten hours every day under the blistering sun, or pouring rain. One old man had been with the company for years, and bread and water had always been his lunch. At one o'clock the men returned to work, a volley of curses serving as warning that the rest period was over. Ceasing their labors at four, the men returned to their ramshackle cars, to cook, eat and sleep. In such an existence there was no religion. In their country it was the fear of God. Now that fear was supplanted by a cringing, all-pervading terror of the boss.

A week after I had arrived at the shanties, the order came from headquarters to move. Saturday evening about five o'clock, just as the men were preparing their suppers, the engine arrived and the men had to seize their cooking utensils lying over the tin-box stoves and retire to the cars without supper. Of course, the company need not see that the men were allowed time to eat. The men were hired to work. None of us slept that night. How could we lose consciousness, with the rickety cars bumping and the brakes squeaking? Next morning, Sunday, the sleepless men arose at three, drank the cups of coffee and departed at half past four to their work. Could these men be efficient, watchful, reliable? Could they be held responsible for errors in repairing the roadway of a great railroad? And could a railroad advertise truthfully that it spared no pains to protect patrons, when it allowed its roadway to be repaired in this fashion, with sleepless, starving, persecuted immigrants? These men build our roads, dig our sewers, perform more than their share in the economic life of our nation; we treat them thus, and then rant of "anarchists" and "dangerous criminal classes." The roadmaster was present that day, but he could not see, nor did he care to see, under what difficulties these men were working. So long as the tyrant cursed and raved, and sweated his men to the limit he was doing his work well, the company applauded, and new men could always be had when the present supply, like potatoes squeezed to a pulp, were ready for the garbage heap. We remained at the new town one day, and that evening, again, the men had to forego their supper and night's rest, and were again forced to rise at three Monday, to go to work for another ten hours.

Such a condition occurred every week, yet most of the men only trudged along and never murmured, for fear of being discharged. But they told me their troubles, of their hatred for the padrone, of their sorrows over their lot; how they wished that they could leave the company. But they had a mother or a wife and children back in Italy, and these "anarchists" and "black-handers" were willing to remain in hell for the sake of their families.

But bear with me for a while. Dante's imagination painted seven hells. My memory wishes to record but one—a real, sordid purgatory, not in the realms of fancy, but here in free America, within one hundred miles of the second greatest city in the United States.

A few weeks later we were in a small Michigan town, and the human cattle were switched to a siding near the county almshouse, near where the gang was required to repair the tracks. The spectacle here was unrivaled. Stinking animal and vegetable matter covered the ground on all sides. Not a farmer would give us water or sell us milk. They appeared to be in fear of the "wops" and we were forced to fetch our water from a filthy trough—water that was covered with algae, greenish and stale, and the taste was an indescribable compound of the prevailing odors. The boss said nothing. He was a "company man" and his motto was "Silence is golden," literally. A few of the human cattle, with a spark of decency still remaining, tried to object, but were threatened with discharge by the padrone, and berated by the American timekeeper as "ingrates." "These dagoes are never satisfied. If they are given a finger they will take the entire hand," said this Christian gentleman. "They should be starved to death. They don't belong here." Such was the response from the American, and the boss, though Italian born, hated and despised his countrymen worse than the timekeeper. Frequently the padrone would sell bread which had become stale and moldy, for nine cents a loaf. If the men protested, he threw it at them and charged it to their accounts. "Take that, you pigs; you never had better bread than that at home," would be his comment, though he knew well that these men had left comfortable homes for hovels.

I would not speak of these things were the situation I have described an exception, but it was common to all the gangs on this road of several thousand miles, and observation and information have proved to me conclusively that the situation is identical on many other great railroads in the United States. Neither would I take the trouble to raise my voice in protest if I could appeal to my own countrymen. But we are of the newly arrived; we have not reached a position of prominence in the community. Few of our leading representatives are wealthy, and many of those blessed with the world's goods, we must sorrowfully admit, have earned their thousands by the cruel exploitation of their compatriots. Our Italian banker and contractor is too frequently a mighty padrone who has had the ability to rise to wealth and prominence by taking advantage of the ignorance of his brother Italian, and by grasping the opportunities for graft that are offered by the contract system of hiring labor.

Exploitation of ignorant men is inexcusable, but what can we say of a company that will be glad to increase its profits at the expense of children? For it must be remembered that each gang had its one or two diminutive fourteen-year-old water-boys, who toiled ten hours a day and lived under the very conditions I have described.

Inspectors and roadmasters visited the gangs often, but not a single official inquired as to the ages of the two lads in our gang. The inspection of our group was more impersonal than a similar examination of a steam hammer, which is at least attended with admiration for its mechanical action.

2. WHEN THE BOSS WENT TOO FAR

Cesidio Simboli

Our boss, Fulvio, was a man 'round forty, of medium height, with broad, Herculean shoulders. His large, apish head, resting upon a solid, bull-like neck, gleamed from a pair of eyes that recalled those of the screech-owl. His whole appearance was calculated to inspire more dread than respect; a man, once you made his acquaintance whom you would walk a mile to avoid. But Fulvio was not without graces. He spoke a beautiful, flowing Southern Italian dialect, howbeit interlarded with many checked and maimed English words. Under excitement he accompanied almost every word with a gesture and won his audience with a torrent of phrases that flowed from his massy lips like a stream of hot lava.

I shall never forget him. The impression he made upon me in Mulberry Street that day will never be effaced. He was recruiting recently arrived immigrants for the building of a railroad and was telling us that the country to which he was going to take us, together with the job, the wages and the board, were the best in the world.

" 'Taliani," he went on to say, "why do you doubt me? We are going to a country abounding in fruit trees, flowers and grass. It is rich in water and game. The surrounding scenery rivals that of Italy itself. The work is easy, the pay good, the board the best to be had, the housing conditions wholesome and comfortable, if not luxurious. What more do you want? Now, how many of you wish to go?"

As he finished, all hands went up and a joyous murmur broke from the crowd. Most of us had landed at Ellis Island but a few weeks earlier eager to work and anxious to redeem our fortunes. Who could wish a better luck? No wonder we all clustered around

Fulvio like flies, desirous to touch his hand and invoke upon him a thousand blessings. Very few, indeed, realize what a staggering thing it is to land in a new world, whose magnitude, differences of customs, law and language are enough to give one the vertigo. And the fact that nearly all of us came without money and without a friend raised a man like Fulvio to the level of a patron saint.

Within two days we were on the job. A little surprised we were to find other Italian laborers there. We greeted each other gladly and felt quite happy to be among our own people, with whom we could associate and talk. I noted, however, a faded look in them all, and they rarely smiled.

"Why are you so despondent, man," I inquired of a young Sicilian, as he wiped from his face the heavy perspiration.

"You will find out in a week or so," was his cryptic reply.

On the morning of the first day our gang was divided in groups of ten and put under the supervision of a boss who was directly responsible to Fulvio and his associate contractors. The treatment for a week was tolerable, but as time wore away, Fulvio's henchman kept applying a pressure which increased almost in geometric ratio. From seven in the morning till seven in the evening you saw nothing, you heard nothing but picks and shovels, rising and falling in incessant monotone. Men sweated like sponges and melted like candles under the blazing sun-heat and the ceaseless admonitions of the bosses to hurry up. Once a man stopped to fill his pipe and was severely reprimanded on the ground that he was wasting time.

One day we were laying some rails. Ordinarily six or eight men with tongs are employed to carry them. Fulvio insisted that four were sufficient. It was the most strenuous work and not without danger. As a huge rail was being moved, one man was borne down by the weight, and the rail fell on his partner, cutting his foot badly.

"Come, come, that is nothing," said the boss.

"Are we slaves, beasts, or men, sir?" inquired a man, his eyes flashing with anger.

"Whatever you like," replied Fulvio, brusquely. "If you don't like the job you may quit."

I saw a fearful struggle going on in the man's face. He quivered all over like a leaf. I heard him mutter, almost in an agony of prayer, "God, if I did not have wife and children in Italy!" and with that he resumed his work with the patience and the resignation of a slave. The word "quit" was the mainspring of terror. To our minds this vile servitude was sweeter than unemployment. It is not an easy thing for a man to throw up a job when he has traveled three thousand miles of sea to find one, and on it has staked the hope of his family and of his future. Stern necessity makes tyranny's yoke bearable, but not easy. We had fallen into the hand of a base tyrant and must make the best of it. What could we do? Unite and offer a stiff resistance? Yes, that would seem the logical thing to do, but there was no head, no hand that braved the monster and dared to stand forward to lead us. The only thing left was to pray —and many and frequent were the fervent supplications that God send a malignant pestilence upon this villain of a boss.

Yet not all were so resigned. Beneath the smooth surface there was brewing a mighty storm. The spirit of dissatisfaction was intensified by the brutal housing and board. To house a gang of nearly a hundred and fifty men a wooden shack had been improvised. It resembled a huge box turned upside down with tiny holes for windows. Cots were arranged in long rows in double file. They nearly touched one another, and not a few were suspended from the ceiling. There was no floor but the hardened soil, which became a mud hole on rainy days. The air at night, poisoned by the fetid smell of garlic and the foulest kind of tobacco smoke became as thick as Spartan broth.

Those of us who had not as yet been thoroughly toughened by life's fierce struggle considered the hardship of the pick, the shovel and the tongs as child's play compared with the torture of sleeping in this infernal box. The eternal symphony of the sleepers snoring, the attacking legions of bed bugs, men swearing by all the saints in the calendar when bitten by gnats or mosquitoes, flies and moths swirling giddily 'round that pestilent kerosene lamp, bats fluttering above one's head, and, on the top of it all, the suffocating heat, were enough to give one St. Vitus' dance.

The food, too, was not even fit for dogs. The bread oftentimes had mould on it, and the beans, sardines, salami, bolognas and macaroni were of the cheapest sort. Fulvio and his brother contractors held the monopoly of all the food supply, and one had either to get what was sold in the contractor's store or starve. Moreover, the matter of buying was a carefully arranged system of graft. No one was allowed, even if he could, to pay cash. Every article was charged oftentimes twice and double its cost. When the end of the month came, our pay was swallowed up by the debts in the store. Protest? To whom?

Yet it seemed that our patience and ability to endure had reached their limits. The strong Italic spirit, cowed and crushed temporarily, gradually reasserted itself. Secret meetings were held under the leadership of a young Sicilian and measures were taken to dethrone these oppressing scoundrels, Fulvio and his feline associates, at the earliest opportunity.

This came on a Friday afternoon. A greasy, shabby-looking Italian came trudging along the uncompleted tracks with a hand-organ on his back. As he approached us, cries of "Eh, countryman, play us a tune" became very insistent. The sun was slowly disappearing behind a high hill, when the ambulant musician, mopping his forehead began to play, with the passion and the devotion of his race for music, the "Anvil Chorus."

As the mighty notes rolled out from the breast of that dingy organ, the crowd listened with such a profound reverence, with such a breathless silence, that they seemed to be hearing mass on Easter Sunday. Work stopped instantly, the picks and shovels were laid aside, and we all sat on the grass without a word, watching and listening intently. The "Chorus" was succeeded by that liberty-inspiring hymn, more religious than patriotic, "L'Inno di Garibaldi."

I never saw such a sudden change wrought in human life by any agency. Men forgot their misery, their weariness. The light which had gone from their eyes during the weary weeks of labor came back with intenser splendor. Unconsciously, spontaneously, the pent-up emotions, like a dam bursting at the surging onrush of a mighty torrent, broke out in song and wild acclamation.

A tall, sunburnt Irishman came along, Fulvio's chief aide, followed by Fulvio himself. With the thundering, arrogant tone of an over-reaching despot Fulvio shouted aloud to the organ-grinder:

"They have had enough. Get away from here!"

"No, no, no; more, more, more," cried the excited crowd.

As the shouts subsided, the young Sicilian who acted as our leader, stepped forward, pale and trembling, and standing between Fulvio and the organ-grinder, he said in a low, choked voice:

"You keep on playing, sir. We do as we please in this place. Let anyone dare send you away."

"You little shrimp, have you the nerve to gainsay my word?" retorted Fulvio, panting like an angered tiger. "You shall never do it again. I'll show you who is boss here," and so saying he dealt the young Sicilian a powerful blow on the face.

It was the signal for a general attack. The outraged gang surged forward like a solid, fearful phalanx. It seized Fulvio, and those of his henchmen who had failed to take to their heels, and dragged them left and right, punching them, kicking them, cursing them, until the cries for mercy died out.

As the evening sun sank slowly behind a thick mass of flaming clouds, the tumult gradually quieted down. When the moon arose, a company of men could be seen wending their way along the valley. Like dark, hushed phantoms they moved, leaving behind them a trackless silence.

THE DIFFERENCES BETWEEN AMERICANS AND ITALIANS

Stefano Miele

[Stefano Miele came to the United States from Naples when he was 23. Like many of his compatriots, he intended to return to Italy to live. This autobiographical sketch on "assimilation through affluence" tells why he remained in America.]

If I am to be frank, then I shall say that I left Italy and came to America for the sole purpose of making money. Neither the laws of Italy nor the laws of America, neither the government of the one nor the government of the other, influenced me in any way. I suffered no political oppression in Italy. I was not seeking political ideals: as a matter of fact, I was quite satisfied with those of my native land. If I could have worked my way up in my chosen profession in Italy, I would have stayed in Italy. But repeated efforts showed me that I could not. America was the land of opportunity, and so I came, intending to make money and then return to Italy. This is true of most Italian emigrants to America. . . .

America wants the immigrant as a worker; but does it make any effort to direct him, to distribute him to the places where workers are needed? No; it leaves the immigrant to go here, there, any place. If the immigrant were a horse instead of a human being, America would be more careful of him; if it loses a horse it feels it loses something, if it loses an immigrant it feels it loses nothing. At any rate, that is the way it seems to the immigrant; and it strengthens his natural disposition to settle among people of his own race.

A man needs to be a fighter to come to America without friends.

From *World's Work*, December, 1920.

I was more fortunate than many: I had a brother in America. He worked in a private bank. He met me when I landed and took me to his home in Brooklyn. I looked for a job for about a month. I tried to get work on the Italian newspapers; I tried to get work in a law office. Finally a friend took me to a Jewish law office, and I was employed—I was to get 25 per cent of the fees from any clients that I brought in. I stayed there two months and got $5. Three months after I arrived in New York, I was given the kind of a place that I had looked for in vain in my native land—one that would enable me to support myself and study my chosen profession. I was given a place on an Italian religious newspaper. I worked from eight in the morning to six in the evening, and attended the night course of the New York Law School.

It was about August when I landed in America, and already there was election talk. (It was the year McClellan ran for Mayor.) I met some of the Italian-American politicians. It is said that I have a gift for oratory. The politicians asked what would be my price to talk in the Italian sections of the city. I said that I did not want anything. I made speeches for McClellan, and I have made speeches in every campaign since.

That was one of the first things that struck me in America—that everyone working in politics was working for his own pocket. Another thing that also amazed me was that most of the men elected to an office in which they are supposed to deliberate and legislate, were in reality only figureheads taking orders from some one else. They had no independence, no individuality. Another discovery was that the Italians with most political influence were men of low morality, of low type. Then I discovered the reason: the politicians needed repeaters and guerillas, and that was why "the boss had to be seen" through a saloon- or dive-keeper.

A thing that seemed very strange was the way the American newspaper magnified crime in Italian districts, how they made sensational stories out of what were really little happenings, how they gave the Italians as a people a character for criminality and violence. No less strange was the way the Italian newspapers answered the American press. They were both building up a barrier of prejudice. If I were to judge America through the American newspapers, I would not have become an American citizen; or if I could know America only through the Italian-American newspapers I would say that the Americans are our enemies.

It must be frankly admitted, however, that there is a change in the second generation, a change that is too frequently not for the better. As I have said, the majority of Italian immigrants come from the rural districts of Italy, and because there is no policy of distribution, most of them settle in the big cities. They are not prepared to meet the situation presented in a big industrial centre. They think to apply the same principle in bringing up children that had been applied in the little village or on the farm in Italy. They let the children run loose. And in the streets of the crowded tenement districts the children see graft, pocketpicking, street-walking, easy money here, easy money there, they see the chance to make money without working. The remedy is to be found in distributing the newly arrived immigrants.

Most of what I have said has been of the faults of America. I have spoken of them because they are things that hold back Americanization.

America has been good to me. I have prospered here as I could not have prospered in Italy. I came to make money and return; I have made money and stayed. A little more than five years after I had landed at Ellis Island I was admitted to the New York bar. I have already had greater success than I dreamed, when I left Italy, that I should have. And I look forward to still greater success. For me, America has proved itself and promises to continue to prove itself the land of opportunity, but I have not forgotten Italy—it is foolish to tell any Italian to forget Italy. I say Italy; but for me, as for the others, Italy is the little village where I was raised—the little hills, the little church, the little garden, the little celebrations. I am forty years old, but Christmas and Easter never come around but what I want to return to Baiano. In my mind I become a little child again. But I know enough to realize that I see all those old scenes from a distance and with the eye of childhood.

But even if I wanted to return to Italy, my children would not let me. America is their country. My father is dead. I have brought my mother here. When an Italian brings his parents to America, he is here to stay.

America is a wonderful nation. But we make a mistake if we assume that the Anglo-Saxon is the perfect human being. He has splendid qualities but he also has faults. The same thing is true of the Latins. The Anglo-Saxon is preëminently a business man, an executive, an organizer, energetic, dogged. But in the Anglo-Saxon's civilization the Latin finds a lack of the things that go to make life worth living. I remember the returned Italians, the "Americans," that I used to see at Baiano: they had made money in America and were prosperous and independent, but they had also lost something —a certain light-heartedness, a joy in the little things—the old jests no longer made them laugh. The Latin has the artistic, the emotional temperament, a gift for making little things put sunshine into life, a gift for the social graces. If the Latin could get the qualities that the Anglo-Saxon has, and give to the Anglo-Saxon those that he lacks—if all the nationalities that make up America could participate in this give-and-take process—then we would have a real Americanization.

AMADEO P. GIANNINI AND THE BANK OF AMERICA

[Giannini founded his Bank of Italy in San Francisco's North Beach Italian neighborhood to aid immigrant farmers, fishermen, fruit peddlers, and other small businessmen who could not deal with established banks for lack of collateral. The secret of his early success was his ability to attract small investors. As the years went by, he established branch banks throughout the West, but primarily in California, so that by 1930, he controlled thirty per cent of the banking business of the state. By 1948, a year before his death, Giannini's bank, now known as the Bank of America, had become the largest such institution in the United States and it has since become the largest bank in the world. The following article, written in 1928, summarizes Giannini's early career and personal views on banking.]

Amadeo P. Giannini is well-known in Italy as President of the Bancitaly Corporation of New York, which acquired and owns control of the Banca d'Italia e d'America.

Giannini's name is very popular, but what is not known well enough is his life and philosophy.

Giannini was not born in Italy, although some people believe so. Indeed he was born of an old Italian family at San Jose, California, fifty-eight years ago. His father died when Giannini was a boy. He began to enter the business world hardly twelve years old, showing in it an unusual aptitude and becoming very useful to his stepfather, L. Scatena (genuine Italian from Lucca), a fruit and produce commission merchant.

Adapted from "La vita e la filosofia di Amadeo P. Giannini" ["Amadeo P. Giannini: His Life, His Philosophy"], in: *La Rivista d'Italia e d'America*, May, 1928.

Giannini's life at that time has something of the incredible: he was well up in his classes, but at once was fascinated by work: getting up shortly after midnight, he remained on the docks until school-time, gathering facts and figures about the day's market. His precious indications allowed Scatena's firm to realize enormous advantages on the other commission merchants. To avoid his mother's objections, Giannini tiptoed downstairs in his stockings and put on his shoes in the sidewalk and passed the whole early morning at work. Immediately after school he went back to business until late in the afternoon; then home for supper and study, and early to bed.

When nineteen, he left the school and became a partner in the stepfather's growing firm. He refused to go to higher school; his mind eminently practical brought him on the only subjects which could be of some direct interest to him. Thus he did not learn the dead languages.

During this period Giannini devoted himself to develop his affairs. Driving a horse and buggy for miles through the neighbours of San Francisco, he visited every day hundreds of growers and shippers, explaining the facilities the firm offered to them and emphasizing that their business would receive his own personal attention. To save time, he stocked up his buggy with crackers and sardines, and took his frugal lunch while on the way. The opposition which he met from stronger rivals stimulated and redoubled his energies. He always held his ground, unless any adversaries were defeated or bought.

At the age of thirty one, he felt that in such a business firm he had nothing to do but count the profits. The success was as full as one could wish. No more creative work was offered to him. He needed to work. It had been said of him "He would rather fight than eat." Therefore he turned over to his associates his shares of the firm.

But Giannini's retirement was a beginning, not an end. Some opportunities arose for him to purchase real estate. One profitable affair followed to another. Almost unconsciously he found himself taken in a new business net.

First, he accepted the place of bank director, but his own suggestions in conducting the bank were not adopted by the powers dominating the institution. Giannini proceeded to fulfil his plans and principles on his own account.

Giannini's bank was opened in October 1904. It was called the Italian bank of California; then changed the name to the Bank of Italy. Giannini had a very definite vision: no speculative exploits with the bank's money. Neither was any officer allowed to speculate or become interested in any other business. By opening branches in different localities, his business was to be diversified; one district would pay off loans at the time another section needed funds.

Local banks must be taken over, and their best officers kept in their places. This conversion of little established banks into branches would facilitate a much better line of credit to be given to the increasing industrial enterprises.

This was a simple plan, but it called for special qualities and abilities for its accomplishment. Giannini was determined to reach at any rate in the banking world the same position he had attained in the produce commission business.

This was completely accomplished in 1906 when Giannini's bank opened its first branch. . . . It was the moment that Giannini crossed his crucial point. His institution was only a year and a half old, when the San Francisco disaster happened.

Giannini had to meet an unprecedented situation. Through the maze of desolation he reached the bank about noon. Threatening flames were already a few yards off. Two horsedrawn rigs commandeered from his old firm were rapidly loaded, one with money and securities, the other with a supply of stationery and furniture to resume work without delay.

Indeed a desk was raised on the docks and a clerk was entrusted with taking deposits. Among the bankers in the city Giannini was the first to re-establish his business. While the fire was still smoldering, Giannini sent a circular letter to all depositors of his bank, announcing that a great part of their money was available in cash. He offered also to lend money to those who intended to rebuild their houses destroyed by the fire and shock. In spite of the confusion, those letters reached their destinations. Thousands of people took advantage of this offer, with the result that the Italian quarter, Phoenix-like, sprang up from its own ashes, before any other. In the midst of the chaos, the "Bank of Italy" sign was hung out on the home of Giannini's brother, Van Ness Avenue, and the bank records show that not one, of all those to whom money was lent, failed to pay back the full amount.

Giannini became more and more popular in San Francisco.

Another event revealed Giannini's business prescience. It was the tremendous financial panic of the fatal 1907. Giannini, just returning from a trip to New York, realized with his infallible foresight that serious financial trouble was coming. Orders were issued that the bank would gather the largest possible stock of gold. The vaults of the bank were filled and the overflowing yellow metal was stored in the vaults of another bank.

When the panic broke out, banks everywhere were obliged to limit or stop gold payments. Only the Bank of Italy, solid as a rock, could meet every demand made by its customers.

The success was unimaginable and the echo of it attracted to the bank such a legion of new depositors that Giannini could spare intact the gold he had stored outside the bank and let this gold be used by the other bank.

The Italian Chamber of Commerce of New York invited him in

1911 to open there a bank. This invitation was accepted only in 1918, because Giannini had still much creative work to do at home. The sum of $1,500,000 was quickly subscribed by over 1000 stockholders. The East River National Bank was acquired, whereof the presidency was assumed by Dr. A. H. Giannini, A. P.'s brother.

Under the aegis of Giannini another institution arose in New York: it was the Bancitaly Corporation, originally organized as a holding company, and now controlling the most conspicuous number of banks in the United States. It has a paid-in capital and surplus of $250,000,000. It includes the Bank of Italy of San Francisco, the Bowery East River National Bank of New York recently fused with the Bank of America, one of the oldest Banks in New York, and finally the Banca d'Italia e d'America in Italy. The Bancitaly Corporation purchased in 1919 the Banca dell'Italia meridionale, whose name has since been changed to Banca d'Italia e d'America. The head office was removed from Naples to Rome. Giannini's son, L. M. Giannini, spent almost an entire year in Italy assisting in the installation, as far as possible, of American systems in the new Italian bank. At present the bank headquarters are being installed in Milan.

Mr. Giannini was the first to organize a special women's banking department, and to cultivate school-savings. He built up the largest school-saving group in the United States, including some thousands of schools.

Mr. Giannini has a very clear philosophy, which may be related in a few propositions.

Don't waste time, and go straight after the object: "Too many people waste time in useless ways. I was never interested in the local gossips or scandals, nor in anything whatsoever foreign to my business. When you have a clear-cut object, go after it promptly and efficaciously. Don't dawdle. My method is concentration. I have always avoided loading my mind and memory with useless stuff. I don't try to keep track of baseball records or golf championships or the late developments in any activity not connected with the banking business. I can let a conversation of no interest to me go in by one ear and go out from the other without ever interfering with my own mental machinery. I don't care for details. If I think of putting up a structure, I know just what kind of a building I want and what facilities must be provided. I leave the execution to others, more expert judges of stones or other building materials."

Love work, not money: "I am not a millionaire, and never expect or hope to be one. I have no ambition to become exceedingly rich. I have seen too many ultra-rich persons who were constantly afraid that some one would put poison in their food or knock them over the head or something else to get rid of them. There is no fun in working merely for money. I like to do things, to create things, to be a builder. To build is a very fascinating thing.

When the difficulties have been overcome, the job has been licked. Having won the fight, I lost any interest. The idea of leaving millions for other people to spend is the height of foolishness. I believe in using money to help worthy causes while one is still living and thus get some satisfactions out of it. Of course, it is every man's duty to give his children the best equipment for life. But to leave millions to young sons is dangerous. We are so much better as we must make our own way. God meant us to work. Those who don't work never amount to anything. To take from any one the incentive to work is a bad service."

Ask the advice of some trusted friends and discover talent everywhere it may be found: "While I do most of my own thinking and usually make my own decision, whenever anything of a particularly ticklish nature comes up and I am not positive as to the best course to follow, I go to some friend and lay the whole matter before him. I tell him what I propose to do and then ask him to knock holes in it. Incidentally, I say that I am turning more and more of the executive responsibilities over to younger men. One reason I moved my office from San Francisco to Los Angeles was that I wished my principal associates to begin making decisions for themselves. I shall pick out the most promising of my vice-presidents and make him president. I don't want to delay taking such a resolution until I am an old man. This gathering together of brainy executives I have always regarded as one of the most important parts of my job. One youth caught my eye; I watched him and when I figured he was ripe, I got him to become one of us. You can't sit down and wait for talent to come to you. You have to be constantly on the lookout for it and catch it."

As to strictly banking business, Giannini is decidedly against outside speculating: "The main thing is to run your business absolutely straight. A good clean bank, unentangled in any speculative exploits, has nothing to fear. Whenever banks fail, you find it is because of outside ventures. No man, no bank, no business should put itself into the grip of anything else. Failure comes from doing things that should not have been done—often things of questionable ethics."

This is Mr. Giannini's sound philosophy. Faithful to this philosophy, he has become a financial colossus and the controller of the biggest banking business in the world. . . .

He is now forming a great organization with the only purpose to help Italian commercial or industrial enterprises. It is perfectly in his views; that is that banking work must be separated from speculative business. The new institution has a capital of Lire 500,000,000 which will be rapidly increased, as Giannini enjoys in Italy so full a trust as in the rest of the world.

AMEDEO OBICI, AMERICA'S "PEANUT KING"

Dominick Lamonica

[Although less well-known, even among his fellow Italian Americans, than such entrepreneurs as Giannini and Sbarbaro, the life of Amedeo Obici is, nevertheless, one of America's striking success stories. Born in Oderzo in the province of Treviso, Italy, on July 15, 1877, Obici came to the United States in 1889. The story of his business success was told in a 1931 article by Dominick Lamonica, associate editor of the journal, *Atlantica*.]

In recounting the lives of their successful, self-made millionaires, Americans love to point to the example of Frank W. Woolworth, who built his fortune on the thin American dime. But consider the case of Amedeo Obici, America's "peanut king," who based his fortune on the lowly American nickel. When he arrived in this country at the age of 12, that sum constituted just about all his working capital. Now the Planters Nut and Chocolate Company, of which he is President and General Manager, does more than $12,000,000 of business annually.

The fundamental idea by which Obici has been guided is extremely simple. People think much less of spending 20 nickels, proportionately, than they do of spending a dollar. This the young immigrant noticed immediately after his arrival in the United States, the country where, his mother had told him back at Aderzo, near Venice, in Italy, "everybody made much money." Why, therefore, seek dollars, which were so guarded, when nickels were so plentiful? They are so plentiful, in fact, that now, at 52, Amedeo Obici is one of the wealthiest Italians in America.

From *Atlantica, The Italian Monthly Review*, February, 1931.

At Scranton, Pa., his uncle, who had sent for him, put him to work on his fruit-stand, and sent him to school the following week. But education did not sit well on the young lad's shoulders. "The books," he says, "meant nothing to me. All I could understand was arithmetic. When school ended in June I had learned nothing more than I already knew when I came to America. That was the end of my schooling here."

But this is not altogether true. Obici did continue his education, though it was not of the formal kind. After having worked at Pittston and Wilkes-Barre for fruit-stands and cigar-makers, he got a job in a popular cafe, whose owner, Billy McLaughlin, "taught me about Shakespeare and helped me to learn English. More than that, I learned much about life in Billy McLaughlin's place. The patrons (doctors, lawyers, city officials, and successful business men), discussed everything under the sun, and I listened."

Young Obici was 17 when Mr. McLaughlin died, and for a while he worked for a rival firm. But working for someone else, after having worked for Mr. McLaughlin, was not to his liking. He had made and saved enough money to bring his mother and his two sisters here the previous year in 1896. Accordingly, he decided to go into business for himself. He rented sidewalk space in front of a store, obtained enough lumber to build on credit, and in the same way managed to win over wholesale fruit dealers. "But for my peanut roaster I had to pay cash," he adds.

That humble little peanut roaster was the precursor of what now amounts to one of the great corporations of the United States, with its four great factories at Suffolk, Va., Wilkes-Barre, Pa., San Francisco, and Toronto, over 2,000 employees, and an authorized capital of five million Preferred Stock and ten million Common Stock. But that $4.50 roaster demanded constant attention, lest the peanuts be scorched.

"One day I got hold of an old electric fan motor and rigged up a set of pulleys. I put that fan motor to work turning my peanut roaster. So far as I know, it was the first electrically operated one in the world.

"Then over my stand I put a sign, 'Obici, the Peanut Specialist.' People came from miles around to buy my peanuts."

That was the beginning. Soon he was packing five-cent bags of shelled peanuts for the trade. This he stimulated by placing in the packages coupons bearing the letters of his name, one letter per package, and giving dollar watches to those who spelled out his name with the coupons. "I gave away some 20,000 watches in two years," he admits.

The "peanut specialist" had experimented meanwhile with salted peanuts and peanut candy bars, and, with the business expanding beyond the scope of one man, he determined to make a national market for his product, conceiving the idea of the Planters Peanut

Company. This, however, needed help and capital. The first of these problems was solved by his obtaining as partner M. M. Peruzzi, sales manager for one of the biggest Scranton wholesale confectionery jobbers, who knew his trade and how to develop a market. The other he managed to solve through some friends.

Thus, in 1906, the Planters Peanut Company of Wilkes-Barre was incorporated, with $20,000 capital stock paid in, and with two small store buildings and about 15 employees. When the landlord jumped the rent from $100 to $200, however, "I determined to buy the building, although the price was $39,000 and I didn't have so much as $1000." Upon the recommendation of friends, nevertheless, he managed to secure a loan at the local bank.

A little showmanship occasionally does no harm and may do much good, Mr. Obici has discovered. When he was able to purchase his first carload of peanuts, he unloaded the whole car in wagons and paraded it through the principal streets of Wilkes-Barre, the novelty creating much favorable comment. Fewer people now were skeptical of the idea of selling salted peanuts in five-cent bags. Fewer people, too, were saying that Messrs. Obici and Peruzzi had "gone nutty with peanuts."

In time it became necessary to look to their sources of supply, for the bulk of the nation's peanuts are grown in Virginia and North Carolina.

"I think it was intuition," says Mr. Obici reminiscently, "that brought me to Suffolk, Va., in 1913 with $25,000, all that the Planters Company could venture at the time, to establish a peanut cleaning business. The plan was to buy the nuts direct from the Virginia planters and clean them ourselves.

"It certainly didn't seem like good business judgment to go to Suffolk. We could have bought our nuts from experienced cleaners in Suffolk at the time more advantageously than we could buy them ourselves. But our venture in Suffolk grew into the manufacture of the finished product itself there."

There is hardly a man, woman or child in this country today who is not familiar with the jaunty, be-monocled and top-hatted figure of "Mr. Peanut," with his tempting invitation to munch the product he represents. "Mr. Peanut" is, so to speak, 13 years old, for it was in 1917 that the Company's first national advertising campaign was launched with a series of full page advertisements in the Saturday Evening Post and other magazines and newspapers. During the many years that have passed since "Mr. Peanut's" formal debut, he has made himself a nationally known, nay, an internationally known character.

The enterprise was now growing by leaps and bounds. Since the preparation of the raw peanuts and of the other raw products they were manufacturing as by-products was being carried on more conveniently, efficiently and economically in Suffolk, the center of the peanut belt, where the new buildings had been erected especially to suit the operations, Mr. Obici decided to discontinue all manufacturing in Wilkes-Barre and concentrate it in Suffolk. This decision proved very profitable and made possible further expansion.

Heavy transportation rates seriously handicapped expansion west of the Rockies, so in 1921 a factory site was acquired in San Francisco, and with this added facility the western coast States were supplied as conveniently as the eastern half of the country.

From time to time, efforts had been made to introduce the manufactured products of the Planters Nut and Chocolate Company into Canada, but customs duties made the cost of the merchandise prohibitive. Accordingly, in 1925, after an investigation of conditions in that country, a modern factory building was purchased in Toronto, and a campaign of national advertising in Canada soon made Planters Salted Peanuts popular in the Dominion. Even in England, in 1928, was "Mr. Peanut" introduced, and accepted without reservation.

Sales branches and warehouses are now maintained in several of the largest American cities to facilitate and expedite the distribution of the finished products. Two of these branches, incidentally, are headed by Italians: Mr. J. M. Gargano in New York, and Mr. L. Bencini in Chicago.

The growth of the Company has been prodigious, for besides producing the enormous tonnage needed to supply its salted peanut, peanut butter, and candy departments, large volumes of raw peanuts, shelled and unshelled, are sold to the jobbing and manufacturing interests throughout the United States. It is the largest concern of is kind in the world and it dominates the American market. The 1930 production of peanuts was about 4,000,000 bags, of which 90% passed through the hands of Mr. Obici's Planters Nut and Chocolate Company.

Like many other of the greater corporations in America, it has found it necessary to manufacture practically all its own accessories. There is a complete tin factory manufacturing all tin containers for salted peanuts and peanut butter, which run into the several thousand every day. A great printing plant is also maintained, which prints all the cartons, paper bags, and colored advertising matter used by the company, and where, too, are located machines for the scoring of cartons, and waxing machines where all boxes are waxed before assembled. All paper bags, cartons, cases and crates used for shipping purposes are also manufactured by the company, whose own employees cut trees on the company's own timber tract, ship them to the company's own saw mill, and then store them in the company's own lumber yards.

A far cry, this, from the days of "Obici, the Peanut Specialist," with his $4.50 peanut roaster that demanded his constant attention.

"I have been asked many times," says Mr. Obici, now the "Peanut King," "how I got from where I was to where I am. I should answer, work and friends. I've worked from 16 to 18 hours a day until recent years, and I have never lacked friends. Friends have been one of my biggest assets. I never needed money for my business which I was not able to get."

Now Mr. Obici has been able also to devote more of his time and attention to other things beside business. He has served his adopted city of Suffolk as President of its Chamber of Commerce, he has been made a Commander of the Crown of Italy by His Majesty King Victor Emanuel III, and recently he contributed $10,000 toward the establishment of a Chair of Italian Culture at the University of Virginia.

Not long ago he went to Italy for a much-deserved vacation, and to visit his native town of Aderzo. But vacations, for men of his calibre, are seldom, if ever, untinged with business matters. So it happened that, while there, he saw the possibility of cultivating peanuts in the Italian colonies of Libia and Tripolitania. Peanuts grow only in tropical countries or climate, and these two colonies both fulfill the requirements. To this end he saw many men high in Italian governmental and business circles. The Hon. Giuseppe Bottai, Italian Minister of Corporations, has evinced great interest in the project.

When a man has worked as untiringly, and under such stern, self-imposed discipline, it is bound to have its effect upon him. America's motto is "Business is business," and Mr. Obici's rule is said to be never to smile during business hours. "A business office should be like a graveyard." This sums it up in his own words. Yet his eyes are bright and sparkling and he is not as forbidding as all that, for, though he may look very serious and protest that the request is reasonable, his employees know that none of them ever asked him for a favor without having it granted.

Part Four

THE QUASI-PUBLIC UTILITY: ORGANIZED CRIME AND THE ITALIAN AMERICAN, 1890–1973

The late Saul Alinsky called it a "quasi-public utility"; for others, it is "the Syndicate." There are more romantic, mysterious, conspiratorial-sounding names: Black Hand, Mafia, Cosa Nostra. But "quasi-public utility" is nearer the truth than "organized crime." As the newspapers reveal almost daily, there is plenty of "organized" crime perpetrated by ostensibly respectable corporations, by labor union leaders, and by government officials at all levels.

Alinsky's "quasi-public utility" as it has developed since Prohibition is largely a purveyor of goods and services demanded by the public, made illegal by the public's elected representatives, but not infrequently winked at by the public's law enforcement officers. These goods and services include gambling, narcotics, and prostitution; but those involved in crime have branched out into respectable areas of business such as wholesale houses, banks, savings and loan associations, and labor unions. The legitimate businesses serve as an outlet for surplus, untaxed profits—as a place to employ legally, money that has been obtained illegally.

A hoopla has been made for several decades about the Italian involvement in crime. The real story, though, is a fairly simple one, not the vast mythology of a giant international criminal conspiracy tearing away at the fabric of American life. As Francis Ianni has pointed out in his book, *A Family Business* (1972), Italian American crime first appeared in the immigrant communities as crimes against other Italians. Such were the "Black Hand" outrages that went on for the period 1895–1915. If there was any Mafia or Camorra involvement, it was only to the extent that members of those societies in the Old World had come to the United States and were using the "Black Hand" device of ill-gotten gain. But there was no Black Hand Society; the kidnappings, blackmail, etc., were the work of individuals or small groups of persons operating independently. Nevertheless, even if there was no such society, there was a strong nativist sentiment that made the idea of such an organization seem quite feasible.

The real organized crime of the era before 1920 was mostly in the hands of Irish gangs, where it had been for decades. In the early years of Prohibition, a number of Jewish gangs became prominent, especially in New York, Detroit, and Chicago; but their hegemony was short-lived. By the middle of the 1920's, the Italian organizations began to challenge the Irish and Jewish control of crime until, by 1930, the Italians dominated the rackets. This transfer of power was more evident in the compact geographical area of Chicago than in the multistate New York metropolitan region. And, of course, Chicago had the most flamboyant, public relations–minded of gangsters in Al Capone (aided by pliable city and state administrations). Capone's administrative expertise was such that by the end of the 1920's he was the dominant figure in Cook County crime, having "eliminated" or coerced the competition. The dynasty he put together has never been toppled; it has only changed through the years to accommodate itself to new conditions.

The bulk of Italian American crime has always been in the New York-New Jersey area, partly because there are more Italian Americans there than in any other part of the nation. This area is the home of the notorious "five families" and their gang wars. This is the setting for *The Godfather* and most of the other "Mafia fiction" that threatens to replace the Western as America's favorite form of romanticism. Since none of the five families lives as public a life as Al Capone, the history of crime in this area can only be pieced together. It is known that there was a violent transfer of power from the older generation to the younger in the early 1930's. This "Castellamarese War" ended the dominance of the old immigrant "Mafia" types and brought to positions of leadership younger, more aggressive men like Lucky Luciano and Vito Genovese, whose *modus operandi* was attuned to the conditions of urban America, not the rural folkways of Sicily.

In essence, it was the twin circumstances of Prohibition and the special character of urban America that made the Italian criminal organizations. They were the ones in the right place at the right time. And, in contrast to their Irish and Jewish predecessors, they did it better. But serious students of criminology strongly suspect that the days of Italian American crime are drawing to a close, as blacks and Puerto Ricans move in on the old territories and as the possibility of becoming "legit" grows more appealing.

How extensive is organized crime? No precise answer can be given in spite of the investigations of the professional "Mafia" experts. Most of the sensational exposés of crime end up dealing solely with the New York-New Jersey combine. Every major city has some organized crime, and in a couple of dozen cities Italians are certainly extensively involved. But the description of a national crime syndicate pulling all the strings, with enormous power, earning $50 billion per year, and secretly infiltrating all levels of business and government is just another instance of the history-by-conspiracy mythology that Americans have been fond of since the days of the Founding Fathers. Such theories are ways to rationalize the complex problems of a society that functions less well every year. But they do not offer much help in dealing with real social and economic issues, including crime. Remember the "confessions" of Joe Valachi: while offering us a whole conspiracy legend of no mean proportions, his testimony has never led to the conviction of one felon.

Professor Ianni has summed up the whole matter nicely: "There is no organized crime 'underworld.' Rather, organized crime is an integral part of our cities. It is the result of an individualistic, predatory philosophy of success, the malaise of laissez-faire economic and political pratice. Organized crime is just that part of the business system operative in the illicit segment of American life. The degree and tenure of minority group involvement in this business enterprise is basically a function of the social and cultural integration of the group into American society. . . . As they are acculturated, their crimes become more American and in time merge into the area of marginal legitimate business practice."

Which brings us to one final point. Italians did not introduce organized crime into the United States. It is an indigenous institution bred by a society where affluence, or the possibility of it, was present and where society thought it could afford to wink at its own laws if that seemed the convenient or profitable thing to do. The practices of criminal operatives since 1920 differ hardly at all from the behavior of the nineteenth century railroad magnates, cattle barons, or industrialists. Crime and anti-social behavior were endemic to our nation before the southern Italians arrived. In 1929, historian James Truslow Adams noted that Americans were "already the most lawless in spirit of any in the great modern civilized countries. Lawlessness has been and is one of the most distinctive American traits. . . . It is impossible to blame the situation on 'foreigners.' The overwhelming mass of them were law-abiding in their native lands. If they become lawless here, it must be largely due to the American atmosphere and conditions." (*Our Business Civilization*)

It might also be added that neither Brazil nor Argentina, both with large Italian immigrant populations, ever developed Black Hand Societies or Mafias. Even in the United States, the number of Italians involved with crime has always been minute—scarcely 1 in 500 Italian American stock. But now that the era of Irish and Jewish gangs is past and the predatory nature of industrialists at least mitigated, society has developed historical amnesia. Crime means "Mafia" or "Cosa Nostra."

Lest the case seem overstated, let it be said that there *is* organized crime, and for the past half century Italian Americans have been a dominant force in it. As affluence has increased, so have the incidence and range of criminal activity. But the criminal organizations that thrive in New York, New Jersey, New England, Illinois, Florida, Nevada, New Orleans, California, and other places do not work in isolation. They could not exist without the cooperation of police officials, judges, aldermen, state legislators, U.S. Congressmen, U.S. Senators, and bureaucrats. Mobster-turned-informer Vincent Teresa insists in *My Life in the Mafia* (1973) that "Crooked cops were the mainstay of the New England mob." And not only of New England, but of every mob in the country. A further mainstay of the mobs are the many wealthy and influential citizens who invest their money with criminals in order to make some extra cash that Uncle Sam can't trace. Finally, as Saul Alinsky also noted, the real members of crime syndicates are the millions of Americans who demand and utilize the goods and services available only outside the law.

The selections in this part serve a twofold purpose. They provide a general survey of Italian American involvement in crime—a survey not always accurate because most of the articles are written from the outside looking in. Secondly, they describe the framework within which Americans have developed their mystique of the Mafia.

THE NEW ORLEANS MAFIA
Henry Cabot Lodge

[One of the most
unpleasant incidents of Italo-American history was the lynching
of eleven Italians in New Orleans on March 14, 1891. This affair
and the events leading up to it gained international notoriety,
disrupting diplomatic relations between Italy and the United States.
The focus of the crisis was the hostility of the native American
public toward the Sicilian population of New Orleans and its
alleged proclivity for crime. Even at this early date, the Mafia
legend had come to the United States, and in an era susceptible
to diverse hostilities toward all immigrants, the legend easily took
root and grew. The author of this selection, Henry Cabot Lodge of
Massachusetts, was, in 1891, a member of Congress. Two years
later he was elected to the U.S. Senate where he remained a
persistant advocate of immigration restriction. The utterances of
such authoritative public figures as Lodge, no doubt, added
credence to the Mafia myth that it would not otherwise have had.]

On Sunday, March 15, the people of the United States were startled
and shocked by hearing that on the preceding day a mob in
New Orleans, led by men of good standing in the community,
had broken into one of the prisons and with cool deliberation had
killed eleven Italians who were confined there. The victims of this
attack were accused of complicity in the recent murder of the chief
of police. Two had never been brought to trial, and the trial of the
others had resulted in the acquittal of six and a mistrial as to three.
The mob acted on the belief that these men were guilty of the
crime with which they were charged; that that crime was the

From "Lynch Law and Unrestricted Immigration," in: *North American Review*, May, 1891.

work of a secret society known as the Mafia; and that the failure
of the jury to convict was due either to terror of this secret
organization or to bribery by its agents.

Americans are a law-abiding people, and an act of lawlessness
like the lynching of these Italians is sure to meet with their utmost
disapproval. There is no doubt that every intelligent man deplores
the lawless act of the New Orleans mob. But to stop there would
be the reverse of intelligent. To visit on the heads of the mob all
our reprobation, and to find in its act alone matter of anxiety and
regret, would not only be unjust, but would show a very slight
apprehension of the gravity and meaning of this event. Such acts
as the killing of these eleven Italians do not spring from nothing
without reason or provocation. The mob would have been impossible if there had not been a large body of public opinion
behind it, and if it had not been recognized that it was not mere
riot, but rather that revenge which Lord Bacon says is a kind of
wild justice. The mob was deplorable, but the public sentiment
which created it was more deplorable still, and deserves to have
the reasons for its existence gravely and carefully considered.

What, then, are the true causes of the events of the 14th of
March at New Orleans? One, certainly, was the general belief that
there had been a gross miscarriage of justice in the trial of the
accused Italians. Whether the jury rendered their verdict against
the evidence or not, it is certain that the people of New Orleans
pretty generally thought that they had done so. It is, unfortunately,
only too evident that there is a profound lack of confidence in
the juries of New Orleans. Lawlessness and lynching are evil things,
but a popular belief that juries cannot be trusted is even worse,
for it is an indication that the law is breaking down in its ordinary
operations. This condition of public opinion is, no doubt, due in
very large measure to the extremely bad condition of politics
in New Orleans; a fact of which the country has had for some
time a vague idea, but upon which, since the 14th of March, it
has received a great deal of very definite information. A city in
which political meetings concerned only with the affairs of a
single party are held under the conditions which attended the
caucuses at the time of the struggle between Governors Nicholls
and McEnery, and where a great gambling enterprise has been
sowing the seeds of corruption in every direction, is in a very bad
way. Violence breeds violence, and corruption engenders corruption. Wrong-doing of this sort always returns to plague the
inventors. At the same time, the condition of municipal politics in
New Orleans is something that the people of that city must deal
with themselves. If they do not set matters right in this respect,
no one else can, and they will suffer by their bad city politics
more than anybody else.

The other exciting cause of the mob was the belief that the men
who were killed were members of the Mafia, a secret society

bound by the most rigid oaths and using murder as a means of maintaining its discipline and carrying out its decrees. Of the existence of such a society no reasonable man can, I think, have any doubt. That it has, as a rule, confined its operations to the people who brought it here is, I think, equally beyond question. But there is nothing to keep it necessarily within such bounds. It is anything but self-limited, and in a political soil like that of New Orleans it was pretty sure to extend. Now, if there is one thing more hateful to Americans than another, it is secret, oath-bound societies which employ assassination as a recognized means for carrying out their objects. The killing of the eleven prisoners had in it no race feeling whatever. There has been no hostility to the Italians in America, as such. On the contrary, they have been generally regarded hitherto as an industrious people, prone to fierce quarrels among themselves, but, in the main, thrifty, hard-working, and well behaved. The men were not killed in the New Orleans prison because they were Italians, but because they were believed to be members of a secret-assassination society responsible for a brutal murder. There was a further popular belief that this society was not only responsible for the murder of the chief of police, but that it was extending its operations, that it was controlling juries by terror, and that it would gradually bring the government of the city and the State under its control. This belief, no doubt, was exaggerated, but it was certainly not without foundation.

We have, therefore, three facts here of the gravest import. First, an outbreak of lawlessness which resulted in the death of eleven men; second, a belief that juries could not be depended upon to administer justice and protect the lives of the citizens; third, the existence of a secret society which was ready to use both money and murder to accomplish its objects, even to the point of perverting the administration of the law. It is my purpose to deal only with the last phase of this question. I believe that, whatever the proximate causes of the shocking event at New Orleans may have been, the underlying cause, and the one with which alone the people of the United States can deal, is to be found in the utter carelessness with which we treat immigration to this country.

The killing of the prisoners at New Orleans was due chiefly to the fact that they were supposed to be members of the Mafia, but it would be a great mistake to suppose that the Mafia stands alone. Societies or political organizations which regard assassination as legitimate have been the product of repressive government on the continent of Europe. They are the offspring of conditions and of ideas wholly alien to the people of the United States. Nevertheless, to certain minds they present a permanent attraction, and there are classes of men sufficiently illiterate and sufficiently criminal to reproduce them wherever they may happen to be, even when there is no repressive government to serve as an excuse. The last twenty years have shown the existence of these societies at various times in one form or another in the United States. They have appeared in different parts of the country, and have usually been put down and their deeds punished by ordinary process of law. We have had, for example, the Molly Maguires in Pennsylvania, the Anarchists in Chicago, the Mafia in New Orleans, and, according to a recent statement in the New York *Times*, there is a similar organization among some of the Poles. It is idle to say that, like all other honest citizens, the great mass of men belonging to the races which have been most pointedly connected with these organizations heartily disapprove them. There is no question that this is true; and yet none the less these dangerous societies spring up and commit murders, and are either put down by the law or crushed out by wild deeds of lawlessness and bloodshed like that at New Orleans. They come not from race peculiarities, but from the quality of certain classes of immigrants of all races. If we permit the classes which furnish material for these societies to come freely to this country, we shall have these outrages to deal with, and such scenes as that of the 14th of March will be repeated.

REPORT OF THE WHITE HAND SOCIETY

[In an effort to combat Black Hand crimes, members of Chicago's Italian communities formed a White Hand Society on November 11, 1907, with the cooperation of the local Unione Siciliana. While the society claimed some success in ridding the city of a few criminals in 1908, it never did gain widespread support among the immigrants. They believed the society was powerless to stop crime in the Italian communities. Through lack of financing and popular support, the White Hand Society died out after a few years. The selection below reprints a portion of the society's report for 1908.]

Here in the land of liberty, of labor, of the boldest steps in human progress, there has originated and extended through the Italian colonies such an air of mystery and terror that it disturbs the peace of families, hampers the profitable development of all the industries, dishonors the Italian name, and tends to prolong that state of moral degradation from which the lowest social strain of certain unhappy regions of Italy are just now beginning to emerge. . . . Whole Italian families, in which a blackmailing letter or a threat in another form has been received from the Black Hand, live in continued anxiety and fear of the vague, unknown, but always terrible danger which hangs over them, and nobody knows whom it will fall upon, the father, one of the children, a relative, or all together, in the destruction of the house or little store, demolished and set on fire by the explosion of a dynamite bomb. . . . Even business men of conspicuously strong

From Robert E. Park and Herbert A. Miller, *Old World Traits Transplanted* (New York, 1921), pp. 241–246.

character, and professional men of unusual ability, frankly admit that, after a threatening letter, a certain time has to pass before they are able to attend to their business with all the composure and energy required. . . .

In these last few years the number of threatening letters has been increasing at an appalling rate, and the field of victims has been enlarged to include all: the poor laborer who by means of great sacrifices has suceeded in putting aside a few dollars, or, perhaps, bought a wretched little property not yet entirely paid for; the small merchant who, with others of his family, is his own clerk in his little store, and barely manages to make a living from it; the proprietor who has retired from business and would enjoy in peace the fruit of his toil; the wholesale merchant; the professional man; and even the representative of the Italian government in Chicago.

The letter in its classic form is short, written in an unassuming and sometimes friendly tone. It contains the request for money, with an indication of the place where it is to be delivered, and a threat, sometimes veiled by mysterious allusions, and sometimes expressed with a brutal lack of reserve.

At the place designated the victim does not find anybody; but at the house he finds, a few days later, a second letter, in which the request is repeated, also the threat, in an aggravated form. And thus at brief intervals comes a third and a fourth letter, each containing more violent threats than the preceding, expressed either in words or symbols, such as drawings of pierced hearts, of pistols, daggers, crosses, skulls and crossbones, bombs, etc. All these letters are prepared with a system of progression which shows in the author a mind by no means crude and untrained, but shows, rather, a consummate skill acquired by practice in this class of crime.

In this manner the victim is intimidated to such a point that there is not left in his veins another drop of blood beyond that needed to nourish his fear, and to enable him, in such a depressed condition of mind, to lay hold on the anchor of salvation which is pointed out to him in one of the letters, that is, to apply to "friends." Some phrase in the letter hints vaguely at so-called friends; suggests that whoever seeks will find; gives to understand, in short, that somebody might intervene between the victim and the mysterious and terrible god that has made the demand, and is threatening with all the thunderbolts in his possession, so that the matter might be adjusted in some way. In one letter in the possession of the "White Hand," this "friend" who is to be the intermediary, and who in reality is the accomplice if not the author of the blackmail, is indicated with sufficient precision. He must be a Terminese from Termini, says the letter, meaning from the town of Termini, not from the country, and must live in the same street as the victim, which is a very short street. . . .

So the unfortunate victim finally looks for the "friend" who can save him from the threatening peril, and has no difficulty whatever in finding him. For some time there has been continually at his side somebody who has shown himself more solicitous than ever before, if known for a considerable time; obliging and exceedingly friendly, if of recent acquaintance. This man sometimes guesses, sometimes induces the other to tell him the trouble which has destroyed his peace of mind, and curses the assassins who blackmail poor people and who ought to be hung or put in the penitentiary. He knows some mysterious people, banded together, who live and have a good time with money extorted from honest, industrious people. . . .

The White Hand, which had studied all phases of those cases which had come to its knowledge, finding it extremely difficult to reach the principal actor, directed all its attention toward this so-called friend whose conduct and explanations gave some clue which might furnish a more or less substantial proof of his participation in the crime. Then the tactics of these criminals were changed, and to the common "friend" of the blackmailed and the blackmailer was assigned the role of enemy of the latter, under the necessity of submitting to a humiliation, the humiliation of being obliged himself to carry to the feet of the powerful and mysterious god the tribute of the money extorted and the homage of his own obedience.

In this way every weapon of the prosecution is broken. The go-between did not offer himself, he was appealed to; he always advised against yielding to the imposition; he refused to intervene; they begged him to, entreated, implored; he yielded out of consideration for his friend, being himself a victim of the oppression of the same mysterious enemy. And in the face of this evidence, in fact, no jury can find him guilty. . . .

BLACK HAND, MAFIA, AND CAMORRA

[The crime that flourished within the Italian immigrant communities gained a good deal of public notoriety in the years from 1890 to 1915. Most Americans never really understood that it was a matter of crimes by the poor against the poor: one immigrant taking advantage of another. The exotic names—Black Hand, Mafia, and Camorra—all seemed to indicate the emergence in this country of dark conspiracies being hatched abroad. And, because the truth was so commonplace, it was not likely tò be believed. After World War II started, Americans turned their attention to other international conspiracies for a few years. The three selections that follow concern the existence and operation of crime among Italian immigrants and popular attitudes toward it. Gaetano D'Amato was president of the United Italian Societies; Frank Marshall White was a journalist and editor for various New York newspapers; and Arthur Train had been assistant district attorney of New York City and a close observer of Italian crime. The articles by White and Train were written following the murder, in Palermo, of Calabria-born Giuseppe Petrosino, a New York police detective. Petrosino had gone to Sicily in 1909 to investigate the activities of Italian criminals who had lived in America. For many Americans, the Petrosino murder confirmed their worst fears of Italian criminal conspiracies.]

It is not strange, perhaps, that most Americans believe that a terrible organization named the "Black Hand Society" exists in Italy, and is sending its members to establish branches for the purpose of plundering the United States, since nearly every newspaper in the

From "The 'Black Hand' Myth," by Gaetano D'Amato, in: *North American Review*, April, 1908.

country conveys that impression to its readers. One would think, however, that such men as Frank P. Sargent, Commission-General of Immigration, and Terence V. Powderly, Chief of the Division of Information of that Bureau, would inform themselves on a matter that pertains so closely to their duties. Nevertheless, both of these officials have put themselves on record as believing that such an organization exists. In his last annual report Mr. Sargent says, apropos of the suggestion that legislation be adopted requiring the presentation of a passport as a prerequisite to the examination of an alien applying for admission to the United States: "The current history of the perpetration of heinous crimes throughout the United States by foreigners domiciled therein, especially by the members of the 'Black Hand' and other like societies in evidence," etc. Again, in a recent article on "Undesirable Citizens," he refers to "the introduction into this free country of such hideous and terrifying fruits of long-continued oppression as the 'Black Hand' and anarchist societies."

Mr. Powderly is more specific. In an interview in the New York "Sun," he declared that he had learned in Italy last summer that "on its native heath the 'Black Hand' was organized for good," explaining further: "An Italian who wrongs a woman, and fails to right the wrong, is practically driven from among his fellows. The black hand of ostracism is raised against him. The 'Black Hand' in this country, brought into being for noble purposes across the sea, was prostituted and converted to ignoble purposes when transplanted to the United States." The "Black Hand" has scarcely even been heard of in Italy. It was never heard of until long after the term had been used in the United States, and then only as a distant manifestation of criminal activity regrettable because the good name of the Italians in the New World suffered by it. A society for the protection of women would be superfluous in Italy. . . .

In the United States, the "Black Hand Society" is a myth, in so far as the phrase conveys the impression that an organization of Italian criminals exists in America, or that the Camorra or the Mafia has become naturalized here. By reason of the laxity of the immigration laws, there have crept into this country some thousands of ex-convicts from Naples, Sicily and Calabria, along with millions of honest and industrious Italians; and, owing to the inefficiency of the police in various cities where these Italians are domiciled, the criminals among them are able to live by robbery and extortion, frequently accompanied by murder, their victims being the more helpless of their fellow countrymen.

These fugitives from justice and gallows-birds, from whom it is America's duty to protect the law-abiding Italians who are doing yeoman service in the building of the Republic, are members of the Italian race that have brought disgrace upon the others, and upon whom the sensational press has conferred the title of "Black Hand Society." How many of these criminals there are in the United States it is impossible, for obvious reasons, to estimate with any degree of accuracy. Lieutenant Petrosino, who is in charge of the little Italian Squad in the Police Department of New York and probably knows more about the predatory brotherhood than any one else, says that they may number as many as from three to four per cent of the Italian population. They are no more organized, however, than are the many thousands of lawbreakers of other nationalities in America. Indeed, Robert Louis Stevenson's playful but accurate characterization of the gangs of thieves that preyed upon nocturnal Paris three and a half centuries ago applies to the so-called "Black Hand" today—"independent malefactors, socially intimate, and occasionally joining together for some serious operation; just as modern stock-jobbers form a syndicate for an important loan."

Italian outlaws are enabled to reach this country to-day with almost the same facility as the honest Italian, so far as the laws of the United States are concerned. True, the ex-convict cannot obtain a passport from the Italian Government and sail on an Italian ship, but there is nothing to prevent his crossing the frontier and leaving from any port outside of Italy to which he may make his way. Many of the most dangerous of the Italian criminals in the United States have come here by way of England and Canada, and many others have shipped as sailors from Italian ports and deserted their ships on reaching this country.

The Neapolitan, Sicilian or Calabrian desperado, once he has reached these shores, finds the conditions ideal for levying tribute upon the feebler folk among his countrymen. In nearly all the larger cities, particularly of the East and Middle West, he will find them living in colonies by themselves. Besides the 500,000 Italians in New York, there are 100,000 each in Boston and Philadelphia; 70,000 each in San Francisco and New Orleans; 60,000 in Chicago; 25,000 each in Denver and Pittsburgh; and 20,000 in Baltimore. In smaller cities are colonies that will number from 5,000 to 10,000.

Conditions are much the same in these colonies all over the country. They are generally located in a poor quarter of the town, which is not policed as well as those where the native American lives. The newcomers, moreover, are timid in their strange surroundings; they are ignorant of the law of the land; few of them can speak English, even if they dared to complain of outrages perpetrated upon them. And, when the humble and respectable Italians do appeal to the police and find that the law cannot, or will not, protect them, they are reduced to a pitiful extremity that has driven scores of potential citizens back to Italy, kept many an industrious resident in actual bondage to the lawbreakers, and in some instances even forced hitherto honest men to become criminals themselves.

Aside from the urban Italians, there are some 500,000 laborers of the race distributed throughout the United States, working in mines and vineyards and on railroads, irrigation ditches and farms, who are equally victims of their rapacious countrymen with the dwellers in cities. In fact, there is scarcely a point throughout the length and breadth of the country where a few Italians are gathered together that some criminals of the race have not fastened themselves upon them.

Every reader of the newspaper is familiar with the outrages that, in the name of the "Black Hand," have been perpetrated among the Italians, beginning some ten years ago and increasing coincidentally with the Italian immigration, but reaching a limit two or three years ago. Murder has been a common crime, and the dynamiting of houses and shops, the kidnapping of children, with every species of blackmail and extortion, was of so frequent occurrence that the mind became dulled to the enormity of these offences. In New York conditions have been worse than anywhere else; and yet, with half a million of Italians in the population, there are to-day only forty Italians in the Police Department. Along miles of street in New York there are no guardians of the people who understand the language of the residents. As Marion Crawford says, the employment of Irish policemen in Rome would be an analogous circumstance, since there are more Italians in New York than in the capital of Italy.

How little the police have understood the situation may be gathered from the fact that, during the height of the wave of Italian crime three years ago, respectable members of that race were not allowed permits to carry weapons of defence, even when their lives were threatened. Physicians whose nocturnal duties subjected them to particular peril; bankers and business men, at any time liable to the attentions of scoundrels who did not stop at murder; in fact, all persons with Italian names were prohibited absolutely from carrying arms. Wherefore the police aided and abetted the outlaws, all of whom carried knives and pistols, by making it impossible for the law-abiding Italian legally to prepare for defence in case of attack.

During twenty-nine years of residence in New York, I have found two causes that operate for the blackening of the Italian name in respect of crime: the sensationalism of the yellow press and the ignorance and recklessness of the police in recording arrests. Almost every dark-skinned European, not speaking English, who does not wear the Turkish fez, is put down on the police records as an Italian, and thus the Italian is condemned for much of the crime committed here by persons of other nationalities.

It is impossible to comprehend the attitude of a part of the American press with regard to the Italian, unless the theory is accepted that the truth is a consideration secondary to the publication of sensations that are calculated to increase the day's sales. Last spring, for instance, the newspapers manufactured a "Black Hand" scare, representing that the police were in despair of getting the lawless element under control. Two of the less sensational of the Sunday supplements had articles on the same day devoted to the subject, in each of which it was stated that an organization of Italian criminals under the name of the "Black Hand Society" existed in New York, and that it was growing in power so rapidly as to be an actual menace to the city. . . .

The term "Black Hand" was first used in this country about ten years ago, probably by some Italian desperado who had heard of the exploits of the Spanish society, and considered the combination of words to be high-sounding and terror-inspiring. One or two crimes committed under the symbol gave it a vogue among the rapacious brotherhood; and, as it looked well and attracted attention in their headlines, the newspapers finally applied it to all crimes committed by the Italian banditti in the United States. Thus the press not only facilitates the commission of crime among the Italian ex-convicts, by making it appear that all the evil done by them is the successful work of a single organization, that aids the individual criminal by leading his ignorant countrymen, upon whom he preys, to believe that he makes his lawless demands on behalf of a powerful society.

In spite of the depredations of the thousands of Italian criminals whom this Government has allowed to enter the country and prey upon the honest and industrious of their own race here, the great body of that race has prospered. A quarter of a century ago, there were not more than 25,000 Italians in America, and their entire possessions would have been valued at a trifling sum. To-day, in New York alone, the estimated material value of the property in the Italian colonies is $120,000,000, aside from $100,000,000 invested by Italians in wholesale commerce, $50,000,000 in real estate, and $20,000,000 on deposit in the banks. I doubt whether any other nationality can show as good a record of twenty-five years of achievement.

HOW THE UNITED STATES FOSTERS THE BLACK HAND

Frank M. White

The assassination by the Mafia in a public square in Palermo, last March, of Lieutenant Joseph Petrosino, head of the Italian squad of the New York Police Department, while on a secret mission connected with the identification in the United States of Italian criminals, means something more than the violent taking off of a brave man and an efficient and loyal public servant, lamentable though the occurrence is in itself. No native-born American was ever a more ardent patriot than the chief of the Italian detectives. He considered himself under an eternal and illimitable debt of gratitude to his adopted country for the opportunities it had given him and so many others of his race, and it was primarily his burning indignation against those of his countrymen who come here for purposes of crime that made him so formidable a foe to the Italian malefactor. He may be said to have cherished personal enmity against every native of Italy who violated the laws of the United States.

Petrosino was the son of a tailor in Padua, in the province of Campania, Italy, where he was born forty-eight years ago, coming to New York with his parents when he was nine years of age. He studied in the public schools and sold newspapers and blacked boots out of school hours as a boy. He had worked as a tailor, as a clerk in a bank, and in the Department of Street Cleaning before he became a policeman. It was while he was in charge of one of the "dumping piers" on the Hudson River that Police Captain Williams (as he was then) marked Petrosino as a capable youth, and induced him to "join the force." His rise from patrolman

From *Outlook*, October 30, 1909.

to lieutenant was slow, but he had accomplished an immense amount of work before his death. Petrosino had a record of more convictions for murder than any other five men in the detective bureau, and yet he was a man of unusually kindly disposition. Fate had set him a stern task, and he did not shirk it, and it may be truthfully said that no man in the entire Police Department was more highly respected by those with whom he came in contact. No one knew better than Petrosino the fearful risk he ran when he ventured into the very home of the Mafia, and his doing so is an example of as splendid courage as a man is often called upon to exhibit.

Immigration from Italy into the United States during the last quarter of a century has brought here some of the best elements of our citizenship, sturdy and thrifty men and women who have asked naught but the opportunity to make their way by honest toil. To-day there are one and a half millions of the race in the country. Five hundred thousand of them are in New York—more than in any one city in Italy, with the single exception of Naples. There are 100,000 each in Boston and Philadelphia, 70,000 each in San Francisco and New Orleans, 60,000 in Chicago, 25,000 each in Denver and Pittsburgh, and 20,000 in Baltimore. In the smaller cities colonies numbering from 1,000 to 10,000 bring the number of urban Italians up to 1,000,000, and there are 500,000 Italian laborers distributed over the forty-six States, working in mines, quarries, and vineyards, and on railways, irrigation ditches, and farms.

Bringing with them to America no capital other than health and intelligence, with stout hearts and wiling hands, these immigrants have thriven wonderfully. They are sending back to Italy every year $10,000,000 of savings (which goes partly into home investments, partly to the support of dependent parents and other relatives, and partly to bring relatives here), and to-day in New York City alone the estimated material value of the property in the Italian colonies is $120,000,000, aside from $100,000,000 invested by Italians in commerce, $50,000,000 in real estate, and $20,000,000 on deposit in the banks. Throughout the country the Italians have been equally prosperous. Of the $50,000,000 of value in importations from Italy into the United States during the last year, men of Italian birth are responsible for $40,000,000, and they are concerned in every department of internal trade and commerce, and engaged in every branch of productive labor.

This register of twenty-five years of achievement of the Italians in America—which it is doubtful if any other foreign nationality can equal—is all the more marvelous when the circumstance is taken into consideration that, owing to the preposterous inadequacy of our immigration laws, there have come with them through the gates (according to an estimate made a year ago by Lieutenant Petrosino, who was conceded to be more familiar with conditions among Italian criminals than any one else) something like 50,000 of the riffraff of the Italian prisons. There is no point throughout the length and breadth of the land, in the cities or the rural districts, under the shadows of police stations or in mountain fastnesses or the solitudes of fields and forests, where a few Italians are gathered together, that the banditti of the race have not fastened upon them. It is safe to say that there are not half a dozen Italian workingmen digging a ditch anywhere in the country to-day who are not paying tribute of their earnings to some scoundrel of their race. The poorer and the weaker are the greater sufferers, but it is doubtful if there is one honest Italian among all the hundreds of thousands who have come to the United States who has not at one time or another been despoiled by the ex-convicts of the Mafia and the Camorra, who compose what has come to be known as the Black Hand.

This aggregation of assassins, blackmailers, and thieves have piled up a record of crime in the United States unparalleled in the history of a civilized country in time of peace. Not only is the toll that has been taken in human life appalling in itself, but the fact that these thousands of criminals have been and are living upon the respectable Italians in the New World means a money loss to them that amounts to millions of dollars annually. Of a list of one hundred and twelve murder mysteries committed in New York since January 1, 1906, that was published in the World last July, fifty-four of the victims were Italians, and there have been approximately a score of murders each year for the last ten years in the Italian colonies of the city about which there is no mystery. If, still according to Petrosino's estimate of a year ago, only five thousand of the Italian ex-convicts are in New York, and the other five thousand have kept up the murder average, an idea may be had of the total butchery. Many of these murders have been among the criminals themselves, but the great majority of the victims are honest men who have refused to yield to extortion, or who have in other ways antagonized the Black Hand.

Of other crimes than murder on the part of Italian malefactors —highway robbery, the kidnapping of children, the dynamiting of shops and houses, the throwing of bombs, with every form of extortion and blackmail, in amounts ranging from pennies to thousands of dollars—few ever reach the courts or are heard of outside the Italian colonies.

Conditions in the United States could not have been better contrived for the Italian ex-convict driven from his native land by the rigorous punitive supervision of the police. Not only is he unknown to the authorities of law and order, but wherever he may go he finds himself among the southern Italians (it is estimated that something like eighty-five per cent of the total immigration from Italy is from Naples, Sicily, and Calabria), who are already familiar with the operation of the Mafia and the Camorra, of whose principles many of them were tolerant before those principles were applied to their undoing, and, what is more important than anything else, consider themselves bound by the *omerta,* or conspiracy of silence, and will never think of applying to the police for protection.

While there is little organization among the Italian desperadoes in the United States, the title of Black Hand, conferred upon them by the newspapers, gives them an advantage never before possessed by scattered lawbreakers, in that they are able to make their cruel demands upon ignorant victims in the name of what the latter believe to be a powerful society. Robert Louis Stevenson's whimsical description of the gangs of thieves that preyed upon nocturnal Paris three and a half centuries ago applies to the so-called Black Hand to-day—"independent malefactors, socially intimate, and occasionally joining together for some serious operation, just as modern stockjobbers form a syndicate for an important loan." So thoroughly has a great association of criminals, covering the entire country, been advertised, however, that the individual adventurer need only announce himself as an agent of the Black Hand to obtain the prestige of an organization whose membership is supposed to be in the tens of thousands.

It is time, however, that Americans should realize that the frequency of Italian names in our criminal news is not so much a proof of unfitness in the immigrant as of the failure of the machinery of American justice to give him the protection to which he is entitled. No further argument is needed to prove preposterous misgovernment on the part of the United States than is furnished by statistics of the Bureau of Immigration, which show that, while European criminals have been flocking into the country by thousands concurrently with the great wave of immigration from southeastern Europe since 1901, since that date and up to the first of the present year there have been less than one thousand stopped at the gates or deported from Ellis Island afterward. Of every fifty criminals who make the effort to enter the United States forty-nine are successful!

Responsibility for these conditions, whereby this country has become an arena in which foreign outlaws maintain a continuous reign of terror, lies primarily at the door of the National Legislature; while the failure of the Federal Government properly to co-operate with the police authorities, the refusal of representatives of the Italian Government to render adequate assistance in the deportation of Italian criminals, and, so far as New York City is concerned, the impudent inaction of the Board of Aldermen in the matter of a secret detective service, are contributory factors to the general demoralization. . . .

There is every reason to apprehend an increase of Italian crime in America, and more particularly in New York, this winter. Not only has the unavenged murder of Petrosino been a source of vast encouragement to the ex-convicts of the Mafia and the Camorra on both sides of the water, but his death removes their most active and dangerous foe in the United States. With the general weakening of the morale of the New York City Police Department brought about by its surrender to the politicians, the Italian squad—which in the death of its former head lost fifty per cent of its potency— cannot fail to decrease in efficiency.

It is in the fall and winter months that the bulk of Italian crime is generally committed in the cities, but the miscreants have been more active during the last spring and summer than ever before during the same period. No better proof of their daring and effrontery need be afforded than is found in the fact that at the height of the universal indignation over the murder of Petrosino the ruffians who exulted in his death prevented by threats the Italian singers who had volunteered for the benefit performance to his widow and child at the Academy of Music from taking part, and that they murdered in cold blood a friend of the martyred detective who was attempting to raise a fund for Mrs. Petrosino and her little one.

There have been more than thirty deaths of their countrymen encompassed in New York City and the immediate vicinity by Italian criminals since the assassination of Petrosino. There has also been an increase of Black Hand crimes throughout the country, though to make anything like an accurate estimate of the extent of this increase a canvass of the States would be necessary.

During the ten years' reign of terror in the Italian colonies of America Congress might at any time have brought it to an abrupt ending. Our legislators were not confronted with an insoluble problem. The average town council might have solved it at a sitting. All that is now necessary to rid the United States finally and absolutely of alien malefactors is to adopt some such measure as that advocated by Mr. Braun as Special Immigration Commissioner, and with it an enactment providing for the deportation of *all* criminals from other countries who cannot show that they are living honest lives, whether they have been in the country three years or thirty. Petrosino used to say that, given such laws and authority to execute them, he would guarantee to eradicate the Black Hand from American soil in three months.

IMPORTED CRIME
Arthur Train

There are a million and a half Italians in the United States, of whom nearly six hundred thousand reside in New York City—more than in Rome itself. Naples alone of all the cities of Italy has so large an Italian population; while Boston has one hundred thousand, Philadelphia one hundred thousand, San Francisco seventy thousand, New Orleans seventy thousand, Chicago sixty thousand, Denver twenty-five thousand, Pittsburgh twenty-five thousand, Baltimore twenty thousand, and there are extensive colonies, often numbering as many as ten thousand, in several other cities. So vast a foreign-born population is bound to contain elements of both strength and weakness. The North Italians are *molto simpatici* to the American character, and many of their national traits are singularly like our own, for they are honest, thrifty, industrious, law-abiding, and good-natured. The Italians from the extreme south of the peninsula have fewer of these qualities, and are apt to be ignorant, lazy, destitute, and superstitious. A considerable percentage, especially of those from the cities, are criminal. Even for a long time after landing in America, the Calabrians and Sicilians often exhibit a lack of enlightenment more characteristic of the middle ages than of the twentieth century.

At home they have lived in a tumbledown stone hut about fifteen feet square, half open to the sky (its only saving quality); in one corner the entire family sleeping in a promiscuous pile on a bed of leaves; in another a domestic zoo consisting of half a dozen hens, a cock, a goat, and a donkey. They neither read, think, nor exchange ideas. The sight of a uniform means to them either a tax-gatherer,

From *McClure's Magazine*, May, 1912.

a compulsory enlistment in the army, or an arrest, and at its appearance the man will run and the wife and children turn into stone. They are stubborn and distrustful. They are the same as they were a thousand or more years gone by. . . .

The conditions under which a large number of Italians live in this country are favorable not only to the continuance of ignorance, but to the development of disease and crime. Naples is bad enough, no doubt. The people there are poverty-stricken and homeless. But in New York City they are worse than homeless. It is better far to sleep under the stars than in a stuffy room with ten or twelve other persons. Let the reader climb the stairs of some of the tenements in Elizabeth Street, or go through some of those in Union Street, Brooklyn, and he will get first-hand evidence. This is generally true of the lower class of Italians throughout the United States, whether in the city or the country. They live under worse conditions than at home. You may go through the railroad camps and see twenty men sleeping together in a one-room hut of laths, tar-paper, and clay. The writer knows of one Italian laborer in Massachusetts who slept in a floorless mud hovel about six feet square, with one hole to go in and out by and another in the roof for ventilation—in order to save $1.75 a month. All honor to him! Garibaldi was of just such stuff, only he suffered in a better cause. . . .

Now, for historic reasons, these South Italians hate and distrust all governmental control and despise any appeal to the ordinary tribunals of justice to assert a right or to remedy a wrong. It has been justly said by a celebrated Italian writer that, in effect, there is some instinct for civil war in the heart of every Italian. The insufferable tyranny of the Bourbon dynasty made every outlaw dear to the hearts of the oppressed people of the Kingdom of the Two Sicilies. Even if he robbed them, they felt that he was the lesser of two evils, and sheltered him from the authorities. Out of this feeling grew the "Omertà," which paralyzes the arm of justice both in Naples and in Sicily. The late Marion Crawford thus summed up the Sicilian code of honor:

> According to this code, a man who appeals to the law against his fellow man is not only a fool but a coward, and he who cannot take care of himself without the protection of the police is both. . . . It is reckoned as cowardly to betray an offender to justice, even though the offense be against one's self, as it would be not to avenge an injury by violence. It is regarded as dastardly and contemptible in a wounded man to betray the name of his assailant, because if he recovers he must naturally expect to take vengeance himself. A rhymed Sicilian proverb sums up this principle, the supposed speaker being one

who has been stabbed. "If I live, I will kill thee," it says; "if I die, I forgive thee!"

Any one who has had anything to do with the administration of criminal justice in a city with a large Italian population must have found himself constantly hampered by precisely this same Omertà. The South Italian feels obliged to conceal the name of the assassin and very likely his person, though he himself be but an accidental witness of the crime. . . .

It is impossible to estimate correctly the number of Italian *criminals* in America or their influence upon our police statistics; but in several classes of crime the Italians furnish from fifteen to fifty per cent of those convicted. In murder, assault with intent to kill, blackmail, and extortion they head the list, as well as in certain other offenses unnecessary to describe more fully but prevalent in Naples and the South. . . .

By far the greater portion of these criminals, whether ex-convicts or novices, are the products or by-products of the influence of the two great secret societies of southern Italy. These societies, and the unorganized criminal propensity and atmosphere which they generate, are known as the "Mala Vita."

The Mafia, a purely Sicilian product, exerts a much more obvious influence in America than the Camorra, since the Mafia is powerful all over Sicily, while the Camorra is practically confined to the city of Naples and its environs. The Sicilians in America vastly outnumber the Neapolitans. Thus in New York City for every one Camorrista you will find seven or eight Mafiusi. But they are all essentially of a piece, and the artificial distinction between them in Italy disappears entirely in America.

Historically the Mafia burst from the soil fertilized by the blood of martyred patriots, and represented the revolt of the people against all forms of the tyrannous government of the Bourbons; but the fact remains that, whatever its origin, the Mafia to-day is a criminal organization, having, like the Camorra, for its ultimate object blackmail and extortion. Its lower ranks are recruited from the scum of Palermo, who, combining extraordinary physical courage with the lowest type of viciousness, generally live by the same means that supports the East Side "cadet" in New York City, and who end either in prison or on the dissecting-table, or gradually develop into real Mafiusi and perhaps gain some influence.

It is, in addition, an ultra-successful criminal political machine, which, under cover of a pseudo-principle, deals in petty crime, wholesale blackmail, political jobbery, and the sale of elections, and may fairly be compared to the lowest types of politico-criminal clubs or societies in New York City. In Palermo it is made up of "gangs" of toughs and criminals, not unlike the Camorrist gangs of Naples, but without their organization, and is kept together by personal allegiance to some leader. Such a leader is almost always under the patronage of a "boss" in New York or a *padrone* in Italy, who uses his influence to protect the members of the gang when in legal difficulties and find them jobs when out of work and in need of funds. Thus the "boss" can rely on the gang's assistance in elections, in return for favors at other times. Such gangs may act in harmony or be in open hostility or conflict with one another, but all are united as against the police, and exhibit much the same sort of Omertà in Chatham Square as in Palermo. The difference between the Mafia and Camorra and the "gangs" of New York City lies in the fact that the latter are so much less numerous and powerful, and bribery and corruption so much less prevalent, that they can exert no practical influence in politics outside the Board of Aldermen, whereas the Italian societies of the Mala Vita exert an influence everywhere—in the Chamber of Deputies, the Cabinet, and even closer to the King. In fact, political corruption has been and still is of a character in Italy luckily unknown in America—not in the amounts of money paid over (which are large enough), but in the calm and matter-of-fact attitude adopted toward the subject in Parliament and elsewhere.

The overwhelming majority of Italian criminals in this country come from Sicily, Calabria, Naples, and its environs. They have lived, most of their lives, upon the ignorance, fear, and superstitions of their fellow countrymen. They know that so long as they confine their criminal operations to Italians of the lower class they need have little terror of the law, since, if need be, their victims will harbor them from the police and perjure themselves in their defense. For the ignorant Italian brings to this country with him the same attitude toward government and the same distrust of the law that characterized him and his fellow townsmen at home, the same Omertà that makes it so difficult to convict any Italian of a serious offense. The Italian crook is quickwitted and soon grasps the legal situation. He finds his fellow countrymen prospering, for they are generally a hard-working and thrifty lot, and he proceeds to levy tribute on them just as he did in Naples or Palermo. If they refuse his demands, stabbing or bomb-throwing shows that he has lost none of his ferocity. Where they are of the most ignorant type he threatens them with the "evil eye," the "curse of God," or even with sorceries. The number of Italians who can be thus terrorized is astonishing. Of course, the mere possibility of such things argues a state of medievalism. But mere medievalism would be comparatively unimportant did it not supply the principal element favorable to the growth of the Mala Vita, apprehended with so much dread by many of the citizens of the United States.

Now, what are the phases of the Mala Vita—the Camorra, the

Black Hand, the Mafia—which are to-day observable in the United
States and which may reasonably be anticipated in the future?

In the first place, it may be safely said that of the Camorra in its
historic sense—the Camorra of the ritual, highly organized with a
self-perpetuating body of officers acting under a supreme head—
there is no trace. Indeed, as has already been explained, this phase
of the Camorra, save in the prisons, is practically over, even in
Naples. But of the Mala Vita there is evidence enough.

The majority of the followers of the Mala Vita—the Black
Handers—are not actually of Italian birth, but belong to the second
generation. As children they avoid school, later haunt "pool" parlors
and saloons, and soon become infected with a desire for "easy
money" which makes them glad to follow the lead of some
experienced *capo maestro*. To them he is a sort of demi-god, and
they readily become his clients in crime, taking their wages in
experience or whatever part of the proceeds he doles out to them.
Usually the "boss" tells them nothing of the inner workings of
his plots. They are merely instructed to deliver a letter or to
blow up a tenement. In course of time the assistant becomes a
sort of bully or bad man on his own hook, a criminal "swell," who
does no manual labor, rarely commits a crime with his own hands,
and lives by his brain. . . .

Generally each *capo maestro* works for himself with his own
handful of followers, who may or may not enjoy his confidence,
and each gang has its own territory, held sacred by the others.
The leaders all know each other, but never trespass upon the
others' preserves, and rarely attempt to blackmail or terrorize any
one but Italians. They gather around them associates from their
own part of Italy, or the sons of men whom they have known at
home. . . .

The Italian criminal and his American offspring have a sincere
contempt for American criminal law. They are used by experience
or tradition to arbitrary police methods and prosecutions unham-
pered by Anglo-Saxon rules of evidence. When the Italian crook is
actually brought to the bar of justice at home, that he will "go"
is generally a foregone conclusion. There need be no complainant
in Italy. The government is the whole thing there. But, in America,
if the criminal can "reach" the complaining witness or "call him
off" he has nothing to worry about. This he knows he can easily
do through the terror of the Camorra. And thus he knows that the
chances he takes are comparatively small, including that of conviction if he is ever tried by a jury of his American peers, who are
loath to find a man guilty whose language and motives they are
unable to understand. All this the young Camorrista is perfectly
aware of and gambles on.

LAST STATEMENT IN COURT

Bartolomeo Vanzetti

[Perhaps the most crucial aspect of the Sacco-Vanzetti case was its timing. When two naturalized Italian immigrants were arrested for the April 15, 1920, murder of the paymaster and a guard at a shoe factory in South Braintree, Massachusetts, the United States was pervaded by extreme xenophobia, anti-radicalism, and anti-communism in an emotional hangover from World War I. Niccola Sacco, a native of Puglia, Italy, had come to the United States in 1908, the same year Bartolomeo Vanzetti, a philosophical anarchist, had come from the Piedmont. Both had fled to Mexico during World War I to avoid the draft. After the robbery and murder, their reputations as draft dodgers, anarchists, and radicals combined with their "Italian appearance" to make them prime suspects. In addition, they were both armed at the time of arrest. The trial, before Judge Webster Thayer of the state superior court, began May 31, 1921, and ended July 14 with a verdict of guilty. The evidence convicting Sacco and Vanzetti was circumstantial, but such was the hostility of the court and the public, that they would have been convicted in any case. After six years of appeals that failed, the pair were scheduled to die in April, 1927. Public protests delayed the executions until August 23. The Sacco-Vanzetti trial became one of the landmark cases in twentieth century American jurisprudence, but the details of what actually happened seemed to elude discovery. Lawyers, journalists, and historians have sifted through all the evidence trying to ascertain the truth, but with no great success. Only in early 1973, with the publication of *My Life in the Mafia*, by mobster-turned-informer Vincent Teresa, was the likeliest reconstruction of the crime published. Teresa flatly asserted that the holdup-murder was the work of a gang led by Frank Morelli, the late crime boss of

From *The Sacco-Vanzetti Case* (New York, 1929), Vol. 5, pp. 4896–4904.

Rhode Island. If Teresa is right (and he quotes Morelli's admission).
the Sacco-Vanzetti trial was an even greater miscarriage of justice
than the Chicago Haymarket Trial of 1886. The selection below
reprints a portion of Vanzetti's last statement to the court, on
April 9, 1927.]

What I say is that I am innocent . . . of the Braintree crime . . .
That I am not only innocent . . . but in all my life I have never stole
and I have never killed and I have never spilled blood. That is
what I want to say. And it is not all. Not only am I innocent . . .
not only in all my life I have never stole, never killed, never spilled
blood, but I have struggled all my life, since I began to reason, to
eliminate crime from the earth.

Everybody that knows these two arms knows very well that I did
not need to go in between the street and kill a man to take the
money. I can live with my two arms and live well. But besides that,
I can live even without work with my arm for other people. I have
had plenty of chance to live independently and to live what the
world conceives to be a higher life than not to gain our bread with
the sweat of our brow. . . .

Well, I want to reach a little point farther, and it is this—that not
only have I not been . . . in Braintree to steal and kill and have
never steal or kill or spilt blood in all my life, not only have I
struggled hard against crimes, but I have refused myself the commodity or glory of life, the pride of life of a good position, because
in my consideration it is not right to exploit man. I have refused to
go in business because I understand that business is a speculation
on profit upon certain people that must depend upon the businessman, and I do not consider that that is right and therefore I refuse
to do that.

Now, I should say that I am not only innocent of all these things,
not only have I never committed a real crime in my life—though
some sins but not crimes—not only have I struggled all my life to
eliminate crimes, the crimes that the official law and the official
moral condemns, but also the crime that the official moral and the
official law sanctions and sanctifies—the exploitation and the oppression of the man by the man, and if there is a reason why I am
here as a guilty man, if there is a reason why you in a few minutes
can doom me, it is this reason and none else.

I beg your pardon. [Referring to paper.] There is the more good
man I ever cast my eyes upon since I lived, a man that will last
and will grow always more near and more dear to the people, as
far as into the heart of the people, so long as admiration for goodness and for sacrifice will last. I mean Eugene Debs. I will say that
even a dog that killed the chickens would not have found an
American jury to convict it with the proof that the Commonwealth
produced against us. That man was not with me in Plymouth or
with Sacco where he was on the day of the crime. You can say

that it is arbitrary, what we are saying, that he is good and he applied to the other his own goodness, that he is incapable of crime, and he believed that everybody is incapable of crime.

Well, it may be like that but it is not, it could be like that but it is not, and that man has a real experience of court, of prison, and of jury. Just because he want the world a little better he was persecuted and slandered from his boyhood to his old age, and indeed he was murdered by the prison. He know, and not only he but every man of understanding in the world, not only in this country but also in the other countries, men that we have provided a certain amount of a record of the times, they all still stick with us, the flower of mankind of Europe, the better writers, the greatest thinkers of Europe, have pleaded in our favor. The scientists, the greatest scientists, the greatest statesmen of Europe, have pleaded in our favor. The people of foreign nations have pleaded in our favor.

It is possible that only a few on the jury, only two or three men, who would condemn their mother for worldly honor and for earthly fortune; is it possible that they are right against what the world, the whole world has say it is wrong and that I know that it is wrong? If there is one that I should know it, if it is right or if it is wrong, it is I and this man. You see it is seven years that we are in jail. What we have suffered during these seven years no human tongue can say, and yet you see me before you, not trembling, you see me looking you in your eyes straight, not blushing, not changing color, not ashamed or in fear.

Eugene Debs say that not even a dog something like that—not even a dog that kill the chickens would have been found guilty by American jury with the evidence that the Commonwealth have produced against us. I say that not even a leprous dog would have his appeal refused two times by the Supreme Court of Massachusetts—not even a leprous dog.

They have given a new trial to Madeiros for the reason that the judge had either forgot or omitted to tell the jury that they should consider the man innocent until found guilty in the court, or something of that sort. That man has confessed. The man was tried and has confessed, and the court give him another trial. We have proved that there could not have been another judge on the face of the earth more prejudiced and more cruel than you have been against us. We have proven that. Still they refuse the new trial. We know, and you know in your heart, that you have been against us from the very beginning, before you see us. Before you see us you already know that we were radicals, that we were underdogs, that we were the enemy of the institution that you can believe in good faith in their goodness—I don't want to condemn that—and that it was easy on the time of the first trial to get a verdict of guiltiness.

We know that you have spoke yourself and have spoke your hostility against us, and your despisement against us with friends of yours on the train, at the University Club of Boston, on the Golf Club of Worcester, Massachusetts. I am sure that if the people who know all what you say against us would have the civil courage to take the stand, maybe, Your Honor—I am sorry to say this because you are an old man, and I have an old father—but maybe you would be beside us in good justice at this time.

When you sentenced me at the Plymouth trial you say, to the best of my memory, of my good faith, that crimes were in accordance with my principle—something of that sort—and you take off one charge if I remember it exactly, from the jury. The jury was so violent against me that they found me guilty of both charges, because there were only two. But they would have found me guilty of a dozen of charges against Your Honor's instructions. Of course I remember that you told them that there was no reason to believe that if I were the bandit I have intention to kill somebody, so that they will take off the indictment of attempt to murder. Well, they found me guilty of what? And if I am right, you take out that and sentence me only for attempt to rob with arms—something like that. But, Judge Thayer, you give more to me for that attempt of robbery than all the 448 men that were in Charlestown, all of those that attempted to rob, all those that have robbed, they have not such a sentence as you gave me for an attempt at robbery. . . .

We were tried during a time that has now passed into history. I mean by that, a time when there was a hysteria of resentment and hate against the people of our principles, against the foreigner, against slackers, and it seems to me—rather, I am positive of it, that both you and Mr. Katzman has done all what it were in your power in order to work out, in order to agitate still more the passion of the juror, the prejudice of the juror, against us. . . .

What I want to say is this: Everybody ought to understand that the first of the defense has been terrible. My first lawyer did not stick to defend us. He has made no work to collect witnesses and evidence in our favor. The record in the Plymouth Court is a pity. I am told that they are almost one-half lost. So the defense had a tremendous work to do in order to collect some evidence, to collect some testimony to offset and to learn what the testimony of the state has done. And in this consideration it must be said that even if the defense take double time of the state without delay, double time that they delay the case it would have been reasonable, whereas it took less than the state.

Well, I have already say that I not only am not guilty . . . but I never commit a crime in my life—I have never steal and I have never kill and I have never spilt blood, and I have fought against the crime, and I have fought and I have sacrificed myself even to eliminate the crimes that the law and the church legitimate and sanctify.

This is what I say: I would not wish to a dog or to a snake, to the most low and misfortunate creature of the earth—would not wish to any of them what I have had to suffer for things that I am not guilty of. But my conviction is that I have suffered for things that I am guilty of. I am suffering because I am a radical and indeed I am a radical; I have suffered because I was an Italian, and indeed I am an Italian; I have suffered more for my family and for my beloved than for myself; but I am so convinced to be right that if you could execute me two times, and I could be reborn two other times, I would live again to do what I have done already.

I have finished. Thank you.

AN UNFAIR PRESS

[The Unione
Siciliana was renamed the Italo-American National Union in 1925
because of the society's alleged involvement with organized crime
in Chicago. In June, 1925, the Union's Bulletin carried the following
editorial berating the press for the unfavorable reflection cast on
the Italian community by the frequent playing up of activities by
criminals with Italian names. Unfortunately, there were some fairly
notorious criminals in Chicago at the time, and this selection was
written at the height of a gang war inaugurated by the murder of
Dion O'Banion in November, 1924. In January, 1925, Johnny Torrio
was shot, and in May, Angelo Genna was assassinated. In June,
there was a shoot-out on the south side between members of the
Bugs Moran gang and the Genna family. The newspapers carried
almost daily headlines of some new gang outrage.]

We regret exceedingly to note that from time to time the American
press, due apparently to a false, unfounded, and deplorable race
prejudice, has attacked unmercifully the Italian people of the United
States and, more especially, the Italians coming from Sicily, merely
because some individuals perpetrate a crime.

Crime has no nationality! Crimes have been committed and will
continue to be committed daily, by the score, by the lawless of other
nationalities—Irish, Jews, Germans, Greeks, Americans—and the
newspapers, unless it be an exceptionally sensational case, are contented to report it as a simple news item.

From *Chicago Foreign Language Press Survey*, WPA Project, 1942.

When the crime however, is committed by an Italian, the papers printed in English give it the greatest amount of publicity, using for the purpose, front page space and large headlines, making uncomplimentary remarks that are insulting to the whole Italian race. We do not intend, in the least, to defend those who have killed. The law must take its course and whether or not justice is done, is a matter that concerns the administrators of the law. We only ask that the editors of the Chicago newspapers accord the Italian people fair play; to refrain from attacking them in a group for the misdeeds of the few; to limit themselves to the cases as they happen without drawing into the vortex of crime, indiscriminately—men and institutions of the highest proven honor and integrity. Journalism must educate and not be prejudiced. The so-called "scoops" brought in by some quixotic reporter should be analyzed before being pub lished; reporters should be instructed to bring in straight and correct information and not rubbish, for publication.

The Italians are honest, sober, enterprising, and working people. They love their families, and know how to save and sacrifice, that their children may have a good education. They are law abiding and assimilate as easily as the mythical Nordic. If among them there are some who do not respect the law, it is perhaps because those who should see that the law is enforced, ensconce them.

To have connected the Italo-American National Union, for mutual benefit, with a regrettable affair that happened in this city recently, simply because those implicated happened to be Sicilians, is absurd, unjust and harmful to an institution, that for the past thirty years has carried on a sincere work of Americanization, moral and economic upbuilding.

Imaginary shootings, fabricated by unscrupulous policemen are attributed to Italians. Whenever the perpetrator of some wicked deed makes his escape, the statement in the paper is usually to the effect that, "The assassin is supposed to be an Italian;" as though nobody else is capable of committing a crime and escaping.

By reading some of the Chicago papers the average person might be led to believe that all the crimes committed in this metropolis are perpetrated by Italians and especially by Sicilians; moreover, that the Sicilians are not Italians, because the Straits of Messina separate them from the mainland.

It is a historic and undeniable fact, however, that twice in the history of Italy, Sicily has been the keystone in the completion of Italian unity, aside from having produced some of the best Italian statesmen. A reference to a history of Sicily by Mommsen, and later to one by Prof. A. Pais, might convince the unacquainted what a mighty and important part of the Italian nation's history Sicily has been.

All this; all the good qualities of the Italians, however, do not seem to avail us. In the eyes of some people we are the newest immigrants here and, therefore the line of least resistance. It is up to all decent Italians and to the members of our organization then, to carry on the good work and to spread the tenets of our organization so that the people of this, our adopted nation, learn to appreciate the value of the good Italians and that they are here to stay and make good Americans.

AL CAPONE:
PUBLIC BENEFACTOR

[Since the passing
of the more colorful outlaws of the Wild West, America has had no
more flamboyant criminal than the late Al Capone. Brought to
Chicago from Brooklyn by Johnny Torrio in 1920, Capone quickly
rose in the ranks and became not only the power broker of Chicago
crime, but also virtually the unofficial mayor of Chicago. (It was
Capone who, on one election eve, said, "Vote early and vote often.")
With city, county, and state officials in his pocket, Capone organized
a criminal syndicate in Cook County which has endured to the
present. Unlike most "bosses," he was not afraid of either the public
or the press. In fact, to many Chicagoans, he was a celebrity to be
emulated, a friend of the rich and famous. The interview which
comprises the first selection below was given to the press on Sunday, December 5, 1927, the evening before Capone was to depart
for Florida. His departure was the result of "heat" from the police
department, at the behest of Mayor William Hale ("Big Bill")
Thompson, who had hopes of obtaining the 1928 Republican presidential nomination. Thompson wanted to refurbish his badly tarn-
ished public image by getting Capone out of the way. As it happened,
Capone did not go to Florida, but to Los Angeles, whence he was
unceremoniously returned to Chicago by the police. The second selection is a summary of Capone's first ten years in Chicago by
journalist Frederick Lewis Allen.]

From: 1. *The Chicago Tribune*, December 6, 1927.
2. *Only Yesterday* (New York, 1931), pp. 245–69.

PUBLIC SERVICE IS MY MOTTO
Al Capone

Al Capone, also known as Al Brown, the chief among Chicago's providers of the forbidden vices—wine, revelry, and games of chance—announced last night from his headquarters at the Metropole Hotel that he is going to leave the city high and dry.

"I'm leaving for St. Petersburg, Florida, tomorrow," Capone said. "Let the worthy citizens of Chicago get their liquor the best they can. I'm sick of the job—it's a thankless one and full of grief. I don't know when I'll get back, if ever. But it won't be until after the holidays, anyway. . . ."

As he gently pursued his muse, Capone rather gently reproached the police who had accused him of being one of the principals of a syndicate which has been reaping profits of $75,000,000 annually in exploiting vice in Chicago.

"I've been spending the best years of my life as a public benefactor," he said. "I've given people the light pleasures, shown them a good time. And all I get is abuse—the existence of a hunted man— I'm called a killer.

"Well, tell the folks I'm going away now. I guess murder will stop. There won't be any more booze. You won't be able to find a crap game, even, let alone a roulette wheel or a faro game. I guess Mike Hughes (Chicago's police chief) won't need his 3000 extra cops, after all.

"Public service is my motto. Ninety-nine per cent of the people in Chicago drink and gamble. I've tried to serve them decent liquor and square games. But I'm not appreciated. It's no use."

Why should he want to go to Florida, land of the rum runners, Capone was asked.

"I've got some property in St. Petersburg I want to sell," he said. It's warm there, but not too warm.

"Say, the coppers won't have to lay all the gang murders on me now. Maybe they'll find a new hero for the headlines. It would be a shame, wouldn't it, if while I was away they would forget about me and find a new gangland chief?

"I wish all my friends and enemies a Merry Christmas and a Happy New Year. That's all they'll get from me this year. I hope I don't spoil anybody's Christmas by not sticking around. . . .

"My wife and mother hear so much about what a terrible criminal I am, it's getting too much for them, and I'm just sick of it all myself.

"The other day a man came in here and said that he had to have $3000. If I gave it to him, he said, he would make me the beneficiary in a $15,000 insurance policy he'd take out and then kill himself. I had to have him pushed out.

"Today I got a letter from a woman in England. Even over there I'm known as a gorilla. She offered to pay my passage to London if I'd kill some neighbors she's been having a quarrel with.

"The papers have made me out a millionaire, and hardly an hour goes by that somebody doesn't want me to invest in some scheme or stake somebody in business.

"That's what I've got to put up with just because I give the public what the public wants. I never had to send out high pressure salesmen. Why I could never meet the demand.

"I violate the prohibition law, sure. Who doesn't? The only difference is I take more chances than the man who drinks a cocktail before dinner and a flock of highballs after it. But he's just as much a violator as I am.

"There's one thing worse than a crook and that's a crooked man in a big political job. [A reference to Mayor Thompson?] A man who pretends he's enforcing the law and is really making dough out of somebody breaking it—a self-respecting hoodlum doesn't have any use for that kind of fellow—he buys them like he'd buy any other article necessary to his trade, but he hates them in his heart."

Pridefully the gangster declared he never was convicted of a crime in his life. He has no "record," as the police put it.

"I never stuck up a man in my life," he added. "Neither did any of my agents ever rob or burglarize any homes while they were working for me. They might have pulled plenty of jobs before they came with me or after they left me; but not while they were in my outfit."

Then Capone warmly endorsed Cicero, that village on the southwest of Chicago which has been pictured for years as the cradle of the country's vice. There for a long time Capone and Johnny Torrio, his patron who broke him into the game, made a headquarters from which to direct their vice and booze and gambling traffic.

"Cicero is a city of 75,000 people and the cleanest burg in the USA," declared Capone forcefully. "There's only one gambling house in the whole town, and not a single so-called vice-den."

ALCOHOL AND AL CAPONE
Frederick Lewis Allen

In 1920, when prohibition was very young, Johnny Torrio of Chicago had an inspiration. Torrio was a formidable figure in the Chicago underworld. He had discovered that there was big money in the newly outlawed liquor business. He was fired with the hope of getting control of the dispensation of booze to the whole city of Chicago. At the moment there was a great deal too much competition; but possibly a well-disciplined gang of men handy with their fists and their guns could take care of that, by intimidating rival bootleggers and persuading speakeasy proprietors that life might not be wholly comfortable for them unless they bought Torrio liquor. What Torrio needed was a lieutenant who could mobilize and lead his shock troops.

Being a graduate of the notorious Five Points gang in New York and a disciple of such genial fellows as Lefty Louie and Gyp the Blood (he himself had been questioned about the murder of Herman Rosenthal in the famous Becker case in 1912), he naturally turned to his alma mater for his man. He picked for the job a bullet-headed twenty-three-year-old Neapolitan roughneck of the Five Points gang, and offered him a generous income and half the profits of the bootleg trade if he would come to Chicago and take care of the competition. The young hoodlum came, established himself at Torrio's gambling place, the Four Deuces, opened by way of plausible stage setting an innocent-looking office which contained among its properties a family Bible, and had a set of business cards printed:

ALPHONSE CAPONE
Second Hand Furniture Dealer
2220 South Wabash Avenue

Torrio had guessed right—in fact, he had guessed right three times. The profits of bootlegging in Chicago proved to be prodigious, allowing an ample margin for the mollification of the forces of the law. The competition proved to be exacting: every now and then Torrio would discover that his rivals had approached a speakeasy proprietor with the suggestion that he buy their beer instead of the Torrio-Capone brand, and on receipt of an unfavorable answer had beaten the proprietor senseless and smashed up his place of business. But Al Capone had been an excellent choice as leader of the Torrio offensives; Capone was learning how to deal with such emergencies.

Within three years it was said that the boy from the Five Points had 700 men at his disposal, many of them adept in the use of the sawed-off shotgun and the Thompson submachine gun. As the profits from beer and "alky-cooking" (illicit distilling) rolled in, young Capone acquired more finesse—particularly finesse in the management of politics and politicians. By the middle of the decade he had gained complete control of the suburb of Cicero, had installed his own mayor in office, had posted his agents in the wide-open gambling-resorts and in each of the 161 bars, and had established his personal headquarters in the Hawthorne Hotel. He was taking in millions now. Torrio was fading into the background; Capone was becoming the Big Shot. But his conquest of power did not come without bloodshed. As the rival gangs—the O'Banions, the Gennas, the Aiellos—disputed his growing domination, Chicago was afflicted with such an epidemic of killings as no civilized modern city had ever before seen, and a new technic of wholesale murder was developed.

One of the standard methods of disposing of a rival in this warfare of the gangs was to pursue his car with a stolen automobile full of men armed with sawed-off shotguns and submachine guns; to draw up beside it, forcing it to the curb, open fire upon it—and then disappear into the traffic, later abandoning the stolen car at a safe distance. Another favorite method was to take the victim "for a ride": in other words, to lure him into a supposedly friendly car, shoot him at leisure, drive to some distant and deserted part of the city, and quietly throw his body overboard. Still another was to lease an apartment or a room overlooking his front door, station a couple of hired assassins at the window, and as the victim emerged from the house some sunny afternoon, to spray him with a few dozen machine-gun bullets from behind drawn curtains. But there were also more ingenious and refined methods of slaughter.

Take, for example, the killing of Dion O'Banion, leader of the gang which for a time most seriously menaced Capone's reign in Chicago. The preparation of this particular murder was reminiscent of the kiss of Judas. O'Banion was a bootlegger and a gangster by night, but a florist by day: a strange and complex character, a connoisseur of orchids and of manslaughter. One morning a sedan drew up outside his flower shop and three men got out, leaving the fourth at the wheel. The three men had apparently taken good care to win O'Banion's trust, for although he always carried three guns, now for the moment he was off his guard as he advanced among the flowers to meet his visitors. The middle man of the three cordially shook hands with O'Banion—*and then held on* while his two companions put six bullets into the gangster-florist. The three conspirators walked out, climbed into the sedan, and departed. They were never brought to justice, and it is not recorded that any of them hung themselves to trees in remorse. O'Banion had a first-class funeral, gangster style: a ten-thousand dollar casket, twenty-six truckloads of flowers, and among them a basket of flowers which bore the touching inscription, "From Al."

In 1926 the O'Banions, still unrepentant despite the loss of their leader, introduced another novelty in gang warfare. In broad daylight, while the streets of Cicero were alive with traffic, they raked Al Capone's headquarters with machine-gun fire from eight touring cars. The cars proceeded down the crowded street outside the Hawthorne Hotel in solemn line, the first one firing blank cartridges to disperse the innocent citizenry and to draw the Capone forces to the doors and windows, while from the succeeding cars, which followed a block behind, flowed a steady rattle of bullets, spraying the hotel and the adjoining buildings up and down. One gunman even got out of his car, knelt carefully upon the sidewalk at the door of the Hawthorne, and played one hundred bullets into the lobby—back and forth, as one might play the hose upon one's garden. The casualties were miraculously light, and Scarface Al himself remained in safety, flat on the floor of the Hotel Hawthorne restaurant; nevertheless, the bombardment quite naturally attracted public attention. Even in a day when bullion was transported in armored cars, the transformation of a suburban street into a shooting gallery seemed a little unorthodox.

The war continued, one gangster after another crumpling under a rain of bullets; not until St. Valentine's Day of 1929 did it reach its climax in a massacre which outdid all that had preceded it in ingenuity and brutality. At half-past ten on the morning of February 14, 1929, seven of the O'Banions were sitting in the garage which went by the name of the S. M. C. Cartage Company, on North Clark Street, waiting for a promised consignment of hijacked liquor. A Cadillac touring car slid to the curb, and three men dressed as policemen got out, followed by two others in civilian dress. The three supposed policemen entered the garage alone, disarmed the seven O'Banions, and told them to stand in a row against the wall. The victims readily submitted; they were used to police raids and thought nothing of them; they would get off easily enough, they expected. But thereupon the two men in civilian clothes emerged from the corridor and calmly mowed all seven O'Banions with submachine gunfire as they stood with hands upraised against the wall.

The little drama was completed when the three supposed policemen solemnly marched the two plainclothes killers across the sidewalk to the waiting car, and all five got in and drove off—having given to those in the wintry street a perfect tableau of an arrest satisfactorily made by the forces of the law!

These killings—together with that of "Jake" Lingle, who led a double life as a reporter for the *Chicago Tribune* and as associate of gangsters, and who was shot to death in a crowded subway leading to the Illinois Central suburban railway station in 1930—were perhaps the most spectacular of the decade in Chicago. But there were over 500 gang murders in all. Few of the murderers were apprehended; careful planning, money, influence, the intimidation of witnesses, and the refusal of any gangster to testify against any other, no matter how treacherous the murder, met that danger. The city of Chicago was giving the whole country, and indeed the whole world, an astonishing object lesson in violent and unpunished crime. How and why could such a thing happen?

To say that prohibition—or, if you prefer, the refusal of the public to abide by prohibition—caused the rise of the gangs to lawless power would be altogether too easy an explanation. There were other causes: the automobile, which made escape easy, as the officers of robbed banks had discovered; the adaptation to peacetime use of a new arsenal of handy and deadly weapons; the murderous traditions of the Mafia, imported by Sicilian gangsters; the inclination of a wet community to wink at the by-products of a trade which provided them with beer and gin; the sheer size and unwieldiness of the modern metropolitan community, which prevented the focussing of public opinion upon any depredation which did not immediately concern the average individual citizen; and, of course, the easy-going political apathy of the times. But the immediate occasion of the rise of gangs was undoubtedly prohibition—or, to be more precise, beer-running. (Beer rather than whiskey on account of its bulk; to carry on a profitable trade in beer one must transport it in trucks, and trucks are so difficult to disguise that the traffic must be protected by bribery of the prohibition staff and the police and by gunfire against bandits.)

There was vast profit in the manufacture, transportation, and sale of beer. In 1927, according to Fred D. Pasley, Al Capone's biographer, federal agents estimated that the Capone gang controlled the sources of a revenue from booze of something like $60 million a year, and much of this—perhaps most of it—came from beer. Fill a man's pockets with money, give him a chance at a huge profit, put him into illegal business and thus deny him recourse to the law if he is attacked, and you have made it easy for him to bribe and shoot. There have always been gangs and gangsters in American life and doubtless always will be; there has always been corruption of city officials and doubtless always will be; yet it is ironically true, nonetheless, that the outburst of corruption and crime in Chicago in the nineteen-twenties was immediately occasioned by the attempt to banish the temptations of liquor from the American home.

The young thug from the Five Points, New York, had traveled fast and far since 1920. By the end of the decade he had become as widely renowned as Charles Evans Hughes or Gene Tunney. He had become an American portent. Not only did he largely control the sale of liquor to Chicago's 10,000 speakeasies; he controlled the sources of supply, it was said, as far as Canada and the Florida coast. He had amassed, and concealed, a fortune the extent of which nobody knew; it was said by federal agents to amount to $20 million. He was arrested and imprisoned once in Philadelphia for carrying a gun, but otherwise he seemed above the law. He rode about Chicago in an armored car, a traveling fortress, with another car to patrol the way ahead and a third car full of his armed henchmen following behind; he went to the theater attended by a bodyguard of eighteen young men in dinner coats, with guns doubtless slung under their left armpits in approved gangster fashion; when his sister was married, thousands milled about the church in the snow, and he presented the bride with a nine-foot wedding cake and a special honeymoon car; he had a fine estate at Miami where he sometimes entertained seventy-five guests at a time; and high politicians—and even, it has been said, judges—took orders from him over the telephone from his headquarters in a downtown Chicago hotel. And still he was only thirty-two years old. What was Napoleon doing at thirty-two?

Meanwhile gang rule and gang violence were quickly penetrating other American cities. Toledo had felt them, and Detroit, and New York, and many another. Chicago was not alone. Chicago had merely led the way.

THE CASTELLAMARESE WAR
OF 1930–31

[The Prohibition years saw so much gangland violence that only in later decades was it possible to perceive what actually happened in the Castellamarese War of 1930–31. Originating as a struggle between the "families" of Joseph Masseria and Salvatore Maranzano, it eventuated in a transition of power from one generation to another. The old "mafia-type" leaders were killed or removed from power, and a younger generation of criminals emerged, more intent on operating in the wider scene of American business and political realities. These new leaders were such men as Charles "Lucky" Luciano, Vito Genovese, Joe Bonanno, and Carlo Gambino. Accounts of the "war" are necessarily second-hand reconstructions from a later period. The following somewhat sketchy narrative has been extracted from the voluminous 1963 testimony of Joseph Valachi before a subcommittee of the U.S. Senate. A fuller account has been pieced together by Peter Maas in his book, *The Valachi Papers* (1968). Other witnesses mentioned in the selection are La Vern J. Duffy, a staff member of the subcommittee, and Sergeant Ralph Salerno of the New York Police Department. Chairman of the committee is Senator John L. McClellan.]

The CHAIRMAN. Mr. Duffy, you are a member of the staff of this subcommittee?

Mr. DUFFY. Yes, sir.

The CHAIRMAN. You have been a member of the staff of this committee for how many years?

Mr. DUFFY. Since 1953, sir.

From U.S., Congress, Senate, Permanent Subcommittee on Investigations of the Committee on Government Operations, 88th Cong., 1st sess., 1963, Part 1, pp. 161–233.

The CHAIRMAN. Have you actively participated in the investigation and preparation for the investigation of these hearings that are now underway?

Mr. DUFFY. Yes, sir; I have.

The CHAIRMAN. In the course of that preparation, have you had frequent discussions with the witness, Valachi?

Mr. DUFFY. I have had a number of discussions with him.

The CHAIRMAN. And with others?

Mr. DUFFY. And with others.

The CHAIRMAN. From that discussion, and from other information you have gained, have you prepared certain charts depicting the organization as we speak of it, the different organizations, showing those in power, those in authority, and so forth, with respect to these organizations that we have been talking about?

Mr. DUFFY. With respect to the New York organization only at this time, sir.

The CHAIRMAN. Well, with respect to the New York organization. Very well.

You have a chart before you now; do you?

Mr. DUFFY. I have, Senator.

The CHAIRMAN. What is the title you have placed on it for the purpose of identification?

Mr. DUFFY. The title of this chart is the "Masseria-Maranzano War and Evolution of Gang Control, 1930 to Present."

The CHAIRMAN. The witness has just testified up to incidents and things that occurred prior thereto, his operation prior to the time that this war began?

Mr. DUFFY. That is correct, Senator.

The CHAIRMAN. He called it the war?

Mr. DUFFY. The Castellamarese war. That is another name for the war that took place during 1930, 1931.

The CHAIRMAN. By either name, then, we will know we are talking about the same war?

Mr. DUFFY. The same ganglands war.

The CHAIRMAN. Now you may proceed to describe the chart. I will make this chart—I think it can go in the record all right but I will make it exhibit No. 8 and direct that it be printed in the record if that can be done.

Mr. DUFFY. I will direct your attention, first, to the bottom of the chart. Reading from left to right we have five bosses listed: Vito Genovese, Carlo Gambino, Giuseppe Magliocco, Joseph Bonanno, and Gaetano Lucchese.

The CHAIRMAN. Are they the bosses of the five families operating in the New York area?

Mr. DUFFY. They are.

The CHAIRMAN. Those are all living and the present bosses of those families, is that correct?

Mr. DUFFY. That is correct.

The CHAIRMAN. May I ask you, Mr. Valachi, if you agree that that is correct, according to your knowledge—

Mr. VALACHI. Yes, sir.

The CHAIRMAN. According to your knowledge, that is correct?

Mr. VALACHI. Yes, Senator.

Senator MUNDT. Is Vito Genovese the only one of the five now in the penitentiary?

Mr. DUFFY. That is correct. As indicated by the chart, the gang is now being run by the three men as indicated on the lower left-hand corner, Thomas Eboli, acting boss; Jerry Catena, under-boss; Consigliere Michele Miranda.

The CHAIRMAN. Is that correct, according to your information?

Mr. VALACHI. Yes.

The CHAIRMAN. You know much of this from your conversation with Genovese while you were in prison with him?

Mr. VALACHI. I know it from conversation; I knew it myself.

The CHAIRMAN. You knew it before you went in there?

Mr. VALACHI. Yes, sir.

Mr. DUFFY. I would like to direct your attention upward on the chart tracing the history of these five families.

You can see it evolved directly from a gangland war that took place during the years 1930 and 1931. Now there were two main gangs fighting this war, the Joseph Masseria group made up of a number of gangs. We do not have them all listed here, but there was Ciro Terranova, Dutch Schultz, a number of others, such as Vito Genovese, Al Capone. They are all on the side of Joseph Masseria during the gangland war.

On the Salvatore Maranzano side, we had Salvatore Maranzano, head of the gang; Tom Gagliano, boss of this gang subsequent to Tom Reina being killed.

Now there were two significant dates, Mr. Chairman, on this chart when this war began.

The CHAIRMAN. The war began about what year?

Mr. DUFFY. 1930, Senator. The first significant date on the chart is the death of Tom Reina. He was the boss of this gang. He was murdered on February 26, 1930.

He was murdered, Senator, by a member of the Masseria group over here.

Now, Tom Gagliano wanted revenge for this murder, Senator.

The CHAIRMAN. I did not understand you.

Mr. DUFFY. Tom Gagliano, the underboss of this family, wanted to avenge the death of Reina, who was unjustly murdered. . . .

Mr. DUFFY. Will you tell us now what you learned from Mr. Profaci as to the details of this gangland war, that the Maranzano force had joined up with Reina and the reason for that?

Mr. VALACHI. At the time that the Gagliano group had intentions of going into war, not knowing there was someone else who had the same intentions.

The CHAIRMAN. So that other gang had the same intention that your gang did about going to war with Masseria?

Mr. VALACHI. Right.

The reason why Joseph Profaci explained to me when I did meet him. All the Castellamarese were sentenced to death.

Mr. ADLERMAN. Will you explain what the Castellemarese are?

Mr. VALACHI. I can explain in Italian.

Mr. ADLERMAN. Is it a hamlet or a little town in Sicily?

Mr. VALACHI. In Sicily.

Mr. ADLERMAN. Did Masseria declare or condemn anybody who came from that area, no matter where they were in the United States, to death?

Mr. VALACHI. All Castellamarese. That is the way I was told. I never found out the reason. I never asked for the reason. All I understand is that all the Castellamarese were sentenced to death.

Mr. ADLERMAN. Can you name some of the Castellemarese in New York?

Mr. VALACHI. That I knew. Joseph Profaci, Joe Bonanno. . . .

Mr. ADLERMAN. Did the Gagliano group know at that time that Maranzano was also trying to fight Masseria?

Mr. VALACHI. The way they explained it to me was that somebody got killed. The Gagliano group knew that they didn't do it. In this case they sent somebody else going out for those guys. In other words, somebody else is in trouble with these guys. So I understand that Steve Rinelli, which was one of the groups of Gagliano's, found out that it was Salvatore Maranzano. The other one that was going out warring against Masseria.

Mr. ADLERMAN. At that point, when they found out that Maranzano had killed Morello and I think shortly after that Pinzolo was killed by Gagliano's men, the two of them joined forces against Masseria?

Mr. VALACHI. Yes. I understand that they had given one another a contract. In other words, in order to trust one another and to feel secure with the new friendship, they gave one name, I wouldn't know the name, one gave one name, the other one gave another name.

When these two names are taken care of, then we join together.

Mr. ADLERMAN. Which two names did they pick?

Mr. VALACHI. I don't know. I never did know.

Mr. ADLERMAN. Did they finally join forces?

Mr. VALACHI. They joined forces.

Mr. ADLERMAN. In the Peter Morello killing, who did that?

Mr. VALACHI. Buster.

Mr. ADLERMAN. Buster of Chicago?

Mr. VALACHI. Buster of Chicago. He originally came from Chicago.

Mr. ADLERMAN. Do you know who he was or where he came from?

Mr. VALACHI. Buster was, the way I understand, he was in trouble in Chicago, himself, fighting a mob like an organization like Cosa Nostra, but Buster didn't know what he was fighting. I understood, I wasn't clear on it, but I tried, I knew who killed his father, something like that.

Mr. ADLERMAN. Was he on the outs with Capone?

Mr. VALACHI. He was fighting him.

Mr. ADLERMAN. He had to leave Chicago because he was fighting him?

Mr. VALACHI. No, after Maranzano, when he was, like after the Castellemarese was sentenced, Maranzano somehow got Buster to join in.

Mr. ADLERMAN. Could you describe Buster to us, what type of man he was?

Mr. VALACHI. Buster looked like a college boy, a little over 6 feet, light complexion, weighed about 200 pounds. He also would carry a violin case.

Mr. ADLERMAN. What did he carry in the violin case?

Mr. VALACHI. A machinegun.

Mr. ADLERMAN. He was quite different from the fellow you were working with at that time?

Mr. VALACHI. Yes. He looked collegiatelike.

The CHAIRMAN. He did not look like a hood?

Mr. VALACHI. No.

The CHAIRMAN. All right.

Mr. VALACHI. He was only about 23 years old.

Mr. ADLERMAN. Coming now to the Pinzolo case, who was the killer there?

Mr. VALACHI. Bobby Doyle. That was the Gagliano group.

Mr. ADLERMAN. That killing took place according to the police records on September 9, 1930. Would that be about right, according to your memory?

Mr. VALACHI. Dates I didn't know but that sounds about right.

Mr. ADLERMAN. Mr. Duffy, do you want to take it up from there?

Mr. DUFFY. As I was saying, they came over here to keep this apartment under surveillance. At this time he learned of this secret pact between Maranzano and Gagliano. They were going to join together after two bosses of the Masseria were killed.

Now, Masseria had condemned to death all the Castellamarese Sicilians. All the Castellamarese in the United States wanted to join up with him to save their lives.

This became a nationwide war after these two men were killed. . . .

The CHAIRMAN. When did Masseria try to get peace?

Mr. VALACHI. Now you had to wait until they get Joe Masseria.

The CHAIRMAN. Another one killed?

Mr. VALACHI. You see, we got it that there was an understanding that his own guys are going to set him up.

The CHAIRMAN. I understand, but did he try to make peace?

Mr. VALACHI. Yes.

The CHAIRMAN. Masseria tried to make peace after these two killings?

Mr. VALACHI. I am sorry, I misunderstood the question.

Yes, he offered himself to be a plain soldier. He will give up anything he had if they leave him alone. Maranzano refused.

The CHAIRMAN. What had the situation developed into at that time? How many people did Masseria have that were fighting for him and how many had come over and were fighting for Maranzano?

Mr. VALACHI. I think Maranzano by this time had about 600, Senator. They were coming over.

The CHAIRMAN. That is because they had all joined forces, what was the name of them—they had come into that group?

Mr. VALACHI. Castellamarese?

The CHAIRMAN. Yes.

Mr. VALACHI. They were coming in, more and more.

The CHAIRMAN. How many did Masseria have left that were fighting for him or apparently loyal to him?

Mr. VALACHI. How many did Masseria have?

The CHAIRMAN. Yes.

Mr. VALACHI. Masseria, in the beginning, had his old brigade in the beginning, his whole family.

The CHAIRMAN. I am talking about this time when he is asking for peace.

Mr. VALACHI. He didn't have much then. He didn't have much then.

The CHAIRMAN. He had lost a lot of his following?

Mr. VALACHI. That's right, yes.

The CHAIRMAN. How many? You made some estimate a day or two ago. Do you remember what you gave us?

Mr. VALACHI. Are you referring to how many friends did he have?

The CHAIRMAN. Yes.

Mr. VALACHI. Well, he had Charley, he had Vito, he had not too many. He had about five or six, Senator.

The CHAIRMAN. That were real close to him?

Mr. VALACHI. Right.

The CHAIRMAN. That was Genovese?

Mr. VALACHI. Genovese.

The CHAIRMAN. Who is now your family boss?

Mr. VALACHI. Right.

The CHAIRMAN. Lucky Luciano?

Mr. VALACHI. Right. Joe Strasse or Joe Stretch.

The CHAIRMAN. Joe Stretch, we will call him that.

Mr. VALACHI. Ciro Terranova.

The CHAIRMAN. Very well. Then what happened?

Mr. VALACHI. They finally, after Joe Baker, sometime after Joe Baker, finally got him to come out at Coney Island, in a restaurant.

The CHAIRMAN. I know. But who did it? Did they arrange with Masseria's own men to set him up?

Mr. VALACHI. Yes.

The CHAIRMAN. Who of his own men set him up for the killing?

Mr. VALACHI. Charley, Lucky, and Vito.

The CHAIRMAN. Vito Genovese and Lucky Luciano?

Mr. VALACHI. Yes.

The CHAIRMAN. Those are the two that set up Masseria for his death meal, is that right?

Mr. VALACHI. Right, with the pretense that they were going to get Maranzano.

The CHAIRMAN. They doublecrossed their own boss?

Mr. VALACHI. Right.

The CHAIRMAN. And set him up to be killed?

Mr. VALACHI. The only way they got him out, they pretended that they had Maranzano. In other words, they sent word to him that they were going to get Maranzano, they were going to sit down and talk about it. . . .

The CHAIRMAN. How many were killed during this 14-month period of undeclared war and what you termed "declared war"? Do you know how many people were killed altogether during that time on either side or both sides?

Mr. VALACHI. Senator, I got the score. The score was, we lost 1 and they lost from 40 to 60.

The CHAIRMAN. From 40 to 60?

Mr. VALACHI. Yes.

The CHAIRMAN. From 40 to 60 people killed as a result of this undeclared war and the declared war that followed after the 2 men were killed who identified your group as the killers? Is that correct?

Mr. VALACHI. That is correct. . . .

The CHAIRMAN. Now, what happened after Masseria's death with respect to peace? You said you had peace after that.

Mr. VALACHI. Yes; we had peace after that, Senator.

The CHAIRMAN. Who became the boss?

Mr. VALACHI. I will explain it to you.

I went on a meeting. I just remember it was around Washington Avenue in the Bronx. I just was notified, I don't remember how, but I was notified. I got to this address and it was a hall, a big hall, on Washington Avenue. There was about 400 to 500 people in this hall.

After I was there a while, Maranzano was standing on the platform when he got up to speak. He didn't speak just as soon as I got in there. Naturally, he was hanging around the hall until he was ready to speak. Members were coming. When he did get to speak, then he got up there and he started to explain about Masseria and his groups, that they were killing people without just.

He mentioned some names, names that I didn't know or never even heard of. He mentioned they had killed Don Antonio without just. They killed another name he mentioned which is on the top on the right, Senator, Reina. I didn't know any of these men.

Then he was explaining how the Masseria group was doing these things. "Now, it is going to be different," he said. "We are going to have—first we have the boss of all bosses, which is myself."

The CHAIRMAN. That is Maranzano, now?

Mr. VALACHI. Maranzano is talking. Then we have the boss and then we have an underboss under the boss. Then we have the caporegima. He was explaining all this. Now, if a soldier wants to talk to a boss, he should not take the privilege for him to try to go direct to the boss. He must speak first to the caporegima, and the caporegima, if it is required and it is important enough, the caporegima will make an appointment for the soldier. He went out and explained the rules. . . .

The CHAIRMAN. Now, there was occasion for a banquet. When was the banquet held along about this time?

Mr. VALACHI. The banquet came, say, about maybe a month after peace.

The CHAIRMAN. About a month after the peace?

Mr. VALACHI. About a month after the peace.

The CHAIRMAN. Which came first; this meeting, or the banquet?

Mr. VALACHI. This meeting came first.

The CHAIRMAN. The meeting came first?

Mr. VALACHI. Yes. This meeting came, the first meeting came about a week or two after the peace and the banquet followed right after this meeting.

The CHAIRMAN. How long did the banquet meeting last?

Mr. VALACHI. The banquet lasted—it was a 5-day banquet, Senator. In other words, I don't mean that it ran continuously for 5 days. For instance, you come in early in the evening and close at 3 or 4 or 5 in the morning. Then reopen again the next day.

The CHAIRMAN. For 5 nights you had a banquet?

Mr. VALACHI. Right.

The CHAIRMAN. What occurred with respect to that banquet? What was the purpose of it primarily?

Mr. VALACHI. Well, the purpose was, the money was supposed to be meant for the original soldiers and for himself. The originals, I mean, which was about 15, there were 12. Now, there was 3 of us there, it makes the 15.

It was supposed to be to give these boys a chance, being they were away, now they are broke, and for himself. This was the purpose. And so he would be recognized as the boss and, naturally, they went to a lot of expense. They understand. That was the reason for the banquet. . . .

Senator MUNDT. Looking back at it now, do you think he stole the money, he kept it to himself?

Mr. VALACHI. As I am telling the story, we talked about this money at his house. When I get to that part I will tell you about it.

The CHAIRMAN. Very well.

Mr. VALACHI. It wasn't long after that, Senator, after all, it was so many years ago, Senator—I don't remember how long, when I was down at the office. He told me that I should be at his house at Avenue J. I don't remember whether it was that night or the night after, I don't remember. I was at his house about 9 o'clock either that day or the day after.

When I got to his house, he was bandaging his son's foot, I remember.

I walked in. He greeted me. I waited until he got through with his son.

He said to me, "You know"—now, Senator, I'm telling you.

"You know why I didn't give you any money? You must have been wondering."

I said, "Yes."

He was referring to the banquet.

"I didn't want to lose you. I didn't want you to get loose. But don't worry about the money." He said, "We have to go to the mattress again."

The "mattress" means we have to go back to war, that is what it means.

Senator MUSKIE. Was he trying to suggest that he would need the money for the new war?

Mr. VALACHI. I'll talk about it, Senator. It was in that line, too.

Naturally, I wasn't too happy to hear that. So he told me that we can't get along. He meant he can't get along with Charley Lucky, Vito. He gave me a list. "We have to get rid of these people."

The CHAIRMAN. You have to get rid of them?

Mr. VALACHI. Got to get rid of them. On the list was, I will try to remember as I go along: Al Capone, Frank Costello, Charley Lucky, Vito Genovese, Vincent Mangano, Joe Adonis, Dutch Schultz. These are all important names at the time.

The CHAIRMAN. Some 10 or 12 altogether?

Mr. VALACHI. Ten or twelve.

Now, he tells me—I forgot to tell you, Senator, there was a rumor passed up in the office a little while before, say a week, a few days before—as I am talking now I remember that—not to come up in the office with any guns, nobody come up there with any guns because they expect the police up there.

I got to talking with some of the members and I said I didn't like that order. So he said, this other fellow, whoever it may have been, said, "What do you mean?"

I said, "I don't know. I'm afraid that they are trying to prepare us to be without any guns. I just don't like it." That is the way I talked.

We let it go that way.

Now, when he told me about the mattress, and he told me that he was going to have the last meeting at 2 o'clock in the office tomorrow. . . .

The CHAIRMAN. Who was he to meet with?

Mr. VALACHI. Vito Genovese and Charley Lucky at the office on 46th Street.

The CHAIRMAN. Whose office?

Mr. VALACHI. Maranzano's office.

The CHAIRMAN. He was going to his office to meet them?

Mr. VALACHI. The next day.

The CHAIRMAN. At 2 o'clock?

Mr. VALACHI. At 2 o'clock.

The CHAIRMAN. All right, go ahead.

Mr. VALACHI. He was telling me about what we are going to do, how big we are going to be. I wasn't interested, Senator, at this time. I feel, as I say, I was away, now to back again. I wasn't too happy. I went along. He told me I should call the office at a quarter to 2.

The CHAIRMAN. Were you to be there, to meet him there at 2?

Mr. VALACHI. No, he told me to call the office at quarter to 2. That afternoon I called the office at quarter to 2 and Charley Buffalo answered the phone. He said that everything was all right. He said I need not go down.

So that day, "the Gap" came around and he decided we would go to Brooklyn. We knew a couple of girls in Brooklyn.

I said, "That is a good idea; we have nothing to do." We took a ride to Brooklyn. We were away all that day and we got back in New York about 12:30 or 1 o'clock in the morning. We landed in Charley Jones' restaurant on 14th Street and 3d Avenue. We had the girls with us. When we went in the restaurant, I noticed there was, like some guy walked in and looked us over and walked out again. Then I noticed another guy walking in and looked us over.

I looked at "The Gap" and he looked at me. I said, "I don't know."

So, Charley Jones, which is a sort of a businessman like he ran crap games and he owned dancehalls, he was in that line of business, so he moved over to me. He told me, "Go home." . . .

So, I went home. I lived about two or three blocks away from there.

About 10 or 15 minutes later, three of the boys, that I proposed and put in, were all shot up, they were not hit, they only had powder marks.

The CHAIRMAN. Powder marks?

Mr. VALACHI. Powder marks all over.

The CHAIRMAN. They did not have bullet marks?

Mr. VALACHI. Just powder marks. It is amazing, all three were missed. . . .

The CHAIRMAN. What are their names?

Mr. VALACHI. Buck Jones.

The CHAIRMAN. That was not Charley Jones, the one at the restaurant?

Mr. VALACHI. No; Buck Jones. Petey Muggins and Johnny Dee.

The CHAIRMAN. Johnny who?

Mr. VALACHI. Johnny De Bellis.

The CHAIRMAN. All right, go ahead.

Mr. VALACHI. I had the newspaper under my arm. I still can't figure it out. All of a sudden—you see, when I went in the house I was laying on the couch trying to figure out these moves. I didn't open up the newspaper.

When they came in, all of a sudden I happened to look. I see a headline, "Park Avenue Murder." I jump at it. I knew we had the office on Park Avenue. That is the first time I read about Maranzano being killed in his office that afternoon.

The CHAIRMAN. That was about what time in the morning?

Mr. VALACHI. When I found out?

The CHAIRMAN. Yes.

Mr. VALACHI. I would say it was about, by this time, it must have been 2 or better.

The CHAIRMAN. About 2 o'clock in the morning?

Mr. VALACHI. Yes.

The CHAIRMAN. Now, you had not gone to his office at 2 o'clock that afternoon before?

Mr. VALACHI. No.

The CHAIRMAN. Because you called there as you were instructed to do and Buffalo—who was it?

Mr. VALACHI. Charley Buffalo.

The CHAIRMAN. Charley Buffalo told you everything was all right and not to come.

Mr. VALACHI. Not to come.

THE CHAIRMAN. So you went off with your friend and got the girls and spent that day that way. Until you got to the restaurant, you didn't even know there was anything to be suspicious about?

Mr. VALACHI. That is right.

The CHAIRMAN. You had not heard about the killings?

Mr. VALACHI. Actually I had forgotten about the appointment after that. . . .

In the meantime, I went looking for "the Gap." Remember "the Gap" was a close friend of mine. When I got in touch with "the Gap," I took a ride and said, "Look, what will I do?" I understand Maranzano had been doing a lot of dirty work, and well anyway it looks like it is going to be no comeback.

Now, Tom Gagliano wants me to go back with him, and now Bobby tells me we may go with Vito. What should I do? I don't know what to do, and you give me advice. And he said, "Go with

Vito." I said, "Is that what you advise?" and he said, "Yes." Well, naturally, I waited a few days and I called up Bobby Doyle.

The CHAIRMAN. All right, proceed.

Mr. VALACHI. So I waited a few days and I gave him a few days' time and I called Bobby, and he said that he has made an appointment to meet Vito Genovese. He said, "You know where to get the other guys?" Well, I said, "They give me a number, and you call them. Well, anyway when is the appointment for?" And he said, "Do you want me to make it for tomorrow, and I can call up." And I said, "OK, make it for tomorrow." So he made an appointment and I met Johnny Dee, I don't know how, but I got in touch with him, and we went at a certain time to 25th Street in the Cornish Arms Hotel. Well, when I got there, I was the last one to go, Johnny and I and the other two were already there and so was Bobby; we met Vito Genovese. Well, after we got there, he was speaking to us, and he said, "I want to take you boys along with me because I want to see the respect due you come to you." In other words, we worked so hard, and now all of a sudden we lost our boss, and there would be no more respect. In other words, we have to provide our way through and he said "that is the reason why most of all I want to take you," and he went on to say the things that Maranzano had done, about the trucking, and about the alcohol. I should have told you, Senator, and I just come to a story that I remember, and I should have said something which I forgot, which I can tell you now and piece it together.

It would be all right?

The CHAIRMAN. All right.

Mr. VALACHI. When Maranzano told me about the mattress, did I say he told me not to tell Bobby Doyle anything?

The CHAIRMAN. No.

Mr. VALACHI. Well then I failed to say it. He had warned me not to tell Bobby Doyle anything. And in fact, he told me that night that I belonged to him all of the time, and that Bobby Doyle was acting lieutenant, "but don't feel that he is your lieutenant. You are personally under me. But when you speak with him, let him believe that. But if you tell Bobby Doyle what I told you tonight, you understand." And I said, "Don't worry about it, I never told Bobby Doyle anything." But after Maranzano died, I told Bobby Doyle that, but not before. He said, "Why didn't you tell me that?" And I said, "Why should I tell you and have you go back to him, and I am dead. What are you, kidding, and you are that way." So he wanted to resign as lieutenant and ship the little time that he was lieutenant, and he wanted to turn it over to me. I refused, and I said. "What am I going to do, with nothing in my pocket? Are you kidding?" And he said, "I can tell the old man" and I said, "You tell the old man I will turn it down."

That never came up, and I refused, but then Maranzano gave me a different story which I failed to remember. Now I go back to Vito

Genovese. Now when I told Bobby Doyle the story about the mattress and this and that, which I wasn't supposed to tell before, and
from the way Vito talked, it looked as though that Bobby already
told him, because he was speaking, he goes on to explain. Well,
another thing I have to tell you before that, and I am running away
with it, Senator. Bobby Doyle explained to me and I said what
happened on 46th Street, and he went out to explain to me that there
were four Jews went up there, and they posed as policemen and he
found out, and how he found out I don't know, but he is telling me
the story and they posed as policemen, and I said, "Remember the
time they passed someone up there?" And he said, "Yes, and remember I was suspicious," and he said, "Yes." Well, they brought
Maranzano in the other room, while the other two stood with the
crowd, and there was quite a crowd, and there was quite a crowd
up there. They talked business, and in other words, they posed as
policemen and showed them a badge and they wanted to talk
business with him, and so he agreed. But when they got in the other
room, Maranzano seemed to have gotten wise, and then they
were only to kill him and not to shoot him, and Maranzano went
for a pistol, and he had a pistol, and they were forced to use a
shot on him before they cut his throat. (So I was running away
with it, and now I corrected it.)

The CHAIRMAN. Now, you said some Jews killed him, is that right?

Mr. VALACHI. The Jews, yes.

The CHAIRMAN. Who were dressed as policemen?

Mr. VALACHI. They had dressed as policemen, and they posed as
policemen.

The CHAIRMAN. Were they members of Cosa Nostra?

Mr. VALACHI. No.

The CHAIRMAN. How did they get into the picture?

Mr. VALACHI. Well, they were very close with Charley and Vito
at that time, and that is an allegiance group. Vito and Charley
"Lucky," they were close to them.

The CHAIRMAN. Did you get any information they were employed
to commit this murder?

Mr. VALACHI. Well, Senator, they seem to work together at times.
You see they had trouble of their own later on, which I will explain,
and Vito and Charley helped them when they had trouble among
themselves. You see I am talking about Meyer Lansky.

The CHAIRMAN. Kind of like swapping work. They would do
something for one crowd and the other crowd then would help
them out.

Mr. VALACHI. I go into that later.

The CHAIRMAN. Was it those people who were posing as policemen, that actually did the killing?

Mr. VALACHI. Yes, sir. . . .

The CHAIRMAN. They pretended or they posed as detectives?

Mr. VALACHI. As detectives; yes, sir. Now I go back to Vito

Genovese and I can understand what he is talking about, and he is telling us—

The CHAIRMAN. Now you are in a meeting with Genovese, in which he is asking you to come back into his organization.

Mr. VALACHI. That is right. And he is telling us why he is taking us with him, because due to respect he wants to see us, that we get which he felt now that we lost because we lost Maranzano. In other words, he figured, "By you being with us, you have prestige, and just the same."

The CHAIRMAN. This killing actually you mean that Lucchese and Genovese were taking over? Did they take over after that?

Mr. VALACHI. Charley "Lucky," and Genovese.

The CHAIRMAN. They took over, Luciano?

Mr. VALACHI. Yes, sir. Now, he said, as he is speaking, he said, "We made it by minutes."

The CHAIRMAN. "We made it by minutes." What did that mean?

Mr. VALACHI. Well, that is another thing Bobby told me. You remember I told you Maranzano had an appointment and he never told me what the appointment was about. He had Vincent Coll ready to shoot Charley "Lucky" and Vito Genovese. . . .

It came out that Maranzano had hired or got Vincent Coll—I never knew he was contacting Coll—the purpose was that they were going to kill Vito and Charley, which Vito and Charley never showed up.

CRIME AS AN AMERICAN WAY OF LIFE

Daniel Bell

[The Senate Crime Investigating Committee, under the chairmanship of Estes Kefauver, held a series of hearings in 1950–51 on crime in interstate commerce. Many of these hearings were televised, and the viewing public watched with amazement much of the testimony by individuals reputed to be in high positions in organized crime. The Third Interim Report of the Committee, published on May 1, 1951, assured the American public that "a nationwide crime syndicate does exist in the United States." Some well-informed citizens could not accept the committee's findings, however, claiming they were the result of unproved allegations. Sociologist Daniel Bell, for instance, saw the hearings as but one more in a long series of oversimplified explanations of complex social phenomena. Bell analyzed the committee report in the article from which this selection is taken.]

The criminal world of the last decade, its tone set by the captains of the gambling industry, is in startling contrast to the state of affairs of the two decades before. If a Kefauver report had been written then, the main "names" would have been Lepke and Gurrah, Dutch Schultz, Jack "Legs" Diamond, Lucky Luciano, and, reaching back a little further, Arnold Rothstein, the czar of the underworld. These men (with the exception of Luciano, who was involved in narcotics and prostitution) were in the main industrial racketeers. Rothstein, it is true, had a larger function: he was, as Frank Costello became later, the financier of the underworld—the pioneer big businessman of crime, who, understanding the logic of co-ordina-

From *Antioch Review*, June, 1953.

tion, sought to *organize* crime as a source of regular income. His main interest in this direction was in industrial racketeering, and his entry was through labor disputes. At one time, employers in the garment trades hired Legs Diamond and his sluggers to break strikes, and the Communists, then in control of the cloakmakers union, hired one Little Orgie to protect the pickets and beat up the scabs; only later did both sides learn that Legs Diamond and Little Orgie were working for the same man, Rothstein.

Rothstein's chief successors, Lepke Buchalter and Gurrah Shapiro, were able, in the early '30's, to dominate sections of the men's and women's clothing industries, of painting, fur dressing, flour trucking, and other fields. In a highly chaotic and cut-throat industry such as clothing, the racketeer, paradoxically, played a stabilizing role by regulating competition and fixing prices. When the NRA came in and assumed this function, the businessman found that what had once been a quasi-economic service was now pure extortion, and he began to demand police action. In other types of racketeering, such as the trucking of perishable foods and water-front loading, where the racketeers entrenched themselves as middlemen—taking up, by default, a service that neither shippers nor truckers wanted to assume—a pattern of accommodation was roughly worked out and the rackets assumed a quasi-legal veneer. On the water-front, old-time racketeers perform the necessary function of loading—but at an exorbitant price, and this monopoly was recognized by both the union and the shippers, and tacitly by government.

But in the last decade and a half, industrial racketeering has not offered much in the way of opportunity. *Like American capitalism itself, crime shifted its emphasis from production to consumption.* The focus of crime became the direct exploitation of the citizen as consumer, largely through gambling. And while the protection of these huge revenues was inextricably linked to politics, the relation between gambling and "the mobs" became more complicated. . . .

While gambling has long flourished in the United States, the influx of the big mobsters into the industry—and its expansion—started in the '30's when repeal of Prohibition forced them to look about for new avenues of enterprise. Gambling, which had begun to flower under the nourishment of rising incomes, was the most lucrative field in sight. To a large extent the shift from bootlegging to gambling was a mere transfer of business operations. In the East, Frank Costello went into slot machines and the operation of a number of ritzy gambling casinos. He also became the "banker" for the Erickson "book," which "laid off" bets for other bookies. Joe Adonis, similarly, opened up a number of casinos, principally in New Jersey. Across the country, many other mobsters went into bookmaking. As other rackets diminished, and gambling, particularly horse-race betting, flourished in the '40's, a struggle erupted over the control of racing information.

Horse-race betting requires a peculiar industrial organization. The essential component is time. A bookie can operate only if he can get information on odds up to the very last minute before the race, so that he can "hedge" or "lay off" bets. With racing going on simultaneously on many tracks throughout the country, this information has to be obtained speedily and accurately. Thus, the racing wire is the nerve ganglion of race betting.

The racing-wire news service got started in the '20's through the genius of the late Moe Annenberg, who had made a fearful reputation for himself as Hearst's circulation manager in the rough-and-tumble Chicago newspaper wars. Annenberg conceived the idea of a telegraphic news service which would gather information from tracks and shoot it immediately to scratch sheets, horse parlors, and bookie joints. In some instances, track owners gave Annenberg the rights to send news from tracks; more often, the news was simply "stolen" by crews operating inside or near the tracks. So efficient did the news distribution system become, that in 1942, when a plane knocked out a vital telegraph circuit which served an Air Force field as well as the gamblers, the Continental Press managed to get its racing wire service for gamblers resumed in fifteen minutes, while it took the Fourth Army, which was responsible for the defense of the entire West Coast, something like three hours.

Annenberg built up a nationwide racing information chain that not only distributed wire news but controlled sub-outlets as well. In 1939, harassed by the Internal Revenue Bureau on income tax, and chivvied by the Justice Department for "monopolistic" control of the wire service, the tired and aging Annenberg simply walked out of the business. He did not sell his interest, or even seek to salvage some profit; he simply gave up. Yet, like any established and thriving institution, the enterprise continued, though on a decentralized basis. James Ragen, Annenberg's operations managers, and likewise a veteran of the old Chicago circulation wars, took over the national wire service through a dummy friend and renamed it the Continental Press Service.

The salient fact is that in the operation of the Annenberg and Ragen wire service, formally illegal as many of its subsidiary operations may have been (i.e. in "stealing" news, supplying information to bookies, etc.) gangsters played no part. It was a business, illicit, true, but primarily a business. The distinction between gamblers and gangsters, as we shall see, is a relevant one.

In 1946, the Chicago mob, whose main interest was in bookmaking rather than gambling casinos, began to move in on the wire monopoly. Following repeal, the Capone lieutenants had turned, like Lepke, to labor racketeering. Murray ("The Camel") Humphries muscled in on the teamsters, the operating engineers, and the cleaning-and-dyeing, laundry, and linen-supply industries. Through a small-time punk, Willie Bioff, and union official George Browne, Capone's chief successors, Frank ("The Enforcer") Nitti and Paul

Ricca, came into control of the motion-picture union and proceeded to shake down the movie industry for fabulous sums in order to "avert strikes." In 1943, when the government moved in and smashed the industrial rackets, the remaining big shots, Charley Fischetti, Jake Guzik, and Tony Accardo decided to concentrate on gambling, and in particular began a drive to take over the racing wire.

In Chicago, the Guzik-Accardo gang, controlling a sub-distributor of the racing news service, began tapping Continental's wires. In Los Angeles, the head of the local distribution agency for Continental was beaten up by hoodlums working for Mickey Cohen and Joe Sica. Out of the blue appeared a new and competitive nationwide racing information and distribution service, known as Trans-American Publishing, the money for which was advanced by the Chicago mobs and Bugsy Siegel, who, at the time, held a monopoly on the bookmaking and wire-news service in Las Vegas. Many books pulled out of Continental and bought information from the new outfit, many hedged by buying from both. At the end of a year, however, the Capone mob's wire had lost about $200,000. Ragen felt that violence would erupt and went to the Cook County district attorney and told him that his life had been threatened by his rivals. Ragen knew his competitors. In June 1946 he was killed by a blast from a shotgun.

Thereafter, the Capone mob abandoned Trans-American and got a "piece" of Continental. Through their new control of the national racing-wire monopoly, the Capone mob began to muscle in on the lucrative Miami gambling business run by the so-called S & G syndicate. For a long time S & G's monopoly over bookmaking had been so complete that when New York gambler Frank Erickson bought a three months' bookmaking concession at the expensive Roney Plaza Hotel, for $45,000, the local police, in a highly publicized raid, swooped down on the hotel; the next year the Roney Plaza was again using local talent. The Capone group, however, was tougher. They demanded an interest in Miami bookmaking, and, when refused, began organizing a syndicate of their own, persuading some bookies at the big hotels to join them. Florida Governor Warren's crime investigator appeared—a friend, it seemed, of old Chicago dog-track operator William Johnston, who had contributed $100,000 to the Governor's campaign fund—and began raiding bookie joints, but only those that were affiliated with S & G. Then S & G, which had been buying its racing news from the local distributor of Continental Press, found its service abruptly shut off. For a few days the syndicate sought to bootleg information from New Orleans, but found itself limping along. After ten days' war of attrition, the five S & G partners found themselves with a sixth partner, who, for a token "investment" of $20,000 entered a Miami business that grossed $26,000,000 in one year.

While Americans made gambling illegal, they did not in their hearts think of it as wicked—even the churches benefited from the bingo and lottery crazes. So they gambled—and gamblers flourished. Against this open canvas, the indignant tones of Senator Wiley and the shocked righteousness of Senator Tobey during the Kefauver investigation rank oddly. Yet it was probably this very tone of surprise that gave the activity of the Kefauver Committee its piquant quality. Here were some Senators who seemingly did not know the facts of life, as most Americans did. Here, in the person of Senator Tobey, was the old New England Puritan conscience poking around in industrial America, in a world it had made but never seen. Here was old-fashioned moral indignation, at a time when cynicism was rampant in public life.

Commendable as such moralistic fervor was, it did not make for intelligent discrimination of fact. Throughout the Kefauver hearings, for example, there ran the presumption that all gamblers were invariably gangsters. This was true of Chicago's Accardo-Guzik combine, which in the past had its fingers in many kinds of rackets. It was not nearly so true of many of the large gamblers in America, most of whom had the feeling that they were satisfying a basic American urge for sport and looked upon their calling with no greater sense of guilt than did many bootleggers. . . .

Apart from the gamblers, there were the mobsters. But what Senator Kefauver and company failed to understand was that the mobsters, like the gamblers, and like the entire gangdom generally, were seeking to become quasi-respectable and establish a place for themselves in American life. For the mobsters, by and large, had immigrant roots, and crime, as the pattern showed, was a route of social ascent and place in American life.

The mobsters were able, where they wished, to "muscle in" on the gambling business because the established gamblers were wholly vulnerable, not being able to call on the law for protection. The Senators, however, refusing to make any distinction between a gambler and a gangster, found it convenient to talk loosely of a nationwide conspiracy of "illegal" elements. Senator Kefauver asserted that a "nationwide crime syndicate does exist in the United States, despite the protestations of a strangely assorted company of criminals, self-serving politicians, plain blind fools, and others who may be honestly misguided, that there is no such combine." The Senate Committee report states the matter more dogmatically: "There is a nationwide crime syndicate known as the Mafia. . . . Its leaders are usually found in control of the most lucrative rackets in their cities. There are indications of a centralized direction and control of these rackets. . . . The Mafia is the cement that helps to bind the Costello-Adonis-Lansky syndicate of New York and the Accardo-Guzik-Fischetti syndicate of Chicago. . . . These groups have kept in touch with Luciano since his deportation from the country."

Unfortunately for a good story—and the existence of the Mafia would be a whale of a story—neither the Senate Crime Committee in its testimony, nor Kefauver in his book, presented any real evidence that the Mafia exists as a functioning organization. One finds police officials asserting before the Kefauver committee their *belief* in the Mafia; the Narcotics Bureau *thinks* that a worldwide dope ring allegedly run by Luciano is part of the Mafia; but the only other "evidence" presented—aside from the incredulous responses both of Senator Kefauver and Rudolph Halley when nearly all the Italian gangsters asserted that they didn't know about the Mafia—is that certain crimes bear "the earmarks of the Mafia."

The legend of the Mafia has been fostered in recent years largely by the peephole writing team of Jack Lait and Lee Mortimer. In their *Chicago Confidential,* they rattled off a series of names and titles that made the organization sound like a rival to an Amos and Andy Kingfish society. Few serious reporters, however, give it much credence. Burton Turkus, the Brooklyn prosecutor who broke up the "Murder, Inc." ring, denies the existence of the Mafia. Nor could Senator Kefauver even make out much of a case for his picture of a national crime syndicate. He is forced to admit that "as it exists today [it] is an elusive and furtive but nonetheless tangible thing," and that "its organization and machinations are not always easy to pinpoint." His "evidence" that many gangsters congregate at certain times of the year in such places as Hot Springs, Arkansas, in itself does not prove much; people "in the trade" usually do, and as the loquacious late Willie Moretti of New Jersey said, in explaining how he had met the late Al Capone at a race track, "Listen, well-charactered people you don't need introductions to; you just meet automatically."

Why did the Senate Crime Committee plump so hard for its theory of the Mafia and a national crime syndicate? In part, they may have been misled by their own hearsay. The Senate Committee was not in the position to do original research, and its staff, both legal and investigative, was incredibly small. Senator Kefauver had begun the investigation with the attiude that with so much smoke there must be a raging fire. But smoke can also mean a smoke screen. Mob activities is a field in which busy gossip and exaggeration flourish even more readily than in a radical political sect.

There is, as well, in the American temper, a feeling that "somewhere," "somebody" is pulling all the complicated strings to which this jumbled world dances. In politics the labor image is "Wall Street," or "Big Business"; while the business stereotype was the "New Dealers." In the field of crime, the side-of-the-mouth low-down was "Costello."

The salient reason, perhaps, why the Kefauver Committee was taken in by its own myth of an omnipotent Mafia and a despotic Costello was its failure to assimilate and understand three of the more relevant sociological facts about institutionalized crime in its relation to the political life of large urban communities in America, namely: (1) the rise of the American Italian community, as part of

the inevitable process of ethnic succession, to positions of importance in politics, a process that has been occurring independently
but also simultaneously in most cities with large Italian constitu-
encies—New York, Chicago, Kansas City, Los Angeles; (2) the fact
that there are individual Italians who play prominent, often leading
roles today in gambling and in the mobs; and (3) the fact that
Italian gamblers and mobsters often possessed "status" within the
Italian community itself and a "pull" in city politics. These three
items are indeed related—but not so as to form a "plot."

The Italian community has achieved wealth and political influence
much later and in a harder way than previous immigrant groups.
Early Jewish wealth, that of the German Jews of the late nineteenth
century, was made largely in banking and merchandising. To that
extent, the dominant group in the Jewish community was outside of,
and independent of, the urban political machines. Later Jewish
wealth, among the East European immigrants, was built in the
garment trades, though with some involvement with the Jewish
gangster, who was typically an industrial racketeer (Arnold Rothstein, Lepke and Gurrah, etc.). Among Jewish lawyers, a small minority, such as the "Tammany lawyer" (like the protagonist of Sam
Ornitz's *Haunch, Paunch and Jowl*) rose through politics and occasionally touched the fringes of crime. Most of the Jewish lawyers,
by and large the communal leaders, climbed rapidly, however, in
the opportunities that established and legitimate Jewish wealth provided. Irish immigrant wealth in the northern urban centers, concentrated largely in construction, trucking and the waterfront, has,
to a substantial extent, been wealth accumulated in and through
political alliance, e.g. favoritism in city contracts. Control of the
politics of the city thus has been crucial for the continuance of
Irish political wealth. This alliance of Irish immigrant wealth and
politics has been reciprocal; many noted Irish political figures lent
their names as important window-dressing for business corporations
(Al Smith, for example, who helped form the U.S. Trucking Corporation, whose executive head for many years was William J. Mc-
Cormack, the alleged "Mr. Big" of the New York waterfront) while
Irish businessmen have lent their wealth to further the career
of Irish politicians. Irish mobsters have rarely achieved status in
the Irish community, but have served as integral arms of the politicians, as strong-arm men on election day.
The Italians found the more obvious big city paths from rags to
riches pre-empted. In part this was due to the character of the early
Italian immigration. Most of them were unskilled and from rural
stock. Jacob Riis could remark in the '90's, "the Italian comes in at
the bottom and stays there." These dispossessed agricultural laborers found jobs as ditch-diggers, on the railroads as section hands,
along the docks, in the service occupations, as shoemakers, barbers,
garment workers, and stayed there. Many were fleeced by the

"padrone" system, a few achieved wealth from truck farming, wine growing, and marketing produce; but this "marginal wealth" was not the source of coherent and stable political power. . . .

The children of the immigrants, the second and third generation, became wise in the ways of the urban slums. Excluded from the political ladder—in the early '30's there were almost no Italians on the city payroll in top jobs, nor in books of the period can one find discussion of Italian political leaders—finding few open routes to wealth, some turned to illicit ways. In the children's court statistics of the 1930's, the largest group of delinquents were the Italian; nor were there any Italian communal or social agencies to cope with these problems. Yet it was, oddly enough, the quondam racketeer, seeking to become respectable, who provided one of the major supports for the drive to win a political voice for Italians in the power structure of the urban political machines. . . .

There is little question that men of Italian origin appeared in most of the leading roles in the high drama of gambling and mobs, just as twenty years ago the children of East European Jews were the most prominent figures in organized crime, and before that individuals of Irish descent were similarly prominent. To some extent statistical accident and the tendency of newspapers to emphasize the few sensational figures gives a greater illusion about the domination of illicit activities by a single ethnic group than all the facts warrant. In many cities, particularly in the South and on the West Coast, the mob and gambling fraternity consisted of many other groups, and often, predominantly, native white Protestants. Yet it is clear that in the major northern urban centers there was a distinct ethnic sequence in the modes of obtaining illicit wealth, and that uniquely in the case of the recent Italian elements, the former bootleggers and gamblers provided considerable leverage for the growth of political influence as well. A substantial number of Italian judges sitting on the bench in New York today are indebted in one fashion or another to Costello; so too are many Italian district leaders—as well as some Jewish and Irish politicians. And the motive in establishing Italian political prestige in New York was generous rather than scheming for personal advantage. For Costello it was largely a case of ethnic pride. As in earlier American eras, organized illegality became a stepladder of social ascent. . . .

Ironically, the social development which made possible the rise to political influence sounds, too, the knell of the Italian gangster. For it is the growing number of Italians with professional training and legitimate business success that both prompts and permits the Italian group to wield increasing political influence; and increasingly it is the professionals and businessmen who provide models for Italian youth today, models that hardly existed twenty years ago. Ironically, the headlines and exposés of "crime" of the Italian "gangsters" came years after the fact. Many of the top "crime" figures long ago had forsworn violence, and even their income, in large part, was derived from legitimate investments (real estate in the case of Costello, motor haulage and auto dealer franchises in the case of Adonis) or from such quasi-legitimate but socially respectable sources as gambling casinos. Hence society's "retribution" in the jail sentences for Costello and Adonis was little more than a trumped-up morality that disguised a social hypocrisy.

Apart from these considerations, what of the larger context of crime and the American way of life? The passing of the Fair Deal signalizes, oddly, the passing of an older pattern of illicit activities. The gambling fever of the past decade and a half was part of the flush and exuberance of rising incomes, and was characteristic largely of new upper-middle class rich having a first fling at conspicuous consumption. This upper-middle class rich, a significant new stratum in American life (not rich in the nineteenth century sense of enormous wealth, but largely middle-sized businessmen and entrepreneurs of the service and luxury trades—the "tertiary economy" in Colin Clark's phrase—who by the tax laws have achieved sizable incomes often much higher than the managers of the super-giant corporations) were the chief patrons of the munificent gambling casinos. During the war decade when travel was difficult, gambling and the lush resorts provided outlets for this social class. Now they are settling down, learning about Europe and culture. The petty gambling, the betting and bingo which relieve the tedium of small town life, or the expectation among the urban slum dwellers of winning a sizable sum by a "lucky number" or a "lucky horse" goes on. To quote Bernard Baruch: "You can't stop people from gambling on horses. And why should you prohibit a man from backing his own judgment? It's another form of personal initiative." But the lush profits are passing from gambling, as the costs of coordination rise. And in the future it is likely that gambling, like prostitution, winning tacit acceptance as a necessary fact, will continue on a decentralized, small entrepreneur basis.

But passing, too, is a political pattern, the system of political "bosses" which in its reciprocal relation provided "protection" for and was fed revenue from crime. The collapse of the "boss" system was a product of the Roosevelt era. Twenty years ago Jim Farley's task was simple; he had to work only on some key state bosses. Now there is no longer such an animal. New Jersey Democracy was once ruled by Frank Hague; now there are five or six men each top dog, for the moment, in his part of the state or faction of the party. Within the urban centers, the old Irish-dominated political machines in New York, Boston, Newark, and Chicago have fallen apart. The decentralization of the metropolitan centers, the growth of suburbs and satellite towns, the break-up of the old ecological patterns of slum and transient belts, the rise of functional groups, the increasing middle-class character of American life, all contribute to this decline.

With the rationalization and absorption of some illicit activities into the structure of the economy, the passing of an older generation that had established a hegemony over crime, the general rise of minority groups to social position, and the break-up of the urban boss system, the pattern of crime we have discussed is passing as well. Crime, of course, remains as long as passion and the desire for gain remain. But big, organized city crime, as we have known it for the past seventy-five years, was based on more than these universal motives. It was based on certain characteristics of the American economy, American ethnic groups, and American politics. The changes in all these areas means that it too, in the form we have known it, is at an end.

Enrico Fermi, a native Italian, was awarded a Nobel prize in 1938 for his contribution to theoretical physics. In 1942, in the University of Chicago laboratories, he produced the first sustained nuclear chain reaction.

Frank L. Rizzo, formerly the chief of police and now mayor of Philadelphia, is only one of many Italian Americans who have achieved success in local politics.

Joseph Alioto, Mayor of San Francisco, has been in the public eye for several years as a controversial political leader representative of the important role played in California politics by Italian Americans.

Wide World Photos

After serving several terms in Congress, Fiorello La Guardia was elected mayor of New York City in 1933 on a fusion ticket. A staunch urban liberal, he appealed directly to the voters rather than to the party bosses. An officeholder of substantial accomplishment during the severe Depression years, he was colorful enough to inspire a Broadway musical, *Fiorello,* in 1959.

Wide World Photos

West of the Mississippi, California proved the strongest magnet for Italian immigrants. The colonies that emerged there, both in San Francisco and in rural areas, consisted primarily of northern Italians—many of them from wine-growing regions of Italy. In the rich soil of their new land, they planted vineyards that developed into the prosperous California wine industry.

Amadeo P. Giannini founded his Bank of Italy in San Francisco's North Beach Italian neighborhood to aid immigrant farmers, fishermen, fruit-peddlers, and other small businessmen. By 1948, a year before his death, Giannini's bank, now known as the Bank of America, had become the largest in the United States, and it has since become the largest in the world.

In the course of his voluminous 1963 testimony before a subcommittee of the U.S. Senate, Joseph Valachi, center, outlined the Castellamarese War of 1930–31. Originating as a struggle between the "families" of Joseph Masseria and Salvatore Maranzano, it resulted in a shift of power from one generation to another. This controversial testimony aroused public concern about the extent of organized crime in America and the role played by Italians in the underworld.

Today, the hyphen is gone and they are just Italian Americans. Or, more accurately, they are simply Americans whose names frequently indicate an Italian heritage. Their pursuits are as varied as those of the United States itself. Nick Buoniconti, a star linebacker with the Miami Dolphins, is only one of the many Italian Americans prominent in sports.

Wide World Photos

Rocky Marciano, one of the greatest heavyweights of all times, reveals his championship form.

New York Yankee first baseman Joe Pepitone is called safe at third base.

Joe DiMaggio, the Yankee Clipper, examines crabs with his father, Joe Sr., a retired fisherman. Joe Jr. in some ways epitomizes the American dream. A son of Italian immigrants, he rose to fame through his athletic abilities, and he is still a popular and prominent public figure.

In 1889 Mother Frances Cabrini came to the United States to work among the Italian immigrants. Her first efforts resulted in the founding of a day school and orphanage in New York City. Within a few years, her rapidly growing society had founded orphanages in several other cities and expanded its work into Latin America. In 1909 she became an American citizen, and on July 7, 1946, Mother Cabrini was canonized, the first American to be so honored.

At the time when Italian immigrants began coming to the United States in large numbers, the American Catholic Church was firmly controlled by the Irish, who insisted that American (Irish) priests were preferable to Italian priests. Recently, Francis J. Mugavero became the first Italian American bishop.

Religious News Service Photos

THE STRUCTURE OF ORGANIZED CRIME

[In 1967, a Presidential Commission on Law Enforcement and Administration of Justice updated, but did not repudiate, the 1951 findings of the Kefauver committee. There was still considered to be a national crime organization, be it Mafia or La Costa Nostra (this term became popular after the televised confessions of Joe Valachi). Proof of this crime syndicate seemed assured by the strange "convention" at Apalachin, New York, on November 14, 1957. This selection describes the ways crime purportedly works, its organizational structures, and membership.]

In 1951 the Kefauver committee declared that a nationwide crime syndicate known as the Mafia operated in many large cities and that the leaders of the Mafia usually controlled the most lucrative rackets in their cities.

In 1957, 20 of organized crime's top leaders were convicted (later reversed on appeal) of a criminal charge arising from a meeting at Apalachin, N.Y. At the sentencing the judge stated that they had sought to corrupt and infiltrate the political mainstreams of the country, that they had led double lives of crime and respectability, and that their probation reports read "like a tale of horrors."

Today the core of organized crime in the United States consists of 24 groups operating as criminal cartels in large cities across the Nation. Their membership is exclusively Italian, they are in frequent communication with each other, and their smooth functioning is insured by a national body of overseers. To date, only the Federal

From *The Challenge of Crime in a Free Society* (Washington, D.C., 1967).

Bureau of Investigation has been able to document fully the national scope of these groups, and FBI intelligence indicates that the organization as a whole has changed its name from the Mafia to La Cosa Nostra.

In 1966 J. Edgar Hoover told a House of Representatives Appropriations Subcommittee:

> La Cosa Nostra is the largest organization of the criminal underworld in this country, very closely organized and strictly disciplined. They have committed almost every crime under the sun. . . .
>
> La Cosa Nostra is a criminal fraternity whose membership is Italian either by birth or national origin, and it has been found to control major racket activities in many of our larger metropolitan areas, often working in concert with criminals representing other ethnic backgrounds. It operates on a nationwide basis, with international implications, and until recent years it carried on its activities with almost complete secrecy. It functions as a criminal cartel, adhering to its own body of "law" and "justice" and, in so doing, thwarts and usurps the authority of legally constituted judicial bodies.

In individual cities, the local group may also be known as the "outfit," the "syndicate," or the "mob." These 24 groups work with and control other racket groups, whose leaders are of various ethnic derivations. In addition, the thousands of employees who perform the street-level functions of organized crime's gambling, usury, and other illegal activities represents a cross section of the Nation's population groups.

The present confederation of organized crime groups arose after Prohibition, during which Italian, German, Irish, and Jewish groups had competed with one another in racket operations. The Italian groups were successful in switching their enterprises from prostitution and boot-legging to gambling, extortion, and other illegal activities. They consolidated their power through murder and violence. . . .

The scope and effect of their criminal operations and penetration of legitimate businesses vary from area to area. The wealthiest and most influential core groups operate in States including New York, New Jersey, Illinois, Florida, Louisiana, Nevada, Michigan, and Rhode Island. . . .

Recognition of the common ethnic tie of the 5,000 or more members of organized crime's core groups is essential to understanding the structure of these groups today. Some have been concerned that past identification of Cosa Nostra's ethnic character has reflected on Italian-Americans generally. This false implication was eloquently refuted by one of the Nation's outstanding experts on organized crime, Sgt. Ralph Salerno of the New York City Police Department. When an Italian-American racketeer complained to him, "Why does it have to be one of your own kind that hurts you?", Sgt. Salerno answered:

> I'm not your kind and you're not my kind. My manners, morals, and mores are not yours. The only thing we have in common is that we both spring from an Italian heritage and culture—and you are the traitor to that heritage and culture which I am proud to be part of.

Organized crime in its totality thus consists of these 24 groups allied with other racket enterprises to form a loose confederation operating in large and small cities. In the core groups, because of their permanency of form, strength of organization and ability to control other racketeer operations, resides the power that organized crime has in America today.

Each of the 24 groups is known as a "family," with membership varying from as many as 700 men to as few as 20. Most cities with organized crime have only one family; New York City has five. Each family can participate in the full range of activities in which organized crime generally is known to engage. Family organization is rationally designed with an integrated set of positions geared to maximize profits. Like any large corporation, the organization functions regardless of personnel changes, and no individual —not even the leader—is indispensable. If he dies or goes to jail, business goes on.

The hierarchical structure of the families resembles that of the Mafia groups that have operated for almost a century on the island of Sicily. Each family is headed by one man, the "boss," whose primary functions are maintaining order and maximizing profits. Subject only to the possibility of being overruled by the national advisory group, which will be discussed below, his authority in all matters relating to his family is absolute.

Beneath each boss is an "underboss," the vice president or deputy director of the family. He collects information for the boss; he relays messages to him and passes his instructions down to his own underlings. In the absence of the boss the underboss acts for him.

On the same level as the underboss, but operating in a staff capacity, is the *consigliere*, who is a counselor, or adviser. Often an elder member of the family who has partially retired from a career in crime, he gives advice to family members, including the boss and underboss, and thereby enjoys considerable influence and power.

Below the level of the underboss are the *caporegime*, some of whom serve as buffers between the top members of the family and the lower-echelon personnel. To maintain their insulation from the police, the leaders of the hierarchy (particularly the boss) avoid direct communication with the workers. All commands, information, complaints, and money flow back and forth through a trusted go-between. A *caporegima* fulfilling this buffer capacity, however, unlike the underboss, does not make decisions or assume any of the authority of his boss.

Other *caporegime* serve as chiefs of operating units. The number of men supervised in each unit varies with the size and activities of particular families. Often the *caporegima* has one or two associates who work closely with him, carrying orders, information, and money to the men who belong to his unit. From a business standpoint, the *caporegima* is analogous to plant supervisor or sales manager.

The lowest level "members" of a family are the *soldati*, the soldiers or "button" men who report to the *caporegime*. A soldier may operate a particular illicit enterprise (e.g., a loan-sharking operation, a dice game, a lottery, a bookmaking operation, a smuggling operation, or a vending machine company) on a commission basis, or he may "own" the enterprise and pay a portion of its profit to the organization, in return for the right to operate. Partnerships are common between two or more soldiers and between soldiers and men higher up in the hierarchy. Some soldiers and most upper-echelon family members have interests in more than one business.

Beneath the soldiers in the hierarchy are large numbers of employees and commission agents who are not members of the family and not necessarily of Italian descent. These are the people who do most of the actual work in the various enterprises. They have no buffers or other insulation from law enforcement. They take bets, drive trucks, answer telephones, sell narcotics, tend the stills, work in the legitimate businesses. For example, in a major lottery business that operated in Negro neighborhoods in Chicago, the workers were Negroes; the bankers for the lottery were Japanese-Americans; but the game, including the banking operation, was licensed, for a fee, by a family member. . . .

There are at least two aspects of organized crime that characterize it as a unique form of criminal activity. The first is the element of corruption. The second is the element of enforcement, which is necessary for the maintenance of both internal discipline and the regularity of business transactions. In the hierarchy of organized crime there are positions for people fulfilling both of these functions. But neither is essential to the long-term operation of other types of criminal groups. The members of a pickpocket troupe or check-passing ring, for example, are likely to take punitive action against any member who holds out more than his share of the spoils, or betrays the group to the police; but they do not recruit or train for a well-established position of "enforcer."

Organized crime groups, on the other hand, are believed to contain one or more fixed positions for "enforcers," whose duty it is to maintain organizational integrity by arranging for the maiming and killing of recalcitrant members. And there is a position for a "corrupter," whose function is to establish relationships with those public officials and other influential persons whose assistance is necessary to achieve the organization's goals. By including these positions within its organization, each criminal cartel, or "family," becomes a government as well as a business.

The highest ruling body of the 24 families is the "commission." This body serves as a combination legislature, supreme court, board of directors, and arbitration board; its principal functions are judicial. Family members look to the commission as the ultimate authority on organizational and jurisdictional disputes. It is composed of the bosses of the nation's most powerful families but has authority over all 24. The composition of the commission varies from 9 to 12 men. According to current information, there are presently 9 families represented, 5 from New York City and 1 each from Philadelphia, Buffalo, Detroit, and Chicago.

The commission is not a representative legislative assembly or an elected judicial body. Members of this council do not regard each other as equals. Those with long tenure on the commission and those who head large families, or possess unusual wealth, exercise greater authority and receive utmost respect. The balance of power on this nationwide council rests with the leaders of New York's 5 families. They have always served on the commission and consider New York as at least the unofficial headquarters of the entire organization.

In recent years organized crime has become increasingly diversified and sophisticated. One consequence appears to be significant organizational restructuring. As in any organization, authority in organized crime may derive either from rank based on incumbency in a high position or from expertise based on possession of technical knowledge and skill. Traditionally, organized crime groups, like totalitarian governments, have maintained discipline through the unthinking acceptance of orders by underlings who have respected the rank of their superiors. However, since 1931, organized crime has gained power and respectability by moving out of bootlegging and prostitution and into gambling, usury, and control of legitimate business. Its need for expertise, based on technical knowledge and skill, has increased. Currently both the structure and operation of illicit enterprises reveal some indecision brought about by attempting to follow both patterns at the same time. Organized crime's "experts" are not fungible, or interchangeable, like the "soldiers" and street workers, and as experts are included within an organization, discipline and structure inevitably assume new forms. It may be awareness of these facts that is leading many family members to send their sons to universities to learn business administration skills.

As the bosses realize that they cannot handle the complicated problems of business and finance alone, their authority will be delegated. Decision making will be decentralized, and individual freedom of action will tend to increase. New problems of discipline and authority may occur if greater emphasis on expertise within the ranks denies unskilled members of the families an opportunity to rise to positions of leadership. The unthinking acceptance of rank authority may be difficult to maintain when experts are placed above long-term, loyal soldiers. Primarily because of fear of infiltration by law enforcement, many of the families have not admitted new members for several years. That fact plus the increasing employment of personnel with specialized and expert functions may blur the lines between membership and nonmembership. In organized crime, internal rebellion would not take the form of strikes and picketing. It would bring a new wave of internal violence.

HOW WE ITALIANS DISCOVERED AMERICA AND KEPT IT CLEAN AND PURE WHILE GIVING IT LOTS OF SINGERS, JUDGES, AND OTHER SWELL PEOPLE

Nicholas Pileggi

[In the late 1960's several organizations were founded by Italian Americans to combat the stigma of organized crime and to publicize the positive achievements of the great majority who had no connections with any Mafia, real or imagined. One of these societies, Americans of Italian Descent, patterned after the Jewish Anti-Defamation League, was founded in 1967 and is headquartered in New York. In this selection, journalist Nicholas Pileggi takes a tongue-in-cheek look at the work of A.I.D. and its anti-Mafia campaign.]

The time of condescension has passed and today there is hardly a hyphenated-American alive who does not have some kind of ethnic broker, some promoter of his parochial heritage, some organization somewhere prepared to count his vote, build his temple and protect him from the slights and slanders of which otherwise he might be unaware. American Indian-Americans protest the use of such derogatory words as "squaw." Polish-Americans, protecting their anti-Communist reputations, are organized to prevent the heart of pianist Ignacy Paderewski, at rest in a vault in Brooklyn, from being turned over to "Communist-dominated Poland." Black-Americans—among other things—persuaded television stations to blip out what is blatantly smug and patronizing about films in which Rochester and Stepin Fetchit rolled their eyes. There are hundreds of organizations—telephones poised, stationery and mailing lists ready, distinguished spokesmen waiting in the wings—all prepared to pounce on the first sign of slander, the first snide allusion, the first gratuitous pun.

From *Esquire*, June, 1968.

The Italian-American community is the most recent to enter this national image-watching contest, and already there are more than two dozen Italian-American organizations furiously competing with each other to smite smears. While the motivation of many of these Italian-American groups is obscured by rhetoric, they can be broken down into three categories. There are the Christopher Columbus-everything-Italian-is-beautiful societies, generally made up of older, well-established, conservative, first-generation *padroni* on the threshold of dotage and still struggling with both the English language and Babbitry. Then there are the politically motivated groups run by the ambitious sons of old *prominenti*, who incorporate in their inflated membership lists various Italian-American civil-service societies and fraternal clubs in the hope of gaining a base of political power. And last, there are the Mafia censorship leagues, the groups which protest not so much the Mafia itself but every book with an Italian villain, every television drama with an Italian crook, every newspaper mention of the Mafia, Cosa Nostra, Camorra, or Unione Siciliana.

It is an irony that not one of these Italian-American groups actually represents who and what they claim. For instance, they all publicize a following of twenty-two million Italian-Americans; but the last U.S. census fixed the count at 4,543,935 Americans who were either Italian immigrants or their children. The twenty-two million paper Italians waved about threateningly by these groups as a measure of vote-getting strength and economic-boycott power is actually their own projection of how many offspring Italian immigrants could have spawned after almost a hundred years of residency in the United States. The Italian groups fail to take into account the fact that many of these third-, fourth- and even fifth-generation Americans do not necessarily think of themselves in the hyphenated terms of the first and second generations.

The administration of these groups usually rests in the hands of a few prominent Italian-American lawyers, state representatives and judges. The same names seem to run down the left-hand side of all the heraldic-crested organization stationery. In fact, it is extraordinary how little the leadership in the Italian-American community has changed since the days when Generoso Pope used to pry pennies from poverty-stricken immigrants in order to build statues of such prominent Italians as Guglielmo Marconi. It seems today that the organization leaders spend as much time bickering among themselves, denouncing each other as fakes, hinting at each other's Mafia connections (while denying that such an organization exists) and threatening each other with libel as they do vying with each other for the most members, the largest turnouts and the brightest stars.

What is startling about these groups, however, is that despite their general lack of accord they somehow manage to exert pressure outside their community far out of keeping with their influence within it.

They have managed—without once attempting to deal with the problem of the Mafia directly—to persuade the Justice Department

to reverse an earlier decision and prevent the written memoirs of
Joseph Valachi from being published—despite the convicted felon's
protestations that his book was about *crooks*, not about Italians.
They have attempted to censure statements not only of fact, but often
of common knowledge. The Grand Council of Columbia Associations
in Civil Service forced the New York City Board of Education to
correct a social-studies textbook which stated "a small percentage of
Italians became notorious racketeers and gamblers" upon their
arrival in New York. A book dealing with social problems of the Prohibition era would have been remiss not to have mentioned that
fact, and yet, because these groups refuse to accept anything other
than unrealistic eulogy, they often find themselves in the kind of
untenable position in which the Uniformed Sanitation Men's Association of New York City found itself a year or so ago. The union,
which is made up largely of Italian-Americans, threatened a city-wide
garbage-collection slowdown because they felt the city's choice of
Edgar Croswell, as inspector general, to clean up large-scale corruption in the department was a "slur on Italian-Americans." The
Italian-Americans were slurred, the Sanitation Men's Association
said, because Croswell was the New York State Police Sergeant
credited with having uncovered the original Apalachin Mafia meeting
of November, 1957. It seems the unhappy position of these groups
always to find themselves defending honest Italian-Americans, who
do not need their defense, as well as a small percentage of Italian-
American racketeers, who do not deserve it. Their effctiveness, however, can be seen when, through threats of economic boycott, concentrated letter writing and constant haranguing, the producers of
TV's *The Untouchables* were forced to give all their swarthy Prohibition racketeers names like Brad Thaxter and Buff Ewing. "When
Frank Nitti becomes an Anglo-Saxon," one of the show's method
gunmen said at the time, "I start looking for another job." It was
not long before he did. . . .

Of all these groups, however, Americans of Italian Descent, Inc.,
"United and Dedicated to Combat Defamation" (formerly known as
The American-Italian Anti-Defamation League, which was later
amended to Council when the Anti-Defamation League of B'nai B'rith
objected), whose first president was New York Civil Court Judge
Ross DiLorenzo and whose chairman is Frank Sinatra, must be singled out as Numero Uno among Italian-American image-watching societies. In its less than two years of existence the A.I.D. has been
criticized by The New York *Times* for its choice of leadership; had
its chairman rebuked by a police Mafia expert because of his underworld ties; been disowned by the National Italian-American League
to Combat Defamation, which is run by another New York Judge, S.
Samuel DiFalco; been accused in effect of being *vigilante* rather
than vigilant by the president of the Grand Council of Columbia
Associations in Civil Service, been called "racist" indirectly by Dore
Schary and sued by the Anti-Defamation League of B'nai B'rith for

appropriating its name. The Council, in fact, first used the name
American-Italian Anti-Defamation League for about two years and
through innumerable table-banging court appearances, until finally
B'nai B'rith won its suit. Only recently did it change over to what
we'll shorten to A.I.D.

The A.I.D. shares a Manhattan office with the Joe Jordan Talent
Agency at 400 Madison Avenue. Joseph Jordan, who is listed as
A.I.D.'s Program Coordinator, is actually its public-relations man,
and while his son handles the talent business, he dedicates himself
to A.I.D.'s operation. Four dark-eyed girls, the volunteer daughters of
various *prominenti*, are at electric typewriters, transcribing names
from application blanks to membership cards. A harried professional
secretary clucks over her volunteers, answering their endless questions, stapling their pages and helping them spell Italian names.
Seated behind Jordan's desk, which is piled high with magazines,
newspapers and Jilly's nightclub flyers, the A.I.D.'s president points
to a small sign: "You need the A.I.D. and the A.I.D. needs you."

"What is the important thing," Judge DiLorenzo insists, "is that
the A.I.D. is needed. Look! It is needed because every time three
Italians get together somebody yells out, 'Here comes the Mafia.' It is
needed because every time an Italian is arrested it's always the
Mafia, but when an Irishman robs the Brinks truck, it's no Molly
Maguires, and when a Jew is arrested for a crime, nobody yells,
'Kosher Nostra.' Only us. Only the Italians. Nobody but the Italians.
Well, we're tired up to here with it, and we're going to do something
about it."

Jordan began to say something.

"Wait, Joe," Judge DiLorenzo held up his hand.

"The *Saturday Evening Post* some time ago screamed out, *The
Mafia: Shadow of Evil on an Island in the Sun.* My God! I bought
the magazine and started to read, and I read, and I read, and in
the end I didn't find one Italian name. But still they yelled Mafia.
Well, that kind of cheap stuff must go."

Can it be that the word Mafia has simply become a part of the
English language today? Perhaps the word—while Italian in origin
—can be applied to any conspiracy, no matter who runs it.

"My God, let's hope not," Judge DiLorenzo gasps. "It is a derogatory word, and it smears all Italians whenever it is used. One
reporter told us of an incident that might shed some light on this
whole word business. He was interviewing U.S. Attorney Robert M.
Morgenthau, the son of the former Secretary of the Treasury, and a
member of one of the great Jewish banking families. Well, as a U.S.
Attorney he is giving out a story about Mafia this and Mafia that and
Cosa Nostra loan sharks and Mafia loan sharks, and this guy and
that guy. So when the story is all over the reporter asks Morgenthau if one of the men was known as a shylock. Well, Morgenthau
stops, looks at the guy, and says in dead seriousness, 'We don't use

that term.' Well if shylock is too ugly for Morgenthau, then Mafia is too ugly for us.

"This Mafia business has simply gotten out of hand," he continued. "When some Italians get together and run an affair, have a wedding party, sit down for a big meal, they can get raided. When B'nai B'rith has an affair, they're never raided. In Buffalo there was a bachelor party given for a groom, and three hundred persons were invited. On an anonymous tip that there were a couple of 'gangsters' in the room, Police Captain Kenneth P. Kennedy, who's well-known for being anti-Italian, called the F.B.I., and they raided the place. They sealed all the doors, and everybody had to identify themselves. Forty-eight men without Italian names were let go. Do you understand that? As long as you did not have a name ending in a vowel, you were released. The people with Italian names, and there were judges, lawyers, and doctors in that hall, were detained. That's the climate of disgrace all this Mafia business creates, and it must be stopped."

The incident in Buffalo, and others like it, are a little more complicated than DiLorenzo—or most Italian-Americans—are prepared to admit. Among the three hundred guests were eight men whom Buffalo police have linked with the Mafia. One of them, in fact, was described at the 1963 McClellan Committee Hearings as a leading Mafia figure; another had attended the original Apalachin meeting; and another was the son-in-law and "representative" of the reputed Mafia boss of the whole Buffalo and Western New York area. DiLorenzo would rather not have to deal with the fact that those well-known men were attending the $6-a-man bachelor dinner because they were invited. Their presence did not surprise any of the other guests, many of whom were distinguished men in the area. Those men attended because they knew the prospective groom, because their fathers knew the groom's father, because they were such an integral part of the community that not to attend would have been unthinkable. They, better than anyone, knew how vulnerable they were, yet there are certain familial obligations—totally unrelated to their lives as racketeers—that must be observed, certain weddings that must be attended, certain funerals that must be mourned, regardless of the risk. Vulnerability is not the province of the Mafioso alone. The honest and law-abiding Italian-American leaves himself open to "questioning" as long as he is in contact of any sort with racketeers.

While the question of this vulnerability has long troubled Italian-Americans, they are loath to discuss it. Yet it is an indisputable fact that for the majority of Italian-Americans who were born or raised in predominantly Italian neighborhoods, the social links between doctors, lawyers, legitimate businessmen, church leaders, politicians and *capo Mafioso* are often blurred. In these communities—where even third cousins are members of the immediate family—many persons totally divorced from any real contact with illegal activities are nevertheless related by "blood" to the Mafia mystique. What is to be done with an uncle who happens to be a *capo regime,* or a first cousin whose Mafia membership is known to police, or a father-in-law who has gained national notoriety as a Mafia family ruler? It is impossible for many Italian-Americans to eliminate these relatives from family affairs. One unusually burdened Italian-American mother and father had as sons a distinguished labor leader, a priest and an infamous Mafia boss. It is easy to hate the Mafia when one thinks objectively of the horror and cruelty it has visited upon people through its bankrolling of narcotics alone. But it is another thing to see it personified in a little old man who tends tomato plants, wraps his fig tree in burlap during the winter and has an altar in the basement of his home. And the Mafiosi, to ease their own position within the communities in which they live, always run at least one totally legitimate business which serves as their cover and about which they will talk for hours with non-Mafia friends and relatives. Membership in the Mafia is never discussed. The word is never used within its own community. Mafia is, above all else, a way of life and, to Judge DiLorenzo's chagrin, often the most cohesive force within an Italian-American neighborhood. In the summer of 1966 racial brawls and minor rioting broke out in East New York between gangs of youths, Negro and white, the latter predominantly Italian-American. Local officials and the police proved incapable of controlling this, and assistance from the dozens of thin-skinned Italian-American societies, including the sword-bearing Knights of Columbus, so quick to denounce an insult, was not forthcoming. After a few days, Frank C. Arricale, then Executive Director of the city's Youth Board, asked the Gallo brothers of Brooklyn to lend their support in restoring order. The Gallos, aware that the neighborhood was in turmoil and not unaware that a little good publicity often helps in court, accepted the task. Albert and Larry Gallo were given letters by the Youth Board that identified them as community helpers and allowed them to pass freely through the police lines that had been set up in the area. Soon their Rivieras and Toronados were cruising the streets of East New York and Flatbush.

"Hey you, com'ere!" the Gallos would begin when they saw a young crowd.

The boys did not find policemen, Youth Board workers, priests or parents in the cars, but Larry and Albert Gallo. *The* Gallos. The second and third generation finally had met authority.

"Getaddaheh! Go home!" said authority. "You're screwing it up for everybody!"

The youths usually ran.

Afterward, even Mayor John Lindsay had to acknowledge publicly the Gallos' contribution in ending the disorder. When he was questioned about the propriety of the city using reputed Mafia members to maintain order he said:

"I don't live in a cocoon. It was hot and dangerous at that time, and I am very thankful that all aspects of the neighborhood agreed to cool it. You can't always deal with people who are leaders in the Boy Scout movement. Sometimes you must call upon individuals with fairly rough backgrounds."

While Lindsay was not the first mayor to use the Mafia to quell a neighborhood disorder (a similar incident took place in 1964 during the administration of Robert F. Wagner), he was the first to admit it. For Judge DiLorenzo, however, the Mafia does not exist as either a criminal conspiracy or an urban peace-keeping force. He disagrees with an estimate from a consultant to the Presidential Task Force on Organized Crime that there are about ten thousand Italian-Americans involved in some way with the Mafia. When pressed, Judge DiLorenzo will admit to a thousand, "but they take orders, they're not the bosses. They're sick clowns like Valachi."

Ralph Salerno, the Task Force consultant and a nationally recognized expert on the Mafia, feels that the position of the A.I.D. and most of the other Italian-American organizations is unrealistic and that it is harmful to their own cause.

"I think the Italian-American community has been following the ostrich principle," Salerno said about the A.I.D. "They have been hoping that the problem would go away, and as a result there are millions of fine, decent people who have failed to disassociate themselves from about ten thousand wrongdoers. There is nothing these racketeers like better than to blend in with the millions of honest Italian-Americans, and when anyone points an accusing finger at them, be able to yell, 'You're maligning millions of good Americans.' They've managed to slide right in there nice and comfortable between two perfectly honest men and yell, "They're accusing the three of us.' Nonsense! They are dangerous and cruel and should be shunned rather than apologized for."

Meanwhile, in the offices of the Americans of Italian Descent, Inc., Salerno needs his own league to combat defamation.

"What right does Salerno have to talk?" Judge DiLorenzo asked shortly before his term as president of the A.I.D. was over. "What has he ever done for the Italian-Americans? It is this kind of defamatory attack that made it necessary for us to create our organization." . . .

"Defamation breeds discrimination," the judge exclaimed, and his audience rose, cheered, clapped, and whistled. "The use of the words Mafia and Cosa Nostra in the press and in the movies have made Italian-Americans the patsy in the crime-go-round of American life. We must have the strength to put an end to these vilifications and to investigate whether or not this is a conspiracy.

"We have paid a high price for being light-headed about our own defamation. With only two percent of Italian-Americans currently inmates in jails and prisons. . . . And the United Nations report showing that out of fourteen hundred sixty-seven convictions of narcotics pushers there were only thirty-seven Italians. . . . We will hit them with economic sanctions, we will boycott against their sponsors, and we will stop these people who are filling their pockets with easy cash."

The crowd stands and cheers. Mostly it consists of first and second generations, mostly businessmen, retail and wholesale merchandisers, the owners of small construction companies, produce dealers and restaurateurs. There are a few of the older men's sons—accountants, lawyers, engineers—still close to home, still loyal and reliable enough to help their families fight the family fight. Carl Furillo, the ex-Brooklyn Dodger outfielder, is introduced. He strides onto the stage, a little heavier than remembered, a blue suit, white socks. Carmine DeSapio is introduced. The audience is silent. His awesome political power, though no longer of practical use, remains a part of him. "Everybody in this room," DeSapio begins in his oddly prissy voice, "is aware tonight, more than ever before, of the need there is for a unity of purpose . . . the uselessness of individualism . . . the desire for strength. . . . I have no doubt this organization will carry its message through the length and breadth of the land. We must all play ball, get on the same team and let everyone in this universe be proud of us."

THE MAFIA CRAZE

Vincent Teresa

[Vincent Teresa has been called the highest-ranking crime figure ever to turn state's evidence. But in hearings before Arkansas Senator John McClellan's investigating committee during August, 1971, Teresa denied that he was ever actually a member of "the mob." Rather he worked his own operations around the fringes of it. He had been a loan shark and in the numbers racket, and at the time of his testimony he was serving a sentence (twenty years reduced to five) for securities fraud. He did claim to be the grandson of an old time "Mafia" leader, and as such said he could speak with some authority on the inner workings of organized crime. Like Joe Valachi before him, he insisted there was "one big gang that runs organized crime in this country," of which gambling is the foundation. As of early 1973, when the following article was published, Teresa was living under an alias, with federal protection at an undisclosed location. The article was written in collaboration with Thomas C. Renner.]

The Mafia is big business. In fact, it's two industries these days. There's the one I was in. That one makes billions of dollars each year through stock thefts, loansharking, gambling, drug traffic, and other rackets. And then there's the other Mafia industry—the one that writes about what we do and puts it in bestsellers and on movie screens for the public to lap up. The funny part is that while the Mafia picks the public's pocket, the public is beating down doors to read about how it's being stolen blind. Right now I think there are more books on the Mafia floating around than Joe Namath signature footballs. Everyone's making money on the mob.

From "A Mafioso Cases the Mafia Craze," in: *Saturday Review of Society*, February, 1973.

It's funny. All my adult life, since I was thirteen, I've been around Mafia people. My grandfather was a Mafia don, a crime boss in Boston in the old days. My friends were all street thieves or big Mafia people. When I was in the mob, stealing millions, I never thought about the public's interest in what my friends and I were doing. I only have a ninth-grade education, so reading anything else but numbers-racket odds or loanshark records didn't interest me. Today, though, I have nothing to do but read, because I'm not out hustling anymore. I'm an informer, something I always hated. But the mob stole my money, tried to kill my wife and one of my kids, so I talked. Now that I'm living in seclusion, I have time to think about all the things I did and read the stuff that's being written. I can't get over what I see on the newsstands these days.

If you want to know the truth, I think the American public are sadists at heart. I remember sitting in a moviehouse in Virginia watching *The Godfather*. The audience was actually cheering at times. That shocked me. You'd think that Don Corleone was the Lone Ranger and the other mob were the bad guys. Everytime a guy did something to hurt Corleone and his men, the people would shout: "That louse! Get the bum!" I couldn't believe it. Didn't they understand that *all* the mobsters in the movies were vicious? Just because Don Corleone didn't want to sell dope, or because his son Mike had an Irish girlfriend, that didn't make them any better than the other guys. They were still dumping stiffs around the corner like everybody else. They were still making their money off gambling and loansharking and extortion.

But the public doesn't want to know. They like seeing blood and guts, cheering for good guys and booing bad guys. Look at prize-fighting in this country, or the phony wrestling matches. Millions go to see them and watch them on television. They shout their lungs out while a guy bites another guy's ear off or pounds his head on the floor. They sit there thinking: "O-o-o-o, would I love to do that to that guy." So when someone else does it, it's just like they were sitting there doing it themselves.

It's the same way when people read about the Mafia. They love to read that Joe the Boss got shot in the head or that Tony the Nut got stabbed in the chest. Let's face it: most mob guys wouldn't read this stuff or look at it in a movie. They know what the mob is like. They got to go to bed each night wondering if they'll wake up the next morning, and when they do, they're too busy hustling money to worry about what someone's writing. They don't like to see things written because that makes them too visible, brings heat on them, and they haven't time to waste reading about what they're doing. . . .

For the most part the Hollywood image of a mobster . . . was over-romanticized. So the public has a false idea of the Mafia, which has been built up by writers and filmmakers who haven't been close enough to a mob guy to know what it's all about. They pump out a lot of garbage from newspapers and cops and informers, but they

don't really know. It's a big game, the other Mafia industry. They
feed the public some pabulum about a secret society, and the public
eats it up. But this secret business is over. It's secret to the extent
that mobsters want to stay on the street. If you talk, of course, you're
going to get hurt. Why? Because, if you talk, I'll go to the can, that's
why. Not that you're giving away any big secrets about blood rites
and that kind of thing.

The only time those rites are still used is when a man of pure
Sicilian blood is being made a don. But that isn't the way you become
an ordinary member—what we call a "made man"—of an organization today. Nowadays a mob member sponsors another guy—just
like you're trying to get into a country club. It's a business. The
sponsor goes to his associates and says, "Look, I got a good man here
that we want to have with us; his capabilities are this, that, and the
other thing. I'll vouch for him." As soon as he vouches for the
applicant he puts his head on the block, too. The new guy's taken
into a room with the top men, asked a few questions, told what's
expected of him. Then there's a vote. But if they weren't going to
vote him in, he wouldn't be there in the first place to see who
else was present. You can only come out of that room two ways—
a made man or feet first. I guess that's the main difference between
getting into the mob and joining a country club.

I know old Joe Valachi talked about secret blood rites before a
U.S. Senate committee and in the book by Peter Maas, *The Valachi
Papers*, but that sort of thing went out in the Thirties. I knew Joe,
and he lived in the past. All he had were his memories.

Don't get me wrong. *The Valachi Papers* was accurate, but to me
the book was just a rehash of the story Joe told at the hearings.
And it wasn't Joe talking in the book—not the way he talked to me at
La Tuna Prison in El Paso, when we were both there a few years
ago. I didn't see the movie, but from what I've heard about it Joe
would have had a fit. It was all blood and guts. That's all the public
wants, not the real story about how a guy like Joe had to sweat
bullets to make a living from day to day, or the agony of his death in
prison. The biggest score Joe ever made was $60,000 on counterfeit
ration stamps. Today that's peanuts to a mob money mover. But
Joe went public. He gave the world a lot of history about the mob,
and that was important.

I remember when Joe was testifying before that Senate committee
back in 1963. I was sitting in Raymond Patriarca's office in Providence, Rhode Island. That was the headquarters for the New
England mob. Patriarca was the don then; now he's in jail. We
were all sitting there, Raymond and me and Henry Tameleo, the
underboss, and some other guys, and we were watching Joe on television. I remember Raymond saying: "This bastard's crazy. Who the
hell is he?" Henry knew him. "I remember that guy," Henry said.
"Vinnie and I met him in some café in Manhattan. He was a nothing." At that moment Valachi was testifying about Joseph Bruno,

an old Mustache Pete who used to operate in Boston. Then he went on to talk about meeting Raymond. Raymond still didn't remember Valachi, and he was mad as hell, but everyone else in the room was getting a big kick out of the hearings.

"What the hell's the Cosa Nostra?" someone else said, pointing to Henry.

"I'm a zipper," another guy joked.

"I'm a flipper," someone else said.

It was all a big joke to them. In New England we never used names like "soldiers" or "caporegimes." People in our mob were either "made men," dons, Mustache Petes, bosses, or underbosses. Sure, we all knew about the Commission—the ruling body of the Mafia, or Cosa Nostra—and the crime families that Joe described, but we called them the Ruling Council and "the mobs." Our mob was called the Office. In Buffalo they called it the Arm.

The Valachi Papers was really the first popular book about the mob, and it was something the public liked because it had seen old Joe on television and could identify with him. But the book that really made the mob fashionable was *The Godfather*. As far as I'm concerned, the book was far superior to the movie. What I liked about the book—and what they dropped from the movie—was that it showed how Don Corleone came over to this country intending to work and make an honest buck, but there were prejudices against Italians, so he was forced into doing things the way they were done in Sicily. I know that's accurate because it's what happened to my grandfather, Vincenzo Teresa, when he came to Boston from Sicily. The Irish politicians and the Protestant snobs looked down their noses at the Italians. They squeezed them for every dime they could and made them work like pigs in the dirtiest jobs. I'm not crying "poor Sicilian boy that couldn't make a living." Don't misunderstand me. What I'm saying is that Don Corleone, like my grandfather, showed his Sicilian temper and found another way to make a buck—the way they did in Sicily when outsiders pushed them around.

The one great thing Puzo did in his book was show the Sicilian genius for organization. That's one thing about Sicilians. They might not always be educated people, but if there is one thing they know, it's organization. They know how to take four guys that are ambling around aimlessly with no place to go and make them a tight-knit unit.

Puzo also showed the compassion of a don, the fair way Corleone ruled. That's the way most dons are. I don't care what they say, if you go to a don, even if you're not a member of his mob, and you've got a legitimate beef about someone in his mob, and it proves to be the truth, you'll get justice. That's what makes the dons so important in the mob. They rule fair and square. I don't know who Puzo had in mind when he made up the character of Corleone, but to me it was a little bit of Joe Profaci, who used to be the boss of Brooklyn; Carlo Gambino, who's head of the largest crime family in New York; and Three-Finger Brown, who used to be the boss of the Long Island mob. I even saw a little of Don Peppino, an old Mustache Pete I loved when I was in the New England mob. I realize Puzo didn't know about him, but he captured some of his mannerisms in the book anyway.

When I saw Marlon Brando play the Godfather on the screen, I remember thinking to myself that this guy ought to get an Academy Award. He had the mannerisms of a don, the class of a don, down to perfection. The soft, soft voice, always talking in riddles and parables. Dons are like that. They're elegant people in their own way—princes of crime, so to speak. They might look like old greaseballs. They might be little squirts, like Peppino, who was only five feet tall. But when they open their mouths, they're ten feet tall. They speak in broken English and all that, but I remember that when Don Peppino sat down and spoke in his broken English, it was like the sound of music coming from him. His speech was so nice and soft, and he never swore. If you said a four-letter word in front of him, he'd say: "Hey, what are you, a nigger, you talka lika that? Don'ta you talka lika that in front of me. I no lika that language."

Peppino was an elegant man, and so was Joe Lombardo, the old Massachusetts boss. I was a thirteen-year-old kid and a petty thief when I met him. I thought to myself, here I am, shaking hands with Joe Lombardo, a big Mustache Pete. I'd heard about him from hanging around the North End of Boston and from my Uncle Sandy, who was connected with the mob. It was Don Lombardo this and Don Lombardo that. Hell, Lombardo looked like a banker, not a thief. He dressed very conservatively, mostly in grays. He wore a little pinky star sapphire, a gray fedora, and black shoes. I was ready to meet a big mobster who'd say in a deep gravel voice: "How are ya, kid?" But when he greeted me, it was in a soft, easy voice. "Be a nicea boy. You be a gooda boy. Some day you goa someplace." He was an educated man, even though he spoke broken English. Clean, he smelled clean. I remember that the most, like it was yesterday. I remember that this man smelled like he'd just stepped out of a shower.

Now, while Puzo had the Sicilian don down perfectly, he went haywire in other areas. I remember both the book and movie portrayed a sitdown of the dons. Everything was fine except for one thing—Don Corleone had an Irish *consigliere*. It could never happen. An outsider, a Jew, an Irishman, a black—no one but a Sicilian could sit in on a council of the dons. I can't understand why Puzo, a guy who wrote such a tremendous book, so easy to read, so interesting, and so close to being true on so many things, fouls up with that.

Nobody can be an adviser to a Sicilian if he isn't a Sicilian himself. They don't trust anyone who isn't of their blood, even if they raised him from birth. Not only would a don distrust him, the rest of the mob would, too. They'd say, "What are you doing with this Irish guy here. We don't want him here."

That's the way it was in Boston. I had a black man working for me called Walter. He'd saved my life, and I trusted him, but nobody else in the mob wanted any part of him. I was told point-blank, "We don't want this guy around."

"Why?" I asked. "He's trustworthy."

"He's black," they answered. "Get rid of him."

I'll say one thing. I didn't have to tell Walter. He understood. If I went into Giro's Restaurant, he'd go in, but he'd sit way over in a corner booth all by himself and never come near the table where I was sitting with the boys. He knew that they wouldn't allow me to bring him close enough to overhear the conversation. It wouldn't have mattered if he was Irish or Indian or black—he wasn't Italian, he wasn't Sicilian. So they wouldn't trust him. He ran a small loan-shark racket for me, and he'd do other things for me, but not when it involved other mob members.

In that way, the title of Nicholas Gage's book—*The Mafia Is Not an Equal Opportunity Employer*—is perfect. Blacks, Irish, Jews, or Poles don't have equal status with Mafia members. They work for them, maybe sometimes they make more money than Mafia members, but unless they're Sicilian they're not trusted in the inner circle.

Take Meyer Lansky, the leading Jew in organized crime. Hank Messick wrote about him in his book called *Lansky*. Now Messick has to be spellbound by Lansky. He thinks Lansky is some kind of god. Well, a guy like Lansky has a lot of power. A lot of mobsters admire him. I did myself, but from a different angle than Messick. I think of him as the great money mover, probably the greatest of all time. He had the foresight to organize Las Vegas and Cuba and Europe with casinos, then to skim off the top and wash the mob money through banks all over the world, where he has contacts.

The big trouble with Messick's book is that he makes Lansky into something he isn't—chairman of the board of organized crime. That's nonsense. The truth is that because Lansky's a Jew he can't sit in on a meeting of the Ruling Council. They don't trust him. That's why they had Jimmy Blue Eyes, a *caporegime* in Vito Genovese's family, with Lansky all the time. Jimmy Blue Eyes kept an eye on Lansky to make sure he didn't chisel, and he prevented mob punks from shaking down Lansky. Without Jimmy Blue Eyes, Lansky would have been like a toothpick standing in a forest. But Messick doesn't know that. He's even got Lansky belting Luciano in the old days. If Lansky ever laid a finger on Luciano before or after Luciano became a boss, he would have been whacked out on the spot. Big as he is, Lansky couldn't even order a guy like me around unless he got permission of my boss. To do that, he had to go to Jimmy Blue Eyes, who would ask Patriarca if I could work with Lansky on something. Otherwise, I'd tell Lansky to take a flying leap. . . .

Frankly, I'm disappointed with books like Messick's and Gage's. For the most part, they're ancient history. They repeat what everyone and his brother has written about—the Mafia wars of the Thirties, Prohibition, the Gallo wars, the Purple Gang. What about the mob today? The only book where a writer really talked to the mob guy he's writing about is *Honor Thy Father* by Gay Talese.

Now there is one of the best written books I've ever read. Talese is a real artist with words. And he got close to the mob. He spent a lot of time talking to Bill Bonanno and other people in the Bonanno mob. I'd say he gave a pretty good picture of mob life, the strains on the family, the problems of survival. He did one thing I didn't like, though: he got too close to Bill Bonanno and because of that he didn't see Bill for what he really was. He made Bill out to be a tough guy, a loyal son, a courageous leader—as though Bill got into the mob only to help out his poor old dad, Joe "Bananas." Let me tell you something: Joe Bananas don't need his kid's help to get out of a jam. He never did and never will. Where Talese went wrong—and don't take my word for it, ask any mob guy—is that he took a punk and glamorized him. I think Talese wrote what he believed was a true story. But in plain English, he was conned.

I remember Bill Bonanno. He was a little over six feet, a nice-looking kid. When I first met him, he reminded me of one of those college joes you see on the football field. But he was a jerk who didn't know what time of day it was unless someone shook him and said it's nine in the morning. He was irresponsible and had a loud, sassy mouth. Believe me, the only reason someone didn't whack him out years ago was out of respect for his old man. When I was in La Tuna Prison, a kid named Rinky, who'd been in jail with Bill for a while, told me that if it wasn't for the reputation of Joe Bananas, Bill would have been thrown from a prison tier a dozen times.

I was on the street when the so-called Banana Wars were taking place. The whole mob was buzzing about the way Joe Bananas had tried to whack out Carlo Gambino, Steve Magaddino, and Three-Finger Brown in order to put himself in the chair as the boss of bosses. So what Talese writes about is pretty accurate, except maybe it wasn't the big gang war he makes it out to be. It was really small potatoes. Only about six or seven guys got hit. Hell, in Boston they once whacked out more than fifty in a gang war.

Talese doesn't really say it, but the reason why the mob didn't put Joe Bananas to sleep was because of the loyalty of a lot of his friends, people like Patriarca and Tameleo. Gambino and Magaddino wanted him hit, but the old Mustache Petes who started the mob with guys like Joe Bananas felt different. I remember the Boston mob sent Tameleo, Don Peppino, and Don Nene to Buffalo. I drove them. They met with Magaddino in a restaurant, and it was there that Joe Bananas's life was saved. Tameleo came out after the meeting and said to me: "I think Joe Bananas will be all right now. Everything is going to be okay." And it was. They banished Bananas as a boss, but they let him live.

Talese saw a dying mob in the Bonannos, and so now he thinks the whole Mafia is dying and unimportant. Well, nothing could be further from the truth. It's big, it makes billions of dollars each year, it still corrupts cops and politicians and judges, and it's getting bigger now that so many Sicilians are being smuggled into this country as reinforcement. Go to Chicago or Detroit or New Orleans and see how big they are. Or just look at New York. Carlo Gambino is more powerful than ever. He's doing what Joe Bananas couldn't. He's making the five New York crime families into one and he'll boss them all.

Both Talese and Puzo fell into another trap in their books. They've got the dons grooming their kids to be in the rackets. That's just fantasy. No mobster—especially a boss—wants his kids to follow in his footsteps. To tell the truth, of all the mob people I knew, I can think of only two whose kids got involved, Bill Bonanno and Anthony Zerilli, the son of old Joe Zerilli, the boss of Detroit. And you can bet they never wanted it to happen, it just did. Even Lansky has tried to keep his two kids on the straight and narrow. Look at Gambino or Luchese. Their kids are in legitimate businesses. Sure, their old man helped them get set up. What father wouldn't? But they're not made members of the mob, and that's a fact. I got sons of my own. I'd break my kids' legs rather than see them involved with the mob. I'd like to see them go to college and become, say, attorneys—anything, really, so long as it's straight and on the up. So when Puzo pictures the sons of Corleone taking over his mob with his approval, he's dead wrong.

I don't know how close Talese got to Joe Bananas, but he was right about one piece of advice that Joe gave his son—never let anyone know how you feel. That's a story I had pounded into my head by Tameleo day after day, and it's a lesson he learned from Bananas. In his younger days Tameleo used to lose his temper a lot, and Bananas pulled him aside one day and gave him a little lecture. "Don't ever forget," Bananas told him, "that when you get mad at a guy, smile at him, look him right in the eye, walk over and pat him on the shoulder. Keep patting him there. Eventually you're going to look down and see a big hole where you were patting him." What he meant was that if you keep on your enemy's good side, he's going to trust you like a brother and then you can whack him out whenever you feel like it.

I met Bananas a couple of times, first at the old Red Devil Restaurant in New York with Tameleo and later at the Dream Bar in Miami. I was very impressed with him. He was a very stern man, good-looking, well-built, with hard features. He had those snake eyes —it's a trait of all the old Mustache Petes—eyes that can look right through you. He was a tough piece of work.

Books like Talese's and Puzo's, even Maas's, give the public at least a halfway decent picture of mob life. I think Puzo and Talese got caught up in the excitement and made heroes out of bums, and that's wrong. Maas plays it pretty straight, but he doesn't have the style that gets you interested the way Puzo and Talese do.

Personally, I wish more writers would get close to mob guys and find out what they're really like, what they really do, before they sit down and write books about them. Talese did it. I think Puzo did. It's the only way they could know some of the things they write about. I realize it isn't easy. Mob guys don't like writers or reporters. The writers may get hurt trying to get too close. But if more would really do it, then the public might stop thinking about the Mafia like it was Robin Hood and his Merrie Men.

Not that mobsters are all bad. There are plenty of good things about them the public might be interested in. For instance, does the public know whether mob guys are patriotic or not? The truth is, most are. We don't think about undermining the government. We corrupt politicians, but that's only so we can do business. We cheat on taxes, but let's face it, there isn't a damn business executive who doesn't. If you want to know the truth, I think everyone's entitled to swindle a little on taxes because they're too high and the politicians spend like drunken sailors on all their pet deals to help out their buddies anyhow.

Mob people aren't stupid. We know that none of us could get away with the things we get away with in some other country. It's a land of opportunity for us. Don't forget, most of us grew up with holes in our shoes. What do you think would happen to me or Lansky or any other mob guy in Russia, or Haiti, or Brazil, or some European country? It would be, empty your pockets, stand up against the wall, and boom—that's the end of it. This is the greatest country in the world—particularly for a mob guy. You are a free man. As bad as your reputation may be, you'll normally get a fair trial. That doesn't happen in a lot of countries.

I was against a guy like that George McGovern, and I'll bet most mob guys were, too. Not that I love Nixon. But any guy who wants to give amnesty to a bunch of draft dodgers, to a bunch of cowards who ran away, shouldn't be President. I don't want to see my sons go to war. It would rip my heart out to see them go. But if they get their notices, I'll drive them to the draft board center. Why? They owe it to their country. It's as simple as that.

Another thing I'd like to see is writers paying more attention to the rackets that mob people operate, instead of always talking about the murders they're behind. Anyone can write about a bunch of gangland murders. All you have to do is read a police file. But how about the millions that are swindled in stocks, and how big corporations are taken over, and how the mob washes its money through corrupt bankers? What about how a mob guy with a ninth-grade education outwits big, educated business executives—the rceny that's in a lot of millionaires that makes them easy game for mob swindler?

That kind of information is interesting, and it also does the public some good. There is one thing that all these books and movies and newspaper articles have already done: they've put heat on the Mafia, made it more visible. A few years ago we were all stealing Wall Street blind and nobody was doing much about it. Then there was a lot of publicity about the mob, and guys like myself were busted one after another. Now it isn't so easy to swipe millions in stocks and use them for collateral to take over companies. People are beginning to wise up. So that's a plus.

I just hope that people who write about the Mafia will wise up more. I hope they start pinning down what the mob is doing now, not what it did twenty or thirty years ago. If they do that, if they wake the public up and stop making the mob look like it's romantic and exciting and a treasure house of easy riches, maybe then they'll contribute something. Otherwise, they're only picking the public's pocket just like the mob does.

Part Five

THE CONTROVERSY OVER ITALIAN IMMIGRATION: VIOLENCE AND POLEMIC, 1890–1924

The opposition to Italian immigration, after 1890, was shrill and often violent; it endured almost without respite until the immigration restriction law of 1924 was passed. This opposition was part of the larger nativist movement of the time directed against all immigration from eastern and southern Europe. But in the case of the Italians, nativism bore down especially hard and frequently with a viciousness that seems bizarre today.

It was almost as if the Italians were singled out as a scapegoat who could be blamed for the social and economic ills of the nation: ills of rapid, unplanned, unchecked industrialism, and urban congestion. Italians were victims of a racist pathology that deemed them inferior to the Anglo-Americans and virtually unassimilable. They were held in contempt by most labor unions (who would not accept them as members in any case) because they worked for low pay, were used as strikebreakers, and supposedly took jobs away from deserving Americans. They were condemned because they crowded into city tenements, aggravating an already deplorable urban congestion. And in the popular imagination, they were the importers of exotic criminal conspiracies. Most Americans were unwilling to see the Italians as victims of an unaccommodating society. As for the racism, it was pretty much the same animosity that was visited upon the Irish, Germans, blacks, Mexican Americans, Japanese, Chinese, and Indians in other times.

In the matter of violence, the Italians were singled out for a disproportionate share among European immigrants after 1890. Some were killed by mob violence in the 1870's and 1880's; but beginning with the sensational lynching of eleven Italians in New Orleans in March, 1891, mob action against them became a rather frequent occurrence. There were fatalities in 1893, 1895, 1896, 1899, 1901, 1906, 1910, 1914, and 1915 in such disparate places as Denver; Marion, North Carolina; Tampa, Florida; and Johnson City, Illinois.

Along with the violence, the pros and cons of Italian immigration were debated in the press, the magazines, the pulpits, the halls of Congress, and in every other forum where the issues of the day were discussed. Italians were berated for their looks, their illiteracy, their Catholicism, their clannishness, their customs, and their crime. On the other hand, they were praised as industrious, thrifty, diligent, honest, and God-fearing citizens-to-be.

By 1916, the time of rational debate was passed. During World War I and its "Red Scare" aftermath, the nativists had their day. Xenophobia reached new heights, and Congress was beset with demands to restrict immigration. Most Congressmen were willing to accommodate their constituents, and, in 1917, the literacy test was passed over President Wilson's veto. Deportation of "undesirables" was also made more easily enforceable. In 1921, an emergency law was passed limiting immigration from any country to three per cent of the number of foreign born of that particular nationality in the United States in 1910. Three years later, the National Origins Quota System was devised and written into the comprehensive 1924 immigration and naturalization law. In 1927, the total number of immigrants allowed to enter the country in one year was set at 150,000. The figure was raised slightly in 1929, and the number of arrivals from one country was apportioned on the basis of the 1920 census. This legislation, flagrantly discriminatory, remained in effect until 1965. It favored the "old stock" nations of western and northern Europe over the peoples of the "new immigration."

For all the vehemence of the nativists and their success in obtaining restrictive legislation, the reality of a sizeable Italian population in the United States could not be denied. By the end of the 1920's nearly five million immigrants had arrived from Italy. These, together with a growing second and third generation, firmly established the Italian presence in America.

The selections in this part give some indication of the hostilities that met Italians, the debate over their presence, and the tenor of the restrictive statutes passed over their protests.

THE NEW ORLEANS LYNCHING, MARCH 14, 1891

[In October, 1890, five men killed the superintendent of police of New Orleans, David C. Hennessy. His dying words supposedly blamed Italians for the crime. Of more than 100 suspects arrested, nine Italians were finally brought to trial in an atmosphere of great public hostility, with animosity against the local Italians being fueled by the press. At the trial, the jury found six of the defendants innocent and voted no convictions for the other three. There was simply no evidence against the men that would hold up in court. But the verdict only enraged an already irrational populace. A vigilance committee was formed on Friday, March 13, 1891. The next day, led by one William Parkerson, a mob of local citizens stormed the jail, hanged two suspects, and shot nine more to death. This incident had international repercussions and broke, for a time, the diplomatic relations between Italy and the U.S. In this country, the massacre was generally applauded by press and public alike and served mostly to arouse public hostility toward Italians in all parts of the nation. The following selection is an interview with William Parkerson, the mob leader, explaining his role in the lynchings.]

"Your name is very much before the public just now," the correspondent remarked, as he was offered a seat.

"Yes; we had a thirty-minute experience that Saturday," he said with a smile. "The most wonderful thing about it is that it was over so soon. I take more credit for that than anything else."

He gave his version of the outbreak, bit by bit, and not without reluctance, although he seems to consider his work a public service.

From *New York Illustrated American*, April 4, 1891.

"I did not take the initiative," he said, in answer to questions. "I could not tell who did. It was all done by others. I was in court Friday morning in a distant building, attending to some business, and came back to this office after the verdict acquitting the Italians. When I got here I found a large number of citizens awaiting me, some of them old enough to be my grandfather. With those who came in afterward, there were perhaps sixty or seventy. They were talking about the outrageous verdict, and told me they had come to ask me to take some measure to right it. After fifteen minutes' conversation we adjourned to meet again that evening. I had no connection with the case beyond taking a good citizen's interest in it, and dropping into court once or twice to see how it was getting along. That evening we met in the rooms of a young man, whose name I don't care to give. There were about one hundred and fifty of us, among them the same men who were here in the morning. We stood up and were packed like sardines. They made me chairman. There was some more talking about the verdict and I was again appealed to. None of us drank anything and there were no refreshments in the room. We all signed a call that was published in the next morning's papers, asking the citizens to assemble at 10 o'clock A.M., Saturday, at Clay statue, and saying that we would be prepared to carry out their instructions."

"Meaning that you would be ready to kill the prisoners."

"That was the feeling, we understood, of the public pulse. On Saturday I came to my office at 8:45, and at 9:45 started for the rendezvous at our friend's room. I was a little ahead of time. Four or five of us went from there to the statue, where we found a muttering mob of many thousands. We walked around outside the railings two or three times to give our own people a chance to fall in. Then I went through the gate of the railings and up the steps. As soon as I took off my hat the people began to cheer. I don't remember exactly what I said, but I made a little speech, telling them we had a duty to perform; that it was the most terrible duty I had ever undertaken; that the law had miscarried, and that we were prepared to do whatever they desired. They shouted, 'Come on!' "

"What did you understand from that?"

"That we were to go to the prison."

"Did anybody say so in so many words?"

"Oh, it was known well enough. At the meeting on Friday night they tried to get me to the prison, but I refused to do anything that night. From the statue we started for the prison, I leading, and the crowd following us. We had to walk about a mile, and as we walked along, people came from side streets and fell into the procession. The women were crying, and the men were cheering. It was the most terrible thing I ever saw, the quiet determination of the crowd. There was no disorder. We stopped on the way at our friend's room, where we found guns awaiting us. I had my own gun there. There were about one hundred and fifty Winchesters and shot-

guns, I think, given out. I never carry a revolver, but that morning
I put one in my pocket. I took a Winchester besides. At this
moment I am unarmed. At the prison gate, Lem Davis, I think that
is his name, came to the door. I asked him for the keys to let us in.
He said he could not give them up, and we said if he did not we
would break in the prison. He still refused, and I ordered the crowd
to make ready to break, sent for some gunpowder, and also sent a
detachment to break in at the side door, which was about a block
away, the building being an immense one and covering more than
a square of ground. Meantime, we got some wood and used it to
batter the main door. That resisted, but the side door was forced.
Then I went around to the side door, placed three men on guard,
one a legal officer of this municipality, telling them whom to allow
to enter, and asking the crowd to be orderly. The guards all had
Winchesters.

"The crowd was composed of lawyers, doctors, bankers, and prominent citizens generally. It was the most obedient crowd you ever
saw. They obeyed me implicitly, just as if I was a military commander. If there was any riff-raff it was all on the outside. The
intention had been not to shoot any of them, but when my men
were inside—about fifty of them—they got very furious, and after
the first taste of blood it was impossible to keep them back."

"If you did not mean to shoot, why did you take the guns?"

"Because we did not know what resistance we might encounter
from the officers in charge—from anybody. We meant to get into the
prison, and we would have burned it down if necessary."

"Did you kill anybody with your own hands?"

"No, I did not fire a shot. In fact, at the meeting the night before
I had said that Matranga and another should be spared, the two declared innocent by Judge Baker, in whose integrity we had perfect
confidence. I said I would defend these men with my own life if
necessary, and they were not harmed."

"Did it not strike you as not courageous to shoot the lot of unarmed men in a hole?"

"Well," said the young lawyer, quietly, "there was no doubt of
the courage of any man in our party. Of course, it is not a courageous thing to attack a man who is not armed, but we looked upon
these as so many reptiles. Why, I was told that on Friday, after the
verdict, the Italian fruit and oyster schooners along the wharfs
hoisted the sicilian flag over the stars and stripes, and the prisoners
themselves had an oyster supper."

"Do you regret what you have done?" asked the correspondent
after a pause.

"Not a bit," said Parkerson, promptly. "This was a great emergency; greater than has ever happened in New York, Cincinnati, or
Chicago. I did not act through a sentimental or personal interest for
Hennessy. I knew him well, and asked Mayor Shakespeare to ap-
point him. He was a fine man and an efficient officer, and we felt

that when he was killed there was no telling who would go next. While the Mafia confined itself to killing its own members we did not resort to violence. But Hennessy's killing struck at the very root of American institutions. The intimidation of the Mafia and the corruption of our juries are to be met only with strong measures. Moreover, I recognize no power above the people. Under our constitution the people are the sovereign authority, and when the courts, the agents, fail to carry out the law the authority is relegated back to the people, who gave it. In this case I look upon it that we represented the people—not the people of the whole United States, perhaps, but the people of the state of Louisiana. . . ."

"WHAT SHALL WE DO WITH THE 'DAGO'?"

[Racism and ethnic hostilities were probably no more prevalent during the last century in America than they are in our society now. But they were certainly much more unequivocally expressed. The most vehement ethnic denunciations would no longer appear in the more respectable journals as they did a generation or two ago. The first selection below is from an article by noted Shakespeare scholar J. Appleton Morgan. The response to it, from one of the magazines' readers, appeared two months later. Although both documents are from the winter of 1890–91, it is unlikely that the events in New Orleans were in the mind of either writer.]

There is just now seeking these shores, in extraordinary numbers, a class of laborers who live more meanly than the imagination of the general public, in well-paid and well-fed America, can conceive. Everyone who has visited the northern shore of the Mediterranean, in Italy, is familiar with the class called *lazzaroni*. It may be actually said that this class does not live in houses at all, does now know what a house means: except for shelter against inclement weather; that it has no use for roofs at all. Water, except as it falls from the heavens, it appears to know not in any external sense; and during the long summers and mild winters a wall or an alley is quite as convenient as, and much more available a shelter than, a roof. A gang of these people, "dagoes" as they are nicknamed (a corruption of *hidalgos*, which, though a Spanish and not an Italian word, once came to be sneeringly applied to a foreigner of Latin Europe out of his element), employed in building an American

From *Popular Science Monthly*, December, 1890 and February, 1891.

railroad, will find it necessary, in the new climate, to be provided with quarters of some sort; will herd together as tightly as they can dispose themselves, in anything which is covered by a roof, and every office of nature will be performed together in the same tumbled quarters. I once happened to witness the following incident: A small circus, with a few lions and tigers, exhibiting in a small town, near by where a railroad was being constructed, fed, as a part of its programme, these wild beasts. The bones which the beasts gnawed were left on the ground when the circus departed between two days. And the "dagoes" collected these bones and boiled them for their soup! What terrors have jails and prisons for such human beings? What have they to lose by pilfering, assaulting, robbing, and murdering? So far as creature comforts are concerned, they live better and work about as much, have warmer clothing and better beds, in the meanest jail in the United States than they experience out of it. So far as the duration of life is concerned, they will probably live as long under a sentence of death as they do in the wretched filth they pile up around them, and in the rapid changes of our national weather. The *bric-à-brac* societies who have exhausted Ibsen, Browning, and the entire science of photography, and who are now devoting themselves to the comfort and well-being malefactors, might possibly be in good part, were there any reasonable percentage of reformation in the ordinary penitentiary experience; if the enterprising burglar, after serving out his term, burglarized no more, or the cut-throat, released from a long penalty for his crime—as Mr. Gilbert would say—"loved to hear the little brooks a-gurgling and to listen to the merry village chime"; but, as a matter of fact, he doesn't. But here is a practical problem quite in the line of refinement. Sooner or later, somebody in this country will be obliged to grapple with the problem of the "dago." Can he be kept out of jail? Can he be made a useful citizen by utilizing the leisure he spends in jails to educate him into some sort of comprehension of the new country in which he finds himself? The proposition that every jail and prison should be made reformatory as well as punitory in its character would require, one would be apt to say, some little looking into. The question as to whether states are bound to reform as well as punish, their wrong-doers, depends largely upon the wider question of the duties of a state to its citizens. The other considerations, as to whether a state should make its prisoners comfortable, should watch over their physical welfare, may be disposed of at once by citing the general propositions that, however models of what they ought to be in other respects, our jails ought to be somewhat more uncomfortable to the prisoner than the most comfortless hovel that the poverty of the habitual criminal provides; as, otherwise, there would never be a class of the community to whom a residence within prison walls would not be a change for the better. . . .

What disgrace is a year or ten years in a prison to a nomad, a man from nowhere, who has no character to lose, who goes by as many names as he pleases and changes them as often as he likes? The problem remains. We must build prisons which, somehow or other, will be less desirable abiding-places than the slums. We can not starve prisoners, or turn them on wheels, or distort them with boots of thumb-screws. We can not freeze them nor roast them, nor feed them with miasmatic diseases. But, all the same, we must eventually find some principle, somewhere, by the practice of which, while meting out to the wrong-doer the penalty he has earned, we shall protect the revenues as well as the peace and the safety of the community.

All this is familiar reasoning enough. But the problem seems to increase to formidable dimensions just now with the new class of which we have spoken. What shall we do with the "dago"? This "dago," it seems, not only herds, but fights. The knife with which he cuts his bread he also uses to lop off another "dago's" finger or ear, or to slash another's cheek. He quarrels over his meals; and his game, whatever it is, which he plays with pennies after his meal is over, is carried on knife at hand. More even than this, he sleeps in herds; and if a "dago" in his sleep rolls up against another "dago," the two whip out their knives and settle it there and then; and except a grunt at being disturbed, perhaps, no notice is taken by the twenty or fifty other "dagoes" in the apartment. He is quite as familiar with the sight of human blood as with the sight of the food he eats. His women follow him like dogs, expect no better treatment than dogs, and would not have the slightest idea how to conduct themselves without a succession of blows and kicks. Blows and kicks, indeed, are too common an experience with them for notice among "dagoes." When a woman is seriously hurt, she simply keeps out of sight somewhere till she is well enough for the kicking and striking to begin over again, and no notice whatever is taken of her absence meanwhile. The disappearance is perfectly well understood, and no questions are asked. The male "dago," when sober, instinctively retreats before his employer or boss, or any other man, and has no idea of assaulting him, or indeed of ad-dressing him, or having any relations with him except to draw his pay. But, when infuriated with liquor, he will upon any fancied oc-casion use the only argument which he possesses—his knife. I say the only argument, for it is inevitable experience that he will not talk; however little or however much he may understand of what is said to him, he will pretend not to understand. He has a pretty clear idea of how much money is coming to him, and manages to convey that information to his paymaster. But it is rather dangerous for the paymaster to give him much less than the amount which, in his idea, is coming to him. He will refuse to accept it, withdraw, jabber and gesticulate, and it will be well for that paymaster to be on his guard until something representing that month's wages is accepted.

Now, when (as happens constantly in the course of the grading of a railroad by great swarms of these "dagoes") three or four hundred or less of these human beings are quartered for a month in the vicinity of some prosperous, quiet, and orderly little inland town, where the justice of the peace and the constable are farmers in the field or keepers of the country "store," or the village shoemaker and carpenter respectively—what happens? What, indeed, must happen? The "dago" will not resume work the day after his pay-day, which comes monthly. (Did it come weekly, he would not work at all, as will presently appear.) He takes his wages to the nearest village or community in which spirits, or what is called spirits, is sold. If it is not given him, he fights, is arrested, and locked up; if it is given him, he also fights, is arrested, and locked up. In either case he will be taken by the constable before the justice, and a little experience will convince these officials that the only safety for their community is to "fine" the "dago" what money he may happen to have in his pocket, for, until his money is gone, he will not return to his work. This programme is repeated month by month, until that section of the railroad is finished and the "dago" is moved to another, where another adjacent village must learn, by experience, how to protect itself precisely as did the last one. Local criminal laws seem, therefore, incompetent to deal with this "dago." He has apparently nothing to lose—and from any standpoint except his own, apparently something even to gain—by the most comfortless prison that American ingenuity can devise.

Editor Popular Science Monthly:
Mr. Appleton Morgan's query, in the Monthly for December, What shall we do wiht the "Dago"? suggests many other questions. I presume the writer did not design that his description of the "dago" should be regarded as typical of the Italian people, or of any considerable part of them, but only intended it to apply to a peculiar variety of the dangerous classes that happens to come from Italy; but his paper is, unfortunately, liable to the former offensive interpretation, and has, I happen to know, been taken in that sense in at least one quarter. Few will venture to dispute that Mr. Morgan's *lazzaroni* are as dangerous as he describes them; but it is hardly fair to regard them as the legitimate products of Italian nature. If we review the history of Italy, we shall find that it has been most conspicuous as the progenitor of a very different class of men.

Classes of outlaws, like the bandits and assassins of Italy, rarely appear prominently in any country that enjoys its own government. They are a result of foreign rule, under which even good citizens may come to regard the Government as their enemy. We do not find them in England, or France, or Germany, or Scandinavia, but in Ireland, in Hapsburg- and Bourbon-ruled Italy, and in the European countries under Turkish sway. If we regard them in Italy, we shall find them most prominent and dangerous in those states of the south that were longest and most continuously under Bourbon dynasties, as in Naples, or Austrian, as in the central states.

No European nation, excepting Greece, has done more for civilization and few for liberty than Italy.

How will it be possible, in less than a volume, to do justice to what the Italians have done in the last forty-five years for the freedom of their country and for human liberty? At the beginning of this period Italy was, as Talleyrand had said, with a sneer which was also truth, only a "geographical expression." It was divided up among some dozen or twenty foreign sovereigns, some of whom were of very low degree, and all used their power for dynastic ends only, regardless of the sufferings of the people. This was and had been for centuries just the condition to breed *lazzaroni* and bandits. One sovereign away up in the northwest, a man of the country, had ideas beyond his family, and thought of the people. With him and his son Victor Emanuel as chiefs, and the great native hero to urge them on and compel them when they would not be persuaded, and Cavour to organize, the long battle was fought of the people of Italy against the world. The people of Italy triumphed and founded a kingdom than which no modern state is more enlightened or progressive. This great work of persistent heroism and its crowning success are the achievement of the common people of the country—the "dagoes"—and no one else, with no help except what they compelled. Its champions, Victor Emanuel, Garibaldi—whom Mr. Morgan's "dagoes" in person resident in America have honored with a creditable bronze statue—Cavour, and their associates, are counted today among the world's noblest men. We might speak of Italian music and of Italy's contemporary literature and science, which occupy no mean position, but we have said enough. What shall we do with the dago? Give him a chance.

ITALIANS CAN BE AMERICANIZED

Joseph A. Senner

[Joseph A. Senner
immigrated to America in 1880 from Vienna, Austria. He was a
lawyer and newspaper editor before serving as U.S. Commissioner
of Immigration from 1893 to 1897 under President Cleveland.]

If the expressions of the press be any indication of public opinion,
the heavy immigration from Italy during the last six weeks has
irritated the American people to a great degree. The "Little Italy"
of Ellis Island has enjoyed, from the pictorial standpoint, as well
as from the reportorial and editorial ones, an unusual amount of
attention, although it did not realize the sensational newspaper
anticipations of riots, epidemics, wholesale escapes, fusilades, and
similar occurrences. Innocent readers of our daily papers must have
come to the conclusion that the immigration from Italy was not
only unprecedented in numbers but also extraordinarily undesirable
in character, and that therefore the most heroic measures were
demanded by the public welfare. The assumed conditions, however,
have differed widely from the real ones. To dispel the notion that
this year's influx is unusually large, I need but refer to the facts that
immigration from Italy to the United States amounted in the fiscal
year 1887–8 to 47,622, in 1888–9 to 51,558, in 1889–90 to 52,003, in
1890–91 to 76,055, in 1891–2 to 61,631, in 1892–3 to 69,437, the largest
part of which in each year was crowded into the spring months.

It is quite true that this year's immigration from Italy exceeds
that of the two preceding fiscal years, 1893–4 and 1894–5, of 42,074
and 33,902, respectively; but during that period the tide of all com-

From "Immigration from Italy" in: *The North American Review*, June, 1896.

merce was exceptionally low and immigration was likewise naturally affected. These years cannot, therefore, properly be taken as a
basis for comparisons. It is also true that since about the middle of
March there have been detained at this port an unprecedented number of immigrants, either for special examination or for deportation,
but this condition was not due to any unusual undesirability on the
part of these immigrants, but solely to the strict enforcement of
the latest law (of March 3, 1893), which made it the duty of the
Inspectors of the Immigration Service to detail for special inquiry
every immigrant who was not clearly and beyond doubt entitled
to admission. That it has been possible, with a very small force of
available employees, to preserve order and peace to the fullest
degree upon Ellis Island, although as many as 1,020 immigrants, of
whom over 500 were sentenced to deportation, have been detained
over night, is convincing proof at least of the fact that the Italians,
who form the largest percentage of the detained, are by no means
as unruly, violent, dangerous, or anarchistic as they have been assumed to be by the imaginative newsgatherers of the public
press. . . .

As long as the migration to and fro was entirely unrestricted,
Italians in large numbers were in the habit of crossing and recrossing the ocean, some as many as ten times, as so-called "birds
of passage," and taking out of the United States, or other countries
of America, the gains which their standard of living, far below
that of an American wage earner, made it easy for them to accumulate. The amount of money annually sent home by Italian laborers
or taken back by them has been conservatively estimated at from
$4,000,000 to even $30,000,000. Commissioner-General Stump observed, during his trip abroad as Chairman of the Immigration
Investigating Commission, that "the marked increase in the wealth
of certain sections of Italy can be traced directly to the money
earned in the United States." But these advantages to the old
country are about to cease definitely. The rigid enforcement of the
Federal statutes since 1893 by the United States Immigration Officials has made it very hard for Italian "birds of passage" to come
and go at their pleasure. Besides, quite a large proportion of those
who originally came to the United States with no intention of
acquiring residence, found the country so advantageous and con-
genial to them that they changed their minds, sent for their families
and settled permanently within the United States, acquiring, in
time, rights of citizenship.

Italian immigrants, even in the first generation, succumb sooner
or later, like those of other European nationalities, to the irresistible
influence of freedom and prosperity; while in the second generation,
as a rule, and in the third invariably, they become thoroughly Americanized. . . .

The common opinion as to the inability of Italian immigrants to
assimilate is, I am frank to state, not shared by me. It must be

admitted that Italians who come over in mature years, without education even in their own language, and during their sojourn in the United States move almost exclusively among their country-men, find it exceedingly difficult to acquire even the rudiments of the national language; but such is the common experience with most other non-English speaking immigrants as well. On the other hand, we find that an Italian who has come here younger in years, or who has received a good education, becomes speedily a thorough American, even if his occupation brings him into contact mostly with his own countrymen. And children born in this country of Italian parents can scarcely be distinguished by their speech or their habits from the children of native Americans. The public schools of New York bear testimony to this statement. The Rev. Bonaventure Piscopo, of the Church of the Most Precious Blood (the largest Italian Roman Catholic Parish in the City of New York), is my authority for the statement that all the Italian priests, in their religious services, their Sunday schools, and even in their confessionals, are obliged to use the English if they hope to be understood at all by the second generation. The same priest related to me the story of a boy of eighteen, born in Italy, but brought to this country when fourteen months of age, by the name of Gian-Battista Foppiano, whose parents left Boston some years ago to return to their native town, Ciccagna, in the province of Genoa. The lad entreated his parents in vain to return to America. He also wrote most urgent and pathetic letters to some of his boy companions in America to send him money. They did so, and he tried to return to the United States against the will of his parents, but did not succeed. The poor boy became so homesick for the United States that he fell into melancholy, and can now be seen in the insane asylum of Genoa, longing for the United States. If this pathetic story cannot be taken as proof of the devotion of all young Italians to this country, it at least illustrates how erroneous are the sweeping assertions sometimes made to the contrary.

It would be an easy thing, of course, to exclude all migration from Italy by the enactment of restrictive measures which would be substantially prohibitory; but the quality of such statesmanship may well be seriously doubted. Despots indulge in radical measures, without regard to consequences, and with no other consideration than their own personal pleasure and comfort. Patriotic statesmen, on the other hand, must not hesitate to face every problem, to study it carefully and to try to find the best possible solution. The United States of America are, in my sincere conviction, not yet ripe, and will not be for a long period of years, to exclude any immigrants who are not really undesirable. The Immigration Investigating Commission very properly said in their report that an entire closing of our ports to immigrants would inevitably result in untold injury to, if not in the very annihilation of, our largest transportation and manufacturing enterprises, in a disastrous stoppage in the development of great sections of the country and in a famine of servants and menial laborers. Italians, as a nationality, certainly do not belong *per se* to an undesirable class of immigrants. There are vast regions in the South and West and on the Pacific coast for the colonization of which they are unquestionably and pre-eminently adapted, and as manual laborers for many varieties of work which Anglo-Saxons are very loth to undertake they are beyond a doubt excellently fitted.

If they are hired out in large masses by unscrupulous padrones, let the padrone system be fought and suppressed. If they are uneducated, let our public schools take care of them. If some are afraid of their voting power, on account of their ignorance—an assumption, by the way, which is rather curious in a country with millions of negro voters—let the United States restrict their naturalization. If we do not want to receive absolute illiterates, let us exclude them by a reasonable test, but without separating families, parts of which may be already here. Let us in general exclude all undesirables, whether they are of Italian or any other nationality, but let us beware, most of all, of dangerous and thoughtless generalities which are based only on the ignorance of facts.

ITALIAN FEELING ON AMERICAN LYNCHING

Augusto Pierantoni

[The frequent violence visited upon Italian immigrants in the United States and the casual attitude toward it on the part of public officials resulted in much unfavorable publicity for the United States abroad. The Italian government urged the United States to take some positive legal steps to ameliorate the situation. In spite of occasional resolutions introduced in Congress, nothing was ever done. The fate of one such bill was discussed in an article by an Italian Senator, Augusto Pierantoni, one of Italy's noted authorities on international law.]

I present in this short article the feelings and reasons which the Italian Government and Parliament express, to obtain from the great Federation of the United States, legislative measures sufficient to prevent the slaughter of the so-called lynchings, thus confirming the bonds of brotherhood between these two civilized nations. Public opinion, the true Queen of Humanity, must be illuminated by those who wish the triumph of law over violence, of constitutional order over anarchy. . . .

Up to 1891 Italians knew only confusedly the cases comprised under the word lynching. The popular instinct of revenge is understood, as when criminals guilty of rape, incendiarism, murder, are surprised *in flagrante delicto;* or lynch law can be understood in territories where law, judges, prison, police, are still lacking, and criminals commit all kinds of violence. The facts of California are well known. It is not allowable to regard as such lynching the deliberate slaughter of foreigners who submit themselves to the law,

From *The Independent*, August 27, 1903.

were or are in prison and were acquitted, or are waiting for a sentence. All the lynchings of Italians have been horrid massacres. In 1891, in New Orleans, some Sicilians, tried for the murder of the Chief of Police of the city, were taken from the prison and eleven were put to death. In March, 1895, in Colorado, three Italian prisoners were put to death. In August, 1896, at Hahnville, La., six Italians confined in the parish jail, charged with murder, were taken therefrom and three of them lynched. At Tallulah, La., in 1899, five Italians were removed from the prison and hanged by a mob. In each of these cases it was found impossible, on account of local sentiment, successfully to prosecute the perpetrators of these crimes in the local courts.

For each of these violations of international obligations the Italian Government protested to the President of the United States, as the Federal system cannot relieve America from international responsibility. In fact every State on entering the Union renounces its sovereignty and is subject to the Federal authority, as defined by the Constitution, and the powers vested in the National Government must regulate foreign relations. The National Government has the judicial power in certain classes of cases which Congress must settle by law.

The diplomatic correspondence between Italy and the Government of the United States, presented to the Senate, proves that the then Italian Ambassador Baron Fava, following the instructions received from the Ministry of Foreign Affairs, declared, "that the entire solution of the difficulty is found in the treaty in force between the United States and Italy," and he asked measures "to prevent the repetition of such atrocious crimes and at the same time just and adequate compensation to the families of the victims."

The great agitation that these facts produced in the press of the Peninsula, arousing heated discussion in the Legislative Chambers, calmed down at once when the news circulated that President Harrison, in the yearly message to the two Houses, recalled that since December, 1890, he had said that Congress should be entirely competent to make offenses against the treaty rights of foreigners domiciled in the United States cognizable in the Federal Courts. Mr. Foraker presented a bill to provide for the punishment of violations of the treaty rights of aliens. A bill was introduced in the Senate, March 1st, 1892, and reported favorably March 30th. President McKinley recommended that the subject be taken up during the session.

The Presidential elections first, then the war with Spain, interrupted this legislative work. . . .

I think that there are two principal obstacles that retard the desired bill. Many Americans think it their duty not to yield to the pressure of a foreign state, while Italy merely invokes what is established by international law and existing treaties; and the Italian *Jurisconsults* know that those of America, as well as the Government and the Senate there, recognize the justice of this demand.

The other obstacle is the struggle of each State to preserve its independence of the Federal power until now enjoyed.

The Italians more and more invoke justice from the Federal Legislative Assemblies, since the Parliament of the Peninsula has passed the Emigration bill, by which the emigration of dangerous or unhealthy people is forbidden, and passports and other means to prevent crises and conflicts are rendered obligatory, being in advance of America, which only last March approved the law rejecting unhealthy, ignorant and anarchist immigration. I might now quote the unanimous agreement of scholars on International Law who recognize the justice of the desired bill for the punishment of violation of treaty rights of aliens. I will, however, merely recall that Italy invokes the rule which the United States succeeded in having applied in the Alabama question, which ended with the Geneva arbitration. Then the arbitration verdict, not accepting the arguments of England, established that when the existing laws are not sufficient, and the Government has not enough means to oblige its people to respect international duties, it must take active steps.

May I soon see the claims of Italy satisfied in the name of humanity and of international justice.

HOW IT FEELS TO BE A PROBLEM

Gino Speranza

[American-born Gino Speranza was a lawyer and the corresponding secretary of the Society for the Protection of Italian Immigrants. One of the lessons he learned in the latter capacity was that native Americans, for all their concern to impress on the foreigner the importance of assimilation, very often provided very poor examples of what it is to be an American. The subtitle of this article by Speranza was "A Consideration of Certain Causes Which Prevent or Retard Assimilation."]

The American nation seems to like to do some of its thinking aloud. Possibly this is true of other nations, but with this difference, that in the case of the American, the thinking aloud is not suppressed even when it deals with what may be termed the "country's guests." Older nations, perhaps because they lack the daring self-sufficiency of the young, prefer, in similar cases, to think in a whisper. All countries have problems to grapple with, economic, political, or social; but with America even the labor problem is popularly discussed as if its solution depended on that of the immigration problem.

Now, considering the large percentage of foreign-born in the population of the United States, it is a strange fact how few Americans ever consider how very unpleasant, to say the least, it must be to the foreigners living in their midst to be constantly looked upon either as a national problem or a national peril. And this trying situation is further strained by the tone in which the discussion is carried on, as if it applied to utter strangers miles and miles away, instead of to a large number of resident fellow citizens. Perhaps this attitude may be explained by the fact that to the vast majority of Americans "foreigner" is synonymous with the popular conception of the immigrant as a poor, ignorant, and uncouth stranger, seeking for better luck in a new land. But poverty and ignorance and un-couthness, even if they exist as general characteristics of our im-migrants, do not necessarily exclude intelligence and sensitiveness. Too often, let it be said, does the American of common schooling interpret differences from his own standards and habits of life, as necessarily signs of inferiority. Foreignness of features or of apparel is for him often the denial of brotherhood. Often, again, the fine brow and aquiline nose of the Latin will seem to the American to betoken a criminal type rather than the impress of a splendid racial struggle.

Then there is another large class of "plain Americans" who justify a trying discussion of the stranger within the gates by the self-satisfying plea that the foreigner should be so glad to be in the "land of the free" that he cannot mind hearing a few "unpleasant truths" about himself.

This is not an attempt to show that the tide of immigration does not carry with it an ebb of squalor and ignorance and undesirable elements. It is rather an endeavor to look at the problem, as it were, *from the inside*. For if America's salvation from this foreign invasion lies in her capacity to assimilate such foreign elements, the first step in the process must be a thorough knowledge of the element that should be absorbed.

Many imagine that the record and strength of the American de-mocracy suffice of themselves to make the foreigner love the new land and engender in him a desire to serve it; that, in other words, assimilation is the natural tendency. Assimilation, however, is a dual process of forces interacting one upon the other. Economically, this country can act like a magnet in drawing the foreigner to these shores, but you cannot rely on its magnetic force to make the for-eigner *an American*. To bring about assimilation the larger mass should not remain passive. It must attract, *actively attract*, the smaller foreign body.

It is with this in mind that I say that if my countrymen here keep apart, if they herd in great and menacing city colonies, if they do not learn your language, if they know little about your country, the fault is as much yours as theirs. And if you wish to reach us you will have to batter down some of the walls you have yourselves built up to keep us from you.

What I wish to examine, then, is how and what Americans are contributing to the process of the assimilation of my countrymen who have come here to live among them.

I have before me a pamphlet which a well-known American society prints for distribution among arriving immigrants. On the title page is the motto: *A Welcome to Immigrants and Some Good Advice*. The pamphlet starts out by telling the arriving stranger that this publication is presented to him "by an American patriotic society, whose duty is to teach American principles"—a statement which must somewhat bewilder foreigners. Then it proceeds to advise him. In America, it tells him, "you need not be rich to be happy and respected." "In other countries," it proceeds, "the people belong to the government. They are called subjects. They are under the power of some emperor, king, duke, or other ruler," which permits the belief that the patriotic author of this pamphlet is conversant mostly with medieval history. There are some surprising explanations of the Constitution, showing as wide a knowledge of American constitutional history as of that of modern Europe—but space forbids their quotation. "If the common people of other countries had faith in each other, there would be no czars, kaisers, and kings ruling them under the pretext of divine right." This is certainly a gem of historical exposition.

Then, in order to make the stranger feel comfortable, it tells him, "you must be honest and honorable, clean in your person, and decent in your talk." Which, of course, the benighted foreigner reads as a new decalogue. With characteristic modesty the author reserves for the last praise of his country: "Ours," he says, "is the strongest government in the world, because it is the people's government." Then he loses all self-restraint in a patriotic enthusiasm. "We have more good land in cultivation than in all Europe. We have more coal, and oil, and iron, and copper, than can be found in all the countries of Europe. We can raise enough foodstuffs to feed all the rest of the world. We have more railroads and navigable rivers than can be found in the rest of the civilized world. We have more free schools than the rest of the world. . . . So great is the extent (of our country), so varied its resources, that its people are not dependent on the rest of the world for what they absolutely need. Can there be any better proof that this is the best country in the world? Yes, here is one better proof. Our laws are better and more justly carried out."

Of course, criticism by the stranger within your gates seems ungracious; but whenever it is attempted it is suppressed by this common question: "If you don't like it, why don't you go back?" The answer is never given, but it exists. For the majority of us this is our home and we have worked very hard for everything we have earned or won. And if we find matter for criticism it is because nothing is perfect; and if we institute comparisons it is because, having lived in two lands, we have more of the wherewithal of comparisons than those who have lived in only one country.

Then there is the American press. How is it aiding our assimilation? It would not be difficult to name those few newspapers in the United States which give space either as news or editorially, to non-

sensational events or problems with which Europe is grappling. As
regards Italy, there is such a dearth of information of vital importance that little, if anything, is known by the average American, of
the economic or political progress of that country. Columns on Muso-
lino, half-page headlines on the Mafia, but never a word on the
wonderful industrial development in northern Italy, never a notice
of the financial policies that have brought Italian finances to a successful state!

What is the American press doing to help assimilate this "menacing" element in the Republic?

"Why is it," was asked of a prominent American journalist, "that
you print news about Italians which you would not of other nationalities?"

"Well, it is this way," was the answer, "if we published them about
the Irish or the Germans we should be buried with letters of protest;
the Italians do not seem to object."

It would be nearer the truth to say that they have learned the
uselessness of objecting unless they can back up the objection by a
"solid Italian vote."

One result of the unfriendliness of the popular American press is
that it drives Italians to support a rather unwholesome Italian colonial press. Why should they read American papers that chronicle
only the misdeeds of their compatriots? Better support a local press
which, however poor and ofttimes dishonest, keeps up the courage
of these expatriates by telling them what young Italy is bravely
doing at home and abroad. But this colonial press widens the cleav-
age between the nations, puts new obstacles in the way of assimilation and keeps up racial differences.

To feel that we are considered a problem is not calculated to
make us sympathize with your efforts in our behalf, and those very
efforts are, as a direct result, very likely to be misdirected. My
countrymen in America, ignorant though many of them are, and
little in touch with Americans, nevertheless feel keenly that they are
looked upon by the masses as a problem. It is, in part, because of
that feeling that they fail to take an interest in American life or
to easily mix with the natives. And though it may seem farfetched,
I believe that the feeling that they are unwelcome begets in them
a distrust of those defenses to life, liberty, and property which the
new country is presumed to put at their disposal. They have no
excess of confidence in your courts and it is not surprising, however lamentable, that the more hotheaded sometimes take the law
into their own hands. You cannot expect the foreigner of the hum-
bler class to judge beyond his experience—and his experience of
American justice may be comprised in what he learns in some of
the minor tribunals controlled by politicians, and in what he has
heard of the unpunished lynchings of his countrymen in some parts
of the new land. What appeal can the doctrine of state supremacy

and federal noninterference make to him? Imagine what you would think of Italian justice if the American sailors in Venice, in resisting arrest by the constituted authorities, had been strung up to a telegraph pole by an infuriated Venetian mob, and the government at Rome had said, with the utmost courtesy: "We are very sorry and greatly deplore it, but we can't interfere with the autonomy of the province of Venetia!"

I am aware that the question is often asked: If these people are sensitive about being discussed as a problem and a menace, why do they come here? It is a question asked every day in the guise of an argument, a final and crushing argument. But is it really an argument? Is it not rather a question susceptible of a very clear and responsive answer? They come because this is a new country and there is a great deal of room here, and because you invite them. If you really did not want them you could keep them out, as you have done with the Chinese. . . .

It is true that, as a nationality, Italians have not forced recognition; though numerically strong there is no such "Italian vote" as to interest politicians. They have founded no important institutions; they have no strong and well-administered societies as have the Germans and the Irish. They have no representative press, and well-organized movements among them for their own good are rare. Those who believe in assimilation may be thankful for all these things; for it could be held that it is harder to assimilate bodies or colonies well organized as foreign elements, than individuals held together in imperfect cohesion.

Yet the Italian in America as an individual is making good progress. In New York City, the individual holdings of Italians in savings banks is over $15 million; they have some 4,000 real estate holdings of the clear value of $20 million. About 10,000 stores in the city are owned by Italians at an estimated value of $7 million, and to this must be added about $7.5 million invested in wholesale business. The estimated material value of the property of the Italian colony in New York is over $60 million, a value much below that of the Italian colonies of St. Louis, San Francisco, Boston, and Chicago, but, a fair showing for the great "dumping ground" of America.

But the sympathetic observer will find the most remarkable progress on what may be called the spiritual side of the Italians among us. It is estimated that there are more than 50,000 Italian children in the public schools of New York City and adjacent cities where Italians are settled. Many an Italian laborer sends his son to Italy to "finish his education" and when he cannot afford this luxury of doubtful value, he gets him one of the *maestri* of Little Italy to perfect him in his native language. In the higher education you will find Italians winning honors in several of our colleges, universities, and professional schools. I know of one Italian who saves money barbering during the summer and on Sundays, to pay his way through Columbia University. I know of another who went through one of our best universities on money voluntarily advanced by a generous and farseeing professor. The money was repaid with interest and the boy is making a mark in the field of mathematics. I know of a third, the winner of a university scholarship, who paid his way by assisting in editing an Italian paper during spare hours; a fourth, who won the fellowship for the American School at Rome and thus an American institution sent an Italian to perfect his special scholarship in Italy.

New York City now counts 115 Italian registered physicians, 63 pharmacists, 4 dentists, 21 lawyers, 15 public school teachers, 9 architects, 4 manufacturers of technical instruments, and 7 mechanical engineers. There are two Italian steamship lines with biweekly sailings, sixteen daily and weekly papers, and several private schools. Italians support several churches, one modest but very efficient hospital, one well-organized savings bank, and a chamber of commerce. They have presented three monuments to the municipality, one, the statue of Columbus, a valuable work of art. They are raising funds to build a school in Verdi's honor, under the auspices of the Children's Aid Society, and are planning to organize a trust company.

I have given the statistics for New York City because the Italian colony on Manhattan is less flourishing than those in other large American cities. So that what is hopeful for New York is even more promising in Philadelphia, St. Louis, and Boston. . . .

There is one more question that an Italian, speaking for his countrymen here, may urge upon Americans who are interested in the problem of assimilation. It is this: that you should make my countrymen love your country by making them see what is truly good and noble in it. Too many of them, far too many, know of America only what they learn from the corrupt politician, the boss, the *banchiere*, and the ofttimes rough policeman. I have been in certain labor camps in the South where my countrymen were forced to work under the surveillance of armed guards. I have spoken to some who had been bound to a mule and whipped back to work like slaves. I have met others who bore the marks of brutal abuse committed by cruel bosses with the consent of their superiors. What conception of American liberty can these foreigners have?

This, then, is the duty upon those who represent what is good and enduring in Americanism—to teach these foreigners the truth about America. Remember these foreigners are essentially men and women like yourselves whatever the superficial differences may be. This is the simple fact far too often forgotten—if not actually denied. And this must be the excuse if you discuss these people as a menace, pitching your discussion as if we were beyond hearing, and beneath feeling, and sometimes even as if beyond redemption.

Make us feel that America has good friends, intelligent, clear-sighted friends; friends that will not exploit us; friends that will not be interested merely because of what Italy did in the past for all civilization, but friends that will extend to us the sympathy which is due from one man to another. You will thereby make us not merely fellow voters, but will prepare us for the supreme test of real assimilation—the wish to consider the adopted country as a new and dear fatherland.

THE FLOWER OF
HER PEASANTRY

John Foster Carr

[John Foster Carr
was an educator and author who spent a great deal of time working among the Italian and Jewish immigrants of Manhattan's Lower
East Side. Few more sympathetic voices have ever spoken in
behalf of the newcomers, the "green horns," the Old World peasants
who flocked to our shores around the turn of the century. He
spoke and wrote Italian, dedicated himself to the education of the
immigrant, and founded the Immigrant Publication Society. In
1912, he was awarded the Chevalier Order of the Crown of Italy.
The following selection is from Carr's oft-quoted article "The
Coming of the Italian."]

To understand our Italians we need to get close enough to them
to see that they are of the same human *pasta*—to use their word—
as the rest of us. They need no defense but the truth. In spite of
the diverse character that all the provinces stamp upon their children, our southern Italian immigrants still have many qualities in
common. Their peculiar defects and vices have been exaggerated
until the popular notion of the Italian represents the truth in about
the same way that the London stage Yankee hits off the average
American. Besides, as the Italian Poor Richard says, "It's a bad wool
that can't be dyed," and our Italians have their virtues, too, which
should be better known. Many of them are, it is true, ignorant, and
clannish, and conservative. Their humility and lack of self-reliance
are often discouraging. Many think that a smooth and diplomatic
falsehood is better than an uncivil truth, and, by a paradox, a liar is
not necessarily either a physical or a moral coward. No force can

From *Outlook*, February 24, 1906.

make them give evidence against one another. Generally they have little orderliness, small civic sense, and no instinctive faith in the law. Some of them are hot-blooded and quick to avenge an injury, but the very large majority are gentle, kindly, and as mild-tempered as oxen. They are docile, patient, faithful. They have great physical vigor, and are the hardest and best laborers we have ever had, if we are to believe the universal testimony of their employers. Many are well-mannered and quick-witted; all are severely logical. As a class they are emotional, imaginative, fond of music and art. They are honest, saving, industrious, temperate, and so exceptionally moral that two years ago the Secretary of the Italian Chamber of Commerce in San Francisco was able to boast that the police of that city had never yet found an Italian woman of evil character. Even in New York (and I have my information from Mr. Forbes, of the Charity Organization Society) Italian prostitution was entirely unknown until by our corrupt police it was colonized as scientifically as a culture of bacteria made by a biologist; and today it is less proportionately than that of any other nationality within the limits of the greater city. More than 750,000 Italian immigrants have come to us within the last four years, and during that entire time only a single woman of them has been ordered deported charged with prostitution.

So far from being a scum of Italy's paupers and criminals, our Italian immigrants are the very flower of her peasantry. They bring healthy bodies and a prodigious will to work. They have an intense love for their fatherland, and a fondness for old customs; and both are deepened by the hostility they meet and the gloom of the tenements that they are forced to inhabit. The sunshine, the simplicity, the happiness of the old outdoor ways are gone, and often you will hear the words, "Non c'é piacere nella vita"—there is no pleasure in life here. But yet they come, driven from a land of starvation to a land of plenty. Each year about one-third of the great host of industrial recruits from Italy, breaking up as it lands into little groups of twos and threes, and invading the tenements almost unnoticed, settles in the different colonies of New York. This is a mighty, silent influence for the preservation of the Italian spirit and tradition.

But there are limits to the building of an Italian city on American soil. New York tenement-houses are not adapted to life, as it is organized in the hill villages of Italy, and a change has come over every relation of life. The crowded living is strange and depressing; instead of work accompanied by song in orangeries and vineyards, there is silent toil in the cañons of a city street; instead of the splendid and expostulating *carabiniere* there is the rough force of the New York policeman to represent authority. There is the diminished importance of the church, and, in spite of their set ways, there is different eating and drinking, sleeping and waking. A different life breeds different habits, and different habits with American surroundings effect a radical change in the man. It is difficult for the American to realize this. He sees that the signs and posters of the colony are all in Italian; he hears the newsboys cry "Progresso," "Araldo," "Bolletino;" he hears peddlers shout out in their various dialects the names of strange-looking vegetables and fish. The whole district seems so Italianized and cut off from the general American life that it might as well be one of the ancient walled towns of the Apennines. He thinks that he is transported to Italy, and moralizes over the "unchanging colony." But the greenhorn from Fiumefreddo is in another world. Everything is strange to him; and I have repeatedly heard Italians say that for a long time after landing they could not distinguish between an Italian who had been here four or five years and a native American.

Refractory though the grown-up immigrant may often be to the spirit of our Republic, the children almost immediately become Americans. The boy takes no interest in "Mora," a guessing match played with the fingers, or "Boccie," a kind of bowls—his father's favorite games. Like any other American boy, he plays marbles, "I spy the wolf," and, when there is no policeman about, baseball. Little girls skip the rope to the calling of "Pepper, salt, mustard, vinegar." The "Lunga Tela" is forgotten, and our equivalent, "London bridge is falling down," and "All around the mulberry-bush," sound through the streets of the colony on summer evenings. You are struck with the deep significance of such a sight if you walk on Mott Street, where certainly more than half of the men and women who crowd every block can speak no English at all, and see, as I have seen, a full dozen of small girls, not more than five or six years old, marching along, hand in hand, singing their kindergarten song, "My little sister lost her shoe." Through these children the common school is leavening the whole mass, and an old story is being retold.

Like the Italians, the Irish and the Germans had to meet distrust and abuse when they came to do the work of the rough day-laborer. The terrors and excesses of Native Americanism and Know-Nothingism came and went, but the prejudice remained. Yet the Irish and Germans furnished good raw material for citizenship, and quickly responded to American influences. They dug cellars and carried bricks and mortar; they sewered, graded, and paved the streets and built the railroads. Then slowly the number of skilled mechanics among them increased. Many acquired a competence and took a position of some dignity in the community, and Irish and Germans moved up a little in the social scale. They were held in greater respect when, in the dark days of the Civil War, we saw that they yielded to none in self-sacrificing devotion to the country. Thousands of Germans fought for the Union besides those who served under Sigel. Thousands of Irishmen died for the cause besides those of the "Old Sixty ninth." "Dutch" and "Mick" began to go out of fashion as nicknames, and the seventies had not passed before it was often said among the common people that mixed marriages between Germans or Irish and natives were usually happy marriages.

From the very bottom, Italians are climbing up the same rungs of the same social and industrial ladder. But it is still a secret that they are being gradually turned into Americans; and, for all its evils, the city colony is a wonderful help in the process. The close contact of American surroundings eventually destroys the foreign life and spirit, and of this New York gives proof. Only two poor fragments remain of the numerous important German and Irish colonies that were flourishing in the city twenty-five or thirty years ago; while the ancient settled Pennsylvania Dutch, thanks to their isolation, are not yet fully merged in the great citizen body. And so, in the city colony, Italians are becoming Americans. Legions of them, who never intended to remain here when they landed, have cast in their lot definitely with us; and those who have already become Americanized, but no others, are beginning to intermarry with our people. The mass of them are still laborers, toiling like ants in adding to the wealth of the country; but thousands are succeeding in many branches of trade and manufacture. The names of Italians engaged in business in the United States fill a special directory of over five hundred pages. Their real estate holdings and bank deposits aggregate enormous totals. Their second generation is already crowding into all the professions, and we have Italian teachers, dentists, architects, engineers, doctors, lawyers, and judges.

But more important than any material success is their loyalty to the nation of their adoption. Yet with this goes an undying love for their native land. There are many types of these new citizens. I have in mind an Italian banker who will serve for one. His Americanism is enthusiastic and breezily Western. He has paid many visits to the land of his birth, and delights in its music, art, and literature. He finds an almost sacred inspiration in the glories of its history. Beginning in extreme poverty, by his own unaided efforts he has secured education and wealth; by his services to the city and State in which he lives he has won public esteem. Perhaps no other Italian has achieved so brilliant a success. But as a citizen he is no more typical or hopeful an example of the Italian who becomes an American than Giovanni Aloi, a street-sweeper of my acquaintance.

This honest *spazzino* of the white uniform sent a son to Cuba in the Spanish War; boasts that he has not missed a vote in fifteen years; in his humble way did valiant service in his political club against the "boss" of New York during the last campaign. And yet he declares that we have no meats or vegetables with "the flavor or substance" of those in the old country; reproaches us severely for having "no place which is such a pleasure to see as Naples," and swears by "Torqua-ato-Ta-ass" as the greatest of poets, though he only knows four lines of the *Gerusalemme*. Side by side over the fireplace in his livingroom are two unframed pictures tacked to the wall. Little paper flags of the two countries are crossed over each.

One is a chromo of Garibaldi in his red shirt. The other is a newspaper supplement portrait of Lincoln.

A man like Giovanni Aloi, yearning for the home of his youth, sometimes goes back to Italy, but he soon returns. Unconsciously, in his very inmost being, he has become an American, and the prophecy of Bayard Taylor's great ode is fulfilled. Their tongue melts in ours. Their race unites to the strength of ours. For many thousands of them their Italy now lies by the western brine.

THE NON-AMERICANIZATION OF IMMIGRANTS

Luigi Carnovale

[Luigi Carnovale, a reporter for the Chicago Italian-language newspaper *La Tribuna Italiana Transatlantica* and for *La Gazzetta Illustrata* of St. Louis, wrote the following article in response to an anti-Italian piece in *The Saturday Evening Post* of August 14, 1923. This selection was first published in the monthly journal *La Fiama* in November, 1923.]

Whoever read the article in *The Saturday Evening Post*, August 14th, 1923, entitled "Our Foreign Cities—Chicago," by Elizabeth Frazer, certainly received a most deplorable impression of European immigrants, especially of the Italians, in the United States, because the authoress interests herself, particularly, in the lowest class of emigrant and sets forth its deficiencies and misery only. Her information, no doubt, came from one of the many insignificant labor agencies, whose chiefs are notoriously known as unscrupulous merchants in human flesh, and are not in a position to give just information regarding immigrants in general. On the other hand, the authoress omits mentioning the good qualities of the immigrants and entirely disregards the better element which European emigration, particularly the Italian, has brought to America.

A conscientious writer ought to set forth not only the "cons" but also the "pros," that is to say, the favorable as well as the unfavorable, especially when subjects of such vital social importance are concerned. Otherwise the reader only sees one side of the truth (if the truth exists in Elizabeth Frazer's article), and it is upon this one and only side that he bases his opinion on the subject discussed by a careless and unjust writer.

From *Chicago Foreign Language Press Survey*, WPA Project, 1942.

Elizabeth Frazer treats her subject in such a pessimistic way that she came to the conclusion, that immigrants, the Italian in particular, are absolutely unsusceptible to Americanization and to the assimilation. Consequently, in her conclusion she does not recognize in the immigrant in this country even the natural instinct of an animal towards its own betterment.

I believe I know the Italian immigrants of the United States well enough, having studied their situation for a long time and having published a book covering my impressions entitled: "The Journal of the Italian Immigrants in North America," (Chicago), therefore, I venture to set forth a few facts quite contrary to the foolish, misleading and slanderous assertions of Elizabeth Frazer.

For instance, there are hundreds of thousands of Italians in the United States who are naturalized American citizens.

In agriculture, the industries, in commerce, finance, politics, sport, science, art and education, in fact, in all fields of American activity, the Italian immigrants have demonstrated in the past, and will demonstrate more and more, that they know how to Americanize themselves and assimilate to the fullest extent that which America offers them.

Furthermore, the immigrants of today are not like the ones of the old days, to whom, no doubt, Elizabeth Frazer refers with such posthumous zeal.

Immigration: The American Commissioner of Immigration at Ellis Island is an Italian, Mr. Caminetti, who has held the office for years.

Labor: The members of the American labor organizations are a good part Italians.

Agriculture: The vineyards, the orange and lemon orchards, the very finest of their kind in this country, were grown and developed to their present state by Italian immigrants and are in their hands.

Industries: The Boston fisheries, considered among the most important in the United States, were established and developed to their present flourishing state by Italian immigrants and are in their hands.

Commerce: South Water Street of Chicago, one of the wonders of Chicago and the most important wholesale fruit market in the United States, was established and developed to its present state by Italian immigrants and it is almost entirely in their hands. An Italian immigrant, Mr. Garibaldi, was for years and up to his death, president of the South Water Street wholesale merchants organization.

Among the high grade confectioners in Chicago, the Allegretti Co., has enjoyed a splendid reputation for years.

Finance: The greatest American Bank of the West from Chicago to California, is the Bank of Italy in San Francisco, established and developed to its present state by Italian immigrants and that bank is in their hands. This bank has numerous branches, among them the New York branch, which rivals the greatest banks of that city.

The Italian, Conte Minotto, is Vice-President of the Boulevard Bridge Bank in Chicago.

Politics: The President of the City Council of New York is the Italian, Fiorello La Guardia, who was also candidate for Mayor of New York during the last election.

The District Attorney of New York City is the Italian, Mr. Pecora. A State Senator of New York is the Italian, Mr. Cotillo.

Among the Judges in Chicago there are three Italians, Barasa, Borelli, Gualano. Judge Barasa was also a candidate for mayor during the last election. And in small American cities some of the Mayors are Italian.

Science: The only American Pasteur Institute in Chicago is the one established and directed by the Italian, Dr. Lagorio. One of the best American hospitals in Chicago is the Columbus Hospital facing Lincoln Park, established and owned by Italians. The Italian, John B. Zingrone of Chicago, is one of the greatest American X-ray operators. He was confidential assistant to the famous surgeon, Prof. J. B. Murphy, who appointed him to make the X-ray pictures of President Theodore Roosevelt.

Art: The Italian, Count di Cesnola, was for years, up to his death, the Director of the Metropolitan Museum of New York. The two greatest American opera companies are in the hands of Italians, i.e., the New York Opera Company being directed by the Italian, Gatti-casazza, and the Chicago Opera Company by the Italian, Maestro Polacco. Among the best American moving picture stars is the Italian, Rudolfo Valentino. There are many others. Not counting the myriads of American singers, music teachers, architects, sculptors, artists, who are of Italian blood. The architect of the Union Station of Chicago, now under construction and said to be the greatest railroad station in the world, is an Italian. The American inventor of artificial lightning is the Italian engineer, Mr. Faccioli.

Professions: There are hundreds of Italians, naturalized American citizens, who are practicing law, hundreds of physicians as well as druggists.

Sports: The American Golf champion is the Italian, Sarazen. The American champion of automobile racing is the Italian, De Palma. Among the American ring champions are Italians, Dundee, Wilson, Gennaro and even Dempsey, who is of Italian descent.

The American cowboy winner of the recent horse races at Harlem, New York, is the Italian, Tony Pagona. In swimming, running, bicycling and motorcycle racing, some of the best champions are Italians.

Hygiene: Several of the finest residences in choice sections of Chicago are occupied by Italian millionaires like Cuneo, Costa, Garibaldi, Dr. Lagorio.

Education: One of the greatest American educators is the Italian, Angelo Patri, not counting the numerous Catholic American educational institutions (universities, colleges, high schools), in all parts of the United States, almost all established and directed by Italians. Dozens of professors in the American universities and colleges are Italians.

In the high school examinations in New York City, two Italian boys, Bernard and Vincent Cioffari, exceeded by 5.03 and 3.77, respectively, the very highest average (92%) ever attained by anyone in the history of New York schools.

I could mention many other facts to prove that the Italian immigrants desire and know how to Americanize themselves, that they desire and know how to assimilate the best America has to offer them by securing for themselves American positions of such importance, and in every field imaginable, as to be envied by those Americans whose individuality Elizabeth Frazer so highly praises. Such positions are attained by Italian immigrants notwithstanding the disadvantages they suffer due to the difference in language and, more than anything else, to the cruel prejudice held against them, such as those found in the lines of Elizabeth Frazer's article.

However, I still want to call attention to the many marriages between high class Americans and Italians in America, which naturally indicates that Italian immigrants do become naturalized American citizens, and, that they assimilate the good America offers to them.

In addition, there is not an Italian newspaper in the United States, that does not continually preach to Italian immigrants the gospel of Americanization.

At any rate, if the Italian quarters of any city lack cleanliness the fault lies particularly with the American health authorities who neglect such quarters and do not enforce, with the necessary vigor, the observance of the laws covering public hygiene.

One should not entirely condemn the ignorant, the humble, the poor, and insist that they should spontaneously uplift themselves. Instead, the learned and the rich, who generally neglect the ignorant and the poor, should extend to them a helping hand in order to uplift them to a higher standard of living. This ought to be the mission of real civilization.

This is the most sacred and most beautiful mission that America has to accomplish, since she believes herself, nowadays, to be the leading nation of the world.

IMMIGRATION AND LABOR

Constantine Panunzio

[Before the
comprehensive immigration law of 1924 was passed, there were
months of Congressional committee hearings taking testimony from
all points of view. The proposed legislation, as drawn up under the
sponsorship of Representative Albert Johnson of Washington, was
obviously aimed at keeping out people from eastern and southern
Europe, while favoring the nations of the "old immigration." Much
of the testimony at the House committee hearings denounced this
bias and called for a fair, nonracial means of apportioning immigration. The following section comprises a portion of the testimony
given by Constantine Panunzio, on January 5, 1924, to the House
Committee on Immigration and Naturalization. Besides the chairman, Mr. Johnson, other members of the committee taking part in
the discussion were John E. Raker of California, John C. Box of
Texas, John L. Cable of Ohio, and Arthur M. Free of California. It is
ironic to note that the principles of Panunzio's recommendations,
ignored by the committee, were incorporated into the 1965 immigration law which repealed the 1924 system.]

With the general proposition of restriction I am in agreement. But
I approach the problem from an entirely different point of view,
and it is there where I differed distinctly with the committee—the
committee's attitude as it is illustrated by this bill. My attitude
is that immigration should be restricted because of social and of
economic conditions in this country, and not primarily because of
racial superiority and inferiority, so-called. Immigration should be

From U.S., Congress, House, Committee on Immigration and Naturalization, *Hearings
on H.R. 5,101 and H.R. 561*, 68th Cong., 1st sess., 1924, pp. 585–606.

restricted first because, so far as we can tell, emigration has not solved any of the fundamental problems of the countries of origin. Italy, for instance, has lost over 10,000,000 population during the last 40 years, but Italy's birth rate has increased even more than it would have increased under ordinary circumstances. Emigration from Italy appears to have made no contribution to and the improvement of social and economic conditions in Italy.

But restriction should be based upon scientific data. Any static, unflexible system of admitting a certain number, or a system which admits at any time a large number or a small number regardless of the actual economic conditions of the country, regardless of the social conditions obtaining in these immigrant communities, or in America as a whole is not scientific. I think I voice the judgment of political economists when I say that if some system could be devised which could take into consideration the problem of actual need at a given time, that we would reach a much more equitable solution of the problem than I believe the bill which is before you now can possibly reach.

Mr. RAKER. And what do you mean by the need at a specific time?

Mr. PANUNZIO. The need for labor, if that is what you are admitting people for.

Mr. RAKER. I am not talking about labor. You say it should be decided upon a scientific basis that would reach the needs at a specific time.

Mr. PANUNZIO. Yes, sir.

Mr. RAKER. What do you mean by that?

Mr. PANUNZIO. Just what I said; the need for labor at any particular time. What is the use, for instance, of admitting to this country, as we did during the fiscal year 1919–1920, large numbers of people when we had approximately four and one-half million or five millions of people out of employment at that time? What reason was there for admitting even one?

And you will recall, Mr. Chairman, when I had the privilege of appearing before this committee on a previous occasion that I cited to you some of my findings in Europe, where certain interests in this country were actually depopulating village after village at that time.

Mr. BOX. Was that carried into the hearings?

Mr. PANUNZIO. The chairman asked for certain names and it was thought best that part of the testimony be left out.

Mr. BOX. It is not in here?

Mr. PANUNZIO. No, sir.

Mr. BOX. I did not recall it. I would like to have that information, though, if it is available.

Mr. PANUNZIO. I think that information could be gathered. I do not know whether the consular reports would show it, but I got a good deal of it from the consuls in Italy.

Mr. RAKER. Do you not go any further on the subject than the question of the needs of labor at a particular time?

Mr. PANUNZIO. I have already spoken of social assimilability.

My chief objection to immigration legislation is that it has devoted its attention almost exclusively to the rejected 3 per cent and it has paid no attention whatsoever to the 97 per cent of those who knock at the doors of the United States and who are admitted, so that many of the problems, some of which have been brought to your attention, I believe, are primarily due to the fact that we have followed a *laissez faire* policy with respect to the immigrant after he has been admitted to the country. I repeat, the entire body of immigration legislation deals with the question of rejecting the 3 per cent of all those who knock at the gates of the United States and pays no attention whatsoever to the much larger and more important problem of properly caring for the immigrant after he has been admitted to the coutnry. Over and above any restriction, be it 1 per cent, be it 2 per cent, be it any percentage, or whatever be the basis upon which the restriction is placed, it seems to me that there is nothing that is more greatly needed in this country than a body of legislation, which will make it possible for the immigrant to find himself, to discover his capacity, to discover where he is needed, to discover how he can become an American citizen, how he can fit in American society. And if you will permit me, gentlemen, to refer to a little book of mine, *The Soul of an Immigrant*, it will tell you the story of how it took me 18 years of continuous hunting and searching before I became a citizen of the United States, even though I was educated, in part, in Italy, even though I was yearning and seeking for the privilege of becoming a citizen of the United States. Such was the lack of actual interest on the part of authorities and on the part of those who could have guided me that it took me all those years before I could actually become a citizen of the United States.

Mr. CABLE. Did you apply right away for first papers?

Mr. PANUNZIO. I applied two years after I came to this country.

Mr. CABLE. Then why did you not on your five years' residence become a citizen?

Mr. PANUNZIO. Because of my movements from place to place and of the obstacles placed in the way by the law.

Mr. CABLE. You blame the law then?

Mr. PANUNZIO. I partly blame the law, although I think it has since been corrected in part. I refer to the naturalization law, and not the immigration law.

Mr. CABLE. This is a hearing affecting the immigration bill and not our naturalization law.

Mr. PANUNZIO. No, sir; this affects the entire question of immigration. I say that what we need is a proper system of regulation, that this regulation should be based upon an elastic principle, and this in turn upon the actual conditions of the country at a given time. And more than this, we need a proper system of distribution and a plan for directing assimilation.

Mr. CABLE. Do you want some one man or some group of men to control the number of aliens who should come here year by year?

Mr. PANUNZIO. May I say that I am free from any political or economic interests. If anything, I would be on the other side of the fence from where Mr. Emory was, or the interests that Mr. Emory represents. But after studying the plans followed by the various countries, I have reached almost exactly the conclusion which Mr. Emory presented to this committee yesterday. So it will not be necessary for me to go into it in detail.

Mr. FREE. I was not here at that time. What was it? What was it, in brief?

Mr. PANUNZIO. A system based on an elastic principle, the application of which should be left in the hands of an administrative board composed of the Secretaries of Labor, Agriculture, and Commerce. This board should from time to time forecast the need of labor and if at a given period there was no need of labor, to have no labor whatsoever come into the country through immigration, and if at other times there was a greater need for labor there would be a greater number admitted within specified or upper limit.

ITALOPHOBIA

[The 1920's were a bad decade for Italian Americans. Ordinarily victims of a bad press anyway, they were now saddled with the onus of the notorious Sacco-Vanzetti murder trial and the emergence of organized crime rings in major cities. To counteract their reputation, the April, 1925, *Bulletin* of the Italian American National Union offered some advice on the matter of assimilation.]

"We are being classified," a friend said to me. "Someone is being paid to make a study of the Italians." And it is true. The local press is attempting to analyze certain manifestations of Italianism, classifying us into north, northwest, west, and south groups. Yes, it's a game, a hunt with the Italians as a prize. A game that is becoming more accentuated every day, and with it are increasing the ways and means of discouraging and expelling the Italian. The immigration law, the naturalization law, and the no less vicious Prohibition law were created, it seems, to strike at the Italian. A glance at the list of victims will alarm you.

Is the majority of prevaricators among Italians? Homes of Italians are those most frequently visited by the forces of law and order, even at the risk of their lives.

The situation is alarming, and our people do not fully realize its gravity. They thoughtlessly go on as before, alone, disorganized in their fight for existence, in their daily trials humiliated by others, deceived by those among them who should be their guides and instead are their betrayers.

From *Chicago Foreign Language Press Survey*, WPA Project, 1942.

The mass of our people is eternally infantile and thoughtless. The majority come from the small towns of Italy, where life is confined to the customs and habits within the shadow of the *campanile* and to the veneration of the patron saint, a veneration that is carried over to this country and is pictured on the standards of the mutual benefit societies organized for that purpose. Thus one can observe, at a glance, in the outstanding foreign sections of the city, the various groups, compact and typical of their small town or district. In this way we have made the distinction, even though from these groups there is a continuous falling away of those who have allowed themselves to be assimilated into the American melting pot.

We say "American." The distinction is made by our own people to whom anyone who does not speak Italian is an American. He might be Jewish, Croatian, Polish, Irish, and so forth, but to us he is an "American." And this ingenuous distinction which we owe to the dull observation of the newly arrived, finds an echo in the Italophobic press, which reports with accentuated emphasis the deeds of Italian character and those which it refers to as typically Sicilian.

The problem has many complications, especially for anyone who desires to throw the bright scientific analysis on the situation. But we cannot give this problem the time which it deserves, and can only give a few practical suggestions even at the cost of having some boor burst into jeering laughter.

The fault lies in our excessive Italianism. We wave the Italian flag at a reckless height over a land which we do not dominate, be it by numbers, by inheritance, or for any other reason. That flag we must keep in our hearts. It is unwise to wave it in the face of a native element that, though having reverence for our ancestors, is intolerant of a people which is competing with it in the economic field.

The local Italian press can teach the newcomers, as well as those who have had a longer period of residence, one very important point: that in America one must do as the "Americans," just as our ancestors said, "When in Rome do like the Romans."

The Italian quarters should disappear, as they are disappearing, though very slowly. With the Italian quarters dismembered it will be easy to eliminate that odious classification which is applied to our people.

Discard your Old Country loyalties and your enemy will be left without a target. In fact I am sure that only in this manner can we obtain the dissolution of all animosities. Because your foe is not that which you have imagined him to be, the antithesis of all things Italian. On the contrary he, whom you call an enemy, is the true friend of the Italian.

The "American" desires the Americanization of the Italian, developed and interested in the community, as an integral part and not like a worm that slowly gnaws into its peace and future.

The Italian who knows how to act will never find any animosity directed against him. On the contrary he will be respected. America in the main has learned to appreciate the Italian, to understand, and to hold him in high esteem when he merits it. But it aims to rid itself of all those Italians who know not how, nor want to respect, the laws and customs of this country which has been so hospitable and generous.

The American press in many cases goes to extremes, makes mountains out of molehills, and seems to agitate against the Italian race. Against these abuses we are powerless for various reasons. We cite the principle: to us there is something wanting in a newspaper that is purely "American." The Italian press does not fill the need. Its voice does not carry where it should and where it does reach, it tends to make the situation more difficult. The times require a different reckoning. The older generation of laborers, or of a more promiscuous existence, is disappearing and is being replaced by a better class. The new generation issues from the educational institution and invades the industrial and professional field. Therefore it has no time for the Italian weekly newspaper, or the daily, which is two days behind in reporting the current news. The Italian press has exhausted its reason for being. It would be a meritorious action if our weeklies were to consolidate into a powerful English daily fighting the battle for Americanization, while maintaining the rights of Italians on a par with those of others.

Part Six

EMERGENCE OF THE ITALIAN AMERICAN

The hyphen is gone now: they are just Italian Americans. Or, more accurately, they are simply Americans whose names frequently indicate an Italian heritage. Their pursuits are as varied as those of the nation itself. Many still work the mines, plant the vineyards, drive the trucks, load the ships, assemble the cars, and perform the manifold tasks that keep the economy functioning. What has changed since 1880 is the broadening of opportunity for all ethnic groups that has enabled many Italian Americans to achieve upward social mobility. Some have attained positions of great influence and prestige. Ralph D. De Nunzio became vice chairman of the New York Stock Exchange. Lee A. Iaccoca became president of Ford Motor Company, and John J. Riccardo headed Chrysler. John Volpe served as Secretary of Transportation; Anthony Celebrezze became Secretary of Health, Education, and Welfare; and John Pastore was elected to the U.S. Senate from Rhode Island. Of the many Italian Americans elected to Congress over the last ninety years, none is better known than Fiorello La Guardia, later mayor of New York City. Edward Corsi served as commissioner of immigration. Vincent Impelleteri, Hugh Addonizio, Joseph Alioto, and Frank Rizzo became mayors of major cities. And to compile an adequate list of Italian Americans who have become famous in baseball, football, ice hockey, auto racing, boxing, show business, opera, art and the sciences would entail a sizable "Who's Who."

In short, the descendants of the immigrants have "made it" in the United States. They have lived all their lives as Americans, and they share whatever situations they find themselves in with other Americans and not distinctly as members of an ethnic group. The immigrants themselves were not so fortunate, but it was with them that the process of acculturation and assimilation began.

How difficult that process was, no one but the immigrant himself knows. He was, as Mary Antin pointed out many years ago, as much a pioneer as the colonist who first sought a New World. The nation to which the immigrants came made little effort to accommodate itself to their needs, other than meeting them at the gate. The illusions of easy wealth were soon dissipated under the cruel realities of congested, dirty tenements set among hostile neighborhoods; under the work that was harder than any imagined in the Old World, and, occasionally, under the backbreaking toil of clearing a small plot of land for a farm.

To what extent did the first generation, the Old World arrivals, Americanize? The question presupposes too much, for it suggests that we can really define what Americanization is. Crevecoeur asserted in 1782 that where a man earns his bread is his country. Historian Marcus Lee Hansen felt that the immigrants were "Americans before they landed" because they were so open to what the United States had to offer them in economic opportunity and free institutions.

Most immigrants lived their lives in America in a transitional stage: they never fully let go of the Old World and they were never totally part of the New. It was not that their loyalties were divided, as nativists who used the epithet "hyphenated Americans" were wont to suggest. Loyalties were much more immediate—just as they had been in Italy. For the immigrants, when they arrived, were not Italians as far as they themselves were concerned: they were Neapolitans, Calabrians, Sicilians. In fact, their "patriotism" was even more localized than that: they were members of the families first, then of towns, then of regions. In America this frame of reference was altered only gradually for the first generation. They settled in close proximity to each other based on their Old World places of origin, and in such "urban villages" they adjusted themselves to American conditions in stages. Thus loyalty here was also at first very immediate: to the family, to the *paesani* or fellow townsmen, and to the job. It saved them from being overwhelmed by that great unknown which was America. Only slowly did the immigrants broaden their horizons, and, even so, this was through their own social events, religious festivals, protective associations, theaters, and Italian language newspapers.

Gradually the immigrants were drawn closer to the American "mainstream" through contacts at work, labor unions, settlement houses, local political bosses, fraternal societies, and churches. Even their own newspapers aided acculturation. As one paper put it, they were "foreign in language, but American in spirit." And from the greater society there was certainly enough pressure to conform, to become "100 percent American," especially during that fevered nativist era from 1910 to 1925.

But the greatest agents of assimilation were the children. Born in the New World, yet forced to live largely in terms of their parents' Old World, they channeled the language and customs of America to the parents, often to the great dismay of the latter. The second generation found itself living in a "both-and" situation, but their loyalties, even if seemingly divided, were primarily to the land in which they had been born. Everything they knew was here, and what their parents represented became increasingly outmoded and "foreign."

One thing that has not changed over the decades is the preference of Italian Americans for city life. Over eighty-eight percent still reside in urban areas, with the greatest concentration along the Eastern seaboard, from Boston to Delaware. The regional pattern of settlement established at the turn of the century has only been reinforced by more recent immigration. The "little Italies" persist, although diminished in size and frequently disrupted by urban renewal. But they are still vivid reminders of an era when immigrant pioneers discovered the New World for themselves.

This part is a collage of selections depicting the range of Italian American life through the imperceptible stages of assimilation from the generation of immigrants to the present. The selections deal with religion, politics, education, and social life—all the activities by which assimilation (whatever its meaning) is accomplished. Omitted here are articles dealing with work and the economy, powerful agents of acculturation, but covered briefly in Part Three. The time span of this chapter is long, from 1890 to the present, but it is necessarily so because the generations overlap, expressions of group self-consciousness change, and the nation itself has changed.

LITTLE ITALY, 1888

[Of all America's "little Italies," the one around Mulberry Street in Lower Manhattan is the archetype. This selection depicts life in that area shortly after the great emigration from southern Italy had begun in the 1880's.]

If the title read, "The Italians in New York" [instead of "The Italians of New York"], it would perhaps better accord with the general idea of the relation of this people to our civilization. The feeling is that they are in, but not of it. There is much, but not all the truth in that view. These picturesque foreigners, whom we are so familiar with behind a hand-organ or a fruit stall or a bootblack's stand, but who are still such an unknown quantity to us, and seem so little a part of our normal national or municipal life—these foreigners are not to remain foreign, and their presence bears in a degree upon that most vital question of our national life to-day—the labor problem.

But before looking into the sociological and political significance of their presence, let us look if we can at the people themselves. There are between forty and fifty thousand of them in New York, the estimates varying considerably within these limits because of the absence of any means of really determining their numbers. They live chiefly in two regions—that of which Mulberry Bend, speaking roughly, may be taken as one topographical extreme, and Crosby Street the other; and in the uptown colony, which extends (again making an approximation) from 110th to 129th Street. Many people, who know nothing else of the Italian quarter, have seen in the

From "The Italians of New York," by Viola Roseboro, in: *Cosmopolitan*, January, 1888.

summer from the street cars the delightfully picturesque groups on the Crosby Street sidewalks. The street itself is uncommonly foreign-looking, because of its narrowness, together with the height of its big gloomy tenements. In hot weather its tunnel-like appearance is rather attractive, and then the inhabitants return to their native habits and camp out in domestic platoons on the sidewalk. . . .

I have just completed an unusually careful examination of the lower place in Little Italy, as Mulberry Street, particularly the part known as the "Bend," and the neighborhood blocks are called. The street swings in a dirty curve northwest from Park Row, changes its direction at every foot, and finally runs north parallel with Broadway. The houses are chiefly tumble-down old rookeries not originally built for tenements, and are therefore worse than the worst of those constructed for the purpose. Ancient one-story stables have been converted into cheap shops and drinking places, and everywhere steps lead down from the sidewalk to various low dives in the cellars. The population swarms; the street is full of swarthy, unkempt men; buxom, handsome women with their babies at their breasts; old crones with bundles on back or head; vociferous Jew peddlers selling refuse fish, meat, and vegetables; pretty shy-eyed young girls who seem strangely misplaced, but are altogether at home; and everywhere, and outnumbering every other class, children, children big and little, healthy and sick, children ugly, and particularly, children handsome.

One of the special features of the quarter is the sale of stale bread, which, as a retail trade, is altogether in the hands of women. It is a systematized industry. The bread that used to be thrown away is now taken back by the big bakeries from the retail houses, and is collected by men, who sell it to the women; the latter retail it at from one to three cents a loaf from the curbstone. Happily stale bread is not chemically deteriorated, even when the mold has to be scraped and scrubbed from it; and all white bread is a luxury among these poor people, though it is a luxury now pretty generally indulged in. The economical, however, still purchase the black bread of their youth (metaphorically speaking only, let us hope) at three cents a pound. This, too, is not injurious, as is most such very cheap food, and it is nutritious. It was a cold day when I was last at the Bend, but the bread-sellers were holding their ground and conducting a brisk business.

Perhaps the thing apt to make the greatest impression on an entirely unfamiliar visitor through Little Italy would be the good manners of the people. The Hebrew peddlers and shopkeepers would probably pursue him with some harmless badinage; but from the Italians, if he were discreet, he would receive only that simple, well-bred courtesy that is unmatched among the other peasantries of Europe. There is much that is obscure and disputed about Italian tendencies and character; their reputation for bloodthirstiness has injured them in the eyes of our public, and the justice or injustice of that reputation it is not quite so easy to decide; but whatever evidence is to be derived from their general bearing is greatly in their favor. . . .

Much of the evidence about the Italians as citizens is in their favor. There is no doubt that they do a great deal of slashing and cutting of each other, but that is really not so much because they are more quarrelsome than other people, as because there is established among them here a sort of vendetta. They settle all their difficulties between themselves, it being a part of their code to submit nothing to the jurisdiction of our courts. This is certainly unfortunate; but it is a misfortune very certain to right itself gradually; and, doubtless, if our lower courts inspired a little more respect and confidence than they do, it would right itself the sooner. The Italians are not generally voters, and they are apt to be made to feel their political non-significance pretty severely when, through differences of opinion with their neighbors of other nationalities, they are brought into contact with our institutions. I know a lawyer who has had a number of clients among them in the last half dozen years, and his connection with them came about through the fact that he happened to see a policeman unmercifully clubbing an Italian, and interfered in his behalf. On investigation, he found that members of the force in that neighborhood were in the habit, just by way of keeping "flush," of levying a tax occasionally on its inhabitants, and that any resistance of this imposition was punished as he had seen, as well as in other and more ingenious ways. He was far too skeptical of results to undertake any general campaign for the oppressed; but, being a politician, he was able to obtain something like justice in the single cause he had espoused. This gave him great prestige among the Italians, and numbers of them have since sought him out when they needed a lawyer. He says they pay their bills, and are also grateful—a union of returns so novel that it fills him with amazement. . . .

I have spoken of one thing that interferes with the desire of the Italians for citizenship; but undoubtedly below that lies a certain temperamental indifference to the diversions of politics. They do not naturally care for the petty power and personal aggrandizement that in times of peace make the chief charm of political life under a popular government. Unlike the Irish or Germans, however ready to settle their own quarrels with knives, they take small interest in arranging the affairs of their neighbors with speeches or votes. They are essentially a simple race, whose interests are apt to be comparatively primitive and personal. To be sure their simplicity is quite a different article from that of the Saxon or Anglo-Saxon, and to the genuine member of either branch of that race all Italians are pretty sure to appear dark examples of duplicity. The same things that make the Italian indifferent to politics make him unamenable to the disorganizing influences of "organized labor." I fear, too, that they will make him peculiarly direct in his dealings with the buyer of votes, when, as must soon happen, that market will be fully open to him. There are already signs to that effect. However, all generalizations based on an observation of the foreign-born Italian are but limited data for other generalizations that can not yet be confidently made as to the coming American-born generation.

The Italian-American is to be a considerable part of our population. The immigrant has more interest in America, and intention of remaining, than is generally supposed. If our politics do not attract him, our financial possibilities do. He certainly does not always come to stay; perhaps he does not, generally; yet, nevertheless he very often stays. More remarkable still, if he goes back to Italy, it is in many cases only once more, and finally to return to America. This fact I have from those that have been brought into direct relation with them for a sufficient term of years to make their observations trustworthy.

They first emigrate and then, after they have obtained a foothold, they send for their families, if they have any, or they marry here, and once let children enter into the problem—and, as may be supposed, they usually do—the advantages of America for them exercise a controlling influence. It is only where the women are left altogether behind, as with the Chinese, that there will ever be much returning of our immigrants. . . .

Perhaps the very best thing to be noted of the Italians—because, for one thing, it is susceptible of proof, and for another, it is so antagonistic to all vice—is their thrift. Of that there can be no question. There are about fifty prominent padroni in New York, none of them worth less than ten thousand dollars, and one worth nearly two hundred thousand. In the nature of things the padrone is a self-made man—it is not exactly an occupation for gentlemen —and his charges, his "children" over here, certainly follow his example in money-getting. Around Mulberry Bend, Baxter Bend, and Five Points, names synonymous in the public mind with abject poverty and squalor, there are about sixteen Italian banking and money-making establishments, generally small places, of course, but thriving.

There has been some talk, by the way, about the great improvement in the once notorious Five Points neighborhood being due to the influx of the Italians. Again, some people have claimed it as a triumph for missionary effort. Perhaps both influences have had a wholesome effect. Certainly the missionary churches and schools are salutary, but I fear that the true glory of the change is due to the prosaic fact that Worth Street was cut straight through that net-work of vicious haunts, putting the neighborhood in direct communication with Broadway and its policemen, and opening it up to travel and traffic. Here is a lesson on conditions worth the thoughtful consideration of philanthropists.

Nothing so proves at a stroke the growth of Italians in wealth, power, and numbers as the change of late years in the procession celebrating the Festa di Garibaldi. It takes place on the twentieth of September, and commemorates the occupation of Rome by the Italian Government. It used to be composed of a most forlorn handful of poverty-striken youths. It is now the most striking, picturesque, and one of the most imposing pageants of the year. It is gorgeous with gold lace and silken banners. All the most beautiful uniforms of the Italian army are represented, and they are particularly handsome and brilliant. Most New Yorkers have not yet found out what a fine show it is, but they will soon. It is characterized by a taste and artistic instinct that make our efforts seem rather clumsy.

ITALIANS SHOULD BE REPUBLICANS

[The political party an immigrant supported was not dictated by theoretical considerations or even intelligent choices about candidates. Normally, it was a matter of what the party could do for him personally; or he voted against the party that the hated Irish supported. The early preference among Italians seems to have been for the Republicans, probably because the Irish controlled the local Democratic machinery in major cities. In November, 1894, the Chicago paper *L'Italia*, published an editorial, "The Two Parties Contrasted," making its political stand quite clear.]

When American citizens of foreign birth refuse to ally themselves with the Republican Party, they make war upon their own welfare. The Republican Party stands for all that the people fight for in the Old World. It is the champion of freedom, progress, order, and law. It is the steadfast foe of monarchial class rule.

It contains the bulk of the intelligence of the nation. That part of the Republic in which the Republican Party is the strongest is that part of the Republic which is the most prosperous.

The brightest names in American history during the last forty years are those of men who followed the Republican banner—Lincoln, Seward, Sumner, Greeley, Grant, Garfield, Blaine, and a host of others.

Look at the achievements of the Republican Party since it sprang into existence. It saved the Republic from disunion and destruction.

It crushed the mightiest rebellion in modern times.

From *Chicago Foreign Language Press Survey*, WPA Project, 1942.

It wiped out the foul stain of slavery. It brought the nation back to honest money and specie payments. It has persistently defended the national credit. It has cut down the national debt until that burden is no longer felt.

It has removed a multitude of taxes. It has built up American industries. It has opened a thousand new avenues for the employment of labor. It has made every citizen, no matter of what complexion, race, or creed, equal before the law.

Under Republican rule the United States reached its highest degree of civilization, liberty, and prosperity. Under Republican rule the American flag became honored and feared abroad as never before.

The record of the Democratic Party is directly the reverse. That party steadily upheld and defended slavery. The leaders of the Southern rebellion were Democratic leaders. It was the Democratic Party that pronounced the war a "failure." It was that party that attempted to flood the country with worthless and cheap money.

It is the Democratic Party that has assailed repeatedly the national credit. It is the Democratic Party that has robbed the voter of the ballot by shotguns and fraud. It is the Democratic Party that is now bent upon tearing down American industries, beggaring workmen, and covering the land with ruin.

Every traitor to the nation, from Aaron Burr down to Jefferson Davis, has belonged to the Democratic Party. Where the greatest amount of ignorance and lawlessness exists in the United States today, the Democratic Party will be found the strongest.

The adopted citizens of the Republic should not be misled by the noisy promises and falsehoods of Democratic demagogues and bosses. On every great question that has come before the people for the last two generations, the Democratic Party has been on the wrong side.

Every great act of legislation that has gone on the statute books of the nation for the last two generations has been put there through the aid of the Republican Party.

It is because the Democratic Party is undoing the work of the Republican Party that the country is now in the depths of calamity and want.

Foreign-born citizens should become thoroughly posted in the history of the Republican and the Democratic Party.

These citizens are here to found a home and to rear their children. They cannot afford to support a party which proposes to make such a home impossible and to drive them back to their native land. A party like the Democratic Party, which for half a century was the backbone of slavery, is not a party from which the escaped victims of foreign tyranny need expect sympathy or help.

ITALIAN CHILDREN IN THE PRIMARY GRADES

Jane Addams

[Jane Addams's Hull House, just west of Chicago's Loop, was a social-educational agency to help prepare neighborhood residents, especially immigrants, for the conditions of urban life. Her own educational theories were influenced by the work of John Dewey, who was teaching at the University of Chicago in the 1890's. In July, 1897, she gave an address before the National Educational Association's annual convention on the problems Italian children encountered in the public schools.]

Whatever may be our ultimate conception of education, and however much we may differ in definition, as doubtless the members of this convention do widely differ, we shall probably agree that the ultimate aim is to modify the character and conduct of the individual, and to harmonize and adjust his activities; that even the primary school should aim to give the child's own experience a social value; and that this aim too often fails of success in the brief sojourn of the child of the foreign peasant in the public school.

The members of the nineteenth ward Italian colony are largely from south Italy, Calabrian and Sicilian peasants, or Neapolitans, from the workingmen's quarters of that city. They have come to America with a distinct aim of earning money, and finding more room for the energies of themselves and their children. In almost all cases they mean to go back again, simply because their imaginations cannot picture a continuous life away from the old surroundings. Their experiences in Italy have been that of simple, out-door

From National Educational Association: *Journal of Proceedings and Addresses of the Thirty-sixth Annual Meeting*, Chicago, 1897, pp. 104–112.

activity, and the ideas they have have come directly to them from their struggle with nature, such a hand-to-hand struggle as takes place when each man gets his living largely through his own cultivation of the soil, with tools simply fashioned by his own hands. The women, as in all primitive life, have had more diversified activities than the men. They have cooked, spun, and knitted, in addition to their almost equal work in the fields. Very few of the peasant men or women can either read or write. They are devoted to their children, strong in their family feeling to remote relationships, and clannish in their community life.

The entire family has been upheaved, and is striving to adjust itself to its new surroundings. The men for the most part work on railroad extensions through the summer, under the direction of a padrone, who finds the work for them, regulates the amount of their wages, and supplies them with food. The first effect of immigration upon the women is that of idleness. They, of course, no longer work in the fields, nor milk the goats, nor pick up fagots. The mother of the family buys all the clothing not only already spun and woven, but made up into garments of a cut and fashion beyond her powers. It is, indeed, the most economical thing for her to do. Her house cleaning and cooking are of the simplest; the bread is usually baked outside of the house, and the macaroni bought prepared for boiling. All of those outdoor and domestic activities, which she would naturally have handed on to her daughters, have slipped away from her. The domestic arts are gone, with all their absorbing interests for the children, their educational value and incentive to activity. A household in a tenement receives almost no raw material. For the hundreds of children who have never seen wheat grow there are dozens who have never seen bread baked. The occasional washings and scrubbings are associated only with discomfort. The child of these families receives constantly many stimuli of most exciting sort from his city street life, but he has little or no opportunity to use his energies in domestic manufacture, or, indeed, constructively, in any direction. No activity is supplied to take the place of that which, in Italy, he would naturally have found in his own home, and no new union is made for him with wholesome life.

Italian parents count upon the fact that their children learn the English language and American customs before they themselves do, and act not only as interpreters of the language about them, but as buffers between them and Chicago, and this results in a certain, almost pathetic dependence of the family upon the child. When a member of the family, therefore, first goes to school, the event is fraught with much significance to all the others. The family has no social life in any structural form, and can supply none to the child. If he receives it in the school, and gives it to his family, the school would thus become the connector with the organized society about them.

It is the children aged six, eight, and ten who go to school, entering, of course, the primary grades. If a boy is twelve or thirteen on his arrival in America, his parents see in him a wage-earning factor, and the girl of the same age is already looking toward her marriage.

Let us take one of these boys, who has learned in his six or eight years to speak his native language, and to feel himself strongly identified with the fortunes of his family.

Whatever interest has come to the minds of his ancestors has come through the use of their hands in the open air; and open air and activity of body have been the inevitable accompaniments of all their experiences. Yet the first thing that the boy must do when he reaches school is to sit still, at least part of the time, and he must learn to listen to what is said to him, with all the perplexity of listening to a foreign tongue. He does not find this very stimulating, and is slow to respond to the more subtle incentives of the schoolroom. The peasant child is perfectly indifferent to showing off and making a good recitation. He leaves all that to his schoolfellows who are more sophisticated and who are equipped with better English. It is not the purpose of this paper to describe the child's life in school, which the audience knows so much better than the writer, but she ventures to assert that if the little Italian lad were supplied, then and there, with tangible and resistance-offering material upon which to exercise his muscle, he would go bravely to work, and he would probably be ready later to use the symbols of letters and numbers to record and describe what he had done; and might even be incited to the exertion of reading to find out what other people had done. Too often the teacher's conception of her duty is to transform him into an American of a somewhat snug and comfortable type, and she insists that the boy's powers must at once be developed in an abstract direction, quite ignoring the fact that his parents have had to do only with tangible things. She has little idea of the development of Italian life. Her outlook is national and not racial, and she fails, therefore, not only in knowledge of, but also in respect for, the child and his parents. She quite honestly estimates the child upon an American basis. The contempt for the experiences and languages of their parents which foreign children sometimes exhibit, and which is most damaging to their moral as well as intellectual life, is doubtless due in part to the overestimation which the school places upon speaking and reading in English. This cutting into his family loyalty takes away one of the most conspicuous and valuable traits of the Italian child.

His parents are not specially concerned in keeping him in school, and will not hold him there against his inclination, until his own interest shall do it for him. Their experience does not point to the good American tradition that it is the educated man who finally succeeds. The richest man on Ewing street can neither read nor write—even Italian. His cunning and aquisitiveness, combined with the credulity and ignorance of his countrymen, have slowly brought about his large fortune.

The child himself may feel the stirring of a vague ambition to go on until he is as the other children are; but he is not popular with his schoolfellows, and he sadly feels the lack of dramatic interest. Even the pictures and objects presented to him, as well as the language, are strange.

If we admit that in education it is necessary to begin with the experiences which the child already has, through his spontaneous and social activity, then the city street begins this education for him in a more natural way than does the school.

The south Italian peasant comes from a life of picking olives and oranges, and he easily sends his children out to pick up coal from railroad tracks or wood from buildings which have been burned down. Unfortunately, this process leads by easy transition to petty thieving. It is easy to go from the coal on the railroad track to the coal and wood which stand before the dealer's shop; from the potatoes which have rolled from a rumbling wagon to the vegetables displayed by the grocer. This is apt to be the record of the boy who responds constantly to the stimuli and temptations of the street, although in the beginning his search for bits of food and fuel was prompted by the best of motives. The outlets offered to such a boy by the public school have failed to attract him, and as a truant he accepts this ignoble use of his inherited faculty. For the dynamic force which the boy has within himself, the spirit of adventure and restless activity, many unfortunate outlets are constantly offered.

The school, of course, has to compete with a great deal from the outside in addition to the distractions of the neighborhood. Nothing is more fascinating than that mysterious "down town," whither the boy longs to go to sell papers and black boots; to attend theaters; and, if possible, to stay all night, on the pretense of waiting for the early edition of the great dailies. If a boy is once thoroughly caught in these excitements, nothing can save him from overstimulation, and consequent debility and worthlessness, but a vigorous application of a compulsory-education law, with a truant school; which, indeed, should have forestalled the possibility of his ever thus being caught.

It is a disgrace to us that we allow so many Italian boys thus to waste their health in premature, exciting activity; and their mentality in mere cunning, which later leaves them dissolute and worthless men, with no habits of regular work and a distaste for its dullness.

These boys are not of criminal descent, nor vagrant heritage. On the contrary, their parents have been temperate, laborious, and painstaking, living for many generations on one piece of ground.

Had these boys been made to feel their place in the school community; had they been caught by its fascinations of marching and singing together as a distinct corps; had they felt the charm of manipulating actual material, they might have been spared this erratic development. Mark Crawford, for many years the able superintendent of the Chicago House of Corrections, has said that in looking over the records of that institution he found that of 21,000 boys under seventeen years of age who had been sent there under sentence less than eighty were schoolboys.

The school is supposed to select the more enduring forms of life, and to eliminate, as far as possible, the trivialities and irrelevancies which actual living constantly presents.

But, in point of fact, the Italian child has received most of his interests upon the streets, where he has seen a great deal of these trivialities, magnified out of all proportion to their worth. He, of course, cares for them very much, and only education could give him a clew as to what to select and what to eliminate.

Leaving the child who does not stay in school, let us now consider the child who does faithfully remain until he reaches the age of factory work, which is, fortunately, in the most advanced of our factory states, fourteen years. Has anything been done up to this time, has even a beginning been made, to give him a consciousness of his social value? Has the outcome of the processes to which he has been subjected adapted him to deal more effectively and in a more vital manner with his present life?

Industrial history in itself is an interesting thing, and the story of the long struggle of man in his attempts to bring natural forces under human control could be made most dramatic and graphic. The shops and factories all about him contain vivid and striking examples of the high development of the simple tools which his father still uses, and of the lessening expenditure of human energy. He is certainly cut off from nature, but he might be made to see nature as the background and material for the human activity which now surrounds him. Giotto portrayed the applied arts and industries in a series of such marvelous beauty and interest that every boy who passed the Shepherd's Tower longed to take his place in the industrial service of the citizens of Florence. We, on the contrary, have succeeded in keeping our factories, so far as the workers in them are concerned, totally detached from that life which means culture and growth.

No attempt is made to give a boy, who, we know, will certainly have to go into one of them, any insight into their historic significance, or to connect them in any intelligible way with the past and future. He has absolutely no consciousness of his social value, and his activities become inevitably perfectly mechanical. Most of the children who are thus put to work go on in their slavish life without seeing whither it tends, and with no reflections upon it. The brightest ones among them, however, gradually learn that they belong to a class which does the necessary work of life, and that there is another class which tends to absorb the product of that work.

May we not charge it to the public school that it has given to this child no knowledge of the social meaning of his work? Is it not possible that, if the proper estimate of education had been there; if all the children had been taught to use equally and to honor equally both their heads and hands; if they had been made even dimly to apprehend that for an individual to obtain the greatest control of himself for the performance of social service, and to realize within himself the value of the social service which he is performing, is to obtain the fullness of life—the hateful feeling of class distinction could never have grown up in any of them? It would then be of little moment to himself or to others whether the boy finally served the commonwealth in the factory or in the legislature.

But nothing in this larger view of life has reached our peasant's son. He finds himself in the drudgery of a factory, senselessly manipulating unrelated material, using his hands for unknown ends, and his head not at all. Owing to the fact that during his years in school he has used his head mostly, and his hands very little, nothing bewilders him so much as the suggestion that the school was intended as a preparation for his work in life. He would be equally amazed to find that this school was supposed to fill his mind with beautiful images and powers of thought, so that he might be able to do this dull mechanical work, and still live a real life outside of it. . . .

Those of us who are working to bring a fuller life to the industrial members of the community, who are looking forward to a time when work shall not be senseless drudgery, but shall contain some self-expression of the worker, sometimes feel the hopelessness of adding evening classes and social entertainments as a mere frill to a day filled with monotonous and deadening drudgery; and we sometimes feel that we have a right to expect more help from the public schools than they now give us.

If the army of school children who enter the factories every year possessed thoroughly vitalized faculties, they might do much to lighten this incubus of dull factory work which presses so heavily upon so large a number of our fellow-citizens. Has our commercialism been so strong that our schools have become insensibly commercialized, rather than that our industrial life has felt the broadening and illuminating effect of the schools?

The boy in the primary grades has really been used as material to be prepared for the grammar grades. Unconsciously his training, so far as it has been vocational at all, has been in the direction of clerical work. Is it possible that the business men, whom we have so long courted and worshiped in America, have really been dictating the curriculum of our public schools, in spite of the conventions of educators and the suggestions of university professors? The business man has, of course, not said to himself: "I will have the public school train office boys and clerks for me, so that I may have them cheap;" but he has thought, and sometimes said: "Teach the children to write legibly, and to figure accurately and quickly; to acquire habits of punctuality and order; to be prompt to obey, and not question why; and you will fit them to make their way in the world as I have made mine."

Has the workingman been silent as to what he desires for his children, and allowed the business man to decide for him there as he has allowed the politician to manage his municipal affairs? Or has the workingman suffered from our universal optimism, and really believed that his children would never need to go into industrial life at all, but that his sons would all become bankers and merchants?

Certain it is that no sufficient study has been made of the child who enters into industrial life early, and remains there permanently, to give him some set-off to its monotony and dullness; some historic significance of the part he is taking in the life of the commonwealth; some conception of the dignity of labor, which is sometimes mentioned to him, but never demonstrated. We have a curious notion, in spite of all our realism, that it is not possible for the mass of mankind to have interests and experiences of themselves which are worth anything. We transmit to the children of working people our own skepticism regarding the possibility of finding any joy or profit in their work. We practically incite them to get out of it as soon as possible.

I am quite sure that no one can possibly mistake this paper as a plea for trade schools, or as a desire to fit the boy for any given industry. Such a specializing would indeed be stupid when our industrial methods are developing and changing, almost day by day. But it does contend that life, as seen from the standpoint of the handworker, should not be emptied of all social consciousness and value, and that the school could make the boy infinitely more flexible and alive than he is now to the materials and forces of nature which, in spite of all man's activities, are unchangeable.

FEAST DAYS IN LITTLE ITALY

Jacob Riis

[Few people were as well acquainted with the immigrant neighborhoods of New York as Danish-born Jacob Riis. As a journalist, he documented the slum conditions of the Lower East Side, and, as a social reformer, he prompted efforts to eradicate the worst aspects of tenement life. His book, *How the Other Half Lives* (1890), was a classic exposé of the causes and conditions of urban poverty. The following selection shows that Riis could also portray, with keen insight, the inner life of an immigrant community.]

The rumble of trucks and the slamming of boxes up on the corner ceased for the moment, and in the hush that fell upon Mulberry street snatches of a familiar tune, punctuated by a determined drum, struggled into the block. Around the corner came a band of musicians with green cock-feathers in hats set rakishly over fierce, sunburnt faces. A raft of boys walked in front, abreast of two bored policemen, stepping in time to the music. Four men carried a silk-fringed banner with evident pride. Behind them a strange procession toiled along: women with babies at the breast and dragging little children; fat and prosperous padrones carrying their canes like staves of office and authority; young men out for a holiday; old men with lives of hardship and toil written in their halting gait and worn and crooked frames; lastly, a cripple on crutches, who strove manfully to keep up. The officials in Police Headquarters looked out of the windows and viewed the show indifferently. It was an every-day spectacle. This one had wandered

From *Century Magazine*, August, 1899.

around the block thrice that day. President [Theodore] Roosevelt (of the Police Board), who had come out to go to lunch, was much interested. To him it was new.

"Where do you suppose they are going?" he said, surveying the procession from the steps. He was told that some Italian village saint was having his day celebrated around in Elizabeth street, and he expressed a desire to see how it was done. So we fell in, he and I, and followed the band too, at a little distance.

It led us to a ramshackle old house in Elizabeth street, and halted there in front of a saloon with the appealing announcement on a swinging sign: "Vino, Vino, di California, di Italia. Any Kind of Whiskey for Sale." The band and the fat men went into the saloon. We followed the women, the children, and the scraggy ones through a gap in the brick wall that passed for an alley to the back yard, and there came upon the village of Auletta feasting its patron saint.

It was a yard no longer, but a temple. All the sheets of the tenement had been stretched so as to cover the ugly sheds and outhouses. Against the dark rear tenement the shrine of the saint had been erected, shutting it altogether out of sight with a wealth of scarlet and gold. Great candles and little ones, painted and be-ribboned, burned in a luminous grove before the altar. The sun shone down upon a mass of holiday-clad men and women, to whom it was all as a memory of home, of the beloved home across the seas; upon mothers kneeling devoutly with their little ones at the shrine, and upon children bringing offerings to the saint's glory. His face smiled down benignly upon them from the frame of gaudy colors with the coat of arms of the village—or was it a hint at the legendary history of the saint?—a fox dragging a reluctant rooster by the tail. In his own country the saint is held to be mighty against fever and the ague, of which there is much there. The faith which prompted a stricken mother to hang the poor garments of her epileptic boy close to his hand, in the hope that so he might be healed, provoked no smile in the latter-day spectators. The sorrow and trust were too genuine for that. The fire-escapes of the tene-ment had, with the aid of some cheap muslin draperies, a little tinsel, and the strange artistic genius of this people, been trans-formed into beautiful balconies, upon which the tenants of the front house had reserved seats. In a corner of the yard over by the hydrant, a sheep, which was to be raffled off as the climax of the celebration, munched its wisp of hay patiently, while bare-legged children climbed its back and pulled its wool. From the second story of the adjoining house, which was a stable, a big white horse stuck his head at intervals out of the window, and surveyed the shrine and the people with an interested look.

The musicians, issuing forth victorious from a protracted struggle with a fleet of schooners in the saloon, came out, wiping their mus-tachios, and blew "Santa Lucia" on their horns. The sweetly seductive melody woke the echoes of the block and its slumbering memories. The old women rocked in their seats, their faces buried in their hands. The crowd from the street increased, and the chief celebrant, who turned out to be no less a person than the saloon-keeper himself, reaped a liberal harvest of silver half-dollars. The villagers bowed and crossed themselves before the saint, and put into the plate their share toward the expense of the celebration. Its guardian made a strong effort to explain about the saint to Mr. Roosevelt.

"He is just-a lik'-a your St. Patrick here," he said, and the president of the Police Board nodded. He understood.

Between birthdays, the other added, the saint was left in the loft of the saloon, lest the priest get hold of him and get a corner on him, as it were. Once he got him into his possession, he would not let the people have him except upon payment of a fee that would grow with the years. But the saint belonged to the people, not to the church. He was their home patron, and they were not going to give him up. In the saloon they had him safe. Mr. Roosevelt delighted the honest villagers by taking five shares in the sheep, albeit the suggestion that it might be won by him and conducted in triumph by the band to Police Headquarters gave him pause. He trusted to luck, however, and took chances.

And luck favored him. He did not win the sheep. The names of all who had taken chances were put into a bag with that of the saint, and in the evening drawn out one by one. When the saint's name appeared there arose a great shout. The next would be the winner. Every neck was craned to read the lucky name as it came out.

"Philomeno Motso," read the man with the bag, and there was an answering shriek from the third-floor fire-escape behind the shrine. The widow up there had won the prize. Such luck was undreamed of. She came down forthwith and hugged the sheep rapturously, while the children kissed it and wept for joy. The last of the candles went out, and the shrine was locked in the loft over the saloon for another year.

San Donato's feast-day is one of very many such days that are celebrated in New York in the summer months. By what magic the calendar of Italian saints was arranged so as to bring so many birthdays within the season of American sunshine I do not know. But it is well. The religious fervor of our Italians is not to be pent up within brick walls, and sunshine and flowers belong naturally to it. "Religious" perhaps hardly describes it, yet in its outward garb it is nearly always that. They have their purely secular feasts,—their Garibaldi day and their Constitution day, both in June, their Columbus day, and the day in September commemorating the invasion of Rome and the end of the temporal power of the pope,— and they celebrate them with enthusiasm of which their hundred and fifty-odd societies in New York have always an abundant store. The rigors of our Northern winter and an unfavorable experience with the police have driven the carnival indoors and turned it into a big masquerade ball. Once, on a temptingly sunny February day some eight or ten years ago, Mulberry street started in to keep carnival in the traditional way; but it had forgotten the police regulations. The merrymakers were locked up for masquerading without a permit, and were fined ten dollars each in the police court. Ball tickets are cheaper, and Mulberry street has confined itself to dancing since. But if one wishes to catch a glimpse of the real man, it is not on these occasions that it is to be had. It is when he is "at home" with the saint in the back yard, the church, or wherever it may be.

To the Italian who came over the sea the saint remains the rallying-point in his civic and domestic life to the end of his days. His son may cast him off, but not the father. Occasionally their relations are strained, perhaps. Such things happen in all families. Inattention to duty on the part of the saint may seem to require correction, or even more drastic measures. You may catch your man, after a losing game of cards, shying a boot at the shrine in the corner, with an angry "Why did you let me lose? I gave you a new candle last week"; but that only goes to prove the closeness of the compact between them. To the homesick peasant who hangs about the Mott-street café for hours, hungrily devouring with his eyes the candy counterfeit of Mount Vesuvius in the window, with lurid lava-streams descending and saffron smoke ascending, predicting untold stomach-quakes in the block, the saint means home and kindred, neighborly friendship in a strange land, and the old communal ties, which, if anything, are tightened by distance and homesickness. In fact, those ties are as real as they were at home. Just as the Aulettans flock in Elizabeth street, so in Mulberry, Mott, and Thompson streets downtown, and in the numbered streets of Little Italy uptown, almost every block has its own village of mountain or lowland, and with the village its patron saint, in whose worship or celebration—call it what you will—the particular camp makes reply to the question, "Who is my neighbor?"

THE ITALIAN THEATER
OF NEW YORK
Hutchins Hapgood

[While working as a reporter for the New York *Commercial Advertiser* in the late 1890's, Hutchins Hapgood acquired a fascination for the immigrant settlements of Manhattan. But, unlike Jacob Riis, Hapgood did not enter these neighborhoods as a reformer. He went there to search out their vitality, their human, social, and cultural qualities. He sought out the scholars, poets, actors, artists, and journalists in order to reveal the world of the immigrant at its best for his readers. Most of his articles dealt with the Jewish ghetto and were subsequently collected into a book, *The Spirit of the Ghetto* (1902).]

On Spring Street, within a few blocks of the Bowery, the heart of the Italian quarter is laid open to the stranger. In this little section are concentrated the Italian theater, properly speaking, an Italian puppet show, and a characteristic Italian restaurant. The poor Neapolitan in New York frequents these resorts, and on the stage of the theater and the puppet show he sees what he is accustomed to in the little theaters of Naples, where he goes to pass a lively or a passionate evening. After his spaghetti, chianti, and *fernetbranca* (composed of paregoric, peppermint, wormwood, and varnish, to judge by the taste), the suave and polite man with dark eyes and ragged clothes lights his cigarette, and with his black derby hat fixed permanently on his head he goes to see the continued fight between the armoured puppets, representing Christian knights and Saracen warriors, at Spring Street, or to see *Othello*, some melodrama, or farce, at No. 24 of the same street.

The puppet show is only one of several of the same kind in

From *The Bookman*, August, 1900.

New York, in all of which the Italians, in rags strangely contrasting with their aristocratic lineaments and courteous manners—men mainly, but also noble-featured women and fine-eyed children—crowd with vivid interest in the maneuverings, widow's plaints, heroic deeds, fine sentiments, and all the showy trappings of medieval warfare. The marionettes encased in complete steel—in armor, helmet, and vizor, weigh from forty to seventy pounds, and when they rush together in fight the noise is as tremendous as the resulting excitement in the audience. One solitary Christian knight will often meet the shock of Saracen after Saracen, swung in rapid succession to the boards by mechanical arrangements behind. A fearful meeting of rapid and resounding swords, and the Saracen lies dead in the middle of the stage, where many others are soon piled up by the doughty knight. The rattling armor, the clash of the swords, the swoop of the knight as he flies to meet the iron-harnessed enemy, the cheers of the excitable audience, combine in as exhilarating noise as the most passionate and romantic audience could desire.

Much of the theatrical life of the East Side is realistic, notably that represented on the Yiddish theaters on the Bowery; but of realism in the ordinary sense the Italian understands nothing. He has no respect for exact fact, and sees more compelling interest in these brilliant and noisy puppets than in the most intellectual and convincing comedy of manners or problem play. When, after a street quarrel, the Italian dying in a Naples hospital regains consciousness merely to ask the doctor appealingly whether he will live to stick his knife into his enemy, the same passionate spirit is expressed that is satisfied at these vigorous entertainments.

The regular theater also satisfies the romantic and fiery Italian heart, although less crudely and with greater variety of means. The grace of the race, too, and the spontaneous character of its farce are manifested in a company of actors not particularly endowed with histrionic power, but possessing to the full the natural spirit and honest directness in passion and in fun of the people. Their farce is allied to their serious play in one important respect: it is pure fun, never approaches the comedy of manners, as it lacks entirely the intellectual and critical element; just as the serious play is pure passion and sentiment, without the reflective or philosophic element, which distinguishes the tragedy of the Anglo-Saxon, the German, and the Jew.

The quality of simplicity, of purity in that sense, is what runs through the tragedy, the melodrama, the farce, and the acting at this little box of a theater. The building, indeed, is so small that the constant vociferation of the prompter is heard throughout the audience; he simply reads aloud the entire play; for, since five or six different dramas are given every week, the actors make no pretense of knowing their lines. But the audience, simple and at the same time sensitive to what is fundamentally dramatic, do not mind in the least. Quick to respond to the emotional situation, they do not need realistic setting and devices to make them feel the illusion of the stage. That they ignore what are really trivial incongruities points to feeling and imagination, and in aesthetic competency puts them far ahead of those blasé rounders on Broadway who watch closely the mechanics of the scene. It is, indeed, the human drama only in which the Italians are absorbed. Not only intellectual comedy is absent, but even plays giving the "local color" of the community in New York: all that is given breathes universal passion or simple fun. . . .

In comedy, too, the same quality as in the serious drama is predominant: the intellectual element is largely lacking. It is buffoonery, farce, or simply burlesque pantomime. Often the fun is exquisite in its spontaneity and native drollness. The excellence of the acting here also rests in the naturalness with which the unsophisticated characteristics of the race are rendered. They never play the hard, metallic farce so popular at the uptown theater—the same play may be given, but by the Italians it is softened, made more natural, and more simply enjoyable. The construction of the farce is generally loose, which leaves room for the actors to infuse very fetching fun, roughly felicitous burlesque, and pantomimic characterization.

The Café-Chantant, a play so popular that it received the unusual honor of several consecutive productions, contains elements from the entire scale of Italian mimic fun, and also comes as near intellectual satire as is possible under the simple circumstances. In New York, Harlem, Hoboken, etc., there are many Italian music halls or cafés-chantants, where cheap variety performances are given. As no admission fee is charged, drinks being depended upon for profit, the regular theater (where the price of admission ranges from ten to thirty cents) has keenly felt the unworthy competition; so that the satiric element of The Café-Chantant, although translated from the French, and consequently not aiming directly at New York conditions, is yet held definitely in mind by the actors and keenly understood by the audience. A couple of actors cannot secure an engagement at a regular theater, but they live with their wives in a garret and prefer to starve rather than to go to the café-chantant, the manager of which offers them fabulous sums for their services. Meantime, their wives sell all their stage costumes for twenty-five cents, in order to buy food; the letters that come to them turn out to be bills rather than engagements; they give lessons in acting, for which they are not paid; and finally, in deep humiliation, are forced to go to the manager of the café-chantant, who pays them in advance. The last act represents a performance at the café-chantant, where the two regular actors play a couple of clowns and go through a ludicrous pantomimic show of comic love and jealousy. The other members, however, point to the incompetence of the ordinary music hall performers, who are indiscriminately accepted by the manager and are amateurs and fakes of various sorts. There is a duet between two lovers who have taken only one lesson previously from the actors. Then comes a boy made up as a woman, who sings in a full voice and promenades about the stage, kicking his train majestically from side to side. There is a "fake" strong man who carefully manipulates wooden weights, each labelled 500 pounds. . . .

The "local color" of the Italian quarter is a quality not easily discoverable in this little theater community. Its quality is that of the Italians in general rather than of the Italians under special New York conditions. The audience, the actors, are just the same as they might be in a little theater in southern Italy, and the plays are imported, written by men in Italy. In this respect, again, there is a marked contrast between the Italian and the Yiddish stage in New York. On the latter there is much which portrays the life of the Jews in New York, an original and local element in the plays, for the making of which there are a number of Yiddish playwrights. The reason, no doubt, is that the Yiddish community have become once for all identified with New York and are undergoing changes and modifications incident to a genuine life here; but the Italians remain Italians, dreaming of sunny Naples.

There have been indeed one or two men in the quarter who from time to time have written plays supposedly based on the life here. But the number of these plays can be easily counted on the fingers of one hand. The most famous of them are *Maria Barberi, Jack the Ripper*, and *The Mysteries of Mulberry Street*, the former two written by Eduardo Pecoraro and the latter by Beniemino Ciambelli. *The Mysteries* had a great success, running four successive nights. But even in these plays there is no real originality. A New York episode is merely taken, but the same thing might have happened in Naples and been treated by the playwright in exactly the same spirit—that spirit of simplicity and passion wholly unassociated with intellectual comment. The genre, therefore, the minor picturesque, the character sketch, the "problem" play, the interest generally in special conditions, are lacking, leaving at the base of their drama the poetry of passion.

ITALIAN ASSOCIATIONS OF NEW YORK

Antonio Mangano

[All sizable Italian settlements developed an active social and organizational life with clubs, mutual benefit societies, fraternal organizations, legal and medical societies, and, of course, churches. Most basic were the self-help societies that provided sickness and death benefits, and the "banks" that remitted money to Italy. By 1912 there were at least 250 mutual aid societies in New York. The following report on some of the early New York associations was made by Calabrian-born Antonio Mangano, a Protestant clergyman.]

The New York colony is composed of persons coming from nearly every nook and corner of the old peninsula. It is by no means strange, then, that they should bring with them local prejudices and narrow sympathies; it is not to be wondered that they feel that highest duty consists in being loyal to the handful who come from their immediate section and in manifesting opposition toward those who come from other localities. Thus it comes to pass that while a man may be known as an Italian, he is far better known as a Napoletano, Calabrese, Veneziano, Abbruzese, or Siciliano. This means that the Italian colony is divided into almost as many groups as there are sections of Italy represented.

There are, however, many signs which unmistakably point to a decided change for the better in the near future. There are certain forces at work which have for their ultimate object the development of a larger spirit of co-operation, which will enable the Italians as a whole to unite for the attainment of specific objects. The main purpose of this article, therefore, is to point out the chief Italian

From "The Associated Life of the Italians in New York City," in: *Charities*, May 7, 1904.

institutions which indicate the lines along which Italian organized effort is directed, and to describe briefly their operations.

Among the agencies which have for their ideal united Italian action, there are none more potent than the Italian Chamber of Commerce. This organization, founded in 1887 with but a few members, today embraces in its membership of 201 a majority of the Italian business men in Greater New York. . . .

In addition, the chamber . . . aims at increasing Italian exports to this country and American exports to Italy; it acts as a medium in suggesting to dealers, both Americans and Italians, where they can secure the particular goods desired.

But to my mind, while I would not for a moment detract from the commercial functions of the chamber, its greatest good is achieved along another line—one which is destined eventually to lead the Italians to drop sectional feeling and rejoice in the glory of a common nationality. That the Neapolitan, the Sicilian, the Roman, can all join this organization and have as the one object the advancement of Italian interests, is a step in the right direction and toward another end which is eminently wholesome and greatly to be desired.

The Columbus Hospital is situated on Twentieth street between Second and Third avenues. Organized in 1892 and incorporated in 1895, it has been from its beginning under the direct supervision of the missionary Sisters of the Sacred Heart. . . .

Columbus Hospital is generally known as an Italian institution, yet of the twenty-one physicians on its medical and surgical staff not one is an Italian, but the sisters who carry it on are all native Italians, and ninety-five per cent of the patients treated are of that race.

The Society for the Protection of Italian Immigrants was founded three years ago, and since then has, without a shadow of a doubt, rendered more practical assistance to the thousands flocking to our shores than any other institution working in the interest of Italians.

Speaking of the conditions in which Italians find themselves on arrival, Eliot Norton, president of the society, says in his annual report: "These immigrants are landed at Ellis Island, where they are examined by United States officials. From there some go into the interior of the country and some remain in New York. Almost all of them are very ignorant, very childlike, and wholly unfamiliar with the ways, customs and language of this country. Hence it is obvious that they need friendly assistance from the moment of debarkation at Ellis Island. Those who go into the interior of the country need to be helped in getting on the right train, without losing their way or money; while those coming to New York City need guidance to their destination and, while going there, protection from sharps, crooks and dishonest runners, and thereafter to have advice and employment." . . .

Closely associated with the work of the Society for the Protection of Italian Immigrants is the Italian Benevolent Institute. Within the past two years it has taken on new life. The work was encouraged by gifts from many quarters, the most noteworthy one being from His Majesty the King of Italy, which amounted to 20,000 lire. One of its encouraging features is the fact that it is maintained almost exclusively by Italians.

The institute has its headquarters in a double house, 165-7 West Houston street, which is intended as a place of refuge for the destitute. It often happens that newcomers, bound for interior points, land in New York without a cent in their pockets, expecting to find at the post-office or some bank the sum necessary to carry them to their destination; it also often happens that the money expected does not arrive in time. To such persons as these the Benevolent Institute opens its doors. Then, too, there are immigrants who come with the intention of settling in New York. Such persons may have $8 or $10, but unless they find work at once they too are compelled to seek aid from some source. Further, New York has become, in a sense, a central market for Italian labor, and of those who go to distant points in search of work some fail to find it, and return to the city.

Attention has already been called to the fact that the Italian is lacking in the spirit of unity, and of association in a large sense. The last few years, however, have witnessed a few noteworthy victories in the interest of larger sympathy—mainly through the efforts of a few leading spirits who have been prominent in the affairs of the colony. If one can prophesy, in the light of tendencies already at work, the day is coming when the Italian colony will recognize its responsibilities, and, throwing aside petty jealousies, will launch out upon such a policy as will best enhance the interests of the Italians as a whole.

If we were asked, therefore, whether there is any bond which unites the Italian colony as a whole, we must answer no. Even the Roman Church cannot be considered such a unifying factor in the attitude of indifference taken toward its claims.

It must be observed, however, that the Italian manifests a strong tendency toward organization with small groups for social ends and for the purpose of mutual aid. There are in Manhattan alone over one hundred and fifty Italian societies of one sort or another. "The moral disunity of the old peninsula is transplanted here."

The Italian does not lack the instinct of charity or mutual helpfulness; but at present he lacks the instinct in a broad sense. He would take the bread from his own mouth in order to help his fellow townsman; there is nothing he will not do for his *paesano;* but it must not be expected from this that he will manifest such an attitude toward *all Italians.* Notwithstanding, were it not for this strong feeling, even though limited to small groups, we should have many more calls upon public charity on the part of the Italians than we now do. . . .

As one passes through the Italian quarter and observes the number of windows displaying the sign "Banca Italiana," he is naturally led to think that the Italians do nothing but deposit money. I am told on very good authority that in Greater New York the number of so-called "banks"—distinctively Italian—is beyond three hundred. It should be said, however, that ninety per cent of these banks are nothing more or less than forwarding agencies. They are constantly springing up to meet the needs of this or that group of persons, coming from a particular town or village. For example, here is a group of people from Cosenza. They want a place where they can have their letters directed. They need some one who can assist them in the matter of sending home money now and then. They look for information regarding new fields of labor which are developing. It is in response to these needs that the larger part of these so-called banks have been brought into existence. They are generally attached to a saloon, grocery store, or cigar store—sometimes to a cobbler shop. The "banker" is always a fellow townsman of the particular group that does business with him, and this for the simple reason that the *paesano* is trusted more, no matter how solid, financially, another bank may be.

The one real substantial Italian bank, incorporated in 1896 under the laws of the state of New York, is the Italian Savings Bank, situated on the corner of Mulberry and Spring streets. It has today on deposit $1,059,369.19. Its report shows open accounts to the number of 7,000, and books up to date to the number of 10,844. The moneys deposited in this bank, as might be supposed, are generally in very small sums, but the figures show an average sum on deposit of about $170. The depositors as a rule are Italians, but persons of any nationality may open accounts if they wish.

This institution was started at a time when small Italian banks were failing, and when there was special antagonism to such institutions, both on the part of those who had lost money through the failure of the smaller banks and on the part of those of the small banks which continued to do business. But through determination and perseverance on the part of the officers under the lead of Cav. J. N. Francolini, who was chosen president, and who for two years gave his services free of charge, the institution was placed upon a firm foundation, and is today a credit to the colony.

Any discussion of the associated life of the Italians would be incomplete unless some mention were made of religious organizations. There are on Manhattan, 23 Roman Catholic churches which are entirely or in part devoted to the Italians. As one enters these churches, he is struck by a certain warmth and artistic display which are lacking in many of the other churches. The Italian has had centuries of training in the matter of artistic cathedral decorations and, taking into account the fact that so much of his life has been centered about the church, it is but natural that his places of worship should embody all that art and aesthetic natures can contribute. The church does work for Italians along the lines of parochial schools, and maintains a home in the lower part of the city for female immigrants.

In Manhattan, there are four regularly organized evangelical churches—maintained by the Presbyterian, Methodist, Protestant Episcopal and Baptist denominations. With the exception of the beautiful little Episcopal church on Broome street, the evangelical churches may be said to lack altogether the very elements which the Italian, in view of his past training, deems most essential to his environment for worship. And yet notwithstanding this, these churches are well attended. There are several other missions established for Italians, but results of their work cannot easily be seen, simply because they lack the organization necessary to hold together the people whom they reach in a more or less effective manner.

Probably the institution which has done more than any other for the Italian colony in an educational way is the school on Leonard street, devoted exclusively to Italians and maintained by the Children's Aid Society. This school, with its faithful body of teachers, has exerted a strong influence upon the Italian colony. The day sessions are conducted precisely along public school lines, mainly for children who do not enter the public schools for a variety of reasons. A night school is conducted in the same building, which aims primarily at giving instruction in the English language. There is an average attendance of men and boys at these classes of about three hundred. Besides this, there is a department of Italian instruction. A teacher who has this work in charge is supported by the Italian government. The building is also used for social purposes, and entertainments are held during the winter every Friday evening.

As an evidence of the esteem felt by Italians who have come under the influence of this school, a movement is now on foot among them to secure funds—$3,000 has already been raised—for the establishment of a similar school for the Italians in "Little Italy."

A SURVEY OF BOSTON'S ITALIANS

Robert A. Woods

[The author of this selection, Robert A. Woods, was head of South End House in Boston from 1891 until his death in 1925.]

There is some question as to how the Italians will thrive physically in the New England climate. The death-rate among them increases with the second generation. This is no doubt largely the effect of extremely close tenement quarters upon people who belong out of doors and in a sunny land. Their over-stimulating and innutritious diet is precisely the opposite sort of feeding from that demanded by our exhilarating and taxing atmospheric conditions. This fact suggests the first and perhaps the chief step in bringing about the adaptation of the Italian type to life in America. On the other hand, it is undesirable that the Italians should be in any considerable degree educated away from their love of the open air and their satisfaction in rural existence. Many Italian families have been sent from Boston into the country, with excellent results. The New England farmers are at first suspicious of them, but soon come to regard them as good neighbors.

The large majority of the Italians in Boston are industrious and thrifty. They carry on several kinds of small trade with commendable assiduity. Over two million dollars' worth of real estate in the Italian district is held in the names of Italian owners. The unskilled laborers sustain themselves by accepting a low wage standard; and still lay by money because they have an inconceivably low standard of living. In both of these respects—and particularly the latter—

From "Notes on the Italians in Boston," in: *Charities*, May 7, 1904.

they do a real injury to the community, and give grounds for the enmity which their industrial competitors among the older immigrant elements feel toward them.

The artisan and the small trader among the Italians do not in general make very rapid economic progress. They show a certain lack of self-reliance and "push." Jewish artisans secure the low-grade building work, and the Greeks often get the best fruit and candy stands away from them. We have had Italian barbers for a long time. They increase in number but their shops do not seem to rise to a higher grade as to service and price.

The children of the early north Italian immigrants have now been through the public schools. Many of the stumbling-blocks which embarrassed their parents have been removed for them. They are beginning to take their proportionate place in the skilled trades, in commercial establishments and in the professions. One important industry which has had an educational effect upon the whole country and for which Boston has been the center, that of making plaster casts of the work of great sculptors—has been developed wholly by Italians. A few young people show signs of that genius for which no race has been more distinguished than the Italian.

There is a particular need and opportunity among the Italians for friendly and helpful influence. With no nationality does the right sort of encouragement bring more valuable results. A lack of force of will in their case goes often with unusual skill, intelligence and constructive imagination.

The new generation is many times hindered by the ignorant conservatism of the elders. One way of breaking the unfortunate tradition of illiteracy which exists particularly among the south Italians, and which leads them to put their children to work as soon as possible, will be to provide in the public schools greatly increased opportunities of manual and technical training along with book work. The tendency of parents to take their children away from the schools is in part a just judgment upon the narrow, abstract character of the school curriculum.

There is danger in Boston that with the gradual withdrawal from the Italian colony of the more progressive members who lose themselves in the general community, there will be left a distinct slum residuum. Not much degeneracy is yet evident among the Italians. But there is a steady continuance of a certain amount of violent crime. Among the large number of men without family connections there is gambling, beer-drinking, and licentiousness. The amount and variety of profanity which seems needed in order to promote the street games of some Italian boys is beyond belief.

These evils are to a considerable extent the result of city conditions. The laborers are without work for much of the year. They are huddled together so that self-respect and peace of mind are lost. It would be the work of a moral as well as an industrial reformer to transport the large surplus of Italian laborers to the agricultural regions of the south, and then to secure at least such restriction of immigration as would prevent new immigrants from creating a new city surplus.

When all is said, there is sound reason to believe that the Italians will prove a valuable factor in our composite population. They are beginning to appreciate and take to themselves our industrial standards and our political loyalties. We ought to begin to be deeply thankful for what they bring of sociability, gayety, love of nature, all-round human feeling. The continental peasant has much to teach us. At his best he is a living example of that simple life which too many of us have so far lost that the words of two recent writers— one an Alsatian, the other a Swiss—seem like a breath of inspiration from some other sphere.

THE SONS OF ITALY

[The Order of
the Sons of Italy was founded in New York by Vincent Sellaro in
June, 1905 as a fraternal insurance association. Half a century later,
the order had more than 3,000 lodges in all parts of the United
States. The following selection consists of the preamble and first
article of the order's constitution.]

We, the members of the Order Sons of Italy in America, a fraternal
organization, being a part of the United States of America, which
we serve at all times with undivided devotion, and to whose progress
we dedicate ourselves; united in the belief in God; conscious of
being a representative element of an old civilization which has contributed to the enlightenment of the human spirit, and which
through our activities, institutions, and customs may enrich and
broaden the pattern of the American way of life; realizing that
through an intelligent and constant exercise of civic duties and
rights, and obedience to the Constitution of the United States, we
uphold and strengthen this republic; in order to make known our
objectives and insure their attainment through the harmonious
functioning of all parts of our organization, the said Order Sons of
Italy in America do hereby ordain and establish the following as
our constitution:

Article I. Purposes

The purposes of the order are:
(a) to enroll in its membership all persons of Italian birth or

From U.S. Congress, *Congressional Record*, 91st Cong., 1st sess., March 25, 1969.

descent, regardless of religious faith or political affiliation, who believe in the fundamental concept that society is based upon principles of law and order, and who adhere to a form of government founded upon the belief in God and based upon the Constitution of the United States of America, which government rests upon the proposition that all men are created equal and functions through the consent of the governed:

(b) to promote civic education among its members;

(c) to uphold the concept of Americanism;

(d) to encourage the dissemination of Italian culture in the United States;

(e) to keep alive the spiritual attachment to the traditions of the land of our ancestors;

(f) to promote the moral, intellectual, and material well-being of our membership;

(g) to defend and uphold the prestige of the people of Italian birth or descent in America;

(h) to encourage the active participation of our membership in the political, social, and civic life of our communities;

(i) to organize and establish benevolent and social welfare institutions for the protection and assistance of our members, their dependents, and the needy in general, with such material aid as we are able to give;

(j) to initiate and organize movements for patriotic and humanitarian purposes, and to join in meritorious movements for such purposes which have been initiated by other organizations or groups.

AMERICAN PRIESTS FOR ITALIAN MISSIONS

[When Italian immigrants began coming to the United States in large numbers, the Catholic Church in Italy undertook to see that their spiritual needs were not neglected. In 1887, Bishop Giovanni Battista Scalabrini of Piacenza founded the Apostolic College of Priests to prepare clergy for work in America. Mission societies were also founded in the United States. The American Catholic Church, however, was firmly controlled by the Irish, and they were very reluctant to see Italian (or German, Polish, or Czech) parishioners tended to by an Italian clergy. They insisted that American (Irish) priests were far better qualified to help "Americanize" the immigrants. The following selection by the Rev. John T. McNicholas, bishop of Duluth, presents the position of the American hierarchy.]

Who are the priests best suited for the work of caring for the Italians in this country? The native Italian diocesan priest is not, I think, the best qualified, in all cases, to work as missionary among the immigrants from Italy. In the first place, the Italians cannot be regarded as representing one nation. "United Italy" is an ironical designation. Between a northern Italian and the Neapolitan or Sicilian there exists hardly any bond of sympathy. On the contrary, they often bear each other a racial hatred stronger than that which separates the Irish and the English. When Americans speak of an Italian priest working among his own people, they rarely give any thought to the question whether he be from the North or the South of Italy. Yet to the Italian priest and people it means more than we can appreciate. Unfortunately it must be said that a number

From *Ecclesiastical Review*, December, 1908.

of native Italian diocesan priests, abstracting from racial prejudices, are not disposed to work among what we call "their own people." They prefer to labor among other nationalities. And the pronounced tendency of many to work for pecuniary interests has given this entire class of priests the reputation of being lacking in zeal.

Nor is the native Italian religious necessarily the best qualified missionary for the immigrants from his own country. First, as in the case of the diocesan native priest, because he is apt to have or suffer from the racial antipathies above alluded to; and these are apt to destroy the zeal we expect to find in him. Again, these priests can rarely understand the spirit of liberty which people enjoy in this country, nor have their habits been adapted or their character formed to appreciate the necessity of the constant activity which marks the life of the truly zealous American priest. It must be expected that fitting adjustment to our liberty and activity, when one is advanced in life, will be slow, and not always attended with the desired results. Lastly, there are those American diocesan and religious priests who go to Rome or Italy in the expectation of fitting themselves for advancement, with an ultimate view of honors and titles. They generally return as Doctors of Philosophy or of Divinity and are regarded as representative men in their respective dioceses. They are hardly the men to expect to be sent to insignificant parishes, with the task of working among the poorest from whom little pecuniary compensation can be expected and still less received. This is true especially of the secular clergy who study in Rome. The American religious priest or student who is sent abroad "causa studiorum" is usually intended by his superiors for the work of teaching in his Order or Congregation.

There remains one class of priests that the writer ventures to suggest as best qualified to work among the Italians in the United States. They are diocesan and religious American priests chosen by our bishops and religious superiors definitively for this work. They need to be priests not so much of big heads as of big hearts, not so much of noble intellects as men of deep religious sentiment and zealous activity, men not destined for degrees, but eager to learn the language and to familiarize themselves fairly with the dialects of Italy, especially the Neapolitan and Sicilian; men who are anxious to acquire sympathy for the Italian people without which no work can be done; in fine, men who are willing to sacrifice themselves in their own country, for the sake of the hundreds of thousands of souls they can be instrumental in saving to the Church in the United States.

In the case of diocesan clergy, it may be necessary to make special provision for priests assigned to labor in what might be called "the Italian missions" of the country. For some time to come the revenues from distinctly Italian parishes must be small; but if the Italians be given a little time, they will no doubt prove their generosity. With regard to priests of Religious Orders, the solution is much easier. Their vow of poverty gives them peculiar advantages in this work. Most of the religious priests, during their course of preparation in the many cities of Italy where they would study the different manners and customs of the people, could live with their brethren. On taking up the work after their return to America, if their Order or Congregation has a house in or near the locality where the congested Italian districts are, three or four Fathers could be maintained by the community at very little expense, to serve the Italian missions. The various Religious Orders, once their attention is drawn to the subject, can hardly escape the obligation of taking up the work, and a refusal to do so might revive the often-stated charge made against religious bodies, namely that they will not coöperate in such a field because there is no pecuniary remuneration.

We have many movements in the interest of Catholicity, but none seems more important than this, and none seems easier of success. The American diocesan and regular priests whom I propose for this task as the most fitted and attainable, would have no racial prejudices to contend with and they would be assured of a respect rarely accorded the native Italian priest. In justice it must be said of the Italian that he has inborn respect for the "forestieri." He will show courtesies to the stranger that he will not extend to his own countrymen. These American diocesan and regular priests who go to Italy for the purpose of qualifying themselves to do this work would get correct notions of the many peoples there, and thus be much better qualified to Americanize the Italians who come to us. These Italians are far from being representative. They come from the poorest classes; they have had no educational advantages. Oppression and unjust taxation have given those who are not simple peasants an inborn hatred of government. The Italians in this country often continue for years under the misapprehension that the Church and her officials here are supported by the government, as is the case in Italy. . . .

Can we spare a sufficient number of priests, both diocesan and regular, who will go to Italy to prepare themselves for this work? However overcrowded a diocese is, however numerous a religious community, there is always a demand for zealous, active priests. The supply of such priests will never equal the demand until the end of time. In this sense a scarcity of priests, both diocesan and religious, will always exist. Very probably in many of our large dioceses, where most of the Italians live in congested districts, a few zealous, diocesan clergymen could be spared. Can ten large dioceses spare four priests each? This would total forty priests. Can the many religious Orders and Congregations in the country assign sixty religious to the work? Two years in Italy would fit these priests admirably for the great task. Their duties would be first, to study the language and people, acquiring a sympathy for them; secondly, to prepare sermons and instructions. In caring for foreigners of their dioceses some few bishops and individual members of Religious Orders have adopted this plan with excellent results. In New York State there are 600,000 Italians. In the city of Philadelphia there are over 100,000. Naturally in these large centers the greatest number of workers will be required. While each organization and body looks to its own interests and strives to impress on others the importance of its claims, seeking help to carry on its propaganda, all of which is permissible and commendable, yet the great and vital interests of the entire Church in the United States must not be lost sight of. All should be willing to bear their share of the burden.

THE FOREIGN
LANGUAGE PRESS

[The Italian language newspaper stood, like the immigrant himself, between the Old and New Worlds. Though its language was of the Old, much of the contents derived from the New; and, as such, it became an agent of acculturation for the first generation. The following editorial on the function of the foreign language press appeared in the Chicago newspaper, *L'Italia*, on January 18, 1914.]

Only an immigrant, one who has for years after his arrival been a stranger to language and customs of the country, can fully understand and appreciate the part that the newspapers printed in his own tongue play in acquainting him with conditions adopted in this adopted country of his. It may seem a paradox that a newspaper is of far greater practical value to the newcomer than any books from which he might have acquired whatever amount of education he possesses, but it is nevertheless true. In fact, the fellow who has spent many a night hour trying to put into polished phrases a chapter from Xenophon is no better off, as far as the practical value of his learning is concerned, than the fellow who comes from the peak of the mountains and cannot write script but must print his letters. Both, although coming from the opposite stations in life, are bounced into the midst of unfamiliar turmoil, in which they find themselves on the same level, that is, unable to express themselves in words of the new tongue which is spoken everywhere about them, and if left to find their way alone, unable even to satisfy their most imperative wants. The natural result of this plight, in

From *Chicago Foreign Language Press Survey*, WPA Project, 1942.

which all foreigners find themselves at their arrival, is the tendency
to settle where others of their nationality have already settled, thus
forming those characteristic little foreign colonies in American
towns, which for the better and the younger element, are like
anterooms where their acquisition of the English language and their
assimilation of American customs are little by little prepared and
accomplished and from which they will, sooner or later, step out
into the larger life of the town and become units of the true American population. The older set, or the purely migratory element,
either fossilizes in these segregated communities or returns to the
homeland after a more or less protracted stay here.

It is during this period of incubation, among the members of
these communities, that the foreign-language newspaper plays its
most important, and lasting educational part. The newspaper becomes then for the immigrated, not merely an agency of information
concerning the happenings in the Old Country, but a unique, practical, almost automatic teacher of American ways, American laws,
and American institutions. Because a foreigner exhibits knowledge,
for instance, of American judicial procedure or political organization, or whatnot, it does not argue that that foreigner has received
school instruction on such topics, or that he must necessarily have
been in court, or have voted. Nor could any manual or newspaper
be found which treats these subjects in an academic way. All that
a foreigner comes to know about his new country, he absorbs from
reading the varied happenings of each day in the newspaper printed
in his own tongue. Today it may be the news concerning the strike
of the street cleaners that teaches him about labor organization
and that particular branch of the city administration. Tomorrow,
by reading a sensational case he will come to understand the functions and the mode of procedure of our courts.

In this respect the lawyer from Italy who might possibly have
edited a newspaper there, needs to read the newspaper here as
much as does the mountaineer from Albania, who perhaps never
saw a newspaperman in his country. A tangible evidence of how
indispensable is the newspaper to the foreigner in America is the
extent to which the newspaper of each nationality is circulated
among the people of that nationality. Every literate foreigner is a
constant and attentive reader of the journals in his own tongue.
Of course, it is to be expected, at such times as during the recent
Turkish-Italian war, and during the present Balkan war, that the
members of the races involved who are residing in this country
should be led by their patriotism to a closer scrutiny of the news
than usual. Hence an abnormal increase in the circulation of the
Italian newspapers in the United States during the war of their
mother country with Turkey amounted to no more than 30 percent,
which is small enough considering the vital and enthusiastic interest with which the Italians here followed every step of the conflict's
progress.

As an educational factor, the advertisements of foreign-language newspapers are also of invaluable assistance to the newcomer. There are a lot of wants that he begins to feel after being here a short while, and while at first it is the suggestion of a friend or relative that makes the newcomer adapt himself to a certain branch or quality of goods, the time comes when he feels the necessity of making his own choice in order to satisfy his own taste. Here is where the new arrival turns to newspapers for help, with a confidence which made him, up to four or five years ago, an easy prey of the sharks and the crooks.

But even the advertising of the foreign-language newspapers is now becoming standardized. The readers are warned through editorials to discriminate in their purchases and preferably look for trademarks or trade names of established reputation. Thus the time is not far off when foreign-language newspapers will be as reliable and educating in their advertisements as they are at present in their news.

THE AMERICAN MISSION OF FRANCES XAVIER CABRINI

[In 1889, Mother Cabrini came to the United States to work among the Italian immigrants. Her first efforts resulted in the founding of a day school and orphanage in New York City. Within a few years her rapidly growing society, Missionary Sisters of the Sacred Heart, had founded orphanages in several other cities and expanded its work into Latin America. In 1909 she became an American citizen. Subsequent to her death on December 22, 1917, her followers promoted her for sainthood. Finally, on July 7, 1946, Mother Cabrini was canonized, the first American to be so honored. The following selection, published shortly after her death, sums up the range of her missionary work in the United States.]

If ever there was a social problem so complex as to seem almost hopelessly insoluble and so many-sided as to perplex and bewilder the best intentioned, it was the welfare of the Italian immigrant in this country during the past twenty-five years. Not only schools for the poor were needed, but for the better classes as well, where they might find sympathy with their national aspirations and character; hospitals also were necessary to prevent the pitiable condition of sufferers coming to dispensaries and city hospitals with little or no knowledge of English and subject to being unfortunately misunderstood to their own detriment. The hard manual labor in which their fathers were engaged, involving numerous accidents, left many orphan children to be cared for, and in a thousand other ways,

From "An Apostle of the Italians," by James J. Walsh, in: *The Catholic World*, April, 1918.

also, these willing workers bearing so many difficult burdens of the country, demanded sympathetic assistance. The question was where would one begin, and having begun how carry on and diffuse any social work widely enough to cover these needs not alone in the coast cities of the East, but everywhere where the Italian immigrant had gone or had been brought by others.

Many people, even Catholics, feel that very little has been done, especially by Catholics, for the solution of this vast problem, although it mainly concerns our Italian Catholic brethren. Such a thought, however, betrays ignorance of an immense work that has been developing around us during the last twenty years. The recent death of Mother Frances Xavier Cabrini at the Columbus Hospital, Chicago (December, 1917), has emphatically called attention to the fine results secured in this important matter by her congregation of the Missionary Sisters of the Sacred Heart. Not quite seventy when she died, she had established over seventy houses of her religious. Her institute, less than forty years old, numbers its members by thousands. From Italy, where her foundation was made, it has spread to North, South and Central America, as well as France, Spain and England. No wonder that at her death, she was honored by those who knew her work as a modern apostle whose influence for good proved that the arm of the Lord had not been shortened: that He still raised up great personalities to meet the special needs of the Church in all generations.

Mother Frances Xavier Cabrini was born at St. Angelo di Lodi, July 16, 1850. Her parents belonged to the Italian nobility. From her early years she gave evidence of devout piety, and at the age of thirty undertook the organization of a congregation that would devote itself to teaching especially the children of the poor and of training school teachers. Her first house was founded at Codogno in 1880. A series of houses sprang up, during the following years, in and around Milan, and her work having attracted the attention of Leo XIII., she was invited to open a Pontifical School at Rome. This succeeded so admirably, that the Pope saw in it a great agency for the benefit of Italians all over the world. This great Pontiff had been very much attracted by Mother Cabrini's character and her enthusiastic zeal, which overcame obstacles that to many seemed insurmountable.

Accordingly when the foreign missionary spirit developed among her Sisters, Mother Cabrini, knowing the blessing that always accrued to a congregation for missionary work, applied to the Pope for permission to send her Sisters into the Orient. Pope Leo suggested that her mission lay in exactly the opposite direction. He recommended the Americas, North and South, as a fertile field for the labors of the Missionary Sisters of the Sacred Heart. Mother Cabrini receiving the suggestion as a command from God, proceeded to carry it out. A few months later she embarked for America with her Sisters, and assumed charge of a school for the children of Italian immigrants which was opened in New York in connection with the Church of St. Joachim.

Immigration was then at its height, the social problems of the Italians were at a climax, Americans had scarcely awakened to the need of doing anything, the Italian government was aroused to the necessity of accomplishing something, but politics were blocking the way, and it looked as though a little band of Italian Sisters could accomplish very little. Yet in a few years it became evident that this mustard seed was destined to grow into a large tree whose branches would shelter the birds of the air.

Mother Cabrini very soon realized that despite the importance of teaching, there were other crying needs of our Italian population that must be met if there was to be a solid foundation for the solution of social problems among them. Ailing and injured Italians needed the care that could properly be given them only by their own. Seeing in the celebration of the five hundredth anniversary of the discovery of America by Columbus, then impending, an auspicious moment, Mother Cabrini, in 1892, opened Columbus Hospital in New York. It had an extremely humble beginning in two private houses and with such slender support as would surely have discouraged anything less than the zeal of this foundress, convinced that she was doing God's work on a mission indicated by the Pope himself. Before long, the fortunes of the hospital began to brighten, until now it is one of the recognized institutions of New York, situated in a commodious building that brings it conspicuously to the notice of New Yorkers. Before the outbreak of the War [World War I], plans had been drawn for a ten-story building which should have been finished before this, and would have been one of the most complete hospitals in the country.

But Columbus Hospital was only the beginning. Mother Cabrini's great work of schools for Italian children of the poorer and better classes, was not neglected, but it was now evident that hospitals offered the best chance to win back adult Italians who had abandoned their faith and to influence deeply those who could be brought in no other way under Christian influences. After an Italian had been under the care of these devoted Italian Sisters, it was, indeed, hard for him to neglect his religion as before, and many a family returned to the devout practice of the Faith when the father had had his eyes opened to the practical virtues of religion by his stay in the hospital. Hence, in 1905, Columbus Hospital, Chicago, was founded under extremely difficult conditions. For some time the failure of this enterprise seemed almost inevitable, and Reverend Mother Cabrini's heart was heavy at the prospect of her beloved poor deprived of skilled care. She did not lose courage, however, and she was rewarded, after a particularly trying time in which her greatest consolation and help was prayer, by the assured future of the hospital.

A little later, a branch hospital known as Columbus Extension Hospital, was established for the very poor in the heart of an Italian district in Chicago, at Lytle and Polk Streets. Five years later, Columbus Hospital and Sanitarium in Denver was founded and a few years later Columbus Hospital, Seattle. All of these were in excellent condition, with abundant promise of future usefulness, and healthy development at the time of Mother Cabrini's death. This holy woman brought to the service of her zeal for religion such good sound common sense and business acumen and efficiency, as to call forth the admiration of all who knew her and who realized what she was accomplishing in the face of unlooked-for and almost insurmountable difficulties. . . .

At the time of her death there were, as we have said, more houses of her Congregation than she counted years, though her work as a foundress had not begun until nearly half of her life was run. It is said that as a young woman she had in her zeal for missionary labor asked her confessor for permission to join an order of missionary sisters that would take her far from home, so that home ties should count for little in life, and should surely not disturb her complete devotion to her vocation. Her confessor replied that he knew of none. There were no missionary sisters in the strict sense of the word and so Mother Cabrini founded the Congregation of the Missionary Sisters of the Sacred Heart, which has flourished so marvelously. . . .

Everywhere she emphasized the Italian origin and spirit of her work. No wonder then that the Ambassador from Italy deeply concerned with the problem of making the Italian people here as happy and contented as possible, but above all of keeping them from being imposed upon in any way, called her his "precious collaborator." "While I may be able to conserve the interests of the Italians," he said, "by what I am able to accomplish through those who are in power, she succeeds in making herself loved and esteemed by the suffering, the poor, the children, and thus preserves these poor Italians in a foreign country."

In spite of her devoted Italian sentiments, she drew her postulants from practically every nationality in the country. Many an Irish girl, after looking into Mother Cabrini's wonderful eyes, felt it her vocation to help this wonderful little woman in the work she had in hand. She won all hearts to herself, but only for the sake of the Master, and so it is that in the course of scarcely more than twenty-five years, her Congregation counts nearly five hundred members here in America. It has some three thousand throughout the world, all intent on accomplishing the social work that has been placed in their care, and of solving the problems brought about by the huge Italian immigration to the Americas in the eighties and nineties of the last century.

When the Italians entered the War, Mother Cabrini, by cable, mobilized her Sisters in Italy for the aid of their native country in

every way possible. The houses of the Congregation were trans-
formed into hospitals and refuges for the convalescent, as well as
asylums for the sons and daughters of those who had fallen on the
field of battle. Her devotion to her Italian people was so great,
Il Carroccio, or as it is called in English, *The Italian Review*, published in New York, compares her to Florence Nightingale, for
what she has accomplished both in peace and in war. Nor may
anyone who knows all the circumstances of her work, deny that
the comparison is more than justified.

A SICILIAN COLONY IN MANHATTAN

Gaspare Cusumano

[In 1920, when the survey reprinted below was made, there were about 200 families from Cinisi, Sicily, living along East 69th Street in Manhattan. Other groups from Cinisi were in Harlem, in Brooklyn, and in Lower Manhattan along Bleecker Street. This selection is from a report entitled "Study of the Colony of Cinisi in New York City" by Gaspare Cusumano.]

The colony is held together by the force of custom. People do exactly as they did in Cinisi. If some one varies, he or she will be criticized. If many vary—then that will become the custom. It is by the group, collectively, that they progress. They do not wish the members of the colony to improve their economic conditions or to withdraw. If a woman is able to buy a fine dress, they say: "Look at that *villana* [serf]! In the old country she used to carry baskets of tomatoes on her head and now she carries a hat on it." "Gee! look at the daughter of so and so. In Cinisi she worked in the field and sunburnt her back. Here she dares to carry a parasol."

So strong is this influence that people hesitate to wear anything except what was customary in Cinisi. Everywhere there is fear of being *"sparlata"*—talked badly of. A woman bought a pair of silk stockings and the neighbors talked so much about her that her husband ordered her to take them off. . . . To dress poorly is criticized and to dress sportily is criticized. In this way one had to conform or be ostracized.

A number of families moved from the central group of Brooklyn.

From Robert E. Park and Herbert A. Miller, *Old World Traits Transplanted* (New York, 1921), pp. 147–151.

There they have combined and rent a whole two-story house. They are living better than those in the other groups and I often hear the East Sixty-ninth Street people say: "Look at those *paesani* in Brooklyn. When they were here they were in financial straits. One of them had to flee from the criticism here. He did not have the money to pay his moving van and crowded all his furniture into a small one-horse wagon. He even put his wife on to save car fare. He left a pile of debts and now he dares come around here with a horse and buggy."

If a wife is spied by another Cinisaro talking to a man who is known as a stranger—that is, who is not a relative—she is gossiped about: she has the latent willingness to become a prostitute. They say: "So and so's wife was talking with an American. Eh! She has the capacity to do wrong."

Nothing in the American women surprises them. They have already made an unfavorable judgment. My mother, for instance, was about to say that my wife, who is an American, was an exception to the rule, but when my wife went to Central Park with the baby she said, "They are all alike."

The colony has no newspapers, except one woman who is known as the "*Giornale di Sicilia*," or the "Journal of Sicily." She carries the news and spreads it as soon as said. She has now gone to Italy and the one who takes her place is a gossiper who is known as a "*too-too*"—referring to the "tooting" of a town-crier's horn. She is, moreover, malicious, and gives a version of a story calculated to produce ridicule. She not only talks about the breakers of customs, but about those who are financially low. To be financially low is looked down upon, and the *Giornale di Sicilia* warns people to look out for such and such a person, as he may ask for a loan. To be willing to lend means that one has accumulated money and thus the secret of the lender is out. So this is the reason they refuse to lend to one another and if one is down and out he would rather get money from a Jew than from a *paesano*. So deceptive are they as to their financial standing (partly through fear of blackmail) that it is customary to figure out a Cinisarian's fortune not by what he says, but by how many sons and daughters are working.

Now and then some Cinisarian takes his chances in the business world. He writes to his relatives in Cinisi, has oil, wine, and figs, lemons, nuts, etc., sent to him, and then he goes from house to house. He does not enter in a business way, but goes to visit some family, talks about Cinisi, then informs them that he has received some produce from the home town. And sure enough, the people will say, "You will let us get some, eh?"

"Of course. Tell your relatives. I can get all you want."

In this way the business man makes his sales. He progresses until he gets a place opened and then come his worries. He must forever show that he is poor, that he is barely making a living, for fear of some attempt to extort money from him.

Not many men of the Cinisi group are in business in New York, the reason being that one Cinisarian will not compete with another in the same line of business.

The central group is closely united and there is little possibility that they will adopt any customs of the neighboring peoples, who are mostly Irish and Bohemians. The Irishwomen are considered wives of drunkards and, as all of the husband's salary goes to the bartender, the wives are believed to earn a living in prostituting themselves. The Bohemians are libertines; the girls are free; and, moreover, Bohemians and Hungarians are looked upon as bastard peoples.

In the Cinisi colony there are no political parties. The group has not been interested in citizenship. Of 250, one or two were citizens before the war and now all those who returned from the war are also citizens. These young men sell their votes for favors. The average Cinisaro, like all foreigners, has the opinion that a vote means $5. The Cinisaro knows of corruption at home. In Cinisi there is very much of it. Money is raised to build a water system for Cinisi year after year, and it gets away without a water system coming in exchange.

The Cinisi group are more interested in Cinisarian politics than in American. They talk of the parties of the artisans, of the gentlemen, of the *villani*, of the hunters, in Cinisi.

Most of the Cinisari in the Sixty-ninth Street group intend to return to Sicily. The town of Cinisi is forever in their minds: "I wonder if I can get back in time for the next crop?"—"I hope I can get back in time for the festa"—"I hope I can reach Cinisi in time to get a full stomach of Indian figs," etc. They receive mail keeping them informed as to the most minute details, and about all the gossip that goes on in Cinisi in addition; they keep the home town informed as to what is going on here. They write home of people here who have transgressed some custom: "So-and-so married an American girl. The American girls are libertines. The boy is very disobedient." "So-and-so who failed to succeed at college in Palermo, is here. He has married a stranger"—that is, an Italian of another town. In this way they blacken a man's name in Cinisi, so that a bad reputation awaits him on his return.

The reputation given them in Cinisi by report from here means much to them, because they expect to return. Whole families have the date fixed. Those who express openly their intention of remaining here are the young Americanized men.

When the festival of Santa Fara, the patron saint of Cinisi, was planned (partly as a reproduction of the home custom, partly as an expression of gratitude to Santa Fara for the miracle of ending the war), there was some opposition on the ground that all funds should be sent to Cinisi for the festival there. The festival was held (April 26 and 27, 1919), but was so disappointing that it is said to have increased the desire to return to Cinisi and see the original.

AMERICANIZATION AND REACTION

Alfonso A. Costa

[For all the pressure by nativists and progressives to get the immigrants to Americanize, there were several features in American life that worked against an easy assimilation. The national xenophobia engendered by World War I, the tirades against "hyphenism," and the repressive "Red Scare" in 1919–20 all hindered the real efforts of immigrants to assimilate rapidly. The following article by Alfonso Costa was written only a few weeks after the notorious raids led by Attorney General A. Mitchell Palmer to root out "subversives."]

The two terms of my title form a combination very disagreeable to the ear in Italian, but in America they go together. Ever since the stream of immigration to the United States began to assume its present immense proportions, a vigorous effort has been under way to assimilate the new arrivals. America is often described as a gigantic melting pot where all the nations of the earth lose their distinctive tongues, temperament, and even physical appearance. This process, it is supposed, will result in the production of a new race, a composite of all types that have been mingled to produce it, speaking one language, possessing identical political and social ideals, inspired with ardent American patriotism and having those habits of material and spiritual life that the natives complacently refer to as "the American standard of living."

Such a transformation is relatively easy for those who arrive in childhood with their parents, and for those who are born in the country of foreign parents. The schools are effective agencies for

From *Living Age*, April 10, 1920.

modeling all their pupils to a single type; by the second generation the process of fusion is well under way and in the third generation only the faintest traces of diverse inheritance remain. But those immigrants who arrive at a mature age are less plastic. They encounter the difficulty of learning a new language; they are disposed to live in separate colonies and to seek friendships and associations only among those of their own tongue. They like to eat the same food and to wear the same style of clothing to which they were accustomed in the Old World. Consequently, these older people do not easily adjust themselves to their new surroundings or borrow the characteristics of the Americans. The process is slow, the results unsatisfactory. However, this has hitherto been tolerated in the faith that by the time the second generation came these difficulties would disappear. Consequently, the country was not much embarrassed in times of peace by the vast number of foreigners who lived in its midst.

But when the war came all this changed. In the first place, the spontaneous affection of the immigrants for their native country, the turning back of their hearts to the land they had abandoned, the instinctive impulse to draw nearer to those of their own race, their intense interest in the military success of their native land rather than of their adopted country, all received a new and vigorous impulse. Men that had gradually and insensibly come to think of themselves as Americans, suddenly discovered that they were passionate Italians, Germans, Russians, or Englishmen. At the same time, the necessity of Americanizing the immigrants suddenly became imperious and urgent. It was no longer possible to trust to time and to limit efforts to the children in the schools. It was imperative that the aliens who lived in America should be Americanized, not only provided with naturalization papers, which signify little or nothing, but changed in heart and mind. They must cancel their old allegiance and commit themselves to their new allegiance, without reserve or qualifications.

During the war, and still more, since the armistice, the efforts of the nation have therefore been concentrated upon making the whole population "100 percent American." Lectures, night schools for studying English, the exclusion of unnaturalized citizens from public and private employment, and the personal efforts of well-intentioned proselyters have been brought to bear on this task in every community.

But most unhappily, just when it was peculiarly desirable to make immigrants love and respect their new home and remain there, a conjunction of adverse circumstances and officious blunders went far to nullify this program of Americanization and to substitute for the slow process of assimilation occurring before the war, not more rapid progress, but real aversion to America, accompanied by a revival of affection for the country of birth. Italians were turned in this direction first by America's lack of recognition for Italy's services in the war, and later by the unfavorable attitude of the President and his colleagues toward Italy's claims at the peace conference. The French in the United States are filled with jealousy, because they feel that France alone won the war. The Irish are alienated by the evident partiality shown to England. The hordes of Russian Jews hate America because the press of this country reviles the Bolshevist revolution, which 90 percent of them approve and admire. The Germans are naturally hostile because America entered the war. So, all have some immediate reason for resisting the effort to make them Americans.

Prohibition came to accentuate this antipathy. A fine country of liberty, these foreigners thought, when you cannot drink a glass of wine or a stein of beer! Who is coming here to sing the songs of liberty, when the laws imprison a man who manufactures, sells, possesses, or offers to any person, a drink of spirits? This is really a serious question, more serious than might appear at first glance. Prohibition of wines and spiritous liquors engenders in some people not only aversion but lively hatred of America. Not only that, but the law was enacted after the sort of a campaign that makes one say, "I dislike you for the manner in which you present yourself."

However, all these influences—the revival of patriotism for their own country, Prohibition, and the other things—would have been forgotten as time went on. But there is another influence, of an infinitely more dangerous and lasting character. That is the current of reaction that is sweeping everything before it in America, and that has found expression in the deportation en masse of those who sympathize with communism; denying seats in the legislature to Socialist deputies regularly elected, solely because of their party; proposed laws of extreme severity limiting liberty of speech and freedom of the press; and wholesale dismissals from employment on mere suspicion of radical sympathies. Last of all, the schools are permeated with the same spirit of reaction, and today in many of the principal cities of the United States a graduation diploma will not be granted to a pupil who does not swear allegiance to the government of the United States—something that in itself is perfectly proper and just—and who also has not declared his repudiation and abhorrence of bolshevist, syndicalist, and Communist doctrine.

This situation is serious, and its consequences may seriously imperil the peace and harmony of America. Violent repression is blind. It has never succeeded in doing anything but increase the pressure of subterranean forces. How will it inspire immigrants with loyalty to a country which has boasted of being the most free and democratic in the world, but where newcomers find actually in force laws so repressive as to be worthy of the most tyrannical rulers of ancient times? To be sure, important organs of public opinion and eminent men of all political parties are opposing these repressive measures with all their power. The Bar Association of New York, headed by former Justice Charles E. Hughes, late candidate for the presidency of the United States, has decided to send to Albany, the capital of the state of New York, a committee composed of six of its members, including Mr. Hughes, to defend the six Socialist deputies to the legislature to whom the state assembly has denied their seats. These men carry with them a protest stating that such action is subversive of democratic ideas and is anti-American.

Every American citizen of well-balanced judgment and clear vision is asking himself with concern where this movement is going to end. Arrests and expulsions en masse, like those we have witnessed during the past few days in the United States, special laws proposed and passed lightheartedly by legislative assemblies—such measures as these cannot increase respect for the government in its own citizens or love for that government in those who are not citizens. Neither will such measures check in the least socialism and communism. They will merely strengthen the conviction that free speech, free discussion, and the free publication of opinions—whether by citizens or aliens—are rights to be exercised only by men endorsed by the government and by powerful private interests. If rights guaranteed by the Constitution to every citizen, and by general consent hitherto assured to strangers within the country, are to be placed in peril merely because a few demagogues and agitators have abused those rights, it is practically certain that new and revolutionary doctrines will spring up and flourish under the very effort to suppress them. You cannot safeguard liberty by denying liberty. Neither will it add to the prestige of America in other lands to return to their countries beyond the ocean the disillusioned and nonassimilated people who had come to its shores. In the opinion of many citizens, the only way to heal radically the discontent existing in the United States is to remove the causes for that discontent. To continue in the road of reaction will not only check an inflow of labor which the country needs and prevent the assimilation of the foreign elements already in its midst, but will breed new perils that may threaten the very life of the nation. Those who sow the wind will reap the tempest.

MICHELANGELO IN NEWARK

[The public
school was one of the chief agents of assimilation, teaching the children of immigrants both the language and the values of the dominant
society. In the following selection an art teacher, Grace Irwin, of
Newark, New Jersey, relates her first encounter with the children of
"Little Italy."]

The school is situated in the midst of a typical Little Italy.

I shall never forget the sinking feeling in my heart that first day
as I left American buildings and homes behind and found myself
walking deeper and deeper into a strange and wholly foreign land.

The narrow, crooked streets fringed with refuse, the forlorn and
ramshackle tenements, and the faces of the inhabitants—all were
foreign. Swarms of children screamed shrilly at their play or quarreled furiously over their games. Every corner was decorated with
a group of young loafers of about the age of seventeen. These stared
at me with a bold insolence, due to their proud contempt for work
and a feeling of superiority toward the weaker and subordinate sex.
A question was thrown at me. I ignored it, and my great disdain
was met with loud guffaws. Saloon doors were wide open and fat
men in their undershirts sat around tables playing cards. I must
admit I stared, for I had never seen a saloon so exposed to public
view.

All of the shop signs were in Italian. I passed several bakeries
against whose grimy windows huge rings of bread devoid of any

From *Harper's*, September, 1921.

wrapping were pressed. Small boys carried these big loaves home, clutching them firmly against their soiled clothing.

The florist and undertaking stores displayed elaborate "set pieces" of artificial flowers. These were hired, I learned later on, for the grand occasion of a funeral. A brass band and a gorgeous collection of flowers were a vital part of an important funeral cortege.

My eyes sought everything in bewilderment and curiosity. The cellar ways were dark and odoriferous. One, I noticed, had long poles stretched beneath its ceiling from which hung yards of "marcaronies." This, I discovered, was a "macaroni factory."

As I turned into the narrow street, almost an alley, where the school was situated, I saw the sign of death over a doorbell. The large bunch of artificial flowers was not all, for the entire doorway of the tenement was draped with a black silk curtain, heavily fringed with gold.

In that school of nearly 3,000 pupils there were only eight who were not Italian, and I never met one of the eight.

My first day was, and remains, a nightmare. I came out of it exhausted and dazed. On my homeward journey an acquaintance said to me:

"All Italians? How very interesting! I hear they are very bright."

"Yes," I answered, somewhat dryly. "Very bright. There is nothing that they can't think of to do."

She smiled. "They have been so brave in the war. Such courage!"

"Yes, they have been," I agreed again, but now I realized that I was speaking of the whole Italian nation, our ally in a great cause. However, I added hotly to myself: "Brave? Afraid of neither God, man, nor devil!"

I had met and faced that day about 160 children, four classes of forty each. My elaborately planned introductions to my lessons had all met ignominious and pitiful defeat. I had floundered about trying to discover the whys and wherefores of it.

"Teacher, let him give it to me; it's mine's. He robbed it."

"It ain't my fault. He ebery time bodders me."

It wasn't his fault that he had struck Angelo over the head with a ruler. Angelo had "ebery time boddered him."

Or, again, I had to stop to discover the meaning of: "He ain't going to curse my dead. I'll git 'im! I'll git 'im!"

Cursing one's dead, I soon found, was the signal for a burst of outraged passion; it was a crime which demanded instant and severe justice.

My classroom that day was, to put it mildly, a scene of "artistic abandon." I was ready to resign right then and there with the temperamental promptness of the children around me. I wanted to be with "mine own people" and that sort of thing. I fell to sleep that night muttering "America for Americans." . . .

My subject is loosely termed "drawing." Drawing is a means, not an end, in industrial art. Industrial art includes poster work, applied design, costume design, and interior decoration. Color work runs through them all. . . .

My definite problem is to make industrial art of some very practical use to these children. Costume designing, interior decoration, applied design are not absurd "modern frills." They are definitely related to everyday life.

For instance, costume designing—a people's mode of dress is more an integral part of national life and development than it would seem at first thought. Dress is not merely a vain show. A man or woman in Oriental dress cannot think or feel American. An Italian immigrant woman with her head uncovered, her shawl, her earrings, and her jewelry of all kinds on top of her soiled dress cannot be expected to feel like an American. When the native costume is discarded something deeper than externals has been touched. There has been a mental process involved as well as a material one. . . .

The people of this Little Italy are in the melting pot. But a melting pot, unattended, uncared for, is of no use, the ingredients will remain the same as they were in the beginning. A melting pot on a dead fire, or too hot a fire, is in a sorry plight. King Alfred turned his back and dreamed—and we know what happened. Since we like to speak of the melting pot let us not turn our backs upon it and sit and dream and plan. Charred cakes are nothing to charred lives.

My children love to hear the story of Michelangelo and I love to read it to them. It is good for them and good for me.

A quiet falls upon the room as I begin to read. They stare at me solemnly and a little proudly as I give the title. They are very, very good.

Every Michel, every Angelo, every relation of a Michel or an Angelo basks in a wonderful feeling of kinship with the great master. They feel he belongs exclusively to them—that he is one of them. I can feel that I am quite an outsider. As I watch their expressions I know that I am gazing upon heroes. Although their light is only reflected, they are distinctly shining forth as heroes.

The name "Italy" dances out of every turn in the story; they love that. They smile as I slur over Italian names, as indulgently they softly correct me. I feel self-conscious as I try to give the liquid pronunciation to the Italian names.

Four hundred years lie between us and the great master and over 3,000 miles between the scene of his exploits and my classroom of young "heroes." But what does it matter? And what does it matter that 400 years ago the living Michelangelo was an austere and solitary aristocrat, who held himself severely above his compatriots, demanding of them nothing but veneration and infinite respect, caring nothing for their love? But my warmhearted, emotional young peasants are not concerned with this distinction. He was an Italian—and his name was Michel—and Angelo. He was very, very great. Books are written about him. Even their American teacher gives him homage. They are proud, so proud!

As the story ends I ask to have it repeated to me. They tell it in a tongue which is neither Michelangelo's nor mine.

"Michelangelo was born in Italy. His father don'ts wants him to be a drawer—so he ebery time . . ."

"Mario," I interrupt, "I think it would sound better to say, 'Michelangelo's father didn't want him to become an artist.' People would not know quite what you meant if you spoke of a man's trying to be a drawer." I smiled encouragingly to take the edge off my criticism. "See, Mario, this is one kind of drawer. Michelangelo's father never feared that he would become part of a desk—or a table."

The others were delighted at such a ridiculous thought; they laughed joyously. Yesterday, they might have been noisy with their laughter—but not today with the spirit of Michelangelo upon them.

Our particular version makes the point that the dome of the Capitol in Washington is a copy of Michelangelo's dome on St. Peter's. Mario quotes and finishes with a gusto and a flourish:

"Michelangelo made David and Moses. And the 'nome' of the White House is just the same like Michelangelo. Of every artist Michelangelo is the best between them all."

He scratches his head, shuffles his feet, twists about in perplexity, and sits down with one eye squinted up. Then he is at peace. His recital pleases him as he thinks it over.

After a few minutes of perplexity on my own part I at last decipher some of the forceful conclusion. I cannot permit Mario to speak of the White House having a "nome," even if he is like Michelangelo. I pride myself upon reading distinctly—but "dome" was an unknown word to them. I hastened to explain "domes." Of course Mario had left out many details—hands, waving frantically, protested the omissions.

"Yes, Attilio, Michelangelo did work very hard, very hard. Do you remember just how long he worked each day?"

"Yes, teacher"—his eyes lighted up with excitement—"eight hours."

I felt myself smiling. And those children, intently watching me, smiled in appreciation of what they had no comprehension of and no interest in. They were with me in every thought this day as I read of Michelangelo.

"Michelangelo did not belong to the union. They did not have any union in those days. . . ."

They laughed, and Attilio grinned good-naturedly and a little sheepishly.

But they had not forgotten that it was distinctly stated that Michelangelo worked until darkness made it impossible.

I like to watch their eyes shine with happy pride and passionate devotion as they recall each detail of Michelangelo's life. Poor youngsters! Life isn't very gentle with them. I wonder at their being capable of so much ardor. I should think it would be chilled and crushed by their struggles. They make life hard for others—but their own is not made easy for them.

Who is to blame? Why is it all so hard? I think, after all, the question should be, "What is to blame?" Perhaps it is just one generation piling their hard knocks and ignorance upon the next. But it is going to be different from now on—the schools are mercifully, bit by bit, repairing the damage of the past.

But I rejoice in the emphasis placed upon the rigorous simplicity and the remarkable industry of Michelangelo's life. Since they crave to feel him their hero, I can use him to serve my ends. I can call upon him to stand in judgment upon them.

Only the other day as I read the description of Michelangelo painting the ceiling of the Sistine Chapel my eyes fell upon Michael Abate lying flat on the floor, painting with a ruler on an imaginary ceiling. He was doing it with great care. He would stop now and then to get the right perspective on his work. Finally he quietly took his seat. At the close of the reading Michael burst out:

"Gee, how hard, teacher! Michelangelo was a smart guy."

"Very, Michael. But do you suppose, children, he ever gave up anything he found hard?"

"Oh no, teacher! Oh no!"

They shook their heads in holy horror at Michelangelo's failing at anything.

Of all the old Italian masters, I love him best, for he has lent me a helping hand in bringing art to Little Italy.

AMERICANIZATION IN CHICAGO

[By 1920, there
were at least 90,000 Italians in Chicago, many of them living on the
near West Side, a few blocks from downtown. This article on their
economic and social progress was written by John Valentino in
1922.]

Immigrant children may yearn for freedom to live untrammeled
American lives; but they can do so only by abandoning, physically
as well as intellectually, their own households.

The conflict of ideals between the two generations often comes to
a crisis on the issue of moving. The young Americans are unwilling
to remain behind in what they scornfully call "Little Italy"; they
want to live in a "civilized neighborhood." An estrangement occurs
in many a family on this very point. Either the children move off
by themselves, and family ties are broken, or they stay with the
parents in the old household, but very unwillingly. The hardships
endured by immigrants have often been pictured, but the mental
agonies undergone by the children of immigrants, born in the
United States but of Old World citizens, are ten times more poign-
ant. The young Americans often see the light of their glorious country, but its brightness is dimmed by ineluctable contact with old
ways and old thoughts.

Chicago's Italian colony comprises several distinct groups in many
parts of the city. These groups are not at all continuous, and they
consequently do not constitute such formidable integral foreign
territories as does the Polish district, for instance, on the South

From "Of the Second Generation," in: *Survey,* March 18, 1922.

Side, or the Jewish section on the West Side. There are, however, three extensive and populous Italian sections quite close to the downtown business and central manufacturing areas on three sides of the city. Hull House, Chicago Commons, and the Jackson Public School are some of the centers of recreational activities, where both young and old generations of Italians find the contacts through which they are gradually getting to know their American neighbors. And the newcomers, with their gay religious festivals, their love of music and dancing and fireworks, have added color and brightness to the districts in which they make their homes. . . .

Those who have come to America since the armistice are not in very prosperous circumstances. After having spent almost their last money in paying for passports, visas, and passage to America at the present exorbitant rates, they have been met here by serious conditions of unemployment. The building deadlock and the cessation of road work have especially hit the new immigrants. The consequence is that in many cases, where relatives have not been able to secure employment for the newcomers, acute suffering has resulted. In the crowded Italian sections enormous numbers of men stand about idle. At one corner 140 such unemployed were recently counted.

But the antebellum immigrants are well off. Most of them are very happy. Those who have wanted to go back to Italy have had the opportunity to do so, and have either remained there to pay the penalty or have returned permanently disillusioned. It is difficult and unprofitable to pass judgment on the status and character of the Italians in Chicago. The chronic critic of all foreigners will continue to disparage them as such. Amateur economists and indolent patriots will depreciate their contribution to America. I should rather bear in memory the wholesome spirit shown at a benefit dance given by young Italians of the West Side for one of its girls now studying music in Milan. Or the stirring picture of a military funeral in the heart of the colony, one day last fall. The body of one of the boys had come back from France. Word was sent about the neighborhood for former soldiers to attend the funeral, in uniform. Some 300 Americans of Italian descent were on hand, soldiers, sailors, and marines. Most of them were members of former "gangs," more or less ferocious. And each one of the firing squad, about the flag-draped casket, bore at least one gold stripe on his right sleeve.

In spite of trade depression, labor uprisings, and scarcity of raw materials, two conspicuous industries new to America are flourishing among the more than 50,000 Italian-born who make Chicago their home. The first, which is an inevitable result of the 18th Amendment, and necessarily an extracurricular activity, is that of wine making in the home. A ruling by an Illinois court allows private families to make 200 gallons of wine each year; but Italian families anticipated that decision long ago. No family is too poor to have this beverage on steady tap; it may live in a dark back room with only an oil stove, a few broken chairs, and an oilcloth-covered table as furniture; but it offers the visitor a hospitable glass of *vino fatto in casa.*

The second infant industry is the making of Italian cheese and macaroni. The United States is already exporting spaghetti to Naples, which outdoes the carrying of coals to Newcastle. Since the war, the Italian government has forbidden exports of cheese, and Italians in this country, after a period of serious suffering, began with true American initiative to make it themselves. Now they have American-made *provoloni, mozzarelle,* and *ricotta* which rival those choice products of the Sorrentine peninsula. Thus far, however, they have not been able to make the famous *Gorgonzola* and *Parmeggians.*

Americanization or assimilation of immigrants is best accomplished through beneficent contact with the better classes of native Americans. A chance word across the backyard fence, a casual inspiration from meeting American neighbors along the street, the mere observation of American ways of living—these form the healthy liaison for the foreigner who wishes to adopt the life of his new country. If isolated zones could be prescribed for immigrants, so that those of different nationalities should not be contiguous but interspersed with native American zones, the process of Americanization would operate splendidly. Who can estimate the tremendous effect an American birthday party, for example, may have on an Italian boy: nice girls in neat frocks, and boys with starched collars; a view into an American dining room, and Helen's mother serving cake and joining in the fun? A year of visits by social workers will not work such wonders as that neighborly invitation of the Jones to the kid of the Italian family who live in the rear cottage next door.

MY NEIGHBORHOOD
Edward Corsi

[Edward Corsi
came to the United States from his native Abruzzi in 1907 at the
age of ten. During the 1920's, he worked as a newspaper reporter,
and, from 1928 to 1931, was director of the Haarlem House settlement. From 1931 to 1934 he was commissioner of immigration at
New York. His book, *In the Shadow of Liberty*, 1935, chronicles his
experiences at Ellis Island.]

We were discussing America and American literature over a cup of
black coffee in one of the many Italian coffee-houses of the neighborhood. My friend, a bohemian of decided literary tastes, did most
of the talking, and evidently enjoyed it. With that cynicism characteristic of the East Side intellectual—too often an indication of
dreams unrealized—he reviewed many of our "best sellers," passing
on from Sinclair Lewis's "Main Street" to the Great American Novel.

"In my opinion," he said, "when that novel comes to be written
its background will not be Main Street, but the East Side of New
York. Its central figure, furthermore, will not be a Babbitt or a
New England farmer or a Kentucky colonel, but an immigrant's
son, a child of the melting-pot." He sipped his coffee, puffed at his
cigarette, and continued: "While Main Street is American, the East
Side, with its peoples from many lands, speaking many tongues,
and gradually building a civilization which, in the end, will be ours
and not Europe's, is America. It is the America of to-morrow, or,
if you please, America in the making. And the Great Novel, to be
true to life, to outlive its author and its age, must deal with and

From *Outlook*, September 16. 1925.

interpret that America." He looked squarely at me, his eyes asking, Isn't it so?

My friend is a unique character, very interesting and very entertaining. Without him and his like the coffee-houses, barber-shops, and "wine basements" of the neighborhood would not be the "intellectual" centers they are. He is the Benvenuto Cellini of Little Italy. The words of wisdom that fall from his lips are manna to ignorant minds eager for knowledge. But, though unique as a character, there is nothing unique or strange about what he says of America. In this respect he speaks the mind of his audiences. America, when all is said and done, is but a great melting-pot, a "polyglot boarding-house," and nothing else. Why, then, shouldn't the East Side be the background for the Great American Novel when it comes to be written? Is not the East Side America? . . .

There are twenty-seven nationalities in the neighborhood, including, of course, the Chinese laundrymen, the gypsy phrenologists, the Greek and Syrian storekeepers. East, along the banks of the East River, surrounding Thomas Jefferson Park, are the Italians; on Pleasant Avenue are the Poles, Austrians, and Hungarians. West, where Fifth Avenue loses its dignity but not its charm, are the Jews, sons of many lands; near them are the Turks and Spaniards. North, where "Little Italy" makes room for "Little Africa," are the Negroes, gradually moving down, much to the discomfort of the whites. South, resisting the merciless invasion of the Jews and Italians, are the Germans and Irish, remnants of a stock that once ruled this part of town. Scattered throughout the neighborhood, with limits well defined, are lesser groups—Finns, Russians, French, Swedes, Danes, Rumanians, and Jugoslavs. Here and there, like refugees in exile, are a few Americans of old stock, heroically holding their ground.

The cosmopolitan character of the neighborhood is evidenced, not only in the signs of many languages, the chop suey, rotisseries, and spaghetti houses, the synagogues and Catholic temples, the flags of many colors, the foreign papers on every news-stand, but in the types one meets on the streets—tall blond Nordics, olive-skinned, dark-haired Mediterraneans, long-bearded Semites and Slavs, massive Africans, East Indians, gypsies, Japs, and Chinese.

The Italians and Jews predominate, giving the neighborhood the color of the Roman Ghetto. Few people have less in common than these. They differ in language, religion, custom, and temperament. But they get along, even if now and then there is an unpleasant interchange of "kike" and "wop." Under the protecting aegis of the Irish policeman's club or of the American flag even the brotherhood of man is possible. Indeed, if that brotherhood exists anywhere, it exists here, imperfect as it may be. Our "nations" have learned the meaning and the value of co-operation. We have a "league" that functions. Jew and Gentile, white and black, French and German, Italian and Austrian, meet on common ground. There is no breaking of bones, no boundary disputes or reparation problems. The Great War itself, with its passions and hatreds, could not disturb the peaceful equilibrium of the neighborhood. Life in that trying hour went on as usual. All fighting was done for America. In the last political campaign the Jews and the Italians joined forces. The result was the election of "the lone Progressive Congressman from the East," an American of Italian extraction, and a large vote for La Follette. If in the next campaign there should be no "third party" to unite the "nations," Tammany, always eager to serve, will do the best it can. We can always count on Tammany to maintain harmony in the household, electing Irish Senators with Jewish and Italian votes.

The Italian, by the way, is not much of a politician. He is too poetic for the "game." He prefers loftier pastimes. While the Irishman is organizing the ward and the Jew listens attentively to the platitudes of the soap-box orator on "Trotsky Square" (the Hyde Park of the neighborhood) the Italian is at home, enjoying the rapturous strains of "O Sole Mio." But, if not a politician, he is certainly an artist. Whatever there is of color and poetry in the neighborhood we owe to him. "Little Italy," with its picturesque markets, tenor-voiced venders, Vesuvio restaurants, candle-shops, statuette dealers, religious and patriotic societies, dark-eyed *signorine* and buoyant men, is but a reproduction of Bella Napoli. The feast of Our Lady of Mount Carmel, one of many feasts throughout the year, with its processions of barefoot devotees winding through the decorated and lighted streets, is a dramatic event. There is about it a touch of the Middle Ages.

What is true of the Italian is true, more or less, of others in the neighborhood, of the neighborhood in general. The life of the Old World is reenacted here. Were it not for the "flappers" and the "cake-eaters" of the younger generation, "Americans" to the core, the illusion would be complete. They "Americanize" the picture, but do not destroy it. Paris is not more interesting nor Vienna gayer than this miniature Europe which is Paris, Vienna, and Naples combined. To be sure, we have not the imposing opera houses, theaters, and hotels of those cities; no Boulevard des Italiens. We are a community of workers, and our life is proletarian. But we have our cafés, rathskellers, spaghetti houses, cabarets, dance-halls, and, since the Volstead Act, our "speak-easies" for the "regulars." We have Yiddish theaters and Italian marionette shows, not to mention the movie and vaudeville houses. Our second-hand bookshops are as good as those of Paris. So are our music stores. Were it not for the soul-stifling tenements and the necessity of having to "keep going," we would have great poets, great artists, great musicians. Some day we will have them.

Some day! But some day this neighborhood of mine will be gone. In fact, it is going now. America's doors are fast closing, and the tide of a new civilization, a civilization which is not Anglo-Saxon or Latin or Slav, but "American," is setting in. When the Great American Novel comes to be written, this "polyglot boarding-house" of many "nations," with its old customs and traditions, its alien tongues and creeds, will have lived its day. Out of the crucible a new neighborhood is emerging, and the myriad of little tots crowding the street and packing the school are my neighbors of tomorrow, Americans all.

THE SPEECH OF LITTLE ITALY

Anthony M. Turano

[Anthony Turano came to America from Italy in 1905 to join his father near Pueblo, Colorado. After attending college, Turano became a lawyer and settled at Reno, Nevada, his home when he wrote the following article.]

Some months ago I was called by the judge of a probate court in Nevada to help decipher the provisions of a strangely written will. The document was wholly in the handwriting of the testator, an old Italian-born resident of a mining town, who had attempted to dispose of a considerable estate among his heirs. With the exception of five or six unfamiliar phrases, and aside from a few orthographical errors due to the testator's limited schooling, the document was unmistakably written in what is properly spoken of as the Italian language, as contradistinguished from the various provincial dialects of Italy.

The will had been submitted previously to a professor of Romance languages, a linguist of exceptional learning. He had managed to translate most of it, but had been hopelessly stumped by a number of words and phrases which were nowhere to be found in his dictionaries. For instance, two of the words, *nota* and *morgico*, which appeared several times in the instrument, and occupied important places in the testator's scheme of distribution, seemed to have been borrowed from a strange tongue that was utterly unknown to the professor.

My experience among Italian-Americans enabled me to make short

From: *American Mercury*, July, 1932.

work of the difficult phrases. There was no doubt that the professor's academical knowledge of languages was far superior to mine, but he had missed this new speech for lack of personal contact with those who spoke it. The clauses in question were written in the strange tongue of Little Italy. The words had the general appearance of true Italian, because of their vowel endings, but they would have been understood least of all in the Italian Peninsula.

A mortgage in Italian is called *ipoteca*, but I had learned that in the speech of Italian-Americans it is almost invariably known as a *morgico* or *morgheggio*. The Italian word for a promissory note is *cambiale*, but in Little Italy it is *nota*. Likewise with hundreds of similar terms to be found in the quotidian vocabulary of all seasoned residents of the many Italian communities of the Republic. They are words that suggest a distant English parentage, but they have been Italianized beyond recognition.

The main reasons for the evolution of this curious speech are very simple. The so-called Italian colony is by no means the homogeneous whole that the untutored outsider believes it to be at first glance. It is, instead, a loosely joined assortment of men and women representing every section of the Italian Peninsula. And although the greater number of them are more or less familiar with the standard Italian of the books and newspapers, the speech most familiar to each individual is the peculiar dialect of his native province. The similarity or dissimilarity of one dialect to another is largely a matter of geographical proximity. Thus while a native of Naples may understand, with relative facility, the speech of his co-national from Rome, neither of them could, without a great deal of study, wholly comprehend the peculiar patois of the Genoese, the Venetian, the Calabrian, or, least of all, the Sicilian.

The natural consequence is that each Italian immigrant, upon coming to America, regardless of the region of his birth, must resort to as much as he happens to know of standard Italian, as the only feasible means of intra-colonial communication. If it is remembered, however, that most immigrants belong to working or agricultural classes, whose schooling was not of the best, it will be understood that the sum total of the language so reached does not bear a very close resemblance to school-book Italian. It may be described, rather, as a Babel of dialects struggling laboriously toward the standard speech, each individual contributing as much pure Italian as his limited education will let him, and supplying the difference in the local speech of his native village.

The confusion would be bad enough if it stopped here. But now comes the English language, spoken by the native neighbors of all Italian groups, and demanding representation in the daily oral intercourse of every Italian-American. The result is the jargon which may be called American-Italian, a dialect no less distinct from both English and Italian than any provincial dialect is distinct from that of the Italian language.

It must be borne in mind that the immigrant, in taking up his economic position in the New World, and in his social dealings with Anglo-Americans, is met by a peculiar relationship of things and activities in an industrial nation that were unknown to him in the rural life of his birthplace. He finds that his native vocabulary, which was never very rich, is now more inadequate than ever, whether in substantives or in verbs, to give expression to his new wants and reactions. His immediate impulse is to coin new words to fit the new life. That he does not invent neologisms of Italian parentage is easily understood. Even if he had the linguistic erudition to coin them, he would not do so, for the English language is conveniently near, and fully adapted to the service of the natives he must deal with daily.

What he does, then, is to borrow purely American words, according to need, and to fit them, as phonetically as possible, into his own makeshift Italian. The first English accretion to his daily speech consists of certain words for which a true Italian equivalent is lacking or remote, because of the absence of absolute identity between the American thing or act and its Italian counterpart. Among them are *sexa* for railroad section; *campo* for a lumber camp; *rancio* for ranch; *gliarda* for yard; *visco* for whiskey; *pichinicco* for picnic; *ais crima* for ice cream; *ghenga* for gang; and *rodomastro* for roadmaster.

In the next division are words whose Italian equivalents were generally unknown or unfamiliar to the immigrant before his arrival in America. In this class belongs the hybrid *morgico* which the professor had found untranslatable. The Italian word *ipoteca* would be an exact synonym for mortgage, but in the simple economy of his rural life in Italy the immigrant had no need for the word, because he was unfamiliar with the thing represented. When called upon to use such a term in America, therefore, he finds it easier to Italianize the American *mortgage* to *morgico*, or *morgheggio*—words that may be understood in his dealings with Anglo-Americans when he is called upon to use his small fund of pure English, and which are also well known to his compatriots of the colony. In the same class are *lista*, a lease (It. *atto*); *bosso* for employer or boss (It. *padrone*); and *fensa* for fence (It. *siepe*).

In the third category are a number of English words that win the honors of Italianization by the sheer force of their repetition by the American natives, despite the fact that the Italian language affords familiar and ample equivalents. Among them are *tomate* for tomatoes; *stritto* for street; *carro* for car, automobile; *trampo* for tramp; *gambolo* or *gambolino* for gambler; *loya* for lawyer; *boya* for boy; *bittare* for beat; *faiti* for fight; *loncio* for lunch; *denso* for dance; *cotto* for coat; *draivare* and *ronnare* for driving or running an automobile; *bucco* for book; *storo* for store; and *checca* for cake.

Once an American word has been borrowed, its transformation

does not end with its first changes. It is drafted for full service and made to run through all the genders, tenses, and declensions of Italian grammar, until it presènts the very faintest image of its former self. Thus the word *fight*, which was first changed into *faiti*, can be seen in such unrecognizable forms as *faitare, faitato, faitava, faito, faitasse,* and many more.

The percentage of Italianized English words varies, of course, with individuals, according to their knowledge of Italian and the length of their residence in America. But it is probable that, on the whole, the new expressions comprise as much as one-fourth of the spoken language of Little Italy. When I first took up my residence in America, in the Italian quarter of Pueblo, Col., I found this peculiar dialect so puzzling that, in the simplicity of a child of twelve, I mistook it for the native language of the Americans. For a number of months after my arrival I did not understand more than half of what was said in this curious speech. For as long as a year I was often forced to ask for translations. It was only with time and my increasing knowledge of English that I finally obtained a sufficient familiarity with it.

It sometimes happens that the newly coined words strike the sound and meaning of well-known Italian words, and the result is very humorous. I was both puzzled and amused, for instance, during my first week in America, when I heard a laborer say quite casually, that his daily work involved the use of a *pico* and a *sciabola*, that is to say, a pick and a saber! It took me some study to understand that in the process of Italianization, the American *pick* could be vaguely recognized, but the *shovel* had been turned into a military implement.

As to the further evolution of American-Italian, in the years to come, there is no doubt that its differentiation away from standard Italian will increase rapidly, now that it is no longer retarded by the influx of new immigrants from Italy. Hence it is easy to predict that its growth will be in the direction of additional Americanization, and toward the estate of a distinct sub-language.

But that it will ever develop the tenacity of such a speech as Pennsylvania Dutch appears to be doubtful, if we bear in mind the urban character of most Italian colonies, and the consequent lack of that isolation and economic self-sufficiency which seem to be necessary for the preservation of alien languages within the borders of any nation.

The average and typical Italian immigrant has never maintained any steady aloofness from the native population. This is particularly true of his American-born children, who do not generally preserve any permanent attachment to Little Italy or its language, but prefer to identify themselves, as early as possible, both in attitude and speech, with the Anglo-Americans. The safest prediction, therefore, seems to be the total disappearance, within a few generations, of the peculiar patois of Little Italy.

THE ODYSSEY OF A WOP

John Fante

[The following selection on the problems of growing up as a second generation Italian American was written by novelist John Fante. His best known work, *Dago Red* (1940), has as its central character a man who becomes ashamed of his nationality. The same issue was at the heart of this earlier article, written in 1933.]

From the beginning, I hear my mother use the words Wop and Dago with such vigor as to denote violent disrepute. She spits them out. They leap from her lips. To her, they contain the essence of poverty, squalor, filth. If I don't wash my teeth, or hang up my cap, my mother says, "Don't be like that. Don't be a Wop." Thus, as I begin to acquire her values, Wop and Dago to me become synonymous with things evil. But she's consistent.

My father isn't. He's loose with his tongue. His moods create his judgments. I at once notice that to him Wop and Dago are without any distinct meaning, though if one not an Italian slaps them on to him, he's instantly insulted. Christopher Columbus was the greatest Wop who ever lived, says my father. So is Caruso. So is this fellow and that. But his very good friend Peter Ladonna is not only a drunken pig, but a Wop on top of it; and of course all his brothers-in-law are good-for-nothing Wops.

He pretends to hate the Irish. He really doesn't, but he likes to think so, and he warns us children against them. Our grocer's name is O'Neil. Frequently and inadvertently he makes errors when my mother is at his store. She tells my father about short weights in meats, and now and then of a stale egg.

From *American Mercury*, September, 1933.

Straightway, my father grows tense, his lower lip curling. "This is the last time that Irish bum robs me!" And he goes out, goes to the grocery store, his heels booming.

Soon he returns. He's smiling. His fists bulge with cigars. "From now on," says he, "everything's gonna be all right."

I don't like the grocer. My mother sends me to his store every day, and instantly he chokes up my breathing with the greeting, "Hello, you little Dago! What'll you have?" So I detest him, and never enter his store if other customers are to be seen, for to be called a Dago before others is a ghastly, almost a physical humiliation. My stomach expands and recedes, and I feel naked.

I steal recklessly when the grocer's back is turned. I enjoy stealing from him: candy bars, cookies, fruit. When he goes into his refrigerator I lean on his meat scales, hoping to snap a spring; I press my toe into egg baskets. Sometimes I pilfer too much. Then, what a pleasure it is to stand on the curb, my appetite gorged, and heave *his* candy bars, *his* cookies, *his* apples into the high yellow weeds across the street. . . . "Damn you, O'Neil, you can't call me a Dago and get away with it!" . . .

At I grow older I find out that Italians use Wop and Dago much more than Americans. My grandmother, whose vocabulary of English is confined to the commonest of nouns, always employs them in discussing contemporary Italians. The words never come forth quietly, unobtrusively. No; they bolt forth. There is a blatant intonation, and then the sense of someone being scathed, stunned.

I enter the parochial school with an awful fear that I will be called Wop. As soon as I find out why people have such things as surnames, I match my own against such typically Italian cognomens as Bianci, Borello, Pacelli—the names of other students. I am pleasantly relieved by the comparison. After all, I think, people will say I am French. Doesn't my name sound French? Sure! So thereafter, when people ask me my nationality, I tell them I am French. A few boys begin calling me Frenchy. I like that. It feels fine.

Thus I begin to loathe my heritage. I avoid Italian boys and girls who try to be friendly. I thank God for my light skin and hair, and I choose my companions by the Anglo-Saxon ring of their names. If a boy's name is Whitney, Brown, or Smythe, then he's my pal; but I'm always a little breathless when I am with him; he may find me out. At the lunch hour I huddle over my lunch pail, for my mother doesn't wrap my sandwiches in wax paper, and she makes them too large, and the lettuce leaves protrude. Worse, the bread is homemade; not bakery bread, not "American" bread. I make a great fuss because I can't have mayonnaise and other "American" things.

The parish priest is a good friend of my father's. He comes strolling through the school grounds, watching the children at play. He calls to me and asks about my father, and then he tells me I should be proud to be studying about my great countrymen, Columbus, Vespucci, John Cabot. He speaks in a loud, humorous voice. Students gather around us, listening, and I bite my lips and wish to Jesus he'd shut up and move on.

Occasionally now I hear about a fellow named Dante. But when I find out that he was an Italian I hate him as if he were alive and walking through the classrooms, pointing a finger at me. One day I find his picture in a dictionary. I look at it and tell myself that never have I seen an uglier bastard. . . .

During a ball game on the school grounds, a boy who plays on the opposing team begins to ridicule my playing. It is the ninth inning, and I ignore his taunts. We are losing the game, but if I can knock out a hit our chances of winning are pretty strong. I am determined to come through, and I face the pitcher confidently. The tormentor sees me at the plate.

"Ho! Ho!" he shouts. "Look who's up! The Wop's up. Let's get rid of the Wop!"

This is the first time anyone at school has ever flung the word at me, and I am so angry that I strike out foolishly. We fight after the game, this boy and I, and I make him take it back.

Now school days become fighting days. Nearly every afternoon at 3:15 a crowd gathers to watch me make some guy take it back. This is fun; I am getting somewhere now, so come on, you guys, I dare you to call me a Wop! When at length there are no more boys who challenge me, insults come to me by hearsay, and I seek out the culprits. I strut down the corridors. The smaller boys admire me. "Here he comes!" they say, and they gaze and gaze. My two younger brothers attend the same school, and the smallest, a little squirt, seven years old, brings his friends to me and asks me to roll up my sleeve and show them my muscles. Here you are, boys. Look me over.

My brother brings home furious accounts of my battles. My father listens voraciously, and I stand by, to clear up any doubtful details. Sadly happy days! My father gives me pointers; how to hold my fist, how to guard my head. My mother, too shocked to hear more, presses her temples and squeezes her eyes and leaves the room.

I am nervous when I bring friends to my house; the place looks so Italian. Here hangs a picture of Victor Emmanuel, and over there is one of the cathedral of Milan, and next to it, one of St. Peter's, and on the buffet stands a wine-pitcher of medieval design; it's forever brimming, forever red and brilliant with wine. These things are heirlooms belonging to my father, and no matter who may come to our house, he likes to stand under them and brag.

So I begin to shout to him. I tell him to cut out being a Wop and be an American once in a while. Immediately he gets his razor-strop and whales hell out of me, clouting me from room to room and finally out the back door. I go into the woodshed and pull down my pants and stretch my neck to examine the blue slices across my rump. A Wop! that's what my father is! Nowhere is there an American father who beats his son this way. Well, he's not going to get away with it; some day I'll get even with him.

I begin to think that my grandmother is hopelessly a Wop. She's a small, stocky peasant who walks with her wrists criss-crossed across her belly, a simple old lady fond of boys. She comes into the room and tries to talk to my friends. She speaks English with a bad accent, her vowels rolling out like hoops. When, in her simple way, she confronts a friend of mine and says, her old eyes smiling, "You lika go the Seester scola?" my heart roars, *Mannaggia!* I'm disgraced; now they all know that I'm an Italian.

My grandmother has taught me to speak her native tongue. By seven, I know it pretty well, and I always address her in it. But when friends are with me, when I am twelve and thirteen, I pretend to ignorance of what she says, and smirk stiffly; my friends daren't know that I can speak any language but English. Sometimes this infuriates her. She bristles, the loose skin at her throat knits hard, and she blasphemes with a mighty blasphemy.

When I finish in the parochial school my people decide to send me to a Jesuit academy in another city. My father comes with me on the first day. Chiseled into the stone coping that skirts the roof of the main building of the academy is the Latin inscription: *Religioni et Bonis Artibus.* My father and I stand at a distance, and he reads it aloud and tells me what it means.

I look up at him in amazement. Is this man my father? Why, look at him! Listen to him! He reads with an Italian inflection! He's wearing an Italian mustache. I have never realized it until this moment, but he looks exactly like a Wop. His suit hangs carelessly in wrinkles upon him. Why the deuce doesn't he buy a new one? And look at his tie! It's crooked. And his shoes: they need a shine. And for the Lord's sake, will you look at his pants! They're not even buttoned in front. And oh, damn, damn, damn, you can see those dirty old suspenders that he won't throw away. Say, mister, are you really my father? You there, why, you're such a little guy, such a runt, such an old-looking fellow! You look exactly like one of those immigrants carrying a blanket. You can't be *my* father! Why, I thought . . . I've always thought . . .

I'm crying now, the first time I've ever cried for any reason excepting a licking, and I'm glad he's not crying too. I'm glad he's as tough as he is, and we say good-by quickly, and I go down the path quickly, and I do not turn to look back, for I know he's standing there and looking at me.

I enter the administration building and stand in line with strange boys who also wait to register for the autumn term. Some Italian boys stand among them. I am away from home, and I sense the Italians. We look at one another and our eyes meet in an irresistible amalgamation, a suffusive consanguinity; I look away.

A burly Jesuit rises from his chair behind the desk and introduces

himself to me. Such a voice for a man! There are a dozen thunder-
storms in his chest. He asks my name, and writes it down on a
little card.

"Nationality?" he roars.

"American."

"Your father's name?"

I whisper it, "Luigi."

"How's that? Spell it out. Talk louder."

I cough. I touch my lips with the back of my hand and spell
out the name.

"Ha!" shouts the registrar. "And still they come! Another Wop!
Well, young man, you'll be at home here! Yes sir! Lots of Wops here!
We've even got kikes! And you know, this place reeks with shanty
Irish!"

Dio! How I hate that priest!

He continues, "Where was your father born?"

"Buenos Aires, Argentina."

"Your mother?"

At last I can shout with the gusto of truth.

"Chi-cag-oo!" Aye, just like a conductor.

Casually, by way of conversation, he asks, "You speak Italian?"

"Nah! Not a word."

"Too bad," he says.

"You're nuts," I think. . . .

Time passes, and so do school days.

I am sitting on a wall along the plaza, watching a Mexican fiesta
across the street. A man comes along and lifts himself to the wall
beside me, and asks if I have a cigarette. I have, and lighting the
cigarette, he makes conversation with me, and we talk of casual
things until the fiesta is over. Then we get down from the wall,
and still talking, go walking through the Los Angeles Tenderloin.
This man needs a shave and his clothes do not fit him; it's plain
that he's a bum. He tells one lie upon another, and not one is well
told. But I am lonesome in this town, and a glad listener.

We step into a restaurant for coffee. Now he becomes intimate.
He has bummed his way from Chicago to Los Angeles, and has
come in search of his sister; he has her address, but she is not at it,
and for two weeks he has been looking for her in vain. He talks on
and on about this sister, seeming to gyrate like a buzzard over her,
hinting to me that I should ask some questions about her. He wants
me to touch off the fuse that will release his feelings.

So I ask, "Is she married?"

And then he rips into her, hammer and tongs. Even if he does
find her, he will not live with her. What kind of a sister is she
to let him walk these streets without a dime in his pocket, and
she married to a man who has plenty of money and can give him a
job? He thinks she has deliberately given him a false address so
that he will not find her, and when he gets his hands on her he's

going to wring her neck. In the end, after he has completely demolished her, he does exactly what I think he is going to do.

He asks, "Have *you* got a sister?"

I tell him yes, and he waits for my opinion of her; but he doesn't get it.

We meet again a week later.

He has found his sister. Now he begins to praise her. She has induced her husband to give him a job, and tomorrow he goes to work as a waiter in his brother-in-law's restaurant. He tells me the address, but I do not think more of it beyond the fact that it must be somewhere in the Italian quarter.

And so it is, and by a strange coincidence I know his brother-in-law, Rocco Saccone, an old friend of my people and a *paesano* of my father's. I am in Rocco's place one night a fortnight later. Rocco and I are speaking in Italian when the man I have met on the plaza steps out of the kitchen, an apron over his legs. Rocco calls him and he comes over, and Rocco introduces him as his brother-in-law from Chicago. We shake hands.

"We've met before," I say, but the plaza man doesn't seem to want this known, for he lets go my hand quickly and goes behind the counter, pretending to be busy with something back there. Oh, he's bluffing; you can see that.

In a loud voice, Rocco says to me, "That man is a skunk. He's ashamed of his own flesh and blood." He turns to the plaza man.

"Ain't you?"

"Oh, yeah?" the plaza man sneers.

"How do you mean—he's ashamed? How do you mean?"

"Ashamed of being an Italian," Rocco says.

"Oh, yeah?" from the plaza man.

"That's all he knows," Rocco says. "Oh, yeah? That's all he knows. Oh, yeah? Oh, yeah? That's all he knows."

"Oh, yeah?" the plaza man says again.

"Yah," Rocco says, his face blue. "*Animale codardo!*"

The plaza man looks at me with peaked eyebrows, and he doesn't know it, he standing there with his black, liquid eyes, he doesn't know that he's as good as a god in his waiter's apron; for he is indeed a god, a miracle worker; no, he doesn't know; no one knows; just the same, he is that—he, of all people. Standing there and looking at him, I feel like my grandfather and my father and the Jesuit cook and Rocco; I seem to have come home, and I am surprised that this return, which I have somehow always expected, should come so quietly, without trumpets and thunder.

"If I were you, I'd get rid of him," I say to Rocco.

"Oh, yeah?" the plaza man says again.

I'd like to paste him. But that won't do any good. There's no sense in hammering your own corpse.

MAYOR LA GUARDIA OF NEW YORK

[After serving several terms in Congress, Fiorello La Guardia was elected mayor of New York City in 1933 on a fusion ticket. A staunch urban liberal, his appeal was directly to the voters, not to the party bosses. An office holder of substantial accomplishment during the severe Depression years, he was also a colorful enough figure to inspire a Broadway musical, *Fiorello* (1959). Perhaps he is best remembered as the mayor who, during a newspaper strike, read the "funnies" to children every Sunday over the radio.]

Few people know that for forty years before he took office as mayor in 1934, Fiorello H. La Guardia dreamed of doing something about New York City; that way out in Arizona, back in the Nineties, as a high school boy, he was reading with gusto week-old New York newspapers telling of Dr. Charles H. Parkhurst's battle with Tammany Hall, and of its result in 1895 in the election of William L. Strong and one of the sporadic stable cleanings. To be sure, "little ol' New York" then meant to him only Manhattan Island; but that 1895 eruption greatly expedited the creation of the Greater City.

We need to know something about this squat, sturdy, sometimes smiling but oftener ferociously scrapping second-generation Italian. The first of his "race" ever to hold this office; hitherto, for half a century anyway, New York mayors have been preponderantly of Irish extraction. Like Al Smith, La Guardia represents American democracy functioning appropriately in bringing to the top on his own a son of the ordinary "common people" regardless of racial

From "La Guardia—Portrait of a Mayor," by John Palmer Gavit, in: *Survey Graphic*, January, 1936.

origin or social status. Also the famous melting pot; for he is not only Italian. His father, by name Achilles, was born at Foggia, inland on the Adriatic side of Italy about east of Naples; but his mother, Irene Coen Luzzatti, was a Jew, of that finest "Safardi" type, in the case of her forebears fugitive to Venice from persecution in Portugal. Of that stock came the noted philosopher Spinoza, our own poetess, Emma Lazarus, and Benjamin Cardozo, now a justice of the Supreme Court of the United States. The parents met and were married at Trieste (port-of-call for Java, where La Guardia *padre* had been a band musician), coming thence to New York and Varick Street where Fiorello was born just 53 years ago, December 11, 1882. It was a small family—a brother, Richard, died about a year ago; a sister survives, at Budapest. His father was a musician of taste and skill; he became a bandmaster in the United States Army, and when Fiorello was a year old was ordered out to old Fort Huachuca in the southeast corner of Arizona. So it was after all a New York City boy who got excited, out there by the Mexican border, about Dr. Parkhurst and Tammany Hall. Always he has regarded New York City as "home." And here he is at last, mayor of the city, charged with Augean stable cleaning and administration; challenged by profound desire and opportunity to do something in fulfilment of a lifelong ambition. Already two years deep in the job. . . .

La Guardia, like other mayors, brought to his office *all* of his personality—assets and liabilities. (Did you expect a Superman, without defects?) Among them his grudges, prejudices, and phobias embittering intercourse. Of phobias four in particular. One against bankers. He knows little about banking, finance, economics, though he's a full-length encyclopedia about them compared with some of his recent predecessors. He seems to regard bankers as merely clutching hoarders of their own money; unaware of their function as custodians—even of the deposits of the Little People—restricted by both mathematics and law. It appears difficult for him to imagine a banker as cleanly motivated as himself. Partly that may be because he used to know about the crooked little bankers who fleeced the immigrants. And crooked big ones are not unheard of! Against lawyers. He ought to know about them, for he is a lawyer himself and has some high-grade friends and devoted supporters among them. But here again, so far as immediate contacts go, practical politics is crawling with slimy ones. Against politicians. Yes, he does know about them. Against racketeers, big and little: enough said.

He has no "social" flair or ambition; no taste, aptitude, nor time for "social doings" with the rich and influential, though among them there are a few whom he likes and trusts. It isn't exactly hostility; it's a kind of contempt, not unlike that characterizing his predecessor Judge Gaynor. They do not interest him: he ignores and forgets them. The folks who do interest him are, as one of his intimates put it to me, "the little people, in the little streets, the 80 percent, whose names aren't even in the telephone directory; who in the last analysis pay the taxes. The little people who read the tabloids." To him the unemployed, recipients of relief, are *people*. He cares about them. It was on their account that he had the courage to surrender his previously vociferous opposition to the retail sales tax as the only means of providing unemployment relief; insisting however upon the exemption of foodstuffs and upon a ten cent minimum. Incidentally it was something of a feat—a blood-infusion for the city's credit—to collect that fund and put the cost behind, instead of ahead, by borrowing as most other cities have done.

The settlement and welfare workers have found him heartily accessible and sympathetic—he knows what they are about and understands their language. "For the first time since Mitchel," one of them said to me, "we have in the mayor's office both a head and a heart." He is not a radical in any proper sense of the word. The Communists have no use for him; he calls their bluffs and refuses to have them clubbed by the police. His proposals of municipal competition with public utility corporations arise not from any theory of collectivism but from the belief that by means of their monopoly they impose upon the city and the public and can be disciplined only with a club. He is not a Socialist but an intellectually convinced progressive, and was fighting for the New Deal essentials before Theodore Roosevelt discovered "the New Nationalism."

He has a quick, mordant wit and makes swifter, better, more humane wisecracks than Jimmy Walker. One of his friends and admirers is that redoubtable architect Isaac Newton Phelps Stokes, president of the Municipal Art Commission: perhaps not least because at their first meeting, aware of the aesthetic nature of that commission's responsibility, without cracking a smile the mayor complained to Mr. Stokes that upon assuming his desk in city hall he found three cockroaches under it! In a biting winter wind, last month, dedicating the "First Houses" in the East Side slums, the mayor told of a constitutional lawyer scoffing to him two or three years ago that "it would be a cold day before there would be houses built by federal aid." Adding:

"Well, it's a cold day, and here are the houses!"

He brought his personal charm which at its best is completely winning, disarming; but he brought also his hair-trigger temper and a loose tongue, at its worst most unlovely, frequently crassly brutal —usually swiftly regretted. He terrifies, intimidates, and often fires his personal subordinates; but though fired they do not quit because down deep they adore and believe in the little spitfire. His secretary in Congress, who saw and heard him at his best and worst—who but his wife knows a man as his secretary knows him? . . . well, knowing him like that, said secretary became, and still is, his wife. The mayor's home is a happy one, in which the husband is master by virtue of that definition of such as "one who can make his wife do anything she wants to do." Mrs. La Guardia keeps out of the newspapers, but by signs familiar to me I judge her to be that sort of cipher which, standing beside him at the right, multiplies a man by ten. There are two children—adopted. La Guardia brought also his ardent love of children. He regards himself as in some sort father and guardian of all the kids in the five boroughs.

ITALIAN CULTURE FOR THE SECOND GENERATION

Mario Petruzzelli

[Since the late 1960's, blacks, Chicanos, and American Indians, among others, have asserted their claims to ethnic-cultural consciousness. Such claims are based, in part at least, on an often unvoiced search for identity through knowing and participating in one's heritage. For even an undefined "Americanism," if given free reign, can obliterate a people's sense of its past. This issue was frequently raised among most immigrant groups as the American-born second generation began growing up in an atmosphere of apparent cultural rootlessness. To many observers, the only way to combat this deprivation was to introduce the new generation to the language and heritage of the parents' homeland. This effort, although vigorously pursued in some places, had only a marginal effect on the children of the second generation. The following selection by Mario Petruzzelli is typical of the admonitions concerning the education of young Italian Americans.]

When our immigrant's son looks back at his early life to consider his environment, his recollections in most cases are not very encouraging. The best he can think of is the sight of the East Side of New York or of any other Eastern city where immigrants are massed together. The rich surroundings of traditions characteristic of his race do not exist for him; he experiences a sort of spiritual starvation from which he tries to escape. Often he cannot understand his own parents' thoughts and manners and this situation at times becomes really tragic. He is no longer at home in his own family. That peaceful united homelife which we still believe is the real foundation of happiness and society is never experienced by many of these

From "The Value of Italian Culture in American Citizenship" in: *Atlantica*, May, 1937.

young people. At times, this peculiar psychological condition is aggravated by the rather cold attitude of the other better groups around him.

What has caused this undesirable and unique situation?

The answer is quite obvious: The first generation of children born in America of Italian-born parents have been entirely cut off from the heritage of their race; as individuals, they do not know and feel that they are the heirs of a people that has given the world the greatness of Rome and that of the Renaissance, whose masters are still the spiritual leaders and teachers throughout the civilized world today.

One of the most important factors that have greatly contributed to the material as well as to the cultural growth of the Anglo-Saxon group in this country has undoubtedly been the intellectual and spiritual guidance that these groups have enjoyed since the very beginning of their immigration.

The Italian immigration in this country is comparatively recent. It began about the very beginning of the century and was made of the poorest classes, which saw in this great land the only hope for their economic redemption. Artists, professional men, business men were very seldom seen among the Italian immigrants, who missed that spiritual help which had been very conspicuously present among the other groups that had come here from the northern countries of Europe. No wonder, then, that the American-born children of these immigrants ignored every manifestation of the artistic, scientific and literary life of the country of their fathers and that in contact with other more advanced racial groups felt, to a certain extent, humiliated and sometimes ashamed of their own race.

We all know that an American citizen, be he the direct heir of the first pioneer or the son of the last immigrant, when he adds to his intellectual equipment one or two modern languages, thereby widening his culture, acquires a direct understanding of millions of people with a rich cultural background different from his own. With this new equipment he can directly penetrate and better interpret the very soul of those people and consequently very often becomes a messenger of that international goodwill we have heard so much about.

The teaching of the Italian language to the American youth of Italian extraction has a two-fold aim and value: first, it gives them those opportunities we have just mentioned; second, it re-attaches them to the best historical, artisic and cultural traditions of their fathers, giving them a consciousness of the rich heritage of their race, an indispensable element which distinguishes the civilized man from the savage.

Acquainted with their priceless intellectual patrimony, they will transmit it and contribute it to those among whom they have chosen to live in America.

The spread of the Italian language and culture among American children of Italian parentage and among other groups will un-doubtedly promote a better mutual understanding between American citizens of American ancestry and American citizens of Italian an-cestry and help to remove the general suspicion natural between natives of different races. It will help to do away with much of the spirit of arrogance, of national self-sufficiency and of the attitude of unfriendliness resulting therefrom.

If great American authors such as Longfellow, Lowell, Norton and many other distinguished ones became keen students of Italian, and promoted and encouraged the spread of that language and literature in the United States, how much more important and necessary it is for the sons of Italian parents to follow the footsteps of these great men and re-attach themselves spiritually to that race, two thousand years old but always young, which has given the world an unbroken chain of immortal men, like Cicero, Sallust, Virgil, Dante, Petrarca, Da Vinci, Michelangelo, Raffaello, Columbus, Gali-leo, Volta, Croce, Marconi?

Let us give the American youth of Italian extraction that spiritual patrimony of their race that most of them would otherwise miss, and in turn they will bring to the civilization of this country not a weak and empty soul but the visible signs of a conscientious per-sonality of which America will be proud.

NO. 38 BECOMES CITIZEN
Max Ascoli

[One inestimable benefit to America during the years after 1930 was a side effect of fascism in Italy. Many Italians who disagreed with Mussolini's policies came to the United States in what has been called an "intellectual migration." Among these notable Italians were conductor Arturo Toscanini; physicists Enrico Fermi, Emilio Segrè, and Sergio De Benedetti; economist Franco Modigliani; and historians Giuseppe Antonio Borgese, Robert S. Lopez, and Gaetano Salvemini. Journalist Max Ascoli arrived in 1931 on a fellowship from the Rockefeller Foundation and remained as a teacher at the New School for Social Research. In 1949 he founded and thereafter edited *The Reporter*, a journal of current events. In this selection, he tells of the day he became an American citizen.]

"Number 38. Come in with your witnesses." It is my examination for the second paper which means that, if everything goes well, after a statutory period of ninety days I shall become an American citizen. "Do you know the Constitution of the United States?" "Do you believe in it?" "Do you know why we celebrate the Fourth of July?" "Can you read English? Read here."

" 'We hold these truths to be self-evident, that all men are created equal, that they are endowed by their Creator with certain unalienable rights, that among these are life, liberty, and the pursuit of happiness.' "

"Do you believe in these principles?"

"Yes, I do."

The questioning goes on. The examiner looks straight at my eyes.

From *Atlantic Monthly*, February, 1940.

Yes, I do believe in the democratic form of government. It is just because I believe in the principles of the Declaration of Independence that I left my native country, Italy, of my own will seven years ago. Of course I don't say this to the examiner. He has no business with my private affairs; it is a routine job for him to take in new citizens. I can see a long row of men and women all waiting to have their numbers called. Like me, they are already uprooted from their own country and not yet Americans. "Do you give up your allegiance to your former country?" "Yes, I do." "Are you willing to bear arms for the defense of the United States?" "Yes, I am."

It is a very strange thing to acquire the citizenship of a new country: something like taking a new father and mother. There is no doubt that the natural destiny of every man is to live and die in the land where he was born, among the people of his own language and tradition and customs. How strange it would have sounded to me if, only a dozen years ago, I had been told that one day I might give up being an Italian! I would have said that to leave one's country is a great calamity, a fateful decision that no one could take unless compelled by the utmost necessity. I would have said that I hated fascism, yes, but that not to share the destiny of the other Italians was an act of arrogance for anybody not in danger of his life; and that as long as it was possible to stay and exert some influence it was better to live a hindered life at home than to look for shelter abroad.

Yet here I am—answering questions in an English which is fluent but still heavy with Italian accent; I earn my living by lecturing in English, thanks to the understanding of my students; I write in English, thanks to friends who still occasionally look over my use of prepositions. In a few months I may be traveling in Europe with an American passport. In Europe, but not in Italy. For several years I have had no passport, as the Italian consulate in New York refused to give me any document except one good to take me back to Italy and keep me there. During these years I have been what is called a political refugee, an expatriate.

I know exactly the date and the hour when I first realized that all this was bound to happen. It was the night of April 30, 1928, in the police headquarters of a small town in central Italy. I had been brought there, not in a regular state of arrest, but to be questioned—or, as it is said, under protective custody. In deference to my professorial dignity I had not been· locked in a cell, but was invited to spend the night in the office of a clerk, with the door open and two policemen watching from the corridor. I sat at the desk, smoking and looking out of the window until after dawn. I had been caught. They could not pin anything specific on me, yet their hand was on my neck. It was not a violent hand. Rather, it was trying to push me with impatient clumsiness in the right direction. Could I not, with a positive act of repentance, clear up all malevolent rumors, establish my reputation, and, together with my countrymen, proclaim that the Duce is always right?

That pressure had been going on for years, but privately, coming through the channels of friendship or comradeship. From that night on it was going to be exerted by policemen. The police of a dictatorial country, to keep themselves busy and the opponents scared, can do little more than invent plots: it is their own naïve blundering way of giving bodily reality to the unfathomable crime of thinking. The police do not know individuals, but want to built up cases. My case was very simple: could I change my mind? Otherwise there was going to be trouble. The pincers of the "either-or" were closing on me. The grip on my neck was the cold metallic one of the system, and it is difficult to reason with a system. One thing was sure: that the police were going to stiffen my determination and that from that night on my way of thinking was going to mold my way of living. That night I knew.

At the bottom, I thought, it was a quite simple matter. I had been so far an Italian citizen devoted to his country. Now the police in their rough way were serving notice on me that my citizenship was going to be forfeited unless I strengthened it by taking a second one. To be an Italian was not enough: one had to become a Fascist. An Italian insisting that the old citizenship was good enough for him was a man without security and without rights. I could not become a Fascist. I could not swear allegiance to the Duce. I knew that night that in due course of time fascism was going to make an alien of me. I did not know that in a few years I should have sworn allegiance to the American Constitution and called Italy my former country. But I knew definitely, when the sky over the piazza, out the window of the police headquarters, was all brightened by the fresh clarity of the Italian dawn, that my moorings had been cut and that I was on the move.

Now I am becoming an American citizen. I pass through the first questioning, but I have to wait before going through a second one; and after that I have to wait again and go through a third. Each time they ask me something or put some stamps on my papers. What I heard from a man at dinner a few nights ago comes to my mind: "To an intellectual it must not be hard to shift allegiance from one country to another. An intellectual is a citizen of the world." I like to remember these words now: they sound so silly. I don't know if anyone here, waiting to pass the first, the second, or the third examination, calls himself a citizen of the world. And I don't know how other intellectuals may feel in this moment. I know my own feeling. I know that I had a country—Italy—and now I have put the final seal on the fact that I have lost it. That is all.

This means that I am definitely estranged from the land, the sky, the culture, in which I have lived. Of course there are always good men around, ready to preach about citizens of the world and culture that survives exile—nay, that lives out of exile. I wish I could pat my shoulder and congratulate myself on the little bit of Italian culture that I have brought to new life over here. But unfortunately the American is adult enough in me to scent the bunk. The truth is that my roots are cut, and that whatever Italian sap is left in my nature is living out of contact with the Italian earth. What is the use of tracing down the origins and the responsibilities? Fascist intolerance worked hand in hand with my stubborn sense of self-respect. I don't regret it. I would do it again. I could not become a Fascist. I became an American. Therefore Italy is my former country. The Italian culture is my former culture. These are facts.

There are people who say, "But after all, things may turn out differently, and you will be back someday." Things may certainly become different in Italy, but one cannot change his country as he changes his shirt. It is a great privilege to become an American. All these routine ceremonies are not exactly formalities or red tape. The two friends who are here with me to testify about my moral character are not professional witnesses picked up in the street. They are real friends. I am in a large group of friends over here, a community which is growing out of the work of each one of us, and mutual confidence, and common beliefs. It did not cause me any trouble to become an Italian; but my becoming an American is my own work. To me these ceremonies are a reality which is of my own making. No, I don't imagine I will undo in the future what I am doing today. . . .

In the list of the prospective citizens invited to call at the Immigration Office of the Southern District of New York on June 21, 1939, I have number 38. Among all men and women I know over here there is not a single one, I suppose, whose American origins cannot be traced back to a number like my 38 obtained in some way for an identical purpose. This is why, perhaps, I feel as if the wrench of being uprooted from Italy were soothed by a sense of homecoming. . . .

I think I know this country well enough not to be swayed by any Fourth of July optimism. I earn my living by teaching what is called political philosophy, which (I answer when I am asked, What is it?) is something between Plato and Jim Farley. I am getting more and more familiar with the hard realistic Jim Farley way of turning things around. I don't think anybody has to teach me about Mayor Hague or Hearst or Tom Girdler: I know almost everything that has been written about these gentlemen who generously provide test cases for the defenders of civil liberties. I know about Senator Reynolds and the anti-alien sentiment. I have read everything I could about sharecroppers and labor spies and labor rackets. *The Grapes of Wrath* is still on my desk.

I know about the ways of intolerance in this country, and what

life was like in the Twenties under Prohibition. I have met some
dozen Babbitts and more than one Elmer Gantry. And certainly I
have met here, among native Americans, Fascist types and countless
men and women of no convictions at all who were ready to jump
into the first wagon hitched to a faraway star. All European diseases
and conditions for diseases I have found over here in large or small
samples, and some more which are specifically American. And how
could it be different? There is nothing superhuman about this country and this people.

It is only too natural that all germs and pollutions which may
affect the human breed have found their way and some chance over
here. Sometimes these germs neutralize each other. Racial or religious intolerance may take ominous forms in Alabama, but will not
easily combine with the brand of intolerance which is preached in
Michigan. In some other instances intolerance has taken the character of a disease that by its recurrence has lost something of its
deadly power. There is a definite limit to what the country can
tolerate in the way of labor troubles or red baiting. Men with some
good qualifications for becoming dictators or tyrants have been
rapidly blown to pieces by the mercilessly used technique of bunk-
ing and debunking.

This homespun wisdom, this shrewd biological health of the
American people, is the instinctive wisdom of that part of the race
which in one way or another has so far managed to keep itself free
from monarchies, from state-enforced religions, from dogmas of all
kinds. Therefore it gets from time to time entangled in cheap sub-
stitutes of what it has freed itself from, and it falls under the
fetters of machine politicians, or prohibition crusaders, or of aboli-
tion preachers of all kinds. For a while—and then the instinctive
wisdom manages to get rid of all these fetters one by one.

It is extremely difficult to fool the American people all the time;
it is quite easy to induce them to try anything—as the immigrant
does who grimly wants, with all his determination and, resourcefulness, to start life anew. By becoming collective, this fondness for
experiment and trial has socialized and lessened its risks. The enormous pool of wisdom of plain men who, finding themselves alone
on this continent, managed to get something done has perhaps more
resources in itself than our rational thought can measure. It is also
true that this healthy resourcefulness has sometimes a rare power
of irritating and humiliating the rational thought of the native and
of the imported intellectuals.

Perhaps the freedom and the equality exalted in the Declaration
of Independence mean a shrewd willingness to give to every germ
a chance, until the body becomes self-immunized. Perhaps freedom
here has its foundation in this astutely gained good health. I don't
know whether the rights that the Declaration mentions are unalienable, but I know that they cannot be easily alienated as long

as they are guaranteed by good health, common sense, and good humor. Who knows whether God gave these rights to men? But certainly they are the instinct of the human race.

"It is a very strange thing to be an American," MacLeish wrote. Perhaps it is somewhat less strange to become one. Or at least in becoming one, the man who has been estranged from his own country may have the feeling that he is not doing a strange thing, that he is not the prey of a freak of destiny. He follows a way that other men have trod. Of course he is coming late, and he has to pay his toll. But he finds a country where, out of the pooled experience of plain uprooted men, something healthy and enduring has come forth—a new kind of country.

I have now to pass the last test. I am told to go with my witnesses into a bare courtroom. A thin elderly man in shirt sleeves, sitting on the bench, calls my name. At his side is the American flag. On the grayed walls are two cheap old pictures, one of Washington and the other of Lincoln. With a quick official voice the man on the bench says: "Do you believe in the American Constitution? Do you believe in the principles of the Declaration of Independence? Do you give up your allegiance to your former country? Are you willing to bear arms for the defense of the United States? . . . We shall check all the information and data, and if they are correct after ninety days you will be called to take your final oath."

I become an American citizen. So help me God.

LITTLE ITALY ON JUNE 10, 1940

[On June 5, 1940, Germany invaded France and five days later, Italy also declared war on France. That same day, President Franklin D. Roosevelt was scheduled to deliver an address to the graduating class at the University of Virginia. Hearing of Italy's attack, Roosevelt rewrote some of his speech in fairly harsh terms, announcing the attack to the university audience by saying: "The hand that held the dagger has struck it into the back of its neighbor." Italian Americans were shocked not only by the onset of war, but by the President's unequivocal language, remarks they felt reflected on them. The selection below gives some indication of the state of mind in New York City's Little Italy on that June 10.]

Outdoors in our block the reaction to the news, yesterday, of Mussolini's declaration of war on England and France was a curious, but only seeming, calm, as I [American-born son of Italian immigrant parents, a graduate of Columbia University] returned home from work early in the evening. Everybody was unusually quiet. I missed the shouting and laughter of children on the sidewalks, the cries of boys playing stick ball in the street. The neighborhood iceman sat on the shoe repairer's doorstep, but they were not arguing as is their custom. Men and women in front of stores and tenements looked about almost furtively, as though they were suddenly being watched. Down the street a group of men stood in front of the grocer's. Their discussion was subdued. Their gesticulations were slow, devoid of the usual drama and animation. Some of them looked far off. They tried not to think and talk, or could not. I know

From Louis Adamic, *From Many Lands* (New York, 1940), pp. 334–36.

most of them; nearly all are immigrants who came over shortly before or after the First World War. A small proportion of them are pro-Fascist, but they really express themselves only in the privacy of their homes. . . .

After supper I dropped in on the people next door, a family of three: a man, his wife, and her niece. Forty-six years old, he holds a city civil service job. His wife is the same age. They have been in America since 1920. Her niece is twenty-five, here only six years. The women listen to Italian radio programs all day, read *Il Progresso*, and swallow propaganda hook, line and sinker. The man has two brothers in Paris, both on the dole there. A brother of the wife, father of the girl, was killed in the war in 1918. One of the girl's brothers now is a soldier in Libya. The man is completely dominated by his wife, who makes him support her niece when she is not working.

I said, "What was the idea of Italy going to war?"

The man answered, "She gave France and England an ultimatum: turn over to us Corsica and Malta, let us use Suez, get off Gibraltar —or else! They refused; Italy went to war."

I said, "But did you hear what Roosevelt said on the radio—that Mussolini stabbed France in the back?"

"It isn't true!" the three of them cried in unison.

The girl went on: "Why do we Italians have to emigrate and go begging to other countries? Why does Italy have to pay at Suez? . . . Sanctions! So they wanted forty-five millions of us to starve! They want to keep us bottled up in the Mediterranean, between Suez and Gibraltar, and even there we can't do what we want. England and France have everything. They took everything before we awoke. Now we are awake, and we want—"

Her aunt interrupted her, "Who gives England the right to stop our ships at Gibraltar? Gibraltar belongs to Spain; England stole it from Spain."

"But," I said, "this is not a war merely to get this or that. It's a war for world domination. It's a revolution. . . . If Hitler is not stopped, the whole world may be enslaved."

The man: "What are you talking about!"

His wife: "Hitler is ruled by Mussolini; I heard it on the radio yesterday."

Her niece: "Italy has been the underdog long enough. Now it's our turn."

"If Germany wins," I said, "Hitler will dominate Italy. He does already."

"So we'll be Germans!" laughed the man, feeling stupid. "So what!"

"But Italians will be slaves," I said.

"Oh, you're crazy!"

The women sat tense, tight-lipped. Behind their tenseness, behind all their words, was really only confusion. . . .

The background of these three people is significant. Ever since they have been in America they have had no contact with the country; not really. Work and home, work and home. The women work in a dress factory a few weeks every three or four months. They are not even in contact with the community of "Little Italy" or of our block or immediate neighborhood. They consider themselves a little better than the general run of Italians and Italian Americans. Isolation. The girl especially has been isolated. When she arrived in the United States at nineteen, she started going to night school, but the instructor antagonized her. She developed the notion he did not like Italians and foreigners generally. She quit. Result: isolation, loneliness. She is not particularly good-looking; who cares about her, or what she thinks? People in the factory, which is Jewish-owned, with Jewish bosses, are pretty much like herself; but, to keep up her ego, she holds herself superior to them. She is very aloof. Underneath, of course, she is insecure, scared. . . .

By a slightly different route her aunt has reached the same mental condition. She doesn't want to associate with the general run of people. She and the girl have locked their senses and minds against all impressions except that of the radio and their favorite newspaper, the exciting Fascist propaganda. When they are at home, the dial of their radio is constantly set on the Italian stations. They get broadcasts from Rome. They seldom go out. I think life in the streets scares them. They are a glaring example of the failure of "Americanization."

The man spent some years in Paris. He has read a few books. He now has a semiclerical job which brings him only superficially in touch with other people. He considers himself an intellectual, also superior to the people of the neighborhood.

I asked him, "Would you shoot a Frenchman?"

"No," he replied without hesitancy.

These seeming pro-Fascists do not know the deeper, hidden meaning of fascism. Once they understand it, they will want to fight it.

This is an extreme case; with variations in form and degree, it represents, on a guess, less than ten per cent of the immigrants in our "Little Italy." But even here there is the contradiction: he would not shoot a Frenchman. When he said, "So we'll be Germans! So What!" he meant he might be a German politically. Beyond that his mind was just confusion.

I spoke to other people last night. They all know me, and were frank. Most of them expressed shame and apprehension. Roosevelt was right; "only maybe he should not have said it for our sake. We all voted for him in '32 and '36. But what can we do?" Their mood affected the children; it changed, at least momentarily, the entire texture of the atmosphere of the neighborhood.

I met an ardent Fascist of a few weeks ago. Now he is outraged by the fury and horror of the Germans' total war.

In some of the families the difficulties between the immigrant

parents and their American-born children are considerable. There
are arguments, fights. Most of the youngsters don't give a hang
about Italy. They play ball in the park, dance the boogi-woogi,
shoot dice in the doorways, and—a few—drive around in cheap
cars. They appear not to know what is going on in the world. Now
and then, however, at the supper table, they suddenly say something
about "Musso" and the old man flares up, although, if you examine
him, he really hasn't much use for Mussolini. It is just that in
recent years "Mussolini" and "Italy" have become synonymous
among people incapable of careful thought.

The young Italian Americans, as a rule, are nowhere culturally.
Nice kids, some of them; but, really, neither Italians nor Americans.
They have little notion of democracy. Many are without jobs, without any perceptible future. They are "wops" and "dagoes" when
they get outside the neighborhood. They are up against a vague difficulty in relation to America. Are they part of the country or aren't
they? . . . "What the hell! So what!" . . . They try not to think about
such things. They succeed in this easily. They follow all available
excitements. They do not understand Hitlerism and Mussolini's fascism. They don't give a damn, or so they say if you ask them. But
they are carried forward in the grip of something in the air. A
force. Something is happening in this world. It is affecting America.
Them. Us. In case of a real crisis in this country, I think, the young
Italian Americans will respond if the government and the leaders
will know how to appeal to them. The crux of the problem is not that
they are "Italians," for they are not, but that they are, as I say,
nowhere, in a cultural no man's land.

I spent an hour last night in the corner candy store where a
bunch of young fellows hang out. I caught phrases: "Ford says he
can make a thousand planes a day. . . . La Guardia is a wop, too,
ain't he? . . . Did you hear what Roosevelt said about Musso? The
sonoffa—" meaning the latter.

There is a boy in our block who spends a lot of his free time
in the branch library. He has read up on Italy. A year ago he
dreamed of going over some day for a visit. He wanted to see
Florence. Now that's out. Last night I met him in front of the
library as it closed at ten. I asked him, "How do you feel about all
this?"

He said, "Mussolini's action puts me in position where I am
obliged to fight my own mother."

PRIDE IN AMERICAN CITIZENSHIP

Attilio Piccirilli

[Sculptor Attilio Piccirilli came to the United States from Tuscany in 1888, at the age of 22, after studying at the Royal Academy of Fine Arts in Rome. Within a dozen years, his works gained him an international reputation. He designed the Maine Memorial, the Firemen's Monument in New York City, the War Memorial in Albany, Rockefeller Center sculptures, and the Marconi monument in Washington, D.C., among many others. At the time of writing this selection in 1940, Piccirilli was president of the Leonardo DaVinci Art School.]

I have been an American for so long—50 years—that I often forget that I was born in Italy. When anyone refers to me as a foreigner, or as an Italian, I pretend that I haven't heard and I don't usually answer. Of course I am an American—Look!

Once, when I thought that I would like to travel a little, I went back to my native city and planned to stay there for a year or more. I locked the door of my studio in New York City, said goodbye to all of my friends and went back to the homeland where I had been born. What did I find?

I was a foreigner in Italy. I could speak the language, of course, but I couldn't think Italian. All of my thoughts were those of an American. I had planned to be away a year but in four weeks I was on my return trip to the Bronx.

My brother and I first came over here together. I shan't tell you how old we were for that is not important. We were boys, with big eyes—boys leaning over the boat rail watching New York harbor.

From Robert Spiers Benjamin, ed., *I Am an American* (New York, 1941), pp. 36–40.

I had twenty-five cents in my pocket, I remember, and my brother and I discussed whether, if our uncle didn't meet us that day, it would be enough to buy some bread and cheese.

There's one big difference right there. Today we wouldn't be allowed to land in America with 25 cents in our pockets! They were glad to have us come in those days for there weren't enough Americans to do the work over here. And there's another difference.

I had raised a beard in honor of America for I wanted to look impressive. But I was so young that the result was not as impressive as I had hoped—with a bunch of hair here, and some there. My uncle *was* there to meet us with a friend. Right away they led us off to show us all of the sights. First we went to Castle Gardens. It's the Aquarium now.

Everyone had a clean shirt and a shaved face, and I asked my uncle, "What day is today?" "Tuesday" he told me.

"No. No," I said. "I mean what fete day is it! Everybody is washed and wearing white shirts—it must be a great national holiday!"

My uncle and his friend laughed. "Oh," they told us, "it isn't a fete day. People wear clean shirts every day in America." I was more impressed by that than anything they showed me. Two days later I took out my first citizenship papers, and I think that I have been a good American ever since.

I first *knew* that I was a real American when I brought my mother's body back from Italy where she had died on a visit. We buried her here and I made a statue of motherhood for her grave. I had worked here, and succeeded a little, and taken the oath of allegiance. But it is when you bury one you love in a country's soil that you realize that you belong to that soil forever.

From the beginning I was happy here. I had my work and the friend of my uncle who met us at the boat was good to us. He gave us money to send for my mother and the others, and when they came he rented an apartment and bought furniture. He didn't know whether or not we would ever pay him back, but he took a chance, as we Americans say. He was Jewish and a fine American.

Schools are always asking me to speak to them, and what do they want me to talk to them about? "How I succeeded!" As if you could make a rule for success. And anyhow who says that I have succeeded?

Have I made a big fortune? No. But I have had a good life. I've worked hard from the first, and earned plenty of money, and spent it and been happy. For five years my brother Furio and I only put our mallets and chisels down to eat and sleep. We did not know whether we were making money with our sculpture or not. We didn't even think of money. My parents were good business people and they managed everything, the sale of our work, buying our house in the Bronx, everything! I noticed that we had more furniture as time went on, and we ate better food, but I never knew that in those first five years my brother and I had earned over

$50,000. Perhaps that is the only possible rule for success as an artist—not to think of work in terms of money, but of opportunity and of joy.

I am often asked if I think that a young artist coming to this country now would still find it a land of opportunity? Yes, I do. There is as much opportunity here now as there was when I came, if the people could only see it. Cities and towns and villages from coast to coast and every one of them needing to be beautified. At first everybody was too busy making a country out of wilderness to think of beauty! They built ugly houses and buildings which could be put up in a hurry. Now it must all be done over again. I'm tired of hearing people talk as if America was finished. What has been done? Not much that doesn't need to be torn down and done over again as you know if you've ever traveled in America and have seen its small towns.

There's work for everybody in rebuilding America. Work for carpenters and bricklayers and factory hands, and house painters—and work for the artist, too! We are just awakening to the idea of adorning our homes and schoolhouses and public buildings with frescoes and paintings and sculpture. And yet with a whole nation to make over, with 130,000,000 people to supply with the good modern things of living we talk as if there never would be enough jobs any more. The young artist who comes to America today, or who is born in America has plenty of opportunity. But opportunity is not all outside, you know. It is inside the heart too so we must carry our own opportunity with us. That is why I have had my art school here in New York for thirty years—so that all young people who carry opportunity in their hearts shall find the door open to them. There is no trouble becoming a pupil of Attilio Piccirilli. All a girl or boy has to do is open my door and step inside. I'll tell them, "There is the clay. There is a hook. Hang up your hat and go to work." Then they are my pupils.

ITALIAN AMERICANS, FASCISM, AND THE WAR

Constantine M. Panunzio

[During the late
1920's and the 1930's, probably most Italian Americans admired
Mussolini and the name he was making for Italy in the world. But
the Italian Americans were by no means alone. Millions of other
Americans found much to admire in Fascism and expressed their
sympathies openly. Only after Italy moved into an alliance with
Nazi Germany did the American ardor for Fascism cool rapidly. By
the time the United States entered World War II, the appeal of
Mussolini's style of government had faded for many Americans. In
1942 Constantine Panunzio, professor of sociology at UCLA, surveyed the whole career of Italo-American Fascism. Panunzio, born
in Molfetta in 1884, came to the United States in 1902, and enjoyed
a long and illustrious career in education and public service. Among
his many books is the autobiographical *The Soul of an Immigrant*
(1921).]

The question of the extent to which American culture is dominant
in the life of minority ethnic groups in the United States, important
at all times, is of the greatest moment in this period of international conflict. As the Italian group in this country contains the
largest number of foreign-born people—they numbered 1,623,580 in
1940, the Germans being next with 1,237,772—and as the whole Italian group is composed of comparative newcomers, presumably
more under the influence of their parent country than earlier immigrants, its response to fascism, a non-American system, as contrasted with democracy, an indigenous American pattern, furnishes
an excellent case in point.

From *The Yale Review*, June, 1942.

The response which the Italian Americans have given to fascism, or are giving to it in the present crisis, has passed through three well-marked phases: early indifference, passing interest, and mild antagonism; partial acceptance and participation; and withdrawal and repudiation. During the years in which fascism was in its formative stages, by far the great majority of Italian Americans regarded the movement with indifference, or passing interest, or mild antagonism. Although on this issue no Gallup poll was ever taken, all the available evidence of their literary and social expression points to such a conclusion. At least four factors helped to produce it. First, the Italians who came to the United States before 1920 were almost wholly late nineteenth-century liberals. In their home land they had been influenced by the American and French Revolutions, had participated in the agrarian, proletarian, and co-operative movements, and had in other ways inclined towards democracy.

Residence in the United States had strengthened the original democratic leanings of early Italian Americans. Most of them had been in this country on an average about twelve to fifteen years by the time fascism was forming. Here in democratic America, they had bettered their condition: they had improved their economic situation, enjoyed greater educational advantages for themselves and their children; and many had risen in the social scale. Their labor-union activity and their American-schooled children added their democratic influence. And here also they had had an opportunity to participate in political democracy—an opportunity which they embraced to such an extent that, in those centres where they were numerous, they constituted powerful political blocs, sometimes unscrupulously manipulated by politicians. Residence in America, then, had clearly increased their democratic bent.

The fact that the United States and Italy had fought side by side in the First World War had further intensified that attitude. Italian Americans were aware of and grateful for what the United States had done towards completing the liberation of Italy from Austria. There was a minority which was disappointed that Italy had not been given Dalmatia at the Peace Conference—a failure attributed to Wilson. But what concerned most Italian Americans in those days above all else and made them rejoice was that the Kaiser's régime, Austria, and other autocracies had fallen, that what some Italians called "the Anglo-Saxon and Latin democracies" had triumphed, and that America had been a factor, if not the decisive factor, in bringing about that triumph. So when the fascist dictatorship was looming, their loyalty was unmistakably to democracy and especially to the United States.

In addition to these forces which drew Italian Americans closer to American democracy, there was one which definitely repelled many from fascism. This consisted of the anti-American feeling which the fascists were fostering in Italy. Using the Dalmatian affair, the war debts, and immigration restriction as weapons to create antagonism—their real target was democracy—the fascists kept engendering a feeling of bitterness against the United States in the early 1920's. Their attacks, however, only served to draw the Italians in this country still closer to America. For America, with all its shortcomings, had been good and was dear to them. So when Mussolini howled about the "decomposing body of democracy," many made impolite gestures and deepened their attachment to their adopted country.

That these forces bound the older generation of Italian Americans, as a whole, firmly to America can hardly be doubted. Their everyday conduct, their feasts and celebrations, their organizations and meetings, their newspapers, magazines, pamphlets, the constitutions of their organizations, gave abundant evidence that their loyalty was clearly to America and its democracy. Down to the end of 1926, the present writer encountered far more stubborn opposition to his anti-fascist utterances among native Americans descended from other racial stocks, especially those of legitimist bent, than among Italian Americans. There were some groups of the latter, such as those which were represented in the Italian Chamber of Commerce and the Italian American Society, and a few publications, such as "Il Progresso Italo-Americano" and "Il Carroccio," both of New York, which favored fascism from the first. But the interests of these were, in those years, primarily commercial or "cultural," not in any way political. The mass of Italian Americans were at that time and have remained to this day fundamentally anti-fascist and American to the core.

About 1926 the picture started to change. More Italian Americans began to lean towards fascism. In this shift also several factors were at work.

First among these was the psychological effect of the immigration restriction movement. The restriction movement, it will be recalled, though primarily economic in its purpose, was largely colored by the inferiority-superiority doctrines of Gobineau and company, which labelled the Italians, along with several other peoples, as inferior. Italian Americans did not oppose restriction *per se*, since they themselves, being largely of the laboring classes, were interested in preventing additional workers from entering the country. But they were humiliated by the underlying discrimination, especially when that discrimination was given national expression and confirmation in the Immigration Acts of 1921 and 1924.

The fascist doctrine, on the other hand, gave them strength, endowed them with a sense of ethnic dignity and pride, by proclaiming the greatness of the Italian people and of the contribution they had made to culture. It encouraged Italians the world over to return to their native land and not subject themselves to indignity abroad; it promised them an empire of their own, a new Roman empire, in which they could toil in their own right and reap the fruit of their labor for themselves and the motherland. As a knowledge of these fascist doctrines and promises permeated the thought of the Italians in this country—and the fascists saw to it that it did —many Italian Americans, being human and needing a prop to sustain them in a world where many people with whom they had to deal regarded them as inferior, looked on fascism as their savior. They turned to it simply as a means of recovering their sense of human importance. If the facts were known, it would probably be found that there were many who, like Domenico Trombetta, editor of the New York weekly "Grido della Stirpe" (Cry of the Race), became fire-eating fascists and agitators against democracy as a result of this process. . . .

A second influence which drew Italian Americans to fascism was the rapprochement between the Catholic church and Italian state, as embodied in the Conciliation Treaties of 1929. . . .

Thus fascism, and more particularly Mussolini, appeared in the role of champion of the church and thereby won many devout Italian Americans to fascism. In fact, the negotiations leading up to the treaties, and the treaties themselves, had so great an effect on Italian Americans and on the American Catholic community as a whole that it has been alleged that the entire affair was undertaken by Mussolini with an eye primarily on America. Since fascism was greatly in need of financial aid and looked for it mainly to the United States, it could secure that aid in no better way than by winning the collaboration of American Catholics. In any event, many Italian Americans were won over.

A third pro-fascist influence consisted in the glowing accounts of the "new Italy" which kept reaching this country during the early 1930's. The fascists in those years were very active in promoting the American tourist trade and in exhibiting to unwary foreigners the achievements of the régime. These visitors, seldom examining the reality behind the scenes, were much impressed. On their return, they spread widely reports of trains running on time, of vast public enterprises, of the "tremendous" building projects, new roads and aqueducts, great industrial and commercial activity, slum clearance, marsh drainage, and of the absence of beggars from the streets. Many American press dispatches from Italy in those years added their distortions and exaggerations. And the Italian American newspapers, which had practically no cable service, reproduced the accounts appearing in the American papers and often referred to the American source as evidence of the impeccable authenticity of the facts. As the benefits of fascism were proclaimed in these ways far and wide, some Italian Americans bowed in veneration to the grandeur that was Il Duce.

Even more, the enthusiasm which certain types of Americans in the Twenties evinced for fascism had its effect. At that time, there *was* a sort of "Teddy Rooseveltian big stick" element in Mussolini; and there was such an ardent, messianic condemnation of communism and defense of capitalism in fascism, and so much Hollywood flamboyance in all fascist events, that not a few Americans were swept off their feet. That, of course, caused Italian American chests to swell. With a number of important persons in industry, commerce, and finance, in education and politics, singing Il Duce's praises, what Italian American could resist?

This excellent foundation being laid, early in the Thirties, fascism initiated its own systematic propaganda among the people of Italian extraction in this country. The fascists did not show the skill the Nazis later showed in their fifth-column activities; that is, the fascists did not send over propagandists from Italy, but they worked through organizations already established in this country. The chief organizations used in this manner included the Italian embassy, the consulates, the Dante Alighieri Society, the Fasci Abroad, and the Sons of Italy. All these organizations were specifically mentioned in "The Order of the Day of the National Fascist Party"— the party's official publication, containing its instructions as to its policies and procedures. Fascism also employed various Italian chambers of commerce in this country, and many Italian American newspapers as avenues of propaganda. The organizations held meetings and banquets, published and distributed pro-fascist literature, procured and conferred honors and the like. . . .

This activity continued to gain momentum until about 1935. In 1931 Foreign Minister Grandi came to the United States, ostensibly to discuss peace with President Hoover. Grandi was accompanied by his wife—an unheard-of arrangement for an Italian on a diplomatic mission—to assist in social propaganda. Then in 1933 the fascists sent Italo Balbo flying over the Atlantic to the United States and the Chicago Fair. This glorified propaganda stunt made some converts. Finally, in January, 1934, the fascists confidently sent over Piero Parini, Director General of Italian Fasci Abroad, to consolidate the fascist forces in the United States. There were in this country at that time 125 principal fascist centres, having headquarters, regularly elected officers, and a membership of about 500,000.

The Parini visit, however, marked the turning point in this movement. Instead of consolidating fascism among Italian Americans, it actually sounded the first peal of the death knell of the movement. The anti-fascists, who had been looking for just such an opportunity, warned of the danger. The House Committee investigating un-American activities looked into the matter. Parini was scarcely out of the country when fascist propagandists started to run for cover. Italian Americans all over the land, beginning to realize the full significance of fascism, commenced to withdraw from fascist groups. American reaction to the Ethiopian war accelerated that movement. Many Italians took out their naturalization papers and brought over their families. They knew where they stood.

In 1937 another event helped to liquidate fascism among Italian

Americans. The fascists sent Mussolini's son to this country on a propaganda tour. But the young man, utterly failing to sense the real spirit of the American˙people, went about the country singing "the glories of sprinkling death from bomber planes." A certain group, it is related, in the motion picture colony of Hollywood set a memorable trap for him. It planned a banquet in his honor, sold hundreds of tickets at a handsome price, and broadcast the coming affair, but when the evening of the banquet came, only a handful of people appeared on the scene. The incident was a bad jolt for the young man. But it served to stress the fact that not all America held Mussolini in great admiration or had pictures of the Duce in their homes beside those of President Roosevelt, as Italian newspapers had been claiming. The event caused great defection among Italian Americans, who are very sensitive to general American public opinion.

In 1938 an increasing number of Italian Americans perceived the real meaning of fascism, for Italy as well as for the rest of the world. First came the Austrian *Anschlus* and the occupation of the Brenner Pass by the Nazis in March, with the fascists' tacit acceptance of that fact, and then Hitler's descent into Italy, in May, at the invitation of the fascists. These events made it clear that fascism, wittingly or unwittingly, was betraying Italy. At first, Italian American newspapers and radio programs were on the defensive; later they became half apologetic; and as time passed they gave fainter and fainter praise to fascism. Prominent Italian Americans changed overnight from fascists to ardent advocates of democracy.

Meantime the Italian anti-fascists, who for nearly two decades had been looked down upon and who had waged a losing fight as individuals, now became articulate. They initiated a broad movement to counteract the fascist propaganda. Outstanding in this connection is the Mazzini Society organized in 1939 by such men as Salvemini, Sforza, Venturi, and others, most of whom are American citizens of Italian extraction. The Mazzini Society now has about fifty centres and over 3,000 members or associate members. It devotes itself to educating Italian Americans in the fundamentals of American democracy. It conducts meetings, publishes literature, assists Italians needing services once performed by the consulates; and in other ways, it aids Italian Americans in the name of democracy.

It is safe to assert that at present the Italian American community as a whole is almost to a man disillusioned as to fascism. There are those who are watching the way the wind blows and who still hope for an Axis victory. But they are few and very far between. The vast majority of Italians in this country today are unequivocally for democracy. Even many of those who have been interned as enemy aliens have no love for Mussolini. An editor of an Italian-language newspaper, only a few days before being interned, said to this writer, "Fascism may have been all right for a time over there, but we are through with it. Give us full-fledged democracy."

The cycle of reaction described above indicates, first, that American culture was at all times dominant. The acceptance of democracy, a well-established American pattern, was at all times clear. This was partly because most early Italian immigrants had acquired portions of that pattern in their native country, but more because life in this country made democracy natural and desirable. In this we have an illustration of the confluence of culture.

In so far as fascism, an extraneous culture pattern, did influence the behavior of the immigrants in question, this also was, at least in great part, due to forces inherent in American life. Some Italian Americans accepted fascism from the first for practical reasons of trade and profit, some out of general considerations of ethnic or religious feeling. The mass of them inclined towards fascism when American society itself evinced a certain amount of approval, and became cool or antagonistic when Americans reacted in that manner. Immigrants adjust themselves to the broad trends of American thought and action far more than is generally realized.

But even this response was not at all basic. To the older generation, fascism was mainly a diversion or a means of escape from the feeling of inferiority which the American community imposed on them. Among the middle-aged, the response was perhaps greater because they, being not as yet fully established in this country, suffered most from discrimination. Those who were young in the 1920's, that is, those who are now under thirty, or even forty, have remained fundamentally untouched. American culture has been so influential in their lives, especially through the schools, that many of them "never heard" of fascism and many of those who knew about it regarded it as a vague, far-off, entertaining system. Fascism did not touch even the fringes of their daily lives.

The final test came when American society denounced fascism and unequivocally reasserted its adherence to the dominantly American pattern of democracy. When that occurred, Italian Americans almost to a man, equally unequivocally, repudiated fascism and declared their loyalty to democracy. A genuine adherence to the democratic way of life had its profound influence.

All in all, there is no clearer illustration of the forces at work in the assimilation process or of the dominance of American influences in the lives of immigrants than this chapter of our social history. Now that the test of war has come, there is no question as to where almost one hundred per cent of our Italian immigrant population stands.

LOYALTY OF ITALIAN AMERICANS

Vito Marcantonio

[Vito Marcantonio represented New York's Harlem in Congress for seven terms, finally being defeated for re-election in 1950. For most of his political career he attracted a very loyal following in spite of his controversial stands on many public issues. He was intensely devoted to the welfare of his constituents, but as his social-economic views became increasingly Marxist, he gradually lost support among the voters. The following selection is part of a radio address delivered by Marcantonio on July 20, 1942, a time when feelings against Americans of Italian, German, and Japanese descent were running high in some quarters. Moves to intern or otherwise discriminate against Italian Americans soon evaporated; and it was only the Japanese Americans who bore the brunt of America's wartime xenophobia.]

My fellow Americans, there should be no need for me to speak to you tonight about the role of Italian-Americans in this war. I feel impelled to address the people of the Nation on this subject because of the persistent activities of certain groups in our country who malign the loyalty and dispute the patriotism of Americans of Italian descent, by discriminating against them in industry, by denying them equal opportunity with other loyal Americans, and by regarding them with suspicion because of the sound of their names.

I am speaking to you tonight because I want to say with utmost emphasis that these maligners and detractors are playing Hitler's game in America.

From U.S., Congress, House, *Congressional Record*, 77th Congress, 2 sess., appendix pp. A2848–49.

The personnel manager in a plant who turns down a skilled worker of undoubted loyalty to our country and overwhelming desire to aid the war effort, because this man has an Italian name, is playing Hitler's game in America.

The plants with huge Government contracts which have an established policy of refusing employment to Americans of Italian descent, are playing Hitler's game in America.

The self-styled "superpatriots" who indulge in alien-baiting and foreign-born baiting are playing Hitler's game in America.

These detractors and maligners of our loyal Italian-Americans are, by this most un-American activity, causing disunity in our country, depriving our Nation of the services of skilled men and women, and are standing in the way of that full mobilization of America's manpower that we must have to win this war. In short, it is they who have become a menace to America's victory program. The contributions of Americans of Italian extraction in blood, toil, and wealth is the devastating answer to those who seek to discriminate against them. . . .

Italian-Americans share with the rest of their countrymen the conviction that enemy agents, saboteurs, and spies, whether American born or foreign born, whether citizen or non-citizen, must be ceaselessly guarded against and ruthlessly dealt with. However, history will record that those who denied opportunities to our Italian-Americans, or to any other group because of their race, color, creed, or national origin, were themselves doing the work of enemy agents and saboteurs. They, as much as any Hitler agent smuggled from Berlin, are subverting the all-out effort which is so essential to victory.

On August 6, 1861, Giuseppe Garibaldi, whose struggles and traditions truly represent the people of Italy, wrote to Abraham Lincoln from Caprera, Italy. In inspiring words which are just as applicable during this great conflict as they were during that crisis of 1861, Garibaldi offers his sword to Lincoln in the struggle for freedom and pledges the aid of all free Italians in that conflict against slavery.

> We salute you, Abraham Lincoln, helmsman of liberty; we salute you who for two years have fought and died for your standard of liberation; we salute you, redeemed, oppressed race —the freemen of Italy kiss the glorious links of your chains.

So, we, too, true sons of Garibaldi, to the great democratic leader of this day, to our Commander in Chief, the President of the United States, renew our pledge and rededicate our energies and our lives for the victory of our arms, for the victory of our cause.

ITALIAN AMERICANS VOTE REPUBLICAN

Vincent Tortora

[During the Depression, Italian Americans joined other low income groups of the population in the New Deal coalition put together by Franklin D. Roosevelt, but they never became so overwhelmingly Democratic as the Irish. In 1940, when Roosevelt ran for a third term, many Italians voted Republican. By the time of the Eisenhower landslide in 1952, the Republican trend among Italian American voters had become even more pronounced. In the following article, journalist Vincent Tortora analyzed this voting trend.]

Analyses of election results in our larger cities reveal that over the past fifteen years more and more Italian Americans of the first, second, and third generation have been voting the Republican ticket. The tendency acquires importance from the fact that Italian Americans are concentrated in the states which have the largest representation in the Electoral College and that they have frequently held the balance of power in some of the major cities in those states and thus in the states themselves. Oscar Handlin in his Pulitzer-prize-winning study of immigrants, "The Uprooted," predicts that even Boston will soon have to acknowledge Italian American political supremacy. No statistics are available, but authoritative estimates of the percentage of Italian Americans—ranging from the foreign-born to the second- and third-generation native-born with one Italian parent—in eleven states are as follows: Connecticut, 25 per cent; New York, 20 per cent; New Jersey, 20 per cent; Rhode Island, 20 per cent; Massachusetts, 15 per cent; Pennsylvania, 10

From "Italian Americans: Their Swing to the G.O.P.," in: *Nation*, October 24, 1953.

per cent; Illinois, 9 per cent; California, 8 per cent; Ohio, 5 per cent; Michigan, 3 per cent; and Maryland, 3 per cent.

New York City contains approximately 2,200,000 Italian Americans as defined above; Providence, 70,000; Buffalo, 75,000; Baltimore, 50,000; Philadelphia, 250,000; Pittsburgh, 200,000; Detroit, 155,000; and Chicago, 280,000. Examination of the vote in these cities shows that in the period from 1930 to 1936, inclusive, the average Republican vote in the Italian wards was 26 per cent, while in the whole city it was 38 per cent. The difference was in reality greater to the extent that the Italian American vote tended to pull the overall vote toward itself.

In the period from 1942 to 1946, inclusive, the average Republican vote in these same wards had risen to 35 per cent and the average over-all Republican vote to 43 per cent. Thus the Democratic margin among Italian Americans had dropped from 12 to 8 per cent.

In the period from 1942 to 1946, inclusive, the average Republican vote in Italian wards had risen another 9 percentage points to 44 per cent. The over-all Republican vote averaged but 42 per cent. At this point the Italian Americans voted more strongly for the Republicans than did the other voters in the cities considered. The Democrats were no longer able to take the Italian American vote for granted.

During this 1942–46 period solidly Italian American wards in Brooklyn, Manhattan, and Pittsburgh that had gone Democratic four to one in the 1930's on the average evenly divided their vote between the two parties. Several wards in Philadelphia that had been overwhelmingly Democratic ten years earlier now gave 60 or 65 per cent majorities to the Republicans.

Since the beginning of the post-war period in 1946, the nationality composition of the traditionally Italian wards in these cities has changed in varying degree. In Manhattan, Philadelphia, Baltimore, Detroit, and Pittsburgh, Italian Americans have been moving out of sections long identified with them, and their homes have been quickly reoccupied by new immigrant groups and racial minorities. In Brooklyn, Buffalo, Chicago, and Providence enough Italians are left in the old sections to give them an Italian flavor even if it is somewhat attenuated.

Trends in Italian American voting have thus become more difficult to determine. It has been possible to establish, however, that in the sections into which large numbers of Italian Americans have recently moved the Republican vote, on the average, has increased 2 to 5 per cent. And by taking into account the proportion of other new immigrants and racial minorities—who usually vote Democratic—in the old Italian sections, it can be determined that what is left of the Italian American vote there favors the Republicans, on the average, by 3 to 5 percentage points above the over-all vote.

In one of the East Side districts of Manhattan, for example, 40 per cent of the Italians have moved out and been replaced by new racial groups 90 per cent of whose members are found to vote Democratic. Subtracting the percentage of votes by these groups from the total percentage, we find that the remaining citizens, largely Italian Americans, have cast 49 per cent of their votes for the Republicans. Since during the 1948–52 period the Republicans obtained on the average 44 per cent of the votes cast in all New York, we must conclude that the Italian American trend away from the Democrats is continuing. The figures in other cities bear this out.

Attempting to find the reasons for this trend, I interviewed a number of first-, second-, and third-generation Italian Americans of varying occupations. Some, especially the foreign-born, revealed strong emotional and familial ties with Italy. They considered the unstable politico-economic conditions in post-war Italy and the ignominious Trieste impasse to be largely the fault of the Democrats, who had been in power. A surprising large proportion felt that the McCarren-Walter immigration act discriminated against their nationality. Numerous non-political Italian American organizations campaigned for a protest vote against the act. Since both McCarran and Walter were Democrats, the protest was registered by a vote for the Republicans.

Within the last fifteen years the war, the generally higher economic standard, and the arrival of new, non-Italian immigrants have worked a marked change in the attitude of society toward the Italian American. Large numbers of young men of Italian descent have served in the army, studied in colleges and universities, gone into the professions or into business. With national prosperity high, much less social pressure has been exerted to keep them down. Puerto Rican immigrants have taken the place of Italians in the contempt of society. Exclusive clubs which once refused membership to "Italians, Greeks, Jews, and Colored" now admit the Italian American.

This change in social attitude and the Italian Americans' own improved financial status have enabled them to move away from the Little Italys. And just as they no longer live as a separate group, they no longer vote as a group. The psychology of group identification and group voting used so successfully by Democratic leaders among the Italians no longer applies. Reacting against the poverty and discrimination of their past, they tend now to consider the Democratic Party that of the menial laborer, the slum dweller—the class to which they belonged for so many years. The Republican Party represents the middle class, the suburbanites, which it has tales of many years ago.

Many of the foreign-born and second-generation Italian Americans interviewed mentioned as a factor in their voting switch the resentment they felt toward the Irish Americans. The Irish, having been immigrants themselves only a few years before, still felt insecure in

American society when the mass immigration of Italians began. As the Italians began to compete for their jobs, the rivalry became intense and frequently erupted into violence. As a result of this feeling the church usually assigned one parish in a neighborhood to the Italians and another parish, perhaps only a block away, to the Irish. At the same time the Irish American politicians, realizing the vote potential of the newcomers, went to almost any extreme to curry favor with them. And in response the newly naturalized Italian voted Democratic.

But as the Italian American started on his upward social and economic climb, his dependence on the ward politician diminished. He became a thinking individual. He began to vote as he pleased. By vigorously pulling the Republican lever, he could give an outlet to his deep-seated antagonism to the Irish.

THE PROCESS OF AMERICANIZATON

Laura Fermi

[Physicist Enrico Fermi brought his family to the United States in 1939. Soon after his arrival, he was involved along with other scientists in the experiments on nuclear fission that resulted in the sustained nuclear chain reaction in December, 1942, at the University of Chicago laboratories. After Fermi's death in 1954, his wife Laura began a literary career, first with the autobiographical *Atoms in the Family* and later with the volume *Illustrious Immigrants; The Intellectual Migration from Europe 1930–1941*. The selection below is from an article describing the Fermi family's first few weeks in America.]

"Wake up and dress. We have almost arrived. The children are already on deck."

In reluctant obedience to Enrico's peremptory voice, I emerged out of sleep and the warm comfort of my berth. It was the morning of January 2, 1939, and the *Franconia* was rolling placidly, with no hurry.

On deck Nella and Giulio rushed to me away from the watchful presence of their nurse. "Land," Nella shouted, and Giulio extended a chubby finger in the direction of the ship's bow and repeated, "Land!"

But Enrico said: "We have founded the American branch of the Fermi family."

I turned my eyes to the children. They seemed more thoroughly scrubbed and polished than American children I had seen. On their curly heads the leather helmets we had bought in Denmark against

From *Mademoiselle*, September, 1954.

the first northern rigors appeared alien. I looked at Enrico and at his markedly Mediterranean features, in which I could read the pride and relief of one who has satisfactorily guided his expedition across land and sea. And I looked at the maid who had come along with us, now bravely winking against the wind and rubbing her hands together to make up for the light coat she was wearing, who could talk to none but us because she knew no English.

This is no American family, I thought to myself. Not yet.

But the process of Americanization had started for us ten days before, shortly after we had boarded the *Franconia* in Southampton on December 24. The children and I, exploring the boat, rang for the elevator. When its doors swung open we were face to face with a short old man in a baggy red suit and furry white trimmings, with a long white beard and twinkling blue eyes. The three of us stood still, fascinated. The queer old man said to us with a benevolent smile: "Don't you know me? I am Santa Claus."

Of course, I should have known him from my English teacher's tales of many years ago.

"I hope you'll be coming to my party this evening. I'll have presents for you!" Santa Claus said, bending his white beard toward my children. Their eyes sparkled. They turned to me. "Will you let us go? Please let us go!"

Of course they went.

Later I tried to explain Santa Claus to the children. Giulio could understand little of what I said but his eyes were eager and attentive, as always when grown-ups were speaking.

"In each country of the world," I told them, "once a year children receive presents from a person who is not one of their parents, who comes for the sole purpose of bringing toys and candies."

"The Epiphany!" Nella interrupted.

"Yes, in Italy it is the Epiphany who comes on the 6th of January, the day the Three Kings brought their presents to the Child Jesus. She rides on a broom in the sky—"

"Brings toys to me too," Giulio said. Nella turned to him. "She has a big, big sack on her shoulders," she explained, "and when all children are asleep and it is night, she comes down the chimney or, if there is no chimney, she enters the door and stuffs the children's stockings with toys."

"For me too," Giulio said.

"This happens in Italy. But in America there is Santa Claus. He does not ride a broomstick but a sleigh pulled by reindeer, which are animals with big antlers. So he travels more comfortably and can carry a larger bag of toys. He comes once a year, the day before Christmas."

"Will the Epiphany come to us all the same? She knows we're Italian children."

"No, she will not. She could not get a visa and must remain in Italy," I answered on the inspiration of the moment.

"Poor Epiphany," Nella said wistfully, "I don't think she likes Mussolini too well."

For six months we lived in New York City, within the ten blocks between 110 and 120 streets, where most Columbia University teachers live. Only occasionally did I take a trip downtown, an expedition comparable to that of the villager going to the big city. . . .

Shopping was a cooperative enterprise shared by the maid and me. She could judge the quality of fruit and vegetables, recognize the cuts of meats. I could better translate dollars into lire to decide whether prices were reasonable; I could explore packages and cans, of which I bought large quantities, for, like any newly arrived European, we went on a canned-food spree, which was to last only as long as there were new cans to try.

I patronized the small shops where the clerks could take the time to instruct ignorant foreigners in the marvels of pudding powders and of frozen foods, which had just appeared on the market. In almost every grocery store at least one man was Italian-born, or of Italian descent, and with him my maid and I made friends at once. Not that it helped much: Italians in New York come from the south of Italy and they bring to their speech so much of their Neapolitan or Sicilian dialects that it is hard to understand them, whether they speak Italian or English.

I soon became addicted to dime stores and mail-order houses. There I could obtain what I wanted without talking, even buttons and dress patterns and all the other objects with the unpronounceable double *t* in them. My incapacity for properly pronouncing double *t*'s outlived all other language difficulties. Months later, when I could usually make myself understood and had mustered enough courage to do an occasional bit of shopping over the telephone, I ordered butter and received bird seed.

Among the several traits that make Enrico a strong individualist is his intolerance of living in a home that he does not own. So as soon as we had settled in a furnished apartment we tackled the problem of buying a permanent place in which to live.

It had been simple to buy an apartment in Rome: we had looked at the advertisements in the papers, we had explored a limited number of possible apartments and we had bought one. In New York it was different. In our small section of the city there were no small homes, no cooperative apartments, nothing we could buy. Those of our friends who owned homes lived in the suburbs and practised that un-European activity, commuting.

"Several of my colleagues live in a town called Leonia. It is in New Jersey, just across the George Washington Bridge, on the other side of the Palisades," Enrico said on Sunday. "Let's go see what it looks like." It was February and an ice-cold afternoon. As we got off the bus at the stoplight in Leonia, a gust of wind blew in our faces and blinded us. We did not know where to go.

"Harold Urey, the Nobel prize winner, lives here. Let's go visit him and his wife. I know him well enough." This last sentence of Enrico's was an answer to my doubtful expression.

The Ureys were in their large living room and had a fire going. Our visit was a success. Dr. Urey sold Leonia to us. By the following summer we were the happy owners of a house on the Palisades, with a large lawn, a small pond, and a lot of dampness in the basement. By the time the house had been redecorated for us and was ready for occupancy our furniture had arrived from Italy and war had broken out in Europe. We settled, and this time for good, or so we thought. . . .

In learning the American language and habits, Enrico had a considerable advantage over me: he spent his days at Columbia University among Americans, and inside the physics building he found an obliging mentor in Herbert Anderson, a graduate student who planned to work for his Ph.D. under Enrico's guidance.

No day went by without Enrico's telling me something that Herbert Anderson had taught him.

"Anderson says we should hire our neighbor's children and pay them a penny for each of our English mistakes they correct. He says it is the only way of learning the language efficiently."

"Anderson says that there are no oral examinations in American universities. The multiple-choice tests, Anderson says. . . ."

Some young people are occasionally shy of Enrico. Some students complain that he does not know how to give them a "pat on the back." Anderson had no place for shyness and felt no need of special encouragement. Had I been able to understand Americans at that time I would have recognized in him at least one attribute of the Jeffersonian heritage: the inborn conviction that men are created equal. The older men's position, the public recognition they might receive, the honors shed on them were to him only indications of the goods available to mankind.

So Anderson was not only Enrico's student but his friend and teacher. He learned physics from Fermi and taught him Americana.

I stayed home most of the time and got Anderson's teachings only at second hand. So, for me, learning English was a very slow process. . . .

In the process of Americanization, however, there is more than learning language and customs and setting oneself to do whatever Americans can do. There is the absorbing of the background—the ability to evoke visions of covered wagons, to hear the sound of thumping hoofs and jolting wheels over a mountain pass—the power to relive a miner's excitement in his boom town in Colorado and to understand his thoughts when, fifty years later, no longer a miner but a philosopher, he lets his gaze float along with the smoke from his pipe over the ghostlike remnants of his town. The acceptance of New England pride and the participation in the long-suffering of the South.

And there is the switch of heroes.

Suppose that *you* go to live in a foreign country and that this country is Italy. And suppose you are talking to a cultivated Italian, who may say to you:

"Shakespeare? Pretty good, isn't he? But all those historical figures he brings in . . . not the most important ones . . . we have to look up history books to follow him. Now you take Dante. *Here* is a great poet for you! A universal poet! Such a superhuman conception of the universe! And his history! He has made history alive. Read Dante and you know history. . . ."

In your hero worship there is no place for both Shakespeare and Dante. If you are to live in Italy and be like other people, forget Shakespeare. Let Mazzini and Cavour replace Jefferson and Adams, Carducci and Manzoni take the place of Longfellow and Emerson. Forget that a telephone is a Bell telephone and accept Meucci as its inventor, and remember that the first idea of an airplane was Leonardo's. Once you have made these adjustments in your mind you have become Italianized, perhaps. Perhaps you have not and never will.

When I travel across the immense plains of the Middle West, plowed and harvested at night by gremlins for in the daytime no soul is ever to be seen, I still feel the impact of emptiness. I miss the crowded, terraced fields reclaimed from the stony side of a hill. I miss the many eyes a tourist feels on his back—as an American friend once told me—each time he stops to eat his lunch in the most secluded spot in Italy. I miss the people who materialize from nowhere. . . .

If I still miss them, I ask myself, and still marvel at the vastness of America, at newly discovered sights, at the mention of some great name still unheard of by me, if I fail to understand the humor in Charles Addams' cartoons, can I truly say that I am Americanized?

ITALIAN AMERICANS OF BOSTON'S NORTH END

Norman Thomas di Giovanni

[The author of this selection is a native of Boston's North End, the most populous Italian American settlement in the city.]

The North End—Boston's Italian quarter—is a closed city within a city. Surrounding it like the walls of a medieval town are the waterfront on one side, and on the other an express elevated highway, a two-block-wide aerial ribbon of steel, concrete and asphalt. And as if these enclosing barriers were not enough, there exists beyond the "walls" a no-man's land, inhabited only by day, of commercial buildings, offices, wholesale meat and produce markets, factories, warehouses and wharves, which adds further protection against the encroachment of outsiders. So the quarter is a tiny, closed city resting on a good portion of the heart and soul of colonial-Revolutionary old Boston.

Within these rigid confines, in a postage-stamp area less than a half-mile square (roughly the area of the Boston Common plus the Public Garden), live 16,000 Italians. But a true picture of the prevailing congestion cannot be drawn without noting the large number —dozen upon dozen—of North End buildings and areas used for purposes other than habitation: stores, factories, warehouses, churches, a few schools, many restaurants, single-lot playgrounds, historical sites, minuscule parks and even a pre-Revolutionary burial ground.

The 16,000, then, inhabit great brick tenements, jammed together

From "Tenements and Cadillacs," in: *Nation*, December 3, 1958.

four to five stories high, ancient, dark, dirty, run-down—some so bad they remain boarded up and untenanted. A new facade often conceals structures a hundred or more years old, for in the North End there is a real marriage of American and foreign, and one may see anywhere two or three new stories, with baroque fire escapes, added onto very simple early nineteenth-century buildings. Here is a maze of tiny streets and alleys, the streets bearing in most cases the names they held in colonial times: Prince and Hanover, Charter and Snow Hill and Salutation; twisted little ways wide enough for eighteenth-century man and his horse and cow, but not for today's Italians with their Oldsmobiles and Cadillacs, which they often park jauntily on the sidewalks. Lined with parked automobiles, many streets are plastered with refuse and garbage and the leftovers of the pushcart peddlers and grocers who pour their goods onto the sidewalks and along the curbing. While above this—on the roofs above the clothes hanging to dry between fire escape and fire escape, and dead-end alleys and walls covered with graffiti—a few old men go on fashioning huts and pigeon lofts out of discarded crates and, amid the omnipresent forest of television antennas, attempt to cultivate tomato gardens, an occasional fig tree, perhaps a few flowers.

Inside the tenements, the apartments—always spoken of as "rooms"—are small and dark and as many-celled as hives. Very few have central heating, separate toilets or their own bathing facilities. Every room is usually overburdened: furniture (either uniformly old or uniformly, jazzily modern), framed family photographs, modern appliances, clothing (for there are few closets), plaster statues of saints, holy pictures, and useless, or no longer usable, shabby, broken or run-down items—the accumulated possessions of a have-not people.

As a class, North Enders are working people first and second generation Americans (with a third generation in its infancy), together with a vast number of recent arrivals from the south of Italy. They hold fiercely independent ideas about the work they do— they minimize their labors and, especially among the young men, give the impression of *lazzaroni*—but are nonetheless endlessly industrious. They are also physically clean, well-fed, well-dressed, comfortable and poor. There is general semi-literacy, and in practical affairs it hardly matters whether one speaks English or Italian, since the community is perfectly bilingual. The Italian they speak is more accurately described as a polyglot of southern dialects, incorporating Italianized American words, just as their English is English that will not be heard elsewhere in America. North Enders have this tendency toward being uniquely apart: not quite Italian, not quite American. And despite the work of four churches and several parochial and public schools, spiritually the people remain impoverished.

Gambling fills the spiritual vacuum. It is so general and so open that discussing the "numbers" is second nature to the North Ender. It is not uncommon to be stopped in the street early in the morning by someone half-awake and disheveled, and to be feverishly asked —in much the same way a derelict asks for a cigarette—"What was yesterday's number?" Or to see a $10 bill plummet from a fourth-floor window, from which a mother instructs her young daughter in the street below: "Go to C. the bookie and put it on 'Many Harvests.'" Above the racket of the bustling street, the child yells back: "What horse did you say, Mummy?"

Everyone in town knows you don't have to go a third of a block to book a horse, a dog, a number, or to borrow from "the shylock." Everyone knows that certain florists sell no flowers, that certain dry-cleaning establishments clean no clothes. Everyone has seen bookies openly burning their tickets at the edge of the street. . . .

Enough about gambling. Of crimes of violence—armed robbery, assault—the North End is free. It has to be: the North End must stay clean because so many small-time gangsters and racketeers live here and work to keep their own yards clean so that attention or detection will not fall their way. The visitor's idea of the North End, which is that crime and violence lurk everywhere, just is not so. As a matter of fact, the North Enders sometimes do their own effective policing—and mete out their own justice. At the foot of Hanover Street is a Coast Guard station, and a few years back coast guardsmen were being beaten and robbed on their way home at night by North End hoodlums. Before the police could get to first base in solving the crimes, certain racketeers made an investigation of their own, found the guilty ones and sent them both to the hospital with severe beatings.

This primitive conception of justice is rather natural to the background of a people who in general are suspicious of laws. Theirs is a live-and-let-live idea which North Enders express as "You be a gentleman, I'll be a gentleman."

What cataclysmic effect does all this have on the youth of the North End? Apparently very little, if we can go by the informal record. No statistics are available concerning juvenile problems in the city of Boston, but something may be derived from the fact that the North End area has in its police station only one juvenile officer, while other sections of the city have two and three, and one section has four. Juvenile crimes in the North End are chiefly breaking-and-entering affairs. Lethal weapons appear to be nonexistent; all the juvenile officer has collected from his troop is one bull whip, one dog chain (used as a knuckler), and about fifteen or twenty pocket jackknives of the kind which would be standard gear for any Huckleberry Finn.

The local schools, of course, cooperate with the juvenile officer in every possible way. But his way is a little thorny among families who are not fond of the police and who, moreover, can think of better things to do with the $1,000 they believe any trouble will cost them if they have to go before a court.

It is always difficult to assess the effects of law enforcement before a crime is committed, but much can be said for the prevailingly liberal and understanding attitude shown in the area toward young offenders. At any rate, it is claimed that 85 per cent of the young people in trouble straighten out happily; about 10 per cent go partway bad, and the remaining 5 per cent prove incorrigible and end badly.

This is a relatively bright picture, and one wonders how North End youth can turn out so well considering their physical and moral environment. Many factors are involved, of course; but perhaps there is one which carries more weight than any other: the homogeneity of the neighborhood. The North End is all Italian, so much so that even the pigeons in the streets eat raw macaroni. As a little, closed city of Italians, they are one, with the same religion, money, opportunity and aspirations. And therefore they are at peace.

But the North End, as a community, is a freak, an accident, from which little can be learned that is applicable elsewhere. We cannot very well divide and isolate communities of peoples, and put barriers between them, integrating each community on the basis of origin, income and general capability. That's the criminal work of fascism. We have simply got to shed more and more light on our human oneness in a world that daily becomes smaller and more crowded, a kind of North End of the universe.

LITTLE ITALY SEVENTY-FIVE YEARS LATER

Pietro Di Donato

[Novelist Pietro Di Donato, whose parents came to America from Abruzzi, has written extensively on Italian American themes, both fiction and essays. His best known work is the autobiographical novel *Christ in Concrete* (1939). In *The Penitent* (1962), he told the story of Mother Cabrini, the first American to be canonized by the Catholic Church. The selection below is a portion of an article dealing with a visit to New York's Little Italy of the 1960's.]

On Manhattan's Lower East Side, Little Italy begins and stretches north to south from Prince to Bayard Streets, and east to west from Elizabeth to Baxter Streets. I have memories of going with father to Ellis Island to greet *paesanos* arriving like tagged sheep from Italy and of escorting them to their first lodgings in America on South Mulberry Street, overlooking little Mulberry Park (now Columbus Park), the notorious Five Points, the Miserable Tombs, and "Bye-bye Baciaglupo."

The tenements are still there, standing in continuous rows on narrow streets. They are a brick and stone and tin poem to the architectural conceit of the mushrooming metropolis of a century ago. Irish, English and Italian masons laid up the intricate patterns of bonds, fretted jambs and stately sills, the curved and flat arches, the showy quoins and stone balconies and stoops. Smiths molded and soldered seamless sculptured shapes of tin for badlachins before entrances and for imposing roof cornices. Iron shops hammered and joined the fanciful wrought-iron of fire-escape landings, railings and

From Pietro Di Donato, *Naked as an Author* (New York, 1971).

ladders. Never again in American construction will be seen the imaginative postures, the flaunt, daunt, myth and craftsmanship of the
mask of Tenement.

Behind the mask were dark, airless, disease-breeding cells with
few taps for water and a single latrine in the hallway, basement or
backyard. In the 1890's Little Italy was a soul-crushing quarter of
mud, dirt and filth. In doorways, on stools, on the sidewalks and
out in the streets, women nursed their young, sewed, cleaned the
withered greens which were the only ingredient of their soup,
washed their clothes in grimy tubs, untangled and arranged one
another's hair. They chattered, not in the happy and playful mood
of the old country, but in an angry, importuning way that stung
the heart.

Everything was old and poor—the clothes the people wore, the
displayed merchandise, the fruit, the herbs, the yellowed meat that
hung in the butcher shops, the furniture in the open stalls, the
sordid Italian and American bank notes in the windows of the
banks, even the huge pictures of King Victor, Umberto and Garibaldi, and the tri-color flags that fluttered from the entrances of the
small shops. The flags evoked a sense of tenderness and of national
shame.

Today the interiors of the tenements have been made fit for
humans, with electricity, adequate and sanitary plumbing and
central heating. My immigrants have come a long way in their
struggle to attain self-respect. . . .

A pigeon coop is visible atop a tenement. I climb the seven flights
to the roof. A group of girls in bathing suits are lolling on a blanket
and applying sun-tan lotion to their limbs. By the coop a handsome
man is directing the flight of a pigeon flock with a long, whirring
bamboo pole. He is wearing swim trunks, and about his neck are
a chain and crucifix.

"Brother, you want to know why I stay in Little Italy? I was
born here and lived all my life on this block. There's *something*
about your own block. After my old folks won the fight over
hatred of Italians and lousy conditions for us kids, are we supposed
to run out on them and the place?

"You see the pigeons on the next roof? My birds won't mix with
them; they know this coop is their home. Our kind of people are
clannish too. I got my parents—thank God they're in good health—
my wife, three girls, relatives and *real* friends in this building—and
the TV brings the world to me. I don't have to knock myself out
worrying about a mortgage, car installments and then end up in the
bug house. My rent is cheap, and I got a lot of time to fly my birds.

"Sure, the outside of the building looks crummy, but in my flat
I'm just as well off as the guy on Park Avenue. There are rich guys
commuting four hours every day to New York—four hours a day
they'll never get back. I'm a teamster, and in ten minutes I'm at the
garage.

"We got security here, and there ain't no safer place to live. There's no mugging and rape like in other sections. Our boys are on every corner and look out for the girls. My daughters can come home at any hour and no one can lay a finger on them.

"I stay in Little Italy because I'm proud. We were despised for garlic and pizza and spaghetti. Now the Americans eat more of that stuff than we do. The tourists are crazy about our restaurants here. American singers change their names to Italian to get into the opera, and the biggest names today are like Como and Borgnine and Sinatra and the swanky stores feature Italian-style clothes."

He invites me down to meet his family. There is newish furniture, an air-conditioner, TV, radio, a small piano, a modern kitchen, holy pictures and a glass-encased statuette of the Madonna—all a far cry from the bare, verminous dank flats of my boyhood.

His wife and teen-age girls greet me.

"My girls can even read and write Italian," he says.

His wife tells me that the girls attended the Church of the Transfiguration Parochial School on Mott Street. She points to a picture of a nun and says, "That's Mother Cabrini, my favorite Saint. She started the school. The Maryknoll Sisters are in charge of the school now. We donated a statute of the little saint of purity, Maria Goretti, to the church, and my girls carry her picture in their pocketbooks."

I am given glasses of Strega, introduced throughout the tenement to the old folks and relatives and invited to dinner. I am made to feel completely at home.

One of the questions my new friend asks me, "Why do the movies and TV show so many gangsters as Italians? The people I know don't watch trash like *The Untouchables;* only hood punks look at that program to see what they can learn. Why don't TV show how immigrants raised families and sent kids to college? And what about the boys of Little Italy who died fighting for this country?" . . . .

It is eight o'clock of a June morning in Boccie Park on East Houston Street, and some two hundred old Italians are there. To the *boccie* devotees it is "the countryside," for around the alleys and giving shade are seven plane trees and seven maple saplings.

The enthusiasts gather, sides are chosen by the throwing of odd and even fingers, and the sturdy faces become intent and profound. The small white lead ball is tossed. The team that get their balls nearest the lead ball make points, and the score is noted on a pegboard. The balls are bowled to roll carefully, or daringly looped up into the air to plummet down between close balls; or when the adversary's ball obstructs the lead ball, the desperate cannonading shot is made with a bellow, and the player weaves about to follow each throw with suggestive directing body English.

The old man next to me explains, "It's like the American shuffleboard. Those guys aren't playing the game right. Without rules there is no dignity to the game. Play for money? No, Money in sport makes bad blood.

"I came from Anzio sixty years ago. I was a track hand on the railroad. I got my pension, and I can ride the railroad free. Here, see, my railroad pass with my name and picture."

A group gathers about me. They are retired on pensions and old-age security. It is Italian to expound, to not agree. Among them are a former waiter, a stone-mason and a businessman.

The waiter looks at me dubiously. "You a writer? I bet you haven't the guts to write the truth I tell you. The Italians in America are turn-banners; when Mussolini was the man of the hour, they were on his side. He said, 'Follow me. If I lead you forward, immortalize me; if backward, kill me.' He made the world respect Italy. He made only one mistake—declaring war on America. All right, no one is perfect. But don't believe the propaganda that he begged for his life; he died like a man. It was a disgrace to hang him by the heels in public. Don't ask my name because I won't tell you."

"War did not ruin Italy; war makes progress," says the businessman. Then he adds lamentingly, "What ruins Italy is religion and the flesh. The hand of the priest is too heavy, with church here and church there. The other thing is that the Italian closes his business at noon, runs home to his wife or to his mistress, eats, drinks and makes love like a pig. Where would America be if Wall Street had that habit? The Italian thinks he is a cock in the barnyard. Yes sir, carnal sport in the afternoon is the downfall of Italy."

"That was done away with by Mussolini," persists the waiter, "but with the Christian Democrats in power, sex with lunch has returned. As for the Communists, they are careerists and rose-water revolutionists. Tomorrow they'll be something else."

What about immigrants who dreamed of retiring in the homeland?

"I was one of those who tried it," says the stonemason, "but it was not the bread for my teeth. Returning to my village in Bari I found myself neither large intestine nor small intestine. The dream was nothing more than a dream, for where one spends his youth and strength, that is his country. I walked the two blocks of the village back and forth. My wife and I were disgusted and longed for Mulberry Street. It is more Italian than Italy, and these markets have more and better food than all of Italy.

"In Bari I met returnees who gave up their American citizenship and then cursed themselves for it. If you think America is crooked, corruption and monopoly is ten times worse in the 'good old country.' Only beauty and the art of poverty is left to Italy.

"Then there are those who left wives and children in Bari. When they went back after ten, twenty or thirty years they were bitter strangers to their families. Money is not worth such woe.

"Many went back to find themselves beautifully cuckolded. And what about the illegitimate children their daughters had with German and then American and Negro soldiers?

"To go back is only good for childless couples who want to die there, and widowers and ugly bachelors who can snare themselves juicy young wives. Once you've lived in America the old country is out of the question."

ITALO-AMERICAN TEEN-AGE CULTURE

Francis A. J. Ianni

[At the time this essay
was written, Mr. Ianni was assistant director of the Cooperative
Research Program of the Department of Health, Education, and
Welfare in Washington, D.C. He is currently Professor of Education
at Teachers College, Columbia University.]

The most immediate changes required of the immigrant Italian
family in the United States were physical and economic—where to
live and how to earn a living. Both represented drastic and dramatic
changes. Although most of the immigrants had come from a peasant
agricultural environment, the labor market in the United States drew
them to the cities to become day laborers in industrial, construction,
and transportation sectors of the economy. Very few became
farmers or even farm laborers. The reasons were both economic and
cultural. In Italy, farming had been conducted on small plots outside
the villages in which the peasants lived. In the United States,
however, farming was an individual enterprise with farms dispersed
and isolated in the rural areas. Equally important, of course, was
the fact that most Italian immigrants arrived with barely enough
money to establish households in the cities, let alone enough to
purchase or lease farms.

In these strange and hostile cities, the Italians banded together
into cultural enclaves, and the Little Italies began to grow, often
with old village neighbors as new neighbors here. Because of their
close cultural contact with other Italian families, because of the

From "The Italo-American Teen-Ager," in: *Annals of the American Academy of Political
and Social Sciences*, Vol. 338, November, 1961.

belief of many that they were here for only a brief period before returning to Italy, and in spite of the many immediate pressures toward acculturation, the traditional Italian family pattern remained relatively intact during the first few years in the United States. But soon the realization that ethnicity was economically as well as socially rewarding, the continued strong pressures toward acculturation, and the natural results of culture contact as the children came more and more in contact with Americans began to undermine and weaken the Old World peasant pattern. Now the immigrant family moved into what Campisi has called the "conflict" stage. The family became only fictitiously patriarchal as the children, out of the home for long periods during the day, achieved new independence, and the family-centered educational, recreational, economic, and religious functions were more and more fulfilled by the American community.

The adolescent children of these families in conflict became the teen-agers in conflict popularly identified with the Little Italies of the Twenties and Thirties. The street corner gangs made famous by the press as well as by William Foote Whyte emerged as teen-agers, no longer encompassed by an integrated and need-satisfying family, took to the street corners and peer group associations. The family had neither the means nor the living space to provide recreation to replace the labor previously expected of the teen-ager. New conflicts also appeared in the parent-child relationship as the teenager attempted to transmit his newly acquired American expectations of life into the weakened family structure. The teen-age Italo-American children of the 1920's and 1930's were neither Italian nor American but occupied an uncomfortable and confused position somewhere along this acculturative continuum.

With the emergence of the second generation Italo-American teenager, whose parents were American-born children of Italian-born parentage, the family had moved even further from the traditional Italian pattern. This movement was physical as well as cultural, for, by the 1930's, Italo-Americans had begun to move in increasing numbers out of the colonies. . . .

The forces which molded the second generation teen-ager were as much, if not more, lower-class urban American as traditional Italian. In his childhood, he attended an American public school or a parochial school where the nun-teachers and usually the pastor were Irish-American rather than immigrant-Italian or even Italo-American. The few Italian priests and nuns who had come to the United States were dying off, and they were not being replaced by Italo-Americans in anywhere near sufficient numbers to staff the churches in the colonies. In these churches, he was encouraged to join a host of new church-centered social, religious, and recreational groups, such as the Catholic Youth Organization. Such groups, along with the youth centers, school-centered social groups, and the other civic activities designed to keep him off the streets brought him into increased and intensified contact with parent-substitutes who conveyed the values of urban-American rather than Italo-American culture. For those who had moved out of the colonies, the acculturative contact was even greater. Their peer group associations were with non-Italo-American youngsters. The old immigrant mutual benefit provincial societies and the *Bocce* clubs, organized to keep nostalgic contact with the old country values, were as alien to the second generation teen-ager as to the American young people.

In some cases, the adjustment of the second generation to this conflict was extreme—the name was changed, all association with the colony was cut off, and the individual rushed to become an American. In some cases, the reaction was extreme in the other direction— the second generation families re-embraced the Italo-American cultural pattern, preferred to remain in the colony close to the parental home, and insulated themselves against further pressures toward acculturation. The most common reaction, however, was to attempt some compromise adjustment, earnestly to seek integration into the American culture while still retaining intimate contact with the immigrant family and way of life.

These second generation teen-agers, many of whom married outside their ethnic group and many of whom served in armed services in World War II, are the parents of today's third generation Italo-American teen-agers. The adjustment which they made to the conflict between the small-village peasant Italian culture of their parents and the predominantly lower-class urban-American culture in which they were reared represents the cultural baseline for the third generation teen-ager.

Today's Italo-American teen-ager is, then, the third generation product of this heritage of peasant-village Italian culture exposed to forty-odd years of acculturation in the United States. A third set of forces, the general social change which has taken place in the teen-age culture of the United States over the last half century, combines with the forces previously discussed to shape his cultural milieu. How individual Italo-American teen-agers respond to these forces is, of course, dependent in large part upon the type of adjustment made to them by his second generation parents.

For those teen-age members of second generation families who sought complete integration into the American culture, residual Italian cultural characteristics are minimal or nonexistent. Living outside the ethnic colony, often with new or anglicized names, their only association with the Italo-American culture is the infrequent contact they have with their immigrant grandparents. On these occasions, the grandparents are often proud of the advances made by their "American" descendents but still retain some degree of resentment over the abandonment of the "old family" and its traditions. During a recent visit to a large Italian colony in Pennsylvania, the writer was introduced to the immigrant grandfather of a popular Italo-American rock-and-roll singer. The old man gave a lengthy de-

scription of the beautiful and costly home bought by the young star
for his parents. His obvious pride in the accomplishment of his
grandson was somewhat conditioned, however, by ill-hidden dis-
appointment, for he added, "Of course, in that beautiful house with
all those paintings and pictures he didn't put up one saint or even
a crucifix."

For those "Capobiancos" who became "Whiteheads" and the
"Campagnias" who became "Bells," the transition is almost complete. This total rejection of Italo-American ethnicity has been
relatively rare, but, where it does exist, it necessarily becomes even
more complete in the third-generation teen-ager. His parents have
rejected Italo-American culture, and he has been reared as an American. If his parents were accepted as Americans, then he has no
ties with the immigrant culture. These teen-agers are Italo-American
only in ancestry and are virtually indistinguishable from their non-
Italo-American peers.

In those few families which sought to maintain and, indeed, to
re-embrace the Italian cultural pattern by a closer orientation with
the Italian neighborhood, the course of social change and the compelling forces of acculturation have worked against any further re-
Italianization. As movement out of the colonies continues, along with
increasing dilution of the cultural baseline of their ethnicity, they
are now forty years removed from the traditional environment.
Warm, family-centered life remains, but the importance of inter-
familial community relationships has all but disappeared. The traditional religious *festas* where *paisani* from the same province celebrated the feast of the patron saint, the provincial mutual benefit
societies, and the interlocking system of god-parenthood are becoming rarities. And, even where they do exist, the bonds they once
signified are alien and meaningless to today's teen-ager. Even the
neighborhoods are beginning to disappear as Italo-Americans move
up the ladder of social acceptance and are replaced in the slum
areas by recent Spanish-speaking immigrants and Negroes. As the
immigrant grandparents die off in increasing numbers, there is no
place to turn but to greater integration into the American culture.
These teen-agers may well become the new Italo-American generation in conflict for the decision of their parents to resist acculturation has merely postponed its inevitable occurrence.

The vast majority of today's teen-age Italo-Americans, however,
come from neither of these two types of second generation families
but, rather, from the marginal families which, both in and outside
the colonies, sought Americanization while still retaining a bond
with the old family and culture. The teen-agers of this group are best
described as typically American while still retaining certain elements
of ethnic identification.

Since these Italo-American families fall predominantly in the
lower socio-economic classes, their teen-age children have greater
representation in the earlier phases of teen-age culture. By late

adolescence, they have usually entered the labor market, and those who do go on to college have no distinctive ethnic patterns to follow. Italo-Americans are still underrepresented in the higher-socioeconomic classes, and, so, Italo-American teen-agers are not a significant group in the middle- and upper-class oriented later-teen culture.

The role of the younger Italo-American teen-ager in the family is much the same as in other lower class families. There is, perhaps, greater warmth and a stronger affectional bond, but only the affectional function remains of the once strong family. The family is slightly more patriarchal than other lower class families but still strives toward the "democratic family" ideal.

Today's Italo-American teen-ager is also much more Irish-American in religious orientation than either his father or grandfather. The effect of religious and often academic education by the predominantly Irish-Catholic Church in the United States has been to give this generation of Italo-American teen-agers a much stronger religious orientation to life than previous generations. It is this orientation, more than any other, which will shape their attitudes toward family life and the rearing of the coming fourth generation.

Another factor which affects Italo-American participation in teen-age culture is their high degree of urbanization. Most Italo-American families continue to live in large and medium-sized cities, so that third generation teen-agers are underrepresented in the suburban and rural patterns of teen-age culture. In these cities, many of the characteristics associated with the Italo-American youth of the Thirties and Forties are beginning to disappear. Street corner gangs are still to be found in the larger cities but have nearly vanished from the smaller cities. Even in the larger cities, however, the structure and the functions of the gang has changed. The well-organized street corner society which had a locus in a particular neighborhood and a specific territory to "protect" has given way to an organization which is likely to include non-Italo-Americans and even nonneighbors. Neither does the street corner gang serve the same status conferring function it did in earlier generations. . . .

The declining importance of the Italo-American teen-age gangs results from the disappearance of the factors which originally led to their formation. Culturally, the sudden break from a strong, family-centered adolescence made strong peer-centered associations inevitable. These conditions simply do not exist for the third generation teen-ager. Psychologically, a large element in the formation of the neighborhood gangs was a sense of cultural inferiority to which the teen-agers responded by banding together. As Italo-American social mobility has increased, this basis for gang organization has lessened in importance.

The final factor which preserves some element of ethnicity in the Italo-American teen-ager is the fact that he is still identified as being an Italian American by his peers and their parents. Attitudes toward Italo-Americans have changed over the last forty years, and social acceptance is much greater today than in the past. Certainly, active discrimination against the group is no greater than that for similar groups such as the Poles, Ukrainians, and Greeks. But, while there is not the same hostility and social distance that existed for the second generation teen-ager, Italo-Americans are still considered to be "different." Most Italo-American teenagers accept this differentiation as a relatively minor part of American life. Being considered as different, however, cannot help but influence the teen-ager's self-concept, and so he does not participate as an equal in teen-age culture.

Most of these changes have been the result of the acculturative experience of the Italian family in the United States. Equally important, however, has been the role of the general social change which has taken place during this half century. Recent visits to Italy by the writer have indicated that many of the changes described above are also taking place among teen-agers in the Italian cities. In fact, the orientation of Italian urban teen-agers is almost as much to American teen-age culture as it is to Italian culture.

Over the last forty-odd years, then, Italo-American teen-age culture has changed to the point where the third generation teen-ager is quite similar to other lower class teen-agers. Those characteristics which do set him apart are the result of the general position of the group in the American social structure. As the process of assimilation continues, even these differences will disappear, and he will soon be indistinguishable from other teen-agers.

ITALIAN AMERICAN SPORTS HEROES

Maurice R. Marchello

[The contribution of Italian Americans to sports have been so considerable that any roster of names must omit more than it includes. Everyone is familiar with the achievements of Mario Andretti in auto racing; Yogi Berra, the brothers DiMaggio, Billy Martin, and Joe Pepitone in baseball; Rocky Marciano, Joey Giardello, and Rocky Graziano in boxing; the Esposito brothers in hockey; and Vince Lombardi in football. This selection by Maurice Marchello brings to mind other early Italian American sports figures. Marchello, a Chicago lawyer, frequently contributes to the newspaper, *Fra Noi.*]

Baseball is unquestionably a typical American sport. For any ethnic group to attain some degree of fame in this popular game is a sure sign of recognition along the ethnic trail into the American way of life. At least, it so appeared to the youthful *paesani* who were accustomed to see their elders engaged in their native game of bocce ball, which was unknown in America.

This talent to attain eminence in baseball proved true even with our black brethren. Jackie Robinson really opened the door for the many current fine baseball stars of his race—in fact, too numerous to mention here. One must mention the champion pitcher of them all, Bob Gibson, and the base-stealer, Lou Brock, as excellent examples of our black athletes' progress.

So it was earlier with the Italian, except that the first Italian in American baseball was made to change his name from Francesco Pezzolo to Ping Bodie by his White Sox manager.

From Maurice R. Marchello, *Crossing the Tracks* (New York, 1969), pp. 173–78.

Ping Bodie played centerfield for the Chicago American League team from 1911 until their downfall in 1919 following the World Series scandal. Few know that he was of Italian origin, except we Illinois *paesani* neighbors who worshipped him as our first baseball ethnic hero. Another earlier ethnic pioneer was Oscar Melillo, the flashy short-stop of the St. Louis Browns.

Later, Ping Bodie was a teammate of Babe Ruth with the New York Yankees. Here came a switch in misnomers. Everyone began calling Ruth "The Great Bambino." This led many to believe that the mighty Sultan of Swat was indeed of Italian origin. The press, usually not too generous to the *paesano* boys, did not bother much to correct this illusion; so that even now many fans of the older Italian-American generation really believe that Ruth was one of them. In appearance, temperament and talent he really was like an Italian.

Just to prove that a real *paesano* boy would duplicate him, along came Joe Di Maggio. This lad quickly became to our baseball fans an acceptable Italian-American. Even the announcers made sure they pronounced his name correctly (Italian style) with a broad sound of "a" and the soft double "g".

Di Maggio responded with many home runs and became a three-time winner of the most valuable player award from the Baseball Writers' Association. Other great *paesani* baseball players followed Di Maggio (too many to mention here), so that we can forget and forgive the role played by Francesco Pezzolo in records of American baseball. . . .

American football, on the other hand, did not attract the *paesani* youth until in the 1920's. The reason is that, prior to the current interest in professional football, this sport for many years really belonged to the college boys and became famous because of the fierce rivalries existing between the various American universities. During the first quarter of this century, only about 5% of all high school graduates attended college, as there was not too much of an opportunity for the first Italian-American generation to participate in college football.

The University of Chicago Maroons, under Alonzo Stagg, had two of the author's classmates, Felix Caruso and Adolph Toigo on the team. Stagg often referred to Toigo as one of his three immortals, the other two being Walter Eckersall and Wally Stephen.

Notre Dame University, being Catholic-oriented, deserves some award for giving the *paesani* boys a start. However, there appeared to be one condition attached to this opportunity for college gridiron fame. The alumni fans and the game announcers gratuitously made every Italian-American star a "Fighting Irishman."

Frank Carideo and Joe Savoldi, during the school's golden Rockne era of the Thirties, were never referred to as "The Fighting Italians." It took the Italian-born father of "Jumping Joe" Savoldi to put the record straight.

Papa Savoldi was attending his first Notre Dame game, where his son Joe and quarterback Carideo were performing brilliantly. Frantically gesticulating on the sidelines, he kept yelling in Italian: *"Bravo, Francesco! Bravo, Giuseppe!"* A nearby radio announcer decided to put him on the air, and in handing the mike to the proud Italian father, asked him: "Mr. Savoldi, what do you think of the Irish boys on the team?"

His reply was: "They's-a good too, but not-a like the Italians."

We cannot help but muse on what Papa Savoldi would do and say about the greatest *paesano* football hero of them all, Coach Vince Lombardi of the Green Bay Packers. A real coach, strict, honest and upright, he is one American of whom all ethnic groups could join to call their own.

Now promoted as head coach of the Washington Redskins, Lombardi was truly one of football's most successful coaches. In his early years he was one of "The Seven Blocks of Granite." He formed the Packers in 1959; and after they suffered a 1-10-1 year . . . his team went on to win six Western Divisions and five championships, to amass a 141-39-4 record for a .783 inning percentage.

Other All-American football players of Italian descent who should be mentioned are Trippi of Georgia, Macaluso of Colgate, Bellino of Navy, Nomellini of Minnesota and Getto of Pittsburgh. There were two leading coaches who changed or Anglicized their names —Luigi Piccolo became Lou Little of Columbia, and Giordano Olivieri became Jordan Oliver of Yale. Joe Paterno of Penn State deserves an accolade for 1968 coaching. In the last minute at the Orange Bowl his team won.

Golf is another popular pastime in which the sons of Italian immigrants have done well. A few of them will be mentioned: Gene Sarazen, Will Turnesa, Ken Venturi, Vic Ghezzi. With no parents to teach them, they rose from caddy boys to highly esteemed professionals.

In Italy, the sport of boxing has been fostered. It produced its first Heavyweight Champion in 1933, when Primo Carnera knocked out Jack Sharkey. Carnera in no way can be compared with our own Rocky Marciano, the champion of champions in boxing. We should not forget Tony Canzonieri, who won his title in three different categories.

The fine performance of these Italian-American athletes is due to the fine discipline and training they received from their American coaches. The *paesani* boys were indeed rugged, with potential talents which the expert sports-minded Americans soon turned into excellent athletic abilities.

ITALIAN AMERICANS TODAY
Richard Gambino

[The publication
of Mario Puzo's *The Godfather* in 1969, followed in 1971 by Gay
Talese's *Honor Thy Father*, gave rise to a spate of "mafia" books
and movies. Organized crime, Italian style, caught the imagination
of the public as the film version of Puzo's novel became the biggest
money-maker in movie history. Whether the "image" or reputation
of Italian Americans was damaged by this popularization is difficult
to assess. But there is no doubt that many Italian Americans felt
that the adventures of the Corleone family reflected badly on them.
Italian American civic organizations disparaged the film and its
popular reception as well as other stereotypes shown in the mass
media. They desired the public to regard Italian Americans not in
terms of any "mafia myth" but simply as the fellow citizens they
are, with a heritage no more peculiar than that of any other ethnic
group. The following selection is taken from an article by Richard
Gambino, who teaches at Queens College, the City University of
New York.]

To understand the special identity problems of Italian-Americans,
we must begin with a very popular Sicilian proverb quoted by
Leonard Covello in "The Social Background of the Italo-American
School Child": *"Che lascia la via vecchia per la nuova, sa quel che
perde e non sa quel che trova"*—"Whoever forsakes the old way
for the new knows what he is losing, but not what he will find."

In Sicily, *la via vecchia* was family life. The Sicilian immigrants
to America were mostly *contadini* [peasants] to whom there was
one and only one social reality, the peculiar mores of family life.
La famiglia and the personality it nurtured was a very different

From *Chicago Tribune*, Sunday, May 7, 1972.

thing from the American nuclear family with the personalities that are its typical products.

The *famiglia* was composed of all one's "blood" relatives, including those relatives Americans would consider very distant cousins, aunts, and uncles, an extended clan with a genealogy traced thru paternity. The only system to which the *contadino* paid attention was *l'ordine della famiglia*, the unwritten but all-demanding and complex series of rules governing one's relations within, and responsibilities to, his own family and his posture toward those outside the family. All other social institutions were seen within a spectrum of attitudes ranging from indifference to scorn and contempt.

One had absolute responsibilities to family superiors and absolute rights to be demanded from subordinates in the hierarchy. All ambiguous situations were arbitrated by the *capo di famiglia* [head of the family], a position held within each household by the father, until it was given to—or taken away by—one of the sons, and in the larger clan, by a male "elder."

The *contadino* showed calculated respect to members of other families which were powerful, and haughtiness or indifference toward families less powerful than his own. He despised as a *scomunicato* [pariah] anyone in any family who broke the *ordine della famiglia* or otherwise violated the *onore* [honor, solidarity, tradition, "face"] of the family.

Thus, Sicily survived a harsh history of invasion, conquest, and colonization by a procession of tribes and nations. What enabled Sicilians to endure was a system of rules based solely on a phrase I heard uttered many times by my grandparents and their contemporaries in Brooklyn's "Little Italy"; *sangu di me sangu*, Sicilian dialect for "blood of my blood."

It was a norm simple and demanding, protective and isolating, humanistic and cynical. The unique family pattern of Sicily constituted the real sovereignty of that island, regardless of which government nominally ruled it.

As all of us are confronted with the conflicts of our loyalty to a sovereign state vs. our cosmopolitan aspirations, so the Italian-American has found himself in the dilemma of reconciling the psychological sovereignty of his people with the aspirations and demands of being American.

Most Italian-Americans are derived from areas of Italy south of Rome, about 25 per cent of them from Sicily. In his book "The Italians," Luigi Barzini reminds us that "Goethe was right when he wrote: 'Without seeing Sicily one cannot get a clear idea of what Italy is.' Sicily is the schoolroom model of Italy for beginners, with every Italian quality and defect magnified, exasperated, and brightly colored."

This background illustrates the confused situation of Italian-Americans. Altho the problems of Italian-Americans are less desperate than those of groups whose fate in this country has been determined by color, they are no less complicated. And they are rising to a critical point. . . .

To the immigrant generation of Italians, the task was clear. Hold to the psychological sovereignty of the old ways and thereby seal out the threats of the new "conqueror," the American society that surrounded them. This ingrained disposition was strongly reinforced by the hatred and insult with which the Italian immigrant was assaulted by American bigots who regarded him as racially inferior —a "dago," a "wop," a "guinea."

The Italian immigrants admitted in the earlier years responded to an alien, hostile society by clustering together in crowded Italian "ghettos," euphemistically called "Little Italies," and exhausted their energies in America's sweat shops.

Oppression and economic exploitation were woven into the fabric of life in Southern Italy. Most of Sicily's foreign governors had two things in common: the subjugation of Sicilians and systematic exploitation of them and their land. The first was done by force, the second by perennial systems of absentee landlordships.

The complicated customs and institutions developed by the Sicilians were marvelously effective in neutralizing the influence of the various alien masters. The people of the island survived and developed their own identity not so much by overtly opposing the oppressor, a suicidal approach, but by sealing out the influence of the strangers.

The sealing medium was not military or even physical. It was at once an "antisocial" mentality and a supremely social psychology, for it forms the very stuff of Sicilian society. It was a system of social attitudes, values, and customs that is impenetrable to the *sfruttamento* [exploitation] of any *stranieri* [strangers], no matter how powerful their weapons or clever their devices.

The mores the immigrants brought with them from the old land gave them psychological stability, order, and security, and were held to tenaciously. But in the United States, the price was isolation from the ways of the larger society.

The immigrants' children, the "second generation," faced a challenge more difficult to overcome. They could not maintain the same degree of isolation. Indeed, they had to cope with American institutions; first schools, then a variety of economic, military, and cultural environments. What was a successful social strategy for their parents became a crisis of conflict for them. Circumstances split their personalities into conflicting halves.

Part of the second generation compromise was the rejection of Italian ways which were not felt vital to the family code. They resisted learning the Italian culture and language well, and were ill-equipped to teach it to the third generation.

Small numbers of the second generation carried the dual rebellion to an extreme. Some became highly "Americanized," giving their time, energy, and loyalty to schools and companies and becoming estranged from the clan. The price they paid for siding with American culture in the culture-family conflict was a strong sense of guilt and a chronic identity crisis not quite compensated for by the places won in the middle-class society.

The compromise of the second-generation Italian-American thus left him permanently in lower middle-class America. He remains in the minds of Americans a stereotype born of their half-understanding of him and constantly reinforced by the media.

The second-generation Italian-American is seen as a "good employee," i. e., steady, reliable but having little "initiative" or "dynamism." He is a good "family man," loyal to his wife and a loving father vaguely yearning for his children to do "better" in their lifetimes but not equipped to guide or push them up the social ladder.

He maintains his membership in the church, but participates in it little beyond ceremonial observances; while he often sends his children to parochial schools, this represents more his social parochialism than enthusiasm for the American Catholic Church, which has very few Italian-Americans at the top of the hierarchy and has never had an Italian-American cardinal. . . .

We come at last to the compound dilemma of the third- and fourth-generation Italian-Americans, who are now mostly young adults and children with parents who are well into their middle-age or older. [The number of those in the third and fourth generations is estimated as at least 10 million, compared to more than 5 million in the second generation and no more than 5 million living members of the first generation.] The difference between the problems of the second and those of the third generation is great—more a quantum jump than a continuity.

One of my students has problems that are typical. Her parents are second-generation Americans. Her father is a fireman and her mother a housewife. Both want her to "get an education" and "do better." Yet both constantly express fears that education will "harm her morals."

She is told by her father to be proud of her Italian background, but her consciousness of being Italian is limited to the fact that her last name ends in a vowel. Altho she loves her parents and believes they love her, she has no insight into their thoughts or feelings.

She is confused by their conflicting signals: "Get an education, but don't change"; "go out into the larger world but don't become part of it"; "grow, but remain within the image of the 'houseplant' Sicilian girl"; "go to church, altho we are lacking in religious enthusiasm." In short, maintain that difficult balance of conflicts which is the second-generation's lifestyle.

Her dilemma becomes more widespread as unprecedented numbers of Italian-Americans enter colleges today. The 1970s are bound
to see a sharp increase in the number of Italian-American college
graduates.

When the third-generation person leaves school and his parents'
home, he finds himself in a peculiar situation. A member of one of
the largest minority groups in the country, he feels isolated, with
no affiliation with or affinity for other Italian-Americans. This young
person often wants and needs to go beyond the minimum security
his parents sought in the world; in a word, he is more ambitious.
But he has not been given family or cultural guidance upon which
this ambition can be defined and pursued.

Ironically, this descendant of immigrants despised by the old
WASP establishment embodies one of the latter's cherished myths.
He sees himself as purely American, a blank slate upon which his
individual experiences in American culture will inscribe what is to
be his personality and his destiny.

But it is a myth that is untenable psychologically and sociolog-
ically. Altho he usually is diligent and highly responsible, the other
elements needed for a powerful personality are paralyzed by his
pervasive identity crisis. His ability for sustained action with autonomy, initiative, self-confidence, and assertiveness is undermined by
his yearning for ego integrity. In addition, the third generation's
view of itself as a group of atomistic individuals leaves them politically unorganized, isolated, diffident, and thus powerless in a society
of power blocs.

The dilemma of the young Italian-American is a lonely, quiet
crisis, so it has escaped public attention. But [it] is a major ethnic
group crisis. As it grows, it will be more readily recognized as such,
and not merely as the personal problem of individuals. If this is to
be realized sooner rather than later, then these young people must
learn whence they came and why they are as they are.

They may opt for one of the several models that we have served
other ethnic groups. For example, they may choose to cultivate their
Italian culture, pursue personal careers, and fuse the two into an
energetic and confident relationship which has been characteristic
of the Jewish-Americans.

They may also turn toward the church, revive it, and build upon
its power base a political organization and morale, as Irish-Amer-
icans did. Or, they may feel it necessary to form strictly national-
istic power blocs, as some black Americans are doing. On the other
hand, they may forge their own models of individual and group
identity out of an imaginative use of their unique inheritance.

BIBLIOGRAPHY

Readers interested in acquainting themselves with the history of Italian Americans in greater detail will find the following books and articles quite helpful.

AMFITHEATROS, ERIK. *The Children of Columbus.* Boston, 1973.

BARZINI, LUIGI. *The Italians.* New York, 1964.

CONDE, ALEXANDER DE. *Half-Bitter, Half-Sweet: An Excursion into Italian-American History.* New York, 1972.

COVELLO, LEONARD. *The Social Background of the Italo-American School Child.* Leiden, 1967.

ETS, MARIE HALL. *Rosa: The Life of an Italian Immigrant.* Minneapolis, 1970.

FOERSTER, ROBERT F. *The Italian Emigration of Our Times.* Cambridge, Mass., 1919.

GAGE, NICHOLAS. *The Mafia Is Not an Equal Opportunity Employer.* New York, 1971.

———, ed. *Mafia, USA.* Chicago, 1972.

GANS, HERBERT J. *The Urban Villagers.* New York, 1962.

GLANZ, RUDOLPH. *Jew and Italian: Historic Group Relations and the New Immigration.* New York, 1971.

HAWKINS, GORDON. "God and the Mafia" in *The Public Interest*, No. 14, Winter, 1970.

IANNI, FRANCIS A. J. *A Family Business: Kinship and Social Control in Organized Crime.* New York, 1972.

IORIZZO, LUCIANO J. and SALVATORE MONDELLO. *The Italian-Americans.* New York, 1971.

KOBLER, JOHN. *Capone.* New York, 1971.

LEVY, MARK R. and MICHAEL S. KRAMER. *The Ethnic Factor: How America's Minorities Decide Elections.* New York, 1972.

MANGIONE, JERRE. *America is Also Italian.* New York, 1969.

NELLI, HUMBERT S. *The Italians in Chicago 1880–1930.* New York, 1970.

PROCACCI, GIULIANO. *History of the Italian People.* New York, 1970.

ROLLE, ANDREW F. *The Immigrant Upraised: Italian Adventurers and Colonists in an Expanding America.* Norman, Oklahoma, 1968.

SCHIAVO, GIOVANNI E. *Four Centuries of Italian-American History,* 5th ed. New York, 1958.

———. *The Italians in America Before the Civil War.* New York, 1934.

SUTTLES, GERALD D. *The Social Order of the Slum.* Chicago, 1968.

TALESE, GAY. *Honor Thy Father.* New York, 1971.

TERESA, VINCENT with Thomas C. Renner. *My Life in the Mafia.* Garden City, N.Y., 1973.

TOMASI, SILVANO M. and MADELINE H. ENGEL, eds., *The Italian Experience in the United States.* Staten Island, N.Y., 1970

VECOLI, RUDOLPH. "Contadini in Chicago: A Critique of *The Uprooted,*" in *The Journal of American History,* 51, December, 1964.

———. *The People of New Jersey.* Princeton, 1965.

FICTION READINGS

Works of fiction have a way of revealing the inner workings of an ethnic community that the general histories cannot quite match. The works listed below are recommended as both useful and entertaining, although not all are of a comparable quality.

D'AGOSTINO, GUIDO. *Olives in the Apple Tree.* New York, 1940.
D'ANGELO, LOU. *What the Ancients Said.* Garden City, N.Y., 1971.
CAPITE, MICHAEL DE. *Maria.* New York, 1943.
CAPITE, RAYMOND DE. *The Coming of Fabrizze.* New York, 1940.
CARUSO, JOSEPH. *The Priest.* New York, 1956.
DI DONATO, PIETRO. *Christ in Concrete.* Indianapolis, 1939.
————. *Three Circles of Light.* New York, 1960.
FANTE, JOHN. *Dago Red.* New York, 1940.
————. *Wait Until Spring, Bandini.* Harrisburg, Pa., 1938.
HOBART, ALICE TISDALE. *The Cup and the Sword.* New York, 1942.
HOWARD, SIDNEY. *They Knew What They Wanted.* New York, 1928.
   (Later made into the Broadway musical "Most Happy Fella.")
JONES, IDWAL. *The Vineyard.* New York, 1946.
MADALENA, LORENZO. *Confetti for Gino.* New York, 1959.
MANGIONE, JERRE. *Mount Allegro.* Boston, 1943.
MELLER, SIDNEY. *Home Is Here.* New York, 1941.
PAGANO, JO. *The Condemned.* New York, 1947.
————. *Golden Wedding.* New York, 1943.
————. *The Paesanos.* Boston, 1940.
PETROCELLI, ORLANDO R. *The Pact.* New York, 1973.
PUZO, MARIO. *The Fortunate Pilgrim.* New York, 1965.
————. *The Godfather,* New York, 1969.
TOMASI, MARI. *Like Lesser Gods.* New York, 1949.

INDEX

Abruzzi, 74, 106, 358
Accardo, Anthony, 222, 223
Acero, Italy, 191
Adams, James Truslow, 165
Adams, John, 28
Addams, Jane, 45, 306–312
Addonizio, Hugh, 295
Adonis, Joe, 213, 220, 227
agriculture, 67–72, 81–88, 93, 111–116, 122–125, 131 135
Alexandria, Virginia, 62
Alinsky, Saul, 163
Alioto, Joseph, 295
Allen, Frederick Lewis, 197, 200–204
Allivine Company (Vineland, N.J.), 70, 71, 72
Aloi, Giovanni, 282
American Fur Company, 34, 35
American Indians, 3–5, 11–18, 20–21, 24–25, 34–36
American-Italian Defamation League, 237
American Pasteur Institute, 285
American Revolution, 26–30
Americans of Italian Descent, 235–242
Anderson, Herbert, 408
Andreani, Count Paolo, 2
Andretti, Mario, 425
Angellotti, F. M., 138
Annenberg, Moe, 227
Antin, Mary, 296
Anti-Defamation League of B'nai B'rith, 235–237
Apalachin meeting (N.Y.), 229, 237
Apostolic College of Priests, 331
Arizona, 1, 23
Arkansas, 123
Arricale, Frank M., 240

Ascoli, Max, 379–384
associations, Italian, 321–325
Asti, California, 65, 111–116
Atoms in the Family (Fermi), 405
Avellino, Italy, 106

Bahamas, 3
Baiano, Italy, 152
Balbo, Italo, 396
Baltimore, 176, 180, 184, 402
Bandini, Pietro, 131–135
Bank of America, 153–157
Bank of Italy, 137, 154, 155, 156, 284
Bank of Naples, 90
Barber of Seville, The (Rossini), 32, 33
Barzini, Luigi, 429
Basilicata, Italy, 79, 106
Beckley, West Viriginia, 117, 118, 119
Bedford Springs, Pa., 34
Bell, Daniel, 219–228
Belle Isle, Newfoundland, 7
Beltrami, Giacomo, 2
Berra, Yogi, 425
Black Americans, 122–125
Black Hand, 163, 164, 165, 171–183, 188
B'nai B'rith, 237, 238, 239
Bodie, Ping, 425, 426
Bologna, Italy, 77
Boltai, Giuseppe, 162
Bonanno, Joe, 205, 206, 208, 249, 250
Bonanno, William, 249
Borgese, Giuseppe Antonio, 379
Boston, 49–54, 176, 180, 184, 244, 246, 247, 326–328, 410–413
Boulevard Bridge Bank (Chicago), 285
Box, John C., 287
Brando, Marlon, 247

Brazos River (Texas), 62
Brock, Lou, 425
Brooklyn, N. Y., 185, 214, 343, 344
Browne, George, 221
Brumidi, Constantino, 2
Bruno, Joseph, 245–246
Bryan, Texas, 62
Buchalter, Lepke, 219, 220, 224
Buffalo, N. Y., 402
Burlington Railroad, 85
Burr, Aaron, 305
Bushee, Frederick O., 49–54
Businessmen, Italian, 90–91

Cable, John L., 287
Cabot, John (Giovanni Caboto), 7–9
Cabrini, St. Frances Xavier, 338–342, 414, 416
Café-Chantant, The, 319
Calabria and Calabrians, 42, 51, 73, 79, 106, 184, 187
Calhoun, John C., 35
California, 23–25, 38, 64–66, 69, 94, 111–116, 136–139
California Fruit Canners' Asociation, 138, 139
Caminetti, Anthony, 138, 284
Camorra, 164, 174–178, 180, 181, 188
Campania, 179
Cance, Alexander E., 85–88
Canto, Luis del, 25
Canzonieri, Tony, 427
Cape Fear, North Carolina, 17
Capone, Al, 164, 197–204, 207, 209, 213, 221, 222, 224
Cardozo, Benjamin, 373
Caribbean Sea, 10
Carib Indians, 17
Carideo, Frank, 426
Carleton, General Guy, 27–28
Carnera, Primo, 427
Carnovale, Luigi, 283–286
Caroti, Arturo, 127–130
Carr, John Foster, 278–282
Carroccio, Il (N. Y.), 342, 394
Caruso, Felix, 426
Casale, Secchi di, 60, 68
Castellamarese War, 164, 205–218
Castiglione, G. E. Di Palma, 55–58
Catena, Jerry, 207
Catholic Youth Organization, 420
Cavour, Camillo, 263
Celebrezze, Anthony, 295
Cerachi, Giuseppe, 2
Cesnola, Count di, 285
Chicago, 45–48, 93, 106, 164, 172, 176, 180, 184, 194, 197–204, 221–222, 306–312, 339, 340, 341, 355–357, 402
Chicago Confidential (Lait & Mortimer), 224
Chicago House of Corrections, 310
Chicago National Gas-Pipe Company, 102
Chicago (Chicaou) River, 22
Chicago Tribune, 203

Children's Aid Society, 92
Chippewa Indians, 34
Christ in Concrete (Di Donato), 414
Chrysler Corporation, 295
Ciambelli, Beniemino, 320
Cicagna, Italy, 266
Cicero, Illinois, 199
Cincinnati, 93
Cinisi, Sicily, 343–345
Cioffari, Bernard, 286
Cioffari, Vincent, 286
Ciolli, Dominic, 141–145
Clark, George Rogers, 2
Clark, William, 35
Clay County, West Virginia, 117
Cleveland, 93,
Codogno, Italy, 339
Cohen, Mickey, 222
Colbert, Jean, 19
Colorado River, 24
Columbia University, 408
Columbus, Christopher, 3–6
Columbus Hospital (Chicago), 285, 339, 340; (Denver), 341; (New York), 322
Columbus Loan and Savings Society, 137
Commercial Advertiser, (N. Y.), 317
Connecticut, 103
Connecticut Valley, 93
Continental Congress, 29
Continental Press, 221, 222
Cook County, Ill., 164, 197
Coolidge, Calvin, 38
Corbin, Austin, 94, 131
Corné, Michel Felice, 2
Corsi, Edward, 295, 358–361
Cosa Nostra, 163, 209, 217, 229, 230
Cosenza, Italy, 79, 324
Così Fan Tutti (Mozart), 31
Costa, Alfonso A., 346–349
Costello, Frank, 213, 219, 220, 224, 226, 227
Covello, Leonard, 428
Crawford, Marion, 185
Crawford, Mark, 310
crime, organized, 163–252
Crocker, Henry J., 114
Croswell, Edgar, 237
Cuba, 4
Cusumano, Gaspare, 343–345

Dago Red (Fante), 366
D'Amato, Gaetano, 174–178
Dante Alighieri Society, 396
Daphne, Alabama, 45
Da Ponte, Lorenzo, 2, 31–33
Davis, Jefferson, 305
De Benedetti, Sergio, 379
Debs, Eugene, 190, 191
Democratic Party, 305, 401, 402
Dempsey, Jack, 285
De Nunzio, Ralph, 295
Denver, 176, 180, 184, 254
Department of Labor, U. S., 106

De Sapio, Carmine, 242
Detroit, 20, 164, 402
Dewey, John, 306
Di Donato, Pietro, 414–418
Di Falco, Samuel, 237
Dimaggio brothers, 425
Dimaggio, Joe, 426
Don Giovanni (Mozart), 31
Doyle, Bobby, 209, 216, 217
Drake, Sir Francis, 24
Duffy, La Vern J., 205
Durand, Kellogg, 67–72

East River National Bank (N.Y.), 156
Eboli, Thomas, 207
Eckersall, Walter, 426
Eco d'Italia, L' (N.Y.), 41, 68
Ellis Island, 264, 322
Erickson, Frank, 222
Esposito brothers, 425
Ewing, Buff, 237

Family Business, A (Ianni), 163
Fante, 366–371
Farley, James, 227
Fasci Abroad, 396
fascism, Italian, 379, 385–388, 392–398
Ferdinand, king of Spain, 3, 11
Fermi, Enrico, 379, 405–409
Fermi, Laura, 405–409
Ferrero, Felice, 81–84
Fiama, La, 283
Fiorello! (Bock and Harnick), 372
Fischetti, Charles, 222
Five Points Gang (N.Y.), 200
Five Points Neighborhood (N.Y.), 302
Florence, Italy, 10, 26, 81, 310
Foggia, Italy, 373
Fontana, New Jersey, 138
Foppiano, Gian-Battista, 266
Ford Motor Company, 295
Fort Crevecoeur, 21
Fort Frontenac, 20
Fort St. Louis, 19
Fort Snelling, Minnesota, 34–36
Fra Noi (Chicago), 425
Francis I, king of France, 17
Francolini, J. N., 324
Franklin, Benjamin, 29
Frazer, Elizabeth, 283, 284, 286
Free, Arthur M., 287
Fresno, California, 65
Frontenac, Count de, 20
Fugazi Bank, 137
Fulton, California, 115
Furillo, Carl, 242

Gaeta, Italy, 19
Gage, Nicholas, 248
Gagliano, Tom, 207, 208, 215
Gale, John, 36
Galena, Illinois, 85
Gallo, Albert, 240
Gallo, Larry, 240
Gambino, Carl, 205, 206, 247, 249, 250

Gambino, Richard, 428–432
Gargano, M. J., 161
Garibaldi, Giuseppe, 42, 68, 263, 400
Gazzetta Illustrata (St. Louis), 283
Genna, Angelo, 194
Genoa, Italy, 3, 34, 111, 266
Genoa, Wisconsin, 85–88
Genoese, 51
Genovese, Vito, 164, 205–218 passim, 248
German Americans, 87–88
Ghezzi, Vic, 427
Giannini, A. H., 156
Giannini, Amadeo P., 153–157
Giannini, L. M., 156
Giardello, Joey, 425
Gibson, Bob, 425
Giotto di Bondone, 310
Giovanni, Norman Thomas di, 410–413
Godfather, The (Puzo), 164, 244, 246, 428
Gold Rush (1849), 64
Gonzales, Manuel, 24
Granite Cutters' National Union, 110
Graziano, Rocky, 425
Green Bay Packers, 427
Greenville, Mississippi, 62
Greve, Italy, 17
Grido della Stirpe (N.Y.), 395
Guadaloupe, 17
Guasti, Secundo, 138

Haarlem House (N.Y.), 358
Hague, Frank, 227
Hahnville, Louisiana, 269
Halley, Rudolph, 224
Hammonton, New Jersey, 61, 68
Handlin, Oscar, 401
Hansen, Marcus Lee, 296
Hapgood, Hutchins, 317–320
Haraszthy, Colonel A., 113
Harlem, N. Y., 399
Hawthorne Hotel (Cicero, Ill.), 202
Haymarket trial (Chicago), 190
Hennepin, Louis, 20
Hennessy, David C., 255
Henry, Patrick, 26
Henry VII, king of England, 7
Hispaniola, 4
Hoboken, New Jersey, 39
Honor Thy Father (Talese), 249, 428
Hoover, J. Edgar, 230
House Committee on Immigration and Naturalization, 287
Houston, Texas, 62
How the Other Half Lives (Riis), 313
Hughes, Charles Evans, 349
Hughes, Mike, 198
Hull House (Chicago), 306, 356
Humphries, Murray, 221

Iacocca, Lee A., 295
Ianni, Francis A. J., 165, 419–424
Illinois, 19, 20

Illustrious Immigrants: The Intellectual Migration from Europe 1930–1949 (Fermi), 405
Impelleteri, Vincent, 295
Independence, Louisiana, 62
Ingolstadt, University of, 25
In the Shadow of Liberty (Corsi), 358
Irish Americans, 49–50, 164, 225
Irwin, Grace, 350–354
Isabella, queen of Spain, 3
Italia, L' (Chicago), 47, 304, 335
Italian American Bank, 137
Italian American Chamber of Commerce, 90, 155, 322, 279
Italian American National Union, 291
Italian American Trust Company, 90
Italian Immigration Bureau, 108
Italian Medical Association, 91
Italian Review, 342
Italian Savings Bank (N. Y.), 90, 324
Italian-Swiss Colony (California), 38, 65, 111–116, 138
Italian Vineyard Company, 138
Italian Women's Mutual Benefit Society, 129
Italians, The (Barzini), 429
Italo-American National Union (Unione Siciliana), 194, 195
Italy, effect of emigration on, 73–80

Jamestown, Virginia, 1
Jefferson, Thomas, 2, 29
Jesuit order, 23
Jews, American, 69, 164, 225
Johnson, Albert, 287
Johnson City, Illinois, 259
Jordan, Joe, 238

Kanawha County, West Virginia, 117
Kearney, Stephen W., 36
Kefauver, Estes, 219, 221, 223, 224
Kennedy, Kenneth P. 239
Kino, Eusebio, 1, 23–25

labor, Italian, 59–63, 73–80, 89–90, 97–162 passim
Labrador, 7
La Guardia, Fiorello, 285, 295, 372–375
Lait, Jack, 224
Lake Erie, 20
Lake Huron, 20
Lake Pepin, 35
Lake Superior, 20
Lamonica, Dominick, 158–162
Landis, Charles, 68
Lansky, Meyer, 217, 248–249, 250
Lansky (Messick), 248
La Salle, M. Cavalier de, 19–22 passim
Las Vegas, Nevada, 222
Lazarus, Emma, 373
Leo XIII, Pope, 339
Leonardo Da Vinci Art School, 389
Leopold, Grand Duke of Tuscany, 26
Lincoln, Abraham, 400
Lindsay, John V., 240

Lingle, Jake, 203
Little, Lou, 427
Little Italy, 38, 293–303, 350–354, 355, 359, 362–365, 385, 414–418
Lodge, Henry Cabot, 167–170
Logansport, Indiana, 102
Lombardi, Jesus, 23
Lombardi, Vince, 425, 427
Lombardo, Joe, 247
Lombardy, 86
Long Island, 93
Lopez, Robert S., 379
Los Angeles, 65, 222
Louisiana, 38, 93–94, 123
Lucca, Italy, 153
Lucchese, Gaetano, 206, 250
Luciano, Charles "Lucky," 164, 205–218 passim, 219, 248
Luzzatti, Irene Coen, 373

Maas, Peter, 205, 245, 251
McClellan, John L., 205
McCormack, William J., 225
McGovern, George, 251
McKinley, William, 269
McNicholas, John T., 331–334
Mac Rae, Hugh, 82
Mafia, 60, 163–165, 167–170, 174–183, 186, 188, 223, 224, 229, 235–252
Mafia Is Not an Equal Opportunity Employer, The (Gage), 248
Magaddino, Steve, 249
Maglioco, Giuseppe, 206
Mangano, Antonio, 73–80, 321–325
Maranzano, Salvatore, 205–218 passim
Marcantonio, Vito, 399–400
Marchello, Maurice R., 425–427
Marciano, Rocky, 425, 427
Marion, North Carolina, 254
Marriage of Figaro, The (Mozart), 31
Martin, Billy, 425
Massachusetts, 38, 69
Masseria, Joseph, 205–218 passim
Mastro-Valerio, Allessandro, 45–48
Mazzei, Filippo, 2, 26–30
Mazzini, Giuseppe, 68
Mazzini Society, 397
Melillo, Oscar, 426
Memoirs on La Salle's Discoveries (Tonti), 19
Memphis, Tennessee, 62
Messick, Hank, 248
Metropolitan Museum of Art (N.Y.), 285
Mexico, 23
Mezzogiorno, 136
Miami, Florida, 222
Michelangelo, 350
Miele, Stefano, 150–152
Milan, Italy, 156, 339
Minotto, Conte, 285
Miranda, Michele, 207
Missionary Sisters of the Sacred Heart, 338–339, 341

Mississippi, 123
Mississippi River, 22
Mississippi Valley, 19–22
Mobile, Alabama, 62
Modigliani, Franco, 379
Molise, 74
Monroe, James, 34
Moran, Bugs, 194
Morelli, Frank, 189
Morello, Peter, 208
Moretti, Willy, 224
Moretti Cafe (N.Y.), 44
Morgan, J. Appleton, 259–262
Morgenthau, Robert M., 238
Morsani, Adriano, 134
Mortimer, Lee, 224
Mozart, Wolfgang A., 31
Mulberry Street (N.Y.), 39, 100, 127,
    299, 300, 316, 414
Murder, Inc., 224
Mussolini, Benito, 386, 388, 392, 395,
    397
My Life in the Mafia (Teresa), 166, 189
Mysteries of Mulberry Street, 320

Napa, California, 65, 112
Naples, Bank of, 90
Naples, Italy, 75, 76, 106, 187
Naples, University of, 77
National Educational Association, 306
National Italian American League, 237
National Origins Quota System, 254
Neapolitans, 42, 51
New Amsterdam (N. Y.), 1
Newark, New Jersey, 350
Newfoundland, 17
"new immigration," 98
New Jersey, 38, 60, 67–72, 93
New Orleans, 1, 167–170, 176, 180, 184,
    254, 255–258, 269
New School for Social Research, 379
newspapers, Italian American, 92–93,
    335–337
New York City, 39–44, 56, 89–95, 102–
    104, 126–130, 151, 164, 176, 180, 185,
    186, 205–218, 276, 313–316, 321–325, 343–
    345, 359–361, 372–375, 402, 407, 414–418
New York City Board of Education,
    237
New York Law School, 151
New York Police Department, 176, 179
New York State, 17–18, 38, 69
New York Stock Exchange, 295
New York Yankees, 426
Niagara, 20
Nitti, Frank, 221, 237
North Carolina, 81–84
North End (Boston), 50
North Street (Boston), 49–54
Norton, Eliot, 322
Notre Dame University, 426

O'Banion, Dion, 194, 201, 202
Obici, Amadeo, 158–162

Oderzo, Italy, 158
Ohio, 93
Oliver, Jordan, 427
Olivieri, Giordano, 427
opera, 31–33
organizational life, 321–325
Our Business Civilization (Adams),
    165

Paderewski, Ignace, 235
padrone system, 44, 99–110
Padua, Italy, 179
Pagona, Italy, 285
Palermo, Sicily, 174, 179, 186
Palmer, A. Mitchell, 346
Palo Alto, California, 113
Panunzio, Constantine, 287–290, 392–
    398
Pardo, Bernardo, 25
Parini, Piero, 396
Parkerson, William, 255–259
Parkhurst, Charles H., 372
Pasley, Fred D., 203
Pastore, John, 295
Paterno, Joe, 427
Patri, Angelo, 285
Patriarca, Raymond, 245–246, 248
Patti, Adelina, 2
Pecora, Ferdinand, 285
Pecoraro, Eduardo, 320
Pecorini, Alberto, 89–95
Pellico, Silvio, 42
Penitent, The (Di Donato), 414
Pennsylvania, 38, 69, 93
Pepitone, Joe, 425
Peruzzi, M. M., 160
Petrosino, Giuseppe, 174, 179–183
Petruzzelli, Mario, 376–378
Pezzolo, 425, 426
Philadelphia, 56, 176, 180, 184, 334, 402
Piacenza, Italy, 331
Piccirilli, Attilio, 389–391
Piccolo, Francesco M., 23
Piccolo, Luigi, 427
Piedmont, 85–88, 189
Pierantoni, Augusto, 268–270
Pileggi, Nicholas, 235–242
Pimo Indians, 23
Piscopo, Bonaventure, 266
Pittsburgh, 176, 180, 184, 402
Planters Peanut Company, 158–162
Pope, Generoso, 236
Powderly, Terrence V., 175
Prairie du Chien, Wisconsin, 35
Presidential Commission on Law En-
    forcement, 229
Primeria Alta, 23
Profacci, Joseph, 208, 246
Progresso Italo-Americano, Il (N.Y.),
    394
Prohibition, 163, 205
Protestant churches, 92
Providence, Rhode Island, 245, 402
Pueblo, Colorado, 362
Puglia, Italy, 189

Pulsano, Italy, 76
Puzo, Mario, 246, 250, 251, 428

Quebec, 20

Ragen, James, 221, 222
railroad workers, 141–149
Raker, John E., 287
Raleigh County, West Virginia, 117
"Red Scare," 346
Red Wing, Minnesota, 35
Reed-Johnson Immigration of 1924, 38
Reina, Tom, 207, 212
Renner, Thomas C., 243
Reno, Nevada, 362
Reporter, The, 379
Republicano, Il, 41
Republican Party, 304–305, 401–404
Rhode Island, 69
Ricca, Paul, 221–222
Riccardo, John J., 295
Riis, Jacob, 225, 313–316, 317
Rinelli, Steve, 208
Rio de Janeiro, 10
Rio de la Plata, 10
Rio Grande, 24
Rizzo, Frank, 295
Robinson, Jackie, 425
Roman Catholic Church, 91–92, 331–334
Roosevelt, Franklin D., 385, 401
Roosevelt, Theodore, 314, 315
Rosati, Giuseppe, 2
Rosetto, Pennsylvania, 62
Rossi, Egisto, 108
Rossi, Pietro, 111
Rossini, Gioachinno A., 32, 33
Rothstein, Arnold, 219, 220, 224
Royal Academy of Fine Arts (Rome), 389
Russian River Valley, California, 115
Ruth, Babe, 426

Sacco, Niccola, 189–190
Sacco-Vanzetti case, 291
Saetta, Francesco Saverea, 23
St. Angelo di Lodi, Italy, 339
St. Anthony Falls, Minnesota, 35
St. Helena, North Carolina, 81–84
St. Lawrence River, 20
St. Louis, Missouri, 2
St. Louis Browns, 426
St. Raphael Society, 91
St. Valentine's Day massacre (Chicago), 202
Salerno, Ralph, 205, 230, 231, 241
Salvaterra, Juan Mario de, 23, 24
Salvemini, Gaetano, 379
San Antonio di Padova Church (N.Y.), 43
Sanchez, Raphael, 3
San Francisco, California, 64, 65, 137–139, 153, 155, 176, 180, 184
San Ignacio, Father, 25
San Jose, California, 153

San Mateo, California, 65
San Salvador (island), 3, 4
Santa Barbara, California, 112
Santa Clara Valley, California, 65
Santa Fe, New Mexico, 23
San Xavier del Bac mission, 23
Sarazen, Gene, 285, 427
Sargent, Frank P., 175
Saturday Evening Post, 283
Sault Sainte Marie, 20, 36
Savoldi, Joe, 426, 427
Savoy Trust Company (N.Y.), 90
Sbarbaro, Andrea, 111–116, 137, 138
Scala, Francesco, 2
Scalabrini, Giovanni Battista, 331
Schary, Dore, 237
Schoolcraft, Henry R., 36
Schultz, Dutch, 207, 213, 219
Scranton, Pennsylvania, 159
Segno, Italy, 1, 23
Segrè, Emilio, 379
Senate Crime Investigating Committee, 219
Senner, Joseph A., 264–267
Shapiro, Gurrah, 219, 220, 224
Sharkey, Joe, 427
Shelburne, Lord, 27, 28
Sica, Joe, 222
Sicily and Sicilians, 51, 106, 164, 184, 187, 194, 208, 231, 343–345, 428
Siegel, Bugsy, 222
Silk Weavers' Union, 127
Simboli, Cesidio, 146–149
Sioux Indians, 34
Smith, Al, 372
Society for the Protection of Italian Immigrants, 119, 121, 271, 322–323
Soderini, 10
Soncino, Raimondo di, 7
Sonoma County, California, 112
Sonora, Mexico, 1, 23
Sons of Italy, 329–330, 396
Sora, Italy, 2
Soul of An Immigrant (Panunzio), 289, 392
South, Italians in, 59–63, 122–125
South America, 10
South Braintree, Massachusetts, 189
South Carolina, 103
South End House (Boston), 49, 326
Spadoni, Adriana, 126–130
Spain, 3
Speranza, Gino C., 117–121, 271–277
Spinello, Mario J., 64–66
Spirit of the Ghetto (Hapgood), 317
Stagg, Amos Alonzo, 426
Stanford, Leland, 112
Stanford University, 113
Stapleton, Staten Island, 68
Stephen, Wally, 426
Stockton, California, 65
Stokes, Isaac Newton Phelps, 374
Stone, Alfred, 122–125
Strasse, Joe, 210
Strong, William L., 372

Suffolk, Virginia, 159, 160
Sunnyside Colony, Arkansas, 94, 131

Talese, Gay, 249, 250, 251
Taliaferro, Lawrence, 34–36
Tallulah, Louisiana, 269
Tameleo, Henry, 245, 250
Tampa, Florida, 254
Taylor, Bayard, 282
Tehama County, California, 112
Tennessee, 69
Teresa, Vincent, 166, 189, 190, 243–252
Terranova, Ciro, 207
Texas, 69
Thaxter, Brad, 237
Thayer, Webster, 189
theater, immigrant, 317–320
Thompson, William Hale, 197
Toigo, Adolph, 426
Tonti, Enrico di, 1, 19–22, 131, 132
Tontitown, Arkansas, 38, 59, 131–135
Toronto, Canada, 159
Torrio, Johnny, 194, 197, 199, 200, 201
Tortora, Vincent, 401–404
Train Arthur, 174, 184–188
Trans American Publishing, 222
Treviso, 158
Tribuna Italia Transatlantica, La (Chicago), 45, 283
Tulare, California, 65
Turano, Anthony M., 362–365
Turkus, Burton, 224
Turnesa, Will, 427
Tuscany, 26, 389
Tuscon, Arizona, 23

Unione Siciliana, 171, 194
unions, labor, 126–130
University of Chicago, 306
Untouchables, The, 237, 416
Uprooted, The (Handlin), 401
Urey, Harold, 408

Valachi, Joe, 165, 205–218, 229, 243, 245
Valachi Papers, The (Maas), 205, 245, 246
Valentino, John, 355–357

Valentino, Rudolph, 285
Vanzetti, Bartolomeo, 189–193
Venice, Italy, 7, 31, 158
Venturi, Ken, 427
Vernon County, Wisconsin, 86
Verrazzano, Giovanni da, 17–18
Vespucci, Amerigo, 10–16
Victor Emmanuel II, king of Italy, 2, 68
Victor Emmanuel III, king of Italy, 162, 263
Vigo, Francesco, 2
Vina, California, 112
Vineland, New Jersey, 38, 60, 67–72
Virginia, 26, 34
Volpe, John, 295

Wabasha, Minnesota, 35
Wagner, Robert F., 241
Waldenses, 1
Wampanoag Indians, 17
Washington County, Arkansas, 132
Washington Redskins, 427
West Virginia, 117–121
White, Frank Marshall, 174, 179–183
White Hand Society, 171–173
Whyte, William F., 420
Wiley, Alexander, 223
Wilkes Barre, Pennsylvania, 159
Wilmington, North Carolina, 82
Wilson, Woodrow, 254
wine making, 65, 111–116
Wirt County, West Virginia, 117
Wisconsin, 85–88
women, Italian, 126–130
Women's Trade Union League, 127, 128, 130
Woods, Robert A., 326–328
Woolworth, Frank W., 158

Xavier, San Francesco, 25

Yorkville, N.Y., 39

Zerilli, Anthony, 250
Zerilli, Joe, 250
Zingrone, John B., 285